Pentecostal Aspects
of
Early Sixteenth-century Anabaptism

Pentecostal Aspects
of
Early Sixteenth-century Anabaptism

CHARLES HANNON BYRD II

Foreword by Allan H. Anderson

WIPF & STOCK · Eugene, Oregon

PENTECOSTAL ASPECTS OF EARLY SIXTEENTH-CENTURY ANABAP

Copyright © 2019 Charles Hannon Byrd II. All rights reserved. Except for brief quotations in critical publications or reviews, no part of this book may be reproduced in any manner without prior written permission from the publisher. Write: Permissions, Wipf and Stock Publishers, 199 W. 8th Ave., Suite 3, Eugene, OR 97401.

Wipf & Stock
An Imprint of Wipf and Stock Publishers
199 W. 8th Ave., Suite 3
Eugene, OR 97401

www.wipfandstock.com

PAPERBACK ISBN: 978-1-5326-5474-9
HARDCOVER ISBN: 978-1-5326-5475-6
EBOOK ISBN: 978-1-5326-5476-3

Manufactured in the U.S.A.   04/02/19

This is dedicated to the memory of my beloved wife,
Patsy W. Gower Byrd, 1942–2018, the love of my life.

Our father, the author, followed his wife, our mother, to Heaven on January 8, 2019, prior to publication. He worked so diligently, with Mom constantly at his side, through serious illness, to finish writing. We could not be more proud of their legacy to us and so many others.

—*his loving children, Mikal Ann, Patty, and Charles*

Contents

Foreword by Allan H. Anderson • ix

Acknowledgments • xiii

Introduction • xv

    Chapter 1
    Luther, Erasmus, and the Foundation of Reformation Radicalism • 1

    Chapter 2
    Zwingli's Reformation and Anabaptist Radicalism • 43

    Chapter 3
    Restitutio in Integrum: Restoring the Fallen Church • 68

    Chapter 4
    Evangelism, Persecution, and Pacifism • 104

    Chapter 5
    Pilgram Marpeck and Early Pentecostalism • 135

Bibliography • 219

Index • 237

Foreword

THIS IS A PARTICULARLY poignant moment for me as one of Charles H. Byrd, II's PhD supervisors, because he succeeded in finishing his PhD thesis despite serious cardiac health issues, and now the resulting book has been published. So, I begin by underlining what an achievement against all odds this book represents. This is not just because of overcoming the obstacles to completion; this study makes a remarkable contribution to understanding the parallels between sixteenth-century Anabaptism and twentieth-century Pentecostalism. Although many have pointed to these parallels, such a detailed study as this one, using both primary (archival) sources and secondary sources, on this fascinating resemblance has never been undertaken. Arising in Huldrych Zwingli's early sixteenth-century Zurich, Switzerland, the Anabaptist ("re-baptizer") movement was originally part of Zwingli's reform. They went much further than Zwingli either intended or allowed, and took the principles of the Reformation, especially *sola scriptura* and *sola fide*, as their appeal to an individual interpretation of the Bible. They rejected pomp and ritual in the church, declared that baptism was only for adult believers, and believed that only the Holy Spirit (and not the institutional church) could interpret the Bible in every believer's conscience. This paved the way for a radical appropriation of another Reformation principle: the priesthood of all believers and the rejection of clerical authority and church-state union. This was known in history as the Radical Reformation, and soon the major Protestant reformers Luther and Zwingli saw its anti-establishment tendencies and turned violently against it. Fast forward almost four centuries and another radical reformation begins, also characterised by extreme individualism, stemming from a firm belief in the priesthood of every believer without the need for clerical class or ecclesiastical hierarchy. The same principles of *sola scriptura* and *sola fide* that motivated the Anabaptists, this study argues, also motivated the early Pentecostals, and they reached similar conclusions. This time, together with a fervent belief in the outpouring of the Spirit in the "last days," there is a greater emphasis on spiritual gifts, which were also found in the Anabaptist movement, so Byrd argues. Although adult baptism was the most prominent tenet of Anabaptism, the spiritual gifts of prophecy, speaking in tongues, and healing were also manifested.

During the Reformation, gifts of the Spirit were rare, but there were occasional reports within the Anabaptist movement of such manifestations that brought them into some disrepute and opposition by the reformers. Luther wrote that tongues were given as a sign to the Jews and had since ceased, and that Christians no longer needed miracles. He used 1 Corinthians 12 and 14 to develop his case for preaching in German. Zwingli took the position that speaking in tongues referred to the ability to read and interpret biblical languages to facilitate the preaching of the gospel. Unfortunately, as far as the Anabaptists were concerned, spiritual gifts were associated with Thomas Müntzer and the apocalyptic fringes, whose alleged excesses and immoralities resulted in Luther and other Reformation leaders totally rejecting the entire Anabaptist movement. However, Müntzer was never seen as representative of Anabaptism by the movement itself. The established Protestant churches were even more firmly opposed to religious enthusiasm than the Roman Catholic Church had ever been, and it took over four centuries for this to change. Spiritual gifts would continue to appear mainly among Catholic saints and in the extreme fringes of Protestantism, and were almost always regarded as sectarian or heretical at the time.

There is a great deal of interesting detail on the Anabaptist movement in this book. First, it shows its origins in the theology of Luther and Zwingli, except that the Anabaptists took the principles of the Reformation to their logical conclusions. In particular, the ideas of Pilgram Marpeck and other early Anabaptists reveal several similarities, if not connections, to the later Pentecostals. The Anabaptists, like the Pentecostals after them, saw their movement as a restoration movement, a return to the spirituality and practices of the early church. No other way was possible for the radical reformation of the church. This included an emphasis on the spiritual gifts as found in 1 Corinthians 12–14, perhaps of greater importance to the Pentecostals than to Anabaptists, however, Pauline pneumatology was central to Anabaptist thought and practice.

This is one of the most important aspects of the argument of this book, which is not an attempt to trace historical connections between Anabaptism and Pentecostalism (this would be impossible to do and would be tenuous at the very least). There were almost four centuries between them and two very different contexts after all. Even if a link can be shown through English Puritanism and German Pietism to Methodism, then to the Holiness movement, and from there to Pentecostalism, any link between Pietism and Anabaptism is doubtful.

Rather than trying to make a case for Anabaptism as being a precedent or progenitor of Pentecostalism, Byrd makes a case for the ethos, the spirituality, the christocentrism, a "literal" biblical hermeneutic, and the charisma that characterised both movements. It is this latter emphasis on the charismatic gifts within early Anabaptism that makes the most significant argument to the continuation of the charismata through the ages. I commend this study to you and to those who would find inspiration in the courageous stand taken by this abused and persecuted Christian minority in early-modern Europe. Pentecostals and charismatics today will find here encouragement to reconnect with the ideas, aims, and convictions of their early predecessors.

Allan H. Anderson
University of Birmingham

Acknowledgments

A GREAT MANY FRIENDS and colleagues, both new and old, have made this dissertation possible. I would like to thank the Marrow Group from Chapel Springs Assembly of God, Dr. Nicholas Tavani, Dr. Randall O'Bannon, Dr. Paul Thee, Rick Bookwalter, and Dr. Scott Cleveland for inviting me to participate in the discussions of our faith that inspired me to begin my graduate education after twenty-seven years.

Thanks go to Rev. Dr. Douglas Chapman for proofreading parts of my work and being a mentor. Dr. Mack Holt, my first graduate professor, who guided me through a very steep learning curve and became a mentor and friend. I greatly appreciate the Open Bible Sunday School class of Chapel Springs Church that provided the first forum for the reading of parts of this thesis. I appreciate the Sixteenth Century Studies Conference and Dr. Geoffery Dipple and Dr. John Roth who encouraged me to read parts of the thesis in the Anabaptist sessions. The help of Lois Bowman, head librarian of the Menno Simons Historical Library Eastern Mennonite University, was invaluable.

I am indebted to Dr. William Kay who made the publication of a significant part of the thesis possible in the Journal of the European Pentecostal Theological Association. Prof. Rev. Diarmaid MacCulloch, Kt. supported and encouraged the proposed study and guided me through my entrance into the University of Oxford. I want to recognize Dr. Kosta Milkov, Dr. Michael Jensen, and Dr. Christian Hofreiter, my Oxford colleagues while at Wycliffe Hall, for taking their time to discuss various topics critical to this dissertation and recommending beneficial avenues of approach. Dr. Charlotte Methuen patiently tutored me successfully through another sharp learning curve at Oxford. Thanks go to Dr. Allan Anderson for convincing me that my proposal was worthy of development at the University of Birmingham. I am particularly grateful for the supervision of Dr. Elaine Fulton at Birmingham. She also patiently and diligently guided me through the preparation of a difficult bit of subject matter that combined Reformation and Pentecostal history and theology.

The greatest of acknowledgments goes to Pat Byrd, my beloved wife of 55 years, who encouraged me in this lifelong goal. She nursed me through a critical health problem that interrupted the work for a year. Her encouragement to continue became a genuine incentive to bring the project to completion. Her love and devotion cannot be overstated.

N.B. American English spelling will be used throughout the thesis.

Introduction

OUT OF A TOTAL world population of 7 billion there are currently 2.18 billion Christians, of which there are 584 million Pentecostals and Charismatics, representing 27 percent of Christians globally.[1] According to the Pew Research Center, it's the fastest growing sect of the faith. The history, theology, and culture of the movement cannot be overestimated.[2] This thesis is not a comprehensive study of Pentecostalism or of the Reformation. It will take cognizance, however, of the social, political, and cultural evolution that was occurring during the advent of each, noting that the impact of each did not occur in a vacuum, but in concert with the conditions of their respective cultures and societies. A discussion of the historical background of each movement will attempt to understand the environments that existed during the development of each, thus making the comparison of similar religious experiences regarding the manifestations of the gifts of the Holy Spirit, according to 1 Corinthians 12–14, relevant to each other. An analysis of early sixteenth-century Anabaptist spiritual praxes and theology (a Reformation-era religious movement intent on the restitution of the primitive New Testament church), and the resemblance it had to early twentieth-century Pentecostalism (a movement also dedicated to the restitution of primitive New Testament Christianity), will be offered.[3] The purpose

---

1. Pew Research Center, "Global Christianity," 7–8.
2. Anderson, *Introduction to Pentecostalism*, 1.
3. Restitution refers to what is understood by both movements to be the restoration of the New Testament's description of the first-century Christian movement. The terms "primitive church" and "early church" refer to the era encompassing Christianity up until the advent of Constantine when many believed the church to have fallen into apostasy. "Apostolic" refers to those aspects of Christianity that conform to the New Testament teachings of the apostles. The terms described above were used by early Anabaptists and early Pentecostals in much the same way. See, Harder, *Sources of Swiss*

is to identify those aspects of early sixteenth-century Anabaptism that were Pentecostal-like in nature and praxes, and coincidentally establish that their respective biblical hermeneutics were, as introduced by Martin Luther (1486-1546) and Huldrych Zwingli (1486-1531), a common source of similarities.

Pentecostal aspects are those theological and spiritual praxes that defined early or classical Pentecostalism as Paul described in 1 Corinthians 12-14. Of particular import are the praxes of the manifestation of the gifts of the Holy Spirit, particularly speaking in tongues, speaking in tongues and interpretation, divine healing, and prophecy. Theological aspects include: experiential nature of salvation, dreams, visions, catatonic ecstasy (being slain in the spirit), evangelism, adult baptism, piety, pacifism, separation from the world, eschatological expectation, centrality of Christ, biblical supremacy, the priesthood of the believer, and restitution of the primitive New Testament church. Similar phenomena and praxes of early Anabaptism will be analytically compared to those listed above, including those which were not shared.[4] The thesis is primarily arranged as a chronological narrative beginning in the sixteenth century. As spiritual praxes appear with Pentecostal-like aspects, the similarities will be compared and analyzed.

Early Pentecostalism will be defined as the initial Christian movement which appeared in the late nineteenth century that primarily concerned itself with "the experience of the working of the Holy Spirit," and the manifestation of the gifts of the Spirit (the charismata) according to 1 Corinthians 12-14.[5] Early Anabaptism will be defined as the radical movement that emanated from the initial Swiss Reformation that rejected infant baptism and embraced adult rebaptism as well as an experiential understanding of the nature and work of the Holy Spirit according to 1 Corinthians 12-14. C. Arnold Snyder has observed that early Anabaptism was a very "charismatic" movement, particularly some elements of the movement such as South German Anabaptism, which outlined in detail the process of individual yielding to the Spirit.[6]

Anabaptism, 276-79, 300-1; Wacker, *Heaven Below*, 71-72; Littell, *Origins of Sectarian Protestantism*, 47-50.

4. Land, *Pentecostal Spirituality*, 6-7. See also, Menzies, *Anointed to Serve*, 57-59.

5. Anderson, *Introduction to Pentecostalism*, 14.

6. Snyder, *Anabaptist History and Theology*, 1, 368-69. The New International Version of the Holy Bible (1984) will be used throughout this thesis unless otherwise noted.

Numerous scholars have observed that there are similarities between early sixteenth-century Anabaptism and early twentieth-century Pentecostalism, but none have provided a detailed and comprehensive explanation of why their observations may have been valid. It must be emphasized that this work is not about establishing Anabaptism as a progenitor of Pentecostalism or proving that Pentecostalism was derivative thereof. It is about identifying and analyzing the abovementioned similarities and determining the sources and catalysts.

In 1955, Dr. Van Dusen, then President of Union Theological Seminary, opined that, according to some scholars, the growing Pentecostal phenomenon was derived from sixteenth-century Anabaptism. He concluded that it represented a revolution of equal importance to the original apostolic church as well as the Reformation.[7] John Howard Yoder observed in 1967 that, "Pentecostalism is in our century the closest parallel to what Anabaptism was in the sixteenth."[8] Twelve years later, Kenneth R. Davis was still able to conclude:

> Clearly sixteenth century Anabaptism was a charismatic movement. . .the core of Anabaptism from the beginning held firmly to a Tertullian version—moderate, "orthodox," and biblical—which complements the Anabaptists' ascetic emphases on brotherhood, lay participation and holy living.[9]

In 1992, George H. Williams pejoratively described Anabaptism in St. Gallen, Switzerland, in 1525, as degenerating into a "rank spiritualism of charismatic vagaries."[10] Three years later, C. Arnold Snyder noted that of the theological and ecclesiological features of Anabaptism, the most important was its pneumatology, and he agreed with Karl Holl's contention that without a strong pneumatic base, Anabaptism would probably have not been a movement at all.[11] Adrian Chatfield has noted the similarity between the sixteenth-century Anabaptist experience of "falling in love with Jesus [as] the source of supreme spiritual confidence which [gave] them the enthusiasm, the passion and the will to face a devastating

---

7. Davis, "Anabaptism as a Charismatic Movement," 219; Van Dusen, "Third Force in Christendom," 122–24.

8. Yoder, "Concern 15," 77.

9. Davis, "Anabaptism as a Charismatic Movement," 233.

10. Williams, *Radical Reformation*, 1290. Williams has expressed a personal observation here notwithstanding similar scriptural manifestations of the Spirit.

11. Snyder, *Anabaptist History and Theology*, 96.

world" and twentieth-century Pentecostalism was that it developed the same kind of intimate and passionate love for Christ.¹² Finally, Mathew Clark identified three areas of similarities between sixteenth-century Anabaptism and twentieth-century Pentecostalism.¹³ He observed that scholars had variously attributed the roots to African-Americans of the Holiness movement, the Holiness and revival movement of the nineteenth century, and German Pietism:

> However, a remarkable omission has been any persistent interest in the historical roots of Pentecostalism in sixteenth century Anabaptism and the intriguing parallels between the ethos of the Anabaptists and that of Pentecostalism.¹⁴

Although John T. Nichol has observed the same similarities between Anabaptism and Pentecostalism, he also failed to provide any detailed research or analysis to substantiate any observations of similitude.¹⁵ These astute, and perhaps passing, observations made after the advent of early twentieth-century Pentecostalism, raises the question: Did early sixteenth-century Anabaptism manifest similar aspects of early Pentecostalism over four hundred years earlier? If Anabaptism did, was there a common denominator, and why didn't the movement evolve into an early twentieth-century-type Pentecostalism? An affirmative answer would place Anabaptism in the genre of historical Christian sectarian movements which attempted the restitution of the primitive New Testament church's charismatic Pentecostal pneumatological nature, based on the Pauline Scriptural model of 1 Corinthians 12–14.

This dissertation will argue that there are many similarities between the two movements and that they stem from the initial Reformation theologies of both Martin Luther and Huldrych Zwingli. After both had abandoned their initial theological positions, radical elements of both reformers—the Lutheran *Schwärmer* and Zwingli's Anabaptists, respectively—continued to embrace their initial theological positions. The context of those initial theologies, particularly the Petrine doctrine of the Priesthood of the Believer, convinced reformation radicals that only

---

12. Chatfield, "Zealous for the Lord," 107–8.

13. Clark, "Pentecostalism's Anabaptist Roots," 198–99. The areas are Anabaptist ethos and hermeneutics, Pentecostal ethos and Anabaptist ethos, and Pentecostal hermeneutics and evangelism (198, 201, and 205).

14. Clark, "Pentecostalism's Anabaptist Roots," 194–95.

15. Anderson, *Spreading Fires,* 18. See also, Nichol, *Pentecostalism,* 3.

the restitution of the primitive New Testament church would suffice to restore biblical Christianity. Reformation of the Roman Church was out of the question. Finally, it will be shown that early Pentecostalism and early Anabaptism developed a similar spiritual-prophetic, literal (natural sense of the text), biblicist hermeneutic. This led to the belief that the manifestation of the charismata, particular as described in 1 Corinthians 12–14, was necessary if there was to be a true church.[16] There is little evidence, however, that Pentecostals were historically aware of the nature of sixteenth-century Anabaptism, but that which has been found will be mentioned. This was primarily due to the fact that sixteenth-century primary sources were not as available as they are today.

Primary source material for each individual movement is available and prolific. Pertinent sources both in English and German translations are also readily accessible. There was no primary source material found that attempted to compare Pentecostalism and Anabaptism, but there is much available regarding the movements separately.[17] Included are books, pamphlets, journals, letters, court records, disputations, reports and records from both historical periods. Secondary literature is abundant, but likewise limited to the history of each movement separately, with very little of it concerning any similarities.

A critically important issue at Pentecostalism's foundation was the refusal of many Christians to accept principal Protestant denominations' devolution into modernism, liberalism, materialism, and social justice in the place of a literal biblical gospel. Their intellectual decent into biblical "higher criticism," began to strip away traditional "textual criticism's" acceptance of the spiritual nature of Scripture and rendered Bible spirituality irrelevant.[18] Those disaffected by the perceived fall of modern Protestantism sought to recapture what became known as the old-time religion of the great awakenings and spiritual revivals, which tapped into the experiential nature of biblical Christian spirituality. It was in that milieu of religious experience that a personal relationship with Christ and the empowerment of the Holy Spirit was to be realized in their

---

16. Williams, *Radical Reformation*, 1257. See also, Archer, *Pentecostal Hermeneutic*, 126; Myland, *Latter Rain Covenant*, 107; Snyder, *Anabaptist History and Theology*, 162–63.

17. Pentecostal "primary source material" refers to any late-nineteenth-century or early-twentieth-century writings that concerned the similarities between early Pentecostalism and early Anabaptism.

18. Archer, *Pentecostal Hermeneutic*, 48–51.

search for biblical orthodoxy. They saw the solution to the problem in the necessity of restitution or restoration of the primitive New Testament church as it was described in Scripture. The disaffected became known as the Holiness Movement.

THE HOLINESS MOVEMENT AND THE ADVENT OF PENTECOSTALISM

Scripture, the Holy Bible, was returned to its perceived rightful place as the final arbiter of the faith by the Holiness Movement, very much like Luther's doctrine of *sola scriptura*. God the Holy Spirit was the one to lead a believer into the truth of the Christian confession through the word; salvation was a personal and emotional experience of the presence of the Holy Spirit, the possibility of living a holy life empowered by the Spirit, and the ability to evangelize the world through the same power. The readoption of the Petrine doctrine of the Priesthood of the Believer, according to 1 Peter 2:9, with all the authority of the biblical priesthood (i.e., authority to read and interpret Scripture as empowered by the Holy Spirit, to manifest every gift of the Spirit, and every act of Christian love taught or commanded by Christ himself), was a spiritually empowering and personally confirming biblical principle that emboldened the new movements. This was a liberating experience, first for the Holiness Movement and the Pentecostalism that was to follow. There was no need for a hierarchical clergy steeped in the depths of higher criticism, and their reliance on modern intellectualism. The Spirit had set them free to pursue their desire to restore the New Testament church. It will be demonstrated that although unwittingly, the participants in the rise of Pentecostalism were living through a situation in the history of Christianity much like that of the European Reformation of the sixteenth century and the emergence of radical Anabaptism.

Within 330 years of the successful establishment of both the Lutheran and Zwinglian Reformation churches, success that must include its expansion throughout Europe and much of the Western Hemisphere, Protestantism had devolved into denominated institutions with hierarchical clergies, an intellectualism that embraced the academic biblical hermeneutic of higher criticism, which was dismissive of much of the spirituality of the former methodology of textual criticism.[19] By the mid-

---

19. Archer, *Pentecostal Hermeneutic*, 48–54.

dle of the nineteenth century, the various Protestant denominations had adapted themselves to the growing economic prosperity of an emerging middle class that became more and more separated from the average lower-working-class Christian. The gospel became a social and cultural endeavor and less personally experiential. Gone were the legacies of the great awakenings of Anglicanism, Methodism, and the revivals of Finney, Edwards, and various Calvinists. Materialism and secularism had taken the forefront, replacing personal piety and public ministry. [20] R. M. Anderson observed that

> The Gospel of wealth, a conglomeration of the doctrines of individualism, classical economics, and Social Darwinism, if not advocated by all clergymen was proclaimed by a sufficient number to give it the apparent endorsement of Protestantism as a whole.[21]

R. M. Anderson argued that the first Pentecostal adherents were by and large made up of the culturally and socioeconomically deprived of the late nineteenth and early twentieth centuries. Neo-Pentecostals were primarily women, African-Americans, and rural agrarian and industrial workers. [22] Grant Wacker concurs with Anderson's observation, but goes on to observe that Pentecostalism may have been seen as a way out of their respective life situations.[23] Harvey Cox also gives Anderson's theory another perspective. He questions whether or not Pentecostalism was attractive to these social outcasts not as a social or economic reprieve from poverty and discrimination, but as possibly "a spiritual meaning for the future of the movement." [24]

C. W. Conn also observed that "The Bible was largely forgotten." [25] Out of the emergence of the disaffected rose Holiness groups seeking to restore the experiential revivalism of by gone days. By 1896, the Pentecostal experience began to manifest itself among these various assemblies. They spoke in tongues and identified their experience as identical to that which occurred on the day of Pentecost in Acts 2:4. [26]

20. Anderson, *Vision of the Disinherited*, 29–31.
21. Anderson, *Vision of the Disinherited*, 29–31.
22. Wacker, *Heaven Below*, 199–200.
23. Wacker, *Heaven Below*, 202.
24. Cox, *Fire from Heaven*, 262.
25. Conn, *Like a Mighty Army*, xxv–xxvi.
26. Conn, *Like a Mighty Army*, xxvii.

Grant Wacker has noted that out of the above-described Protestant devolution, many Christians left their mainstream Protestant churches, having rejected doctrinal intellectualism and sociocultural secularism. They began to seek the revivals of the great awakenings, with their personally experienced spirituality, the objective of which was personal piety. They were by and large restorationists, seeking the restitution of the literal New Testament church as described in Scripture. This religious phenomenon is referred to by consensus as the Holiness Movement and is regarded by most scholars as the vanguard of modern Pentecostalism.[27] Edith Blumhofer characterized early Pentecostals, "as restorationists [who] intentionally ignored historical tradition, opting rather for biblical terminology and precedent."[28]

Allan Anderson argues that notwithstanding the historical knowledge of many manifestations of the charismata (Pentecostalism) throughout the history of the church, it was rejected as not being normative Christianity, despite any confirming biblical record.[29] This opposition was similar to that of Martin Luther, who considered the gifts of the Spirit, the charismata, to be in "cessation" and unnecessary, as the church had established a hierarchical clergy to fulfill the same role.[30] This became the prevailing theology of Protestantism as these manifestations, particularly speaking in tongues, were considered heresy, even demon possession. Donald Dayton contends that John Wesley (1703–1791) was the progenitor of the Holiness Movement which was the immediate forerunner of early Pentecostalism.[31]

Within the above context, Wesley placed an emphasis on a doctrine of a "second blessing," one subsequent to conversion, referred to as sanctification. It would be this doctrine that divided the nationally popular Methodist church from its initial positions of emotionalism, personal liberty, and empowerment of the "dispossessed," such as women, former

27. Wacker, *Heaven Below*, 3–4, 71–72.
28. Blumhofer, *Restoring the Faith*, 4.
29. Anderson, *Introduction to Pentecostalism*, 19.
30. Luther, *Commentary on the Epistle*, 238.
31. Luther, *Commentary on the Epistle*, 25. See also, Wesley, *Works of John Wesley: Sermons*, 354; Dayton, *Theological Roots of Pentecostalism*, 38–50. It should be noted here that the relationship between seventeenth-century German Pietism and early-sixteenth-century Anabaptism has been relatively unexplored although many Pietist beliefs and practices were similar to those of the Anabaptists. It can also be noted that early German Pentecostals republished many of the seventeenth-century Pietists' theological works in the early twentieth century.

slaves, and the poor.³² Out of the division came a Holiness Movement of the disaffected, those who accepted the doctrine of sanctification as the second blessing. This became very influential in the early development of Pentecostalism.³³

The literal biblical record was clear enough for the Holiness adherents regarding the charismata and its important role in the first-century church which, to them, was paramount to the restitution of that church. A classic example of this is the work and ministry of A. B. Simpson (1843–1919).³⁴ This in turn caused many to conclude that these gifts of the Spirit should be manifested in the contemporary church if a complete and total restitution was to occur. The baptism in the Holy Spirit became an empowering phenomenon, empowering for service, evangelism, and ministry. It was particularly believed to be critical within the context of the imminent return of Christ. However, it would be some time before the idea of sanctification was separated from the baptism in the Holy Spirit and accepted as a subsequent experience to conversion.³⁵

An important aspect of the Holiness Movement was the attendant belief in divine healing. Allan Anderson points out that divine healing had become an important element by the end of the nineteenth century within the Holiness Movement. The influence of German Pietist Johann Blumhardt (1805–1880) on early Holiness ideas was significant.³⁶ He had operated a healing center in Germany based on linking healing with the power of the Spirit. Divine healing passed on to America, with some mainline denominational adherents following suit. Charles Cullis, an Episcopalian physician from Boston, had visited healing centers in Germany and began praying for the sick in healing conventions back in Boston. He would influence A. B. Simpson, future founder of the Christian and Missionary Alliance Church, who opened a healing home in 1884, linking healing to Christ's atonement. There were also others who became engaged in divine healing ministries, having connected it with the biblical charismata as a gift of the Spirit, as in 1 Corinthians 12–14.³⁷

---

32. Anderson, *Introduction to Pentecostalism*, 26.
33. Wesley, *Works of John Wesley: Sermons*, 2:415–16.
34. Nienkirchen, *A. B. Simpson*, 26–29.
35. Anderson, *Introduction to Pentecostalism*, 26–27.
36. Anderson, *Introduction to Pentecostalism*, 24.
37. Synan, *Century of the Holy Spirit*, 242.

CHARLES FOX PARHAM AND AMERICAN PENTECOSTALISM

Charles Fox Parham (1873–1929), a Methodist holiness preacher, experienced a personal healing and would become an important leader in the emerging Pentecostal movement. Some scholars purport that Parham was the founder of early American Pentecostalism, but others disagree.[38] Whether he was or not does not preclude the impact his initial ministry had on the development of the movement. Parham became disaffected from Methodism after experiencing his healing from rheumatic fever, after which he began his own healing ministry. He had been influenced by John A. Dowie (1847–1907) and Frank Sanford (1862–1948), both leading substantial healing ministries in the U. S. at the time. Parham traveled extensively, visiting various Holiness schools and ministries, looking for answers to the questions "What exactly is the Baptism in the Holy Spirit?" and "How does it differ from sanctification?" He had witnessed many sporadic incidents of glossolalia, speaking in tongues, but no one would take a definitive position on its manifestation as to meaning, purpose, or value. In 1898, the same year he was healed, he established a Bible school, Stone's Folly, in Topeka, Kansas, from which he also taught—among other things—that healing was in the atonement of Christ, premillennialism (with the imminent return of Christ), the coming of a worldwide revival (referred to as the "latter rain" to precede Christ's return), and a "third blessing" beyond "entire sanctification."[39] Students were instructed to determine what the evidence of the baptism in the Holy Spirit was from the Bible alone, and the Acts of the Apostles in particular. Upon his return to the school from an evangelistic trip, the students informed him that they had concluded that the initial evidence of the Spirit baptism was speaking in tongues. After setting aside a night of prayer for the biblical experience of the baptism in the Spirit, according to that described in the book of Acts, Agnes Ozman (1870–1937) received the baptism when Parham laid hands on her and she began to speak in tongues. Parham described Ozman as "speaking the Chinese language." This was a great catalyst for the idea that speaking in tongues was actually being able to speak known but unlearned languages (xenolalia) to evangelize the world.[40]

38. Hollenweger, *Pentecostals*, 22.
39. Anderson, *Introduction to Pentecostalism*, 32–33.
40. Anderson, *Introduction to Pentecostalism*, 34.

Parham developed a theology that incorporated the Stone's Folly experience of speaking in tongues as the evidence of the baptism in the Holy Spirit, xenolalia, the empowerment of the Holy Spirit to speak foreign languages without education or training for world evangelization, and divine healing. He would be and continues to be credited with formulating the doctrine of evidential tongues (speaking in tongues as the initial evidence of the Spirit's baptism), which is still embraced by the broader spectrum of Pentecostalism.

Parham's initial attempt at establishing a movement emphasizing speaking in tongues as the initial evidence of the baptism in the Holy Spirit, and its meaning, purpose, and value, was not widely accepted at first. However, by 1905, his influence had grown to the point where he founded another Bible school in Houston where his new movement, the "Apostolic Faith," was becoming very popular. It was here that one of his most important adherents began to attend his new Bible school. William Seymour (1870–1922) became a Holiness preacher, accepted Parham's doctrine of speaking in tongues, and moved it further down the theological path of experiential biblical Christianity which became the "hall mark of Classical North American Pentecostalism."[41]

WILLIAM JOSEPH SEYMOUR

William Seymour, an African-American son of former slaves, became an adherent of Parham's ministry in Houston. After sitting under Parham's ministry for a time, he assumed the pastorate of a small prayer group meeting in Los Angeles in 1906. That group evolved into the famous Azusa Street Pentecostal mission. Seymour's early work in the movement also earned him notoriety as a father of American Pentecostalism.[42]

Seymour moved to Los Angeles to accept a Holiness pastorate offered to him by some who knew him from Houston. By 1906, he was leading a Pentecostal revival at the Azusa Street mission that swept the nation. Manifestations of the gifts of the Spirit were constantly in evidence and having initially embraced Parham's doctrine of xenolalia, numerous people went out onto the foreign mission field, as well as pioneering other local and state missions across the country. Parham visited Azusa Street, but was highly critical of the emotional nature of the meetings. He

---

41. Anderson, *Introduction to Pentecostalism*, 34.
42. Anderson, *Introduction to Pentecostalism*, 44.

was especially critical of the racially integrated character of the assembly. Walter J. Hollenweger considers Seymour's participation and leadership of the Azusa Street revival particularly important for its introduction of African traditional religion as it came down through the African-American slave religion. Seymour's encouragement of racial integration and adoption of many African-American customs of music, worship, prayer, and emotionalism, had a lasting influence on the movement.[43] It was shortly after his visit to Los Angeles that Parham was scandalized by a sexual indiscretion that cost him his leadership of the Apostolic Faith, which was then assumed by Seymour.[44]

GLOBAL PENTECOSTAL REVIVAL

The Pentecostalism of the Azusa Street mission, particularly the doctrine of speaking in tongues as being the initial evidence of the infilling of the Holy Spirit, attracted not only local, but national and international attention. Holiness leaders from all over the world visited the mission to witness, and in many cases experience, the baptism in the Holy Spirit accompanied by speaking in tongues.

Allan Anderson justifiably advances the origins of Pentecostalism into a more global perspective by pointing out that in the Holiness Movement's attempt to clarify the difference between sanctification and the baptism in the Spirit, the English Keswick movement of 1875 adopted the theology of Charles Finney (1792–1876). Finney did not believe that sanctification was the baptism in the Spirit. The Keswick Convention saw two distinct experiences of "new birth" and the "fullness of the Spirit." The fullness of the Spirit was seen in terms of holiness or a higher Christian life. Andrew Murray, Jr. (1828–1917) was also a great influence at Keswick as he taught that sanctification was a progressive experience and not a one-time event. As the solution to the second blessing question grew closer to resolution, by the end of the nineteenth century there were three positions available: the Wesleyan position that the second blessing was entire sanctification, known as the baptism in the Spirit; the Keswick position that the baptism in the Spirit was an endowment of power for service; and a "third blessing" position which combined the second blessing of sanctification and the baptism with fire, also considered an

---

43. Hollenweger, *Pentecostals*, 2, 18–24.
44. Hollenweger, *Pentecostals*, 35.

endowment with power for service. The first American Pentecostals would embrace this third position, but equated it with the baptism in the Holy Spirit accompanied by speaking in tongues.[45] Additionally, a subsequent but important part of the Holiness faith regarded John N. Darby's premillennial "secret rapture" of the church as believable. Already having accepted the Keswick second position of the baptism in the Spirit as being empowerment for service, early Pentecostals also embraced Darby's secret rapture position as well. As the various Holiness groups accepted the Keswick positions they also embraced the idea of new Pentecostal revival to usher in the return of Christ.[46]

Allan Anderson also cites many examples of Pentecostal manifestations throughout the world in various revival movements. In 1904–5, there was a Welsh revival led by Evan Roberts (1878–1951) where Pentecostal behavior was witnessed, including loud emotional prayer, "singing in the Spirit" prophecies, and visions. Alexander Boddy (1854–1930), an Anglican vicar from Sunderland, England, and first leader of British Pentecostalism, visited the revival as did future adherents to the Pentecostal revival about to occur in Los Angeles. Glossolalia was sporadically experienced during the Welsh revival, but leader Evan Roberts discouraged it. Pentecostal-like revivals had been experienced in southern India since 1860, as well as other places being evangelized by Welsh missionaries. Pandita Ramabai's (1858–1922) Mukti Mission, near Pune and in the Bombay area in 1905, had experienced manifestations of glossolalia. By 1906, other regions of India were witnessing the same phenomena. A Korean revival commencing around 1903 under the leadership of Methodist missionaries confirmed many Pentecostal manifestations.[47]

EARLY SIXTEENTH-CENTURY ANABAPTIST CATALYSTS FOR RADICAL REFORM

Much like the catalysts for the emergence of early Pentecostalism, early sixteenth-century Anabaptism faced very similar theological issues with the Roman Catholic Church, as well as the evolving Reformation churches. A spiritually and politically powerful, corrupt, and materialistic Catholic clergy that redefined the word of God to include historical

---

45. Anderson, *Introduction to Pentecostalism*, 28–29.
46. Anderson, *Introduction to Pentecostalism*, 29–30.
47. Anderson, *Introduction to Pentecostalism*, 36–37.

church tradition, was viewed as a primary reason for the need of reformation. The new reformation churches, both Lutheran and Zwinglian Reformed, began incorporating magistracies for the propagation of the gospel, seeking political influence and power, and hoping for a successful reformation. This was an indication to the Anabaptists that there would be no restitution of the New Testament church.

The Zwinglian and Lutheran Reformations were aimed at reforming the Roman Catholic Church to comply with *sola fide and sola scriptura*. Their initial perspectives were very Pauline in terms of ecclesiology and pneumatology, particularly in regard to conforming to 1 Corinthians and 1 Peter. Both embraced the idea of a Spirit-empowered laity, the priesthood of the believer, that was capable of assuming the role of priest as interpreter of Scripture and spiritually enabled to live a life of Scriptural piety as well. Notwithstanding this highly spiritual and scripturally based beginning, they both veered into a magisterial reformation that would compromise with the magistracies to play a role in propagating the gospel by coercion to ensure success of the reform. This, plus the appearance of antinomianism among the laity within Lutheranism, a misunderstanding of Luther's theology of salvation *iustificatio sola fides,* and the evolution of a Catholic-like clergy whose role became one of attempting to control an emerging charismatic, even Pentecostal-like, radicalism, all contributed to the advent of Anabaptism, as well as many spiritualist sects.

Among Luther's followers, a radical evangelicalism developed, led by Andreas Bodenstein von Karlstadt (1486–1541), Thomas Müntzer (d. 1525), and Caspar Schwenckfeld (1489–1561), each of whom would advocate various aspects of Pauline pneumatology such as the manifestation of the gifts of the Spirit, anti-pedobaptism, and an imminent parousia. Zwingli's Reformation also gave rise to radical elements, Anabaptists, who would also embrace Paulinism, similar to their Lutheran radical counterparts. Spiritualists, however, would step outside of traditional Christian orthodoxy and consider anything that was physical, such as the Bible, water baptism, and the Eucharist, as lacking any efficacy for Christians since being filled with the Holy Spirit rendered physical aspects of the church no longer necessary.

These spiritualists and Anabaptists were not interested in reforming the church as were the magisterial reformers. Their goal was the restitution of primitive New Testament Christianity, a new church. The conflict of objectives that ensued would alienate these radical sectarian elements from both Zwingli and Luther. They, for all intents and purposes, were for the most part traditional orthodox Christians who sought a biblically based *ecclesia* which manifested the gifts of the Holy Spirit according to 1 Corinthians, but sans a Roman-type clergy. Both Lutheran and Reformed Zwinglian elements would consider these radical movements as enemies of their respective reformations and on occasion ally themselves with the Roman Catholic forces to coerce them into conformity by persecution and martyrdom.

It can be posited that Anabaptism was neither Protestant nor Catholic in the strict definition of those terms, as they rejected the reformations of both Luther and Zwingli. Although its adherents were initially followers of Luther and/or Zwingli, they rejected their magisterial reform, opting instead for the restitution of Pauline ecclesiology and charismatic spirituality within the context of *sola scriptura* and biblical literalism. This option was not a unique choice as throughout two millennia of Christian history many examples of restitutionism have occurred.

Before the end of the first century, the need for church restitution was already being advocated by the New Testament writers who repeatedly encouraged the emerging church to continue to manifest the charismata for the edification of the church. They warned of the growing number of false teachers who were displaying counterfeit signs and wonders.[48] As the church began to grow and the number of internal and external spiritual and physical threats increased, the writers emphasized the necessity of exercising the gifts of the Spirit to counter these threats. There were several extra-biblical writings implying either restitution or the continuance of early church charismatic praxes. False teachers and growing apostasy is the subject of the *Didache* (c. AD 70), also known as the *Teaching of the Twelve Apostles*. The teaching set out parameters of conduct for itinerant charismatic apostles, evangelists, prophets, teachers, and for elected bishops and deacons responsible for static congregations.[49] The teaching focused on the growing tension between an evolving hierarchical clergy and itinerant Spirit-led charismatics, and the need to

---

48. Romans 12 and Jude 1.
49. 1 Corinthians 12–14 and 1 Timothy 3.

include both dimensions of Christian service, particularly as they were described in Paul's letters.[50]

The *Epistles of Ignatius of Antioch* (c. 125–150) are most indicative of the rapid nature of the evolution of early church polity and its transition from a charismatic leadership to one of a hierarchical clergy.[51] A very significant attempt at restitution of the church after Ignatius was the anti-clerical charismatic movement of Montanus (c. 165). William Tabbernee characterizes Montanism not as an attempt at the restitution of primitive charismatic Christianity, but as a "reaction to the early church's compromise with secular society."[52] However, his thesis appears to beg the question of whether or not Montanism was an early charismatic movement with Pentecostal traits when he describes the charismatic pneumatic manifestations of Montanism, which appear to comply with the definitions of early Pauline ecclesiology as well as early Pentecostalism. Cecil Robeck concludes in his review of Tabbernee's work that if he is correct in his assessment of Montanism's beliefs and teachings it was a Pentecostal movement.[53] Tertullian (c. 145–220), "the church's first Pentecostal theologian," became a Montanist (c. 207) while maintaining his faith in the Catholic Church. He was convinced of the orthodoxy of Montanism and its biblical adherence to Pauline pneumatology.[54] Tabbernee strikes too fine a line between Montanism's reaction to the early church's compromise with secularism and the intent to restore the charismatic nature of Pauline pneumatology.

The ultimate and final historical "fall" of the church which demanded its restitution was thought to have been Constantine the Great's conversion to Christianity and the consequent secularization of the faith as seen in the eyes of many.[55] Subsequent to this fall, the true church lived in a state of diaspora among the heretical adherents of the Constantinian church. According to Franklin H. Littell, this idea was embraced by Anabaptists who identified themselves with those who had thought the same way and had been condemned for it: John Scotus (800ç877?), Peter Waldo (Vaudes, c 1180–1218?), the Franciscan Fraticelli sect 1315, John

---

50. Draper, "Didache," 13–20. See also, Kleist, "Didache," 3–14, 21–23.

51. Foster, "Epistles of Ignatius of Antioch," 81–108. See also, Ignatius of Antioch, "Epistles," 45–131.

52. Tabbernee, *Fake Prophecy and Polluted Sacraments*, xxxv, 421–24.

53. Robeck, "Montanism and Present Day Prophets," 413–29.

54. Burgess, *Holy Spirit*, 62–68; Schaff, *History of the Christian Church*, 417–21.

55. Alighieri, *Inferno*, Canto xix st. 115; Spinka, ed. *Advocates of Reform*, 224.

Wycliff (1328–1384), and Jon Huss (1372–1415).[56] Critical to initial Anabaptist reform motivations was the restitution of the true church according to the New Testament. The words of Georg Witzel (1501–1573), a Lutheran clergyman and Anabaptist sympathizer, became an Anabaptist distinctive:

> Which is the true [Church]? The ancient apostolic. My wish, my yearning is that the world may go back to a true apostolic church. The *Acts* and the writings of the Great [Church] Fathers and ancient Bishops show the way on which we must go back to it. The apostolic church flourished to the time of Constantine. From then on it was perverted, because Bishops went over to the world.[57]

Early Anabaptism would go on to emulate a Pauline ecclesiology and spirituality as described in Acts and 1 Corinthians 12–14 replete with signs, wonders, miracles, and manifestations of the gifts of the Spirit. Early Pentecostalism, following in the footsteps of the Wesleyans and the Holiness Movement, was likewise devoted to the restitution of the primitive church and the reestablishment of the "Full gospel."[58] What follows is a description of the principles, theories, and methods of research that bring these similarities to light.

ANABAPTIST HISTORIOGRAPHY AND LITERATURE

The most significant sixteenth-century primary historical sources written regarding the Anabaptist movement were principally produced by hostile magisterial reformers such as Zwingli in "Refutation of the Tricks of the Catabaptists" (1527), Philip Melanchthon's book, *Against the Teachings of the Anabaptists: Translated into German by Justus Jonas* (1528), and Heinrich Bullinger's *False Teaching of the Anabaptists* (1531) and *Origins of the Anabaptist Sect* (1560). Typical of these histories was the critical way Anabaptism was associated with the Peasants War of 1525 and the apocalyptic debacle at Münster, (1534–35).[59] These works, among many

---

56. Littell, *Origins of Sectarian Protestantism*, 76.

57. Littell, *Origins of Sectarian Protestantism*, 77–78.

58. Wacker, *Heaven Below*, 71–72. See also Dayton, *Theological Roots of Pentecostalism*, 72–73; Ware, "Restorationism in Classical Pentecostalism."

59. Bender and Oyer, "Historiography, Anabaptist"; Zwingli, *Catabaptistarum Strophas* Elenchus; Melanchthon, *Unterricht wider die Lere der Wiedertauffer*

other extremely critical magisterial histories, were subsequently used as accurate, fair, and definitive histories of Anabaptism, notwithstanding their highly prejudicial views. The first historian to break with the anti-Anabaptist historical convention was German Pietist Gottfried Arnold in his *Unpartisan History of Church and Heresy* (1699).[60] Perhaps owing to his Pietism, he recognized the false depictions of Anabaptism in the previous works and noted the spiritual similarities between Anabaptism and German Pietism.

Mennonite historians first began to publish works that emphasized the Anabaptism of the Netherlands, particularly the republication of the *Martyr's Mirror, 1615* in 1720. The *Mirror* is a historical chronicle of the persecutions and martyrdoms of particular Anabaptists from the inception of the movement in 1525. It is based on contemporary court records and personal correspondence. From 1699 until 1855, Anabaptist history was relegated to various publications of accepted histories, but generally determined to be of little interest to Reformation historians given the perceived sectarian, if not heretical, label assigned to them in general.[61] However, many biographical publications concerning various Anabaptist personalities began to appear from 1855–1950 such as, works about Hans Denck (1500–1527), Wolfgang Capito (1478–1541), Ludwig Haetzer (1500–1529), David Joris (1501–1556), Conrad Grebel (1498–1526), Georg Blaurock (1492–1529), Balthasar Hubmaier (1480/85–1528), and Menno Simons (1496–1561).[62] Ludwig Keller was one of the first to publish a work arguing that Anabaptism was a revival of apostolic church life entitled *The Reformation and the Old Reformationists* (1885).[63]

In addition to the legitimizing work of Keller regarding Anabaptism, Ernst Troeltsch (1865–1923) would publish a sociological analysis of Christian theology and teaching which reinforced the idea of the

---

verdeutscht durch Justus Jonas; Bullinger, *Von dem unverschampten fräfe, ergerlichen verwyrren und unwarhaftem leeren der sebsgesandten Widertouffern;* and *Ursprung, fürgang, secten, wäsen, füreme und gemeine irer Artikel, 1528,* respectively.

60. Gottfried Arnold, *Unparteyische Kirchen-und Ketzer-Historie.* 1703.

61. It should be noted that John R. Rempel described the *Mirror* as the most comprehensive and widely used history of martyrdom in church history. See Rempel, *Jorg Maler's Kunstbuch,* 204.

62. Such as Bender, "Conrad Grebel"; Zwingli, *Zwingli and Bullinger*; Hosek, *Life of Balthasar Hubmaier*; Vedder, *Balthasar Hubmaier.* See also, Hillerbrand, *Bibliography of Anabaptism.*

63. Bender and Oyer, "Historiography, Anabaptist." Also, Keller, *Die Reformation und die Reformparteien, 1885.*

orthodoxy of sectarian Christianity, specifically using Anabaptism as an example.[64] Harold S. Bender (1897–1962) described Troeltsch's work as "epoch-making and influential."[65] Greatly encouraged by the growing acceptance of Anabaptist studies as a legitimate academic pursuit, Mennonite scholars became the primary catalysts of Anabaptist history. In the late nineteenth and early twentieth centuries, they perceived a confessional value in developing a historical foundation for an ecclesiology which incorporated sixteenth-century Anabaptist theological positions, e.g., voluntary religious choice (believer's baptism for adults); a free church (no state affiliation); biblical literalism; non-participation in government (avoidance of moral compromise); suffering servants of Jesus who emphasized piety, persecution, and martyrdom as Jesus did; and restitutionism, trying to restore the pre-Constantinian apostolic church.[66]

The milestone transcription and publication of the abundance of Anabaptist primary archival sources from all of German-speaking Europe, begun by the *Verein für Reformationgeschicte* in 1920, was of incalculable value to researchers developing the field of Anabaptist and Radical Reformation studies.[67] The collection and centralization via publication of primary source material from state, private, and church archives and libraries is still in progress to a certain degree, but the majority was accomplished from 1930–1962. Civil and criminal court records, pamphlets, books, private letters, diaries, chronicles, and journals were collected, as well as birth, death, baptismal, and land records.

However, the Bender methodology became more contentious academically as revisionists began to include persons and entities he felt were outside the pale of normal Anabaptism. His narrow preconceptions, as well as that of his adherents, concerning what true Mennonite Anabaptism consisted of (i.e., those radical Christians who were uniformly nonviolent biblical literalists, anti-pedobaptists, seeking the restitution of the apostolic primitive New Testament church to the exclusion of all others), was contrary to what the new research was revealing. John Roth observed that Bender's pantheon of "normative" and "evangelical" Anabaptists excluded important radical reformers like Müntzer, Hubmaier, Denck, Schwenckfeld, much to the chagrin of historians such as Franklin

---

64. Troeltsch, *Social Teaching*, 694–709. This work was translated into English by Olive Wyon, but not until 1931.

65. Bender and Oyer, "Historiography, Anabaptist," 8.

66. Bender and Oyer, "Historiography, Anabaptist."

67. Neff, "Manuscripts." See also Bender and Oyer, "Historiography, Anabaptist."

H. Littell, Roland Bainton (1894–1984), Hans Hillerbrand, and George H. Williams, who coined the phrase "Radical Reformation" in 1962.[68] It should also be noted that the Bender School's normative and evangelical litmus test for true Anabaptism eliminated those radical reformers who, although anti-pedobaptists, accepted the idea that the age of the Holy Spirit had arrived rendering the rational and physical trappings of traditional Christianity moot. These spiritualists had decided that the Spirit rendered all outer, physical, and natural elements of Christianity (the Bible, the Eucharist, baptism, and the accompanying ceremonies and rituals) null and void. The inner working of the Spirit alone had any efficacy in being Christian as each believer now possessed the Holy Spirit as individuals, thus rendering outer or rational spirituality useless in living a true Christian life. Those identified by the Bender School as non-normative spiritualists, however, were noted for their manifestations of the charismata, particularly prophecy, glossolalia (speaking in tongues), and interpretation, including dreams, visions, and revelations, many naming the gifts of the Spirit listed by the apostle Paul in 1 Corinthians 12–14. Also included were: Melchior Hoffman, Ludwig Haetzer, Andreas Bodenstein von Karlstadt, the Zwickau Prophets, Paracelsus (1493–1541), Valentine Weigel (1533–1588), and Sebastian Franck (1499–1542).[69] Not all the spiritualists were of the same mind regarding the inner and outer word and the efficacy of the Bible, as some still adhered to *sola scriptura* as a failsafe for judging the validity of spiritual revelation according to Pauline pneumatology.

MONOGENESIS OR POLYGENESIS

James Stayer and fellow historians of Reformation radicalism, Werner Packull and Klaus Depperman, published "From Monogenesis to Polygenesis," challenging Bender's Anabaptist paradigm, which focused on the rebellion of Conrad Grebel and the Swiss Brethren against Zwingli in 1525.[70] Stayer's new paradigm advocated the inclusion of Hoffman and the apocalyptic Hans Hut, among many others of like confession, as Anabaptists. It also saw the development of Anabaptist nonviolence and separatism as emerging gradually as outcomes of anticlericalism, apoca-

---

68. Roth, "Recent Currents in the Historiography," 524–25.
69. Williams, *Spiritual and Anabaptist Writers*, 28–35.
70. Stayer, "From Monogenesis or Polygenesis."

lyptic fears, and aspirations for social reform, and not from the Bender theory of the outgrowth of lay Bible conventicles seeking to restore the New Testament apostolic church, discipleship, and nonviolence.[71] By the 1980s, and notwithstanding the support of Bender's students John Howard Yoder (1927–1997) and Heinold Fast, the Bender paradigm had been superseded by the reality that Anabaptism's boundaries were fluid and its theology not easily defined.[72] Roth has concluded that the Stayer, et al., polygenesis theory has been the most significant historiographical paradigm shift in the writing of Anabaptist history, implying that there has been little in the way of dramatic change in the discipline since then.[73] However, there continues to be a very guarded position taken by Mennonite scholars regarding Anabaptist history and its role as a unifying force for the global Mennonite communion around a shared theological and historical point of view.[74]

One important issue a historian has to overcome, given Mennonite early Anabaptist historiography, is the narrow parameters set for the qualification of an Anabaptist under Bender's paradigm. What occurred in the translation work of the Bender school concerning Pentecostal- and charismatic-type behavior and the manifestation of the gifts of the Spirit as it appears in the original German manuscripts in many cases is an anglicized version of the German. The German phrase for speaking in tongues, for example, *Zungen Reden*, (a translation of Erasmus' New Testament Greek *glossolalia*) is used throughout many manuscripts, but is translated as *unintelligible speech* or *language that no one could understand*. These translations are not incorrect, but are perhaps indicative of an effort to avoid any concurrence with early Pentecostal-type terminology. Pentecostal terms such as speaking in tongues and interpretation, glossolalia, and behavior such as weeping, dreams, visions, healings, physical contortions (possibly slain in the Spirit), and other camp-meeting-type phenomena were particularly singled out as being beyond liminal Anabaptism.[75] In order to avoid these kinds of arbitrary exclusions of Anabaptist spirituality, it was necessary to carefully review the pertinent original German manuscripts to determine what exactly

71. Roth, "Recent Currents in the Historiography," 526.

72. Roth, "Recent Currents in the Historiography," 527. See Also, Yoder, *Anabaptism and Reformation in Switzerland*, 194–97.

73. Roth, "Recent Currents in the Historiography," 534.

74. Roth, "Recent Currents in the Historiography," 534.

75. Williams, *Radical Reformation*, 667.

was being described in reference to spiritual praxis and determine if it was similar to Pentecostalism. It must be noted that neither early twentieth-century Pentecostalism nor the charismatic movement of the 1960s were accepted by the Mennonite Church in the USA and Canada. It was initially resisted and discouraged to the point of asking adherents who participated to withdraw from their respective Mennonite fellowships, which lends some perspective to the Bender paradigm in question.[76]

In the more recent past, Anabaptist historiography has moved from a confessional dogmatic to a more objective sociohistorical method which now encompasses social history, theological history, and theology in an indispensable interdisciplinary methodology.[77] A. James Reimer succinctly traces the evolution of Anabaptist historiography from the highly prejudicial descriptions in the contemporary histories of the sixteenth century, mentioned above, to the work of Troeltsch in 1912 that contextualized Anabaptism as sectarian, but in a positive sense for their contribution of the concept of the separation of church and state to modern liberal democracies.

Reimer then proceeds to describe the Bender School as the first effort to legitimize the academic study of Anabaptism with the publication of the *Anabaptist Vision*. The students of this era saw the early Anabaptists as nonviolent critics of *corpus Christianum* and Constantinianism, John Howard Yoder being its most influential student.[78] The third wave of scholars was led by James Stayer, Werner Packull, Klaus Deppermann, and Hans Jürgen-Goertz, who supported the polygenesis of Anabaptism, causing a paradigm shift which is still current. He suggests a fourth stage led by C. Arnold Synder and John Rempel, who concur with the importance of polygenesis and social histories, but have nuanced them to account for the theological history of Anabaptism. They insist that there exists a theological and ecclesiological core of beliefs which binds the various Anabaptist groups together not unlike Allan Anderson's "family resemblance" theory of Pentecostalism.[79]

---

76. Epp, "Blumenhof Mission Hall." See also Thiessen, "Thiessen, Johann, 1869–1953"; Storms, "Eby, Solomon, 1834–1931"; Bender, "Ontario Mennonite Brethren in Christ"; Lederach, "First Mennonite Church, Norristown, Pa."; Del Gingrich, "Koch, Roy Swartz"; Kauffman, "Mennonite Charismatics"; Bauman, "Charismatic Movement"; Mennonite Church, "Holy Spirit in the Life."

77. Reimer, "Denominational Apologetics to Social History," 235.

78. Yoder, *Anabaptism and Reformation in Switzerland*, lii–liv.

79. Anderson, "Varieties, Taxonomies, and Definitions," 15.

Snyder developed a common core of systematic theological and doctrinal categories for examining Anabaptism of the early sixteenth century: the creed (they were primarily traditional orthodox Christians); the Bible (as illuminated by the Spirit) was the sole authority, emphasizing both the inner and outer Word, salvation by grace through faith (a strong view of prevenient grace guarded against Pelagianism); becoming righteous in the power of the risen Christ constituted salvation, not Lutheran *simul Justus et peccator*; anthropology (humans were fallen but the incarnation and atonement freed the human will to accept or reject salvation); discipleship (importance of both faith and works); pneumatology (inward spiritual regeneration was the first step in the process of salvation); ecclesiology (priesthood of all believers, baptism, and the Lord's Supper were outward signs of inner regeneration); the ban as a form of church discipline; mutual aid; and eschatology (the imminence of the end time, when the Holy Spirit will be poured out on all people, accompanied by dreams, visions, direct revelations). [80] Finally, Reimer concludes with a fifth wave of historiographers who are interpreting Anabaptism from an interdisciplinary perspective, including natural and social sciences, history, philosophy, literature, and theology. It is within this last group that consideration is being given to a more ecumenical and comparative historiography and theology of sixteenth-century Anabaptism and early twentieth-century Pentecostalism.[81]

Sixteenth-century Anabaptism will be defined for our purposes by using the doctrinally and ecclesiologically held principles said by C. Arnold Snyder to constitute the theological and ecclesiological core of sixteenth-century Anabaptism in general. A critical element that he highlights among these core principles, which is most pertinent to this dissertation, is the increased emphasis by Anabaptists on pneumatology. "The work of the Spirit provided the essential underpinning for biblical interpretation, for conversion, and rebirth leading to baptism, and for discipleship (as an enabling power which made discipleship possible). Anabaptist ethics and ecclesiology rested on the living presence of the Spirit." [82]

The failure of the Bender School to recognize many of the spiritualists was indicative of their unwillingness to include those who did not fit

---

80. Snyder, *Anabaptist History and Theology*, 83–99.
81. Reimer, "Denominational Apologetics to Social History," 236.
82. Snyder, *Anabaptist History and Theology*, 96.

their normative evangelical model of orthodox Mennonite Christianity, but it also precluded any group or person who advocated that part of the primitive New Testament church that was pneumatologically charismatic. It also encouraged pejorative translations of historical records which reflected the many manifestations of the charismata in Anabaptists' meetings and conventicles. [83] This dilemma has been overcome by the more recent historiography of Anabaptism, particularly the expansion of the definition of the inclusiveness of the movement since the acceptance of a polygenetic origin. It will be shown that early twentieth-century Pentecostals had also embraced the idea of the polygenetic origin of Pentecostalism.

PENTECOSTAL HISTORIOGRAPHY

Current Pentecostal historiography, compared to that on early Anabaptism, concerned itself primarily with late nineteenth- and early twentieth-century origins, rather than with trying to link it with reformation or even earlier antecedents. As seen by some, Pentecostalism is an empowering religious response to contemporary sociological conditions such as poverty, immorality, and racial discrimination, all of which were present in the era of its emergence.[84] But Edith Blumhofer more correctly attributes the advent of the movement to Catholic and Protestant Christian apostasy and the desire for restitution of the New Testament primitive church. This is analogous to the social and cultural situation in sixteenth-century Europe at the emergence of Anabaptism. She suggests that it was also the radical desire for the restoration of the primitive church that motivated both movements.[85]

C. Arnold Snyder's common core of beliefs and principles used to identify Anabaptism will be juxtaposed with Allan Anderson's theory of the nature of Pentecostalism. Both see the difficulty in defining movements of such polygenetic origins—or in Anderson's perspective, "polycentric" origins—but both see the respective movements as being within the context of traditional Christian orthodoxy. Allan Anderson may agree with Robert Mapes Anderson's observation that Western Pentecostalism's self-definition in terms of the doctrine of "initial evidence,"

---

83. Clasen, *Anabaptism*, 90–95.
84. Anderson, *Vision of the Disinherited*.
85. Blumhofer, *Restoring the Faith*, 4–5.

but he considers it more correctly defined in the broader context of the experience of the working of the Holy Spirit and practice of spiritual gifts.[86] Allan Anderson, much like Arnold Snyder (regarding Anabaptism's polygenesis), adopted a Wittgenstein-type "family resemblance" definition for Pentecostalism, and identifies the resemblances within a greater global perspective, incorporating the myriad of Pentecostalism's emerging churches throughout the majority world that also emphasize the general working of the Holy Spirit despite some blurred edges.[87] The term "working of the Holy Spirit" implies conformity to Pauline pneumatology according to 1 Corinthians 12–14 for both.

METHODOLOGY

While there is no intent to establish any historical connection between early sixteenth-century Anabaptism and early twentieth-century Pentecostalism, there is intent to present evidence that early Pentecostalism independently interpreted 1 Corinthians 12–14 with a similar hermeneutic. A chronological narrative will be used to compare those aspects of Anabaptism praxes identified as being similar to those of early Pentecostalism. As each Anabaptist Pentecostal aspect is identified as being believed and practiced, a comparison will be made with the similar beliefs and praxes of Pentecostalism. The comparison will be made within the context of the historical development of the respective movements. However, this will not be a history of the Reformation or of Pentecostalism, but it will discuss the manifestations of the gifts of the Spirit, the charismata, as they were chronologically introduced during the advent of each respective movement beginning with Anabaptism.

It will be argued that the acceptance by both Luther and Zwingli of *sola fide and sola scriptura,* Luther's experimentation with the medieval mysticism of Johannes Tauler and the *Theologia Germanica,* and Zwingli's Erasmianism, the Pauline pneumatology of both, combined with the influence of Luther's radical *Schwärmer*, Karlstadt, Scwenckfeld, and Müntzer, resulted in the emergence of the Pentecostal-like Anabaptist movement. An examination of the origins of Luther and Zwingli's initial theologies will show that what began as their respective attempts

---

86. Anderson, *Introduction to Pentecostalism*, 14.

87. Anderson, "Varieties, Taxonomies, and Definitions," 15. See also, Snyder, *Anabaptist History and Theology*, 5.

to reform the Catholic Church resulted in the unintended establishment of new churches: Lutheran, Swiss reformed, and Anabaptist. An analysis of the influence of the initial theologies of Luther and Zwingli on various radical groups, including the Anabaptists that emerged from their respective reform efforts, will be scrutinized by an investigation of the praxes of those theologies by the Anabaptists. An examination of the various books, pamphlets, and correspondence written against radical elements by Luther and Zwingli will be undertaken.

The examination of pertinent sixteenth-century archival primary source material, secondary sources, and contemporary chronicles and memoirs mentioned above, was done to compare the varied aspects of initial Anabaptist spirituality and theology with similar contemporary sources of early Pentecostalism. This methodology made the analysis and comparison of the two movements most convincing. An added value will be the possibility of proposing a causal explanation for the similarities identified.

Chapter one will argue that the initial Reformation theology of Martin Luther and the catalytic effect of his early consideration of the spiritual efficacy of medieval mysticism, particularly the *Theologia Germanica*, the works of Johannes Tauler (1300–1361), emphasis on the Petrine doctrine of the priesthood of the believer, and inclusion of the magistracy, had a lasting effect on the emergence of reformation radicalism.[88] The radical Lutheran *Schwärmer* also had a significant influence on the emerging Anabaptist movement.[89]

Chapter two will contend that, not unlike Luther, the initial theology of Huldrych Zwingli, its origins, propagation, and influence, made a specific and significant contribution to the rise of Anabaptism. It will argue that as he gravitated toward the inclusion of the magistracy into his reformation, he compromised his initial theological positions to satisfy secular rulers' fear that too much change too fast would upset the civil order. Zwingli, by agreeing to continue the Catholic Mass, infant baptism, use of images, and the ecclesiastical priesthood, alienated his radical adherents who became Anabaptists.

Chapter three will examine Anabaptism's efforts to restore the primitive church and argue that, very similar to early Pentecostalism, the full restitution of the New Testament church would necessitate active and

---

88. Hoffman, *Theologia Germanica of Martin Luther*, 53–54.
89. Luther, "Against the Roman Papacy"; Lehmann, *Luther's Works*.

effective evangelism, the approbation of the gifts of the Holy Spirit according to 1 Corinthians 12–14, the institution of adult rebaptism replacing infant baptism, and the separation of church and state.

Chapter four focuses on the impact of evangelism, persecution, and pacifism in both Anabaptism and Pentecostalism. It will also examine the importance that both placed on the restitution of the primitive apostolic New Testament church. The consequences of magisterial intervention in the sixteenth century, both at the local and imperial levels, and the traumatic affect it had on the diaspora that ensued will be discussed. The purpose is to examine the persecution that took place, including the techniques that were used to enforce the various laws and mandates that were passed to control, suppress, and eliminate Anabaptism and the effectiveness of their evangelism. Additionally, a comparison of pacifistic theologies of Anabaptism and Pentecostalism will be made.

Finally, chapter five will focus on the development of early Anabaptist spirituality and theology and its similarity to that which was developed by early Pentecostalism. A comparative analysis will establish that both radical confessions included parallel theological insights and opinions based on comparable hermeneutical praxes and spiritual experiences. Scrutiny of their respective conclusions and how they were reached, notwithstanding the passing of almost 500 years, will also reveal their similarities.

It will be primarily within the context of the life and work of Pilgram Marpeck that the various Anabaptist attempts at unification will be examined. Alister McGrath has identified Marpeck as one of three of the most significant theologians in the Anabaptist movement, including Balthasar Hubmaier and Menno Simons. Simons would first appear after the collapse of the Münster apocalyptic experiment of 1534–35 and ultimately rescue Anabaptism from extinction.[90]

The most significant overall contribution of this thesis is not only to the history of early sixteenth-century Anabaptism and early Pentecostalism, but to the general history of Christianity's continued praxis of manifestation of the charismata from the first-century church to the Reformation and into the early Pentecostal movement of the nineteenth and twentieth centuries. It argues in support of past, less-detailed observations of many Reformation and Pentecostal scholars that early sixteenth-century Anabaptism was a similar Pentecostal-type movement,

---

90. Simons, *Complete Writings of Menno Simons*, 28–29.

by presenting evidence of the praxis of the charismata according to the Pauline pneumatology of 1 Corinthians 12–14.

CHAPTER 1

Luther, Erasmus, and the Foundation of Reformation Radicalism

THIS CHAPTER WILL CONTEND that Luther had an initial interest in the more mystical, spiritual, and theological ideas of Rhenish mysticism, particularly Johannes Tauler, Erasmus, the *devotio moderna,* and Pauline pneumatology. These interests had a significant impact on the development of the earliest Reformation radicals within the Lutheran movement. But as his reform efforts evolved, he shied away from those early influences.

His anti-clericalism was a critical catalyst that began to shape the developing core of his reform. Moreover, from that perspective he began to focus on the overarching importance of justification by faith alone, *sola fide* and Scripture alone, *sola scriptura,* as the final arbiter of the faith, not the pope.[1] His more radical adherents, however, continued to follow those initial mystical inclinations, even after he began to shy away from them, although they did maintain the practice of the principles of *sola scriptura* and *sola fide.* This gave rise to the idea of the possibility of the restitution of the primitive New Testament church and consequently the abandonment of any effort to reform the Roman Catholic Church.

The polemic that developed from Luther's initial interest in mysticism and Pauline spirituality as juxtaposed against the radical anti-Lutheranism of his early adherents Andreas Bodenstein von Karlstadt (1480–1531), Thomas Münzter (1489–1525), and Caspar Schwenckfeld

---

1. Lohse, *Martin Luther's Theology,* 187–88. See also, McGrath, *Reformation Thought,* 152–53.

(1489–1561)—the *Schwärmer* (fanatics)—would be detrimental to his original reform intent.[2] These Lutheran radicals would loom instrumental in the emergence of other radical elements of the Reformation, particularly for the purpose of this thesis, the Swiss Anabaptists.

The term "radical" will be generally defined for the purposes of this thesis as the advocacy of fundamentally innovative and/or extreme changes in the accepted philosophy and theology of the Roman Catholic Church. This includes the attempted restitution of primitive New Testament Christianity, in the Pauline perspective, notwithstanding 1,500 years of Church history and tradition.[3] Not only Anabaptists', but Huldrych Zwingli's (1484–1531) and Martin Luther's (1483–1546) early theological concepts of ecclesiology and spirituality certainly conform to this definition and therefore identify them as radical protestors in the eyes of the Catholic Church. Although they may not necessarily have foreseen the idea of restitution of the New Testament church as being part of their reforms, Luther and Zwingli did open the door to that theology for Anabaptist radicals. Historians and theologians of Luther argue that if Anabaptist radical elements meet the above definition "Luther was by far the most radical reformer."[4] George H. Williams described the Radical Reformation as a "tremendous movement at the core of Christendom during the sixty years following Luther's three great Reformation tracts of 1520." That being the case, "it was as much an entity of the Reformation" as the magisterial reformations of Luther in Germany, Zwingli in Switzerland, and the Catholic Counter-Reformation, notwithstanding the radicals' rejection of all three.[5]

Luther would soon realize that his early interest in the *Theologia Germanica* of the *devotio moderna*, the sermons of Rhenish mystic Johannes Tauler (1300–1361), and a literal interpretation of the apostle Paul, would have a very different impact on those who considered his concept of *sola scriptura* as opening the door to a New Testament spirituality that needed

---

2. "Schwärmer" is the German word that Luther used to identify those who embraced the manifestation of the gifts of the Holy Spirit as listed by Paul in 1 Corinthians 12–14, specifically and initially Karlstadt, Müntzer, and Schwenckfeld.

3. This definition of radicalism is my own. Paulinism will be defined as the utilization of the biblical writings and theology of the apostle Paul in support of fundamental and or extreme changes to the philosophy and theology of the sixteenth-century Roman Catholic Church.

4. Stayer, "Radical Reformation," 249. See also, Bainton, *Here I Stand*, 90; Methuen, *Luther and Calvin*, 24. And Zwingli's Swiss reformation will be explored in chapter 2.

5. Williams, *Radical Reformation*, 1289.

restitution of Christianity in general. The three protagonists—Karlstadt, Müntzer, and Schwenckfeld—were chosen for this analysis as they have been identified as the first radical leaders emanating from the context of Lutheranism and the profound impact they had not only on Lutheranism but on radicalism in its broader sense. C. Arnold Snyder identifies Karlstadt, Müntzer, and Schwenckfeld as "evangelical" radical reformers as opposed to the Anabaptist radicalism of Swiss origin. He has observed that there is great difficulty in clearly differentiating the radical reformers from each other in that although there are similarities, there was much in the way of theological disagreement that caused conflicts. The evangelical radicals—the *Schwärmer*—are uniquely of Lutheran origin and not Anabaptists. However, this does not preclude a substantial exchange of ideas and influence in many theological areas.[6] Luther and Zwingli were also radicals within the contexts of their respective German and Swiss Reformations. But even they rejected various aspects of one another's theology, notwithstanding many similarities and a mutual conflict with the Anabaptists, Catholics, and other radical elements.

Luther had sensed the spiritual dysphoria that existed within the Roman Catholic Church during his early Christian experience, and began an anxious search of Scripture hoping to explain and rectify his lack of personal peace regarding his salvation. He determined that in spite of his absolute dedication to the church as an Augustinian monk, the absence of the primitive faith, pneumatologies, and praxes, as described in the New Testament, were the missing elements.[7] He would gain spiritual peace only when he concluded that what Paul meant in Romans 5:1 was that Christians were justified (made righteous) by faith in Christ alone; thus rendering irrelevant the works-oriented soteriology of the church.[8] He commented in his lectures on Romans:

> Being justified therefore by faith, let us have peace with God, through our Lord Jesus Christ. But it must be noted how the apostle bases the spiritual peace on righteousness. Therefore, he says first: "being justified by faith" and then only, "we have peace."[9]

---

6. Snyder, *Anabaptist History and Theology*, 43–49.
7. Luther, "Table Talk No. 4007," 308–9.
8. Bainton, *Here I Stand*, 65.
9. Pauck, *Luther*, 153–54.

This was the hermeneutic epiphany that brought the peace he felt salvation should have provided him in the first place. Wilhelm Pauck observed that Luther had learned to distinguish between two literal meanings of biblical text, the historical-literal and the prophetic-literal interpretations. He opted for the latter of the two which appeared to him to be eminently inspired by the Holy Spirit, while the other was more prone to be a product of human imagination.[10] Martin Brecht agrees with Pauck regarding Luther's hermeneutics, although he did not set aside the scholastic fourfold standard of interpretation, he began to reveal a new style not only in Romans, but in Galatians and Hebrews as well. The more exegesis he did, the more he emphasized the prophetic-literal hermeneutic as being a more spiritual, christological, and moral sense of the Scripture.[11] The consequence of this new interpretive method would show up later in the Reformation when Anabaptists began to use the same method, following Luther's lead, while implementing the praxis of the priesthood of the believer.

The purpose of this fresh analysis is to contextualize the ensuing radical perspectives of those who saw a different reformation than that of Luther. Based on Luther's early spiritual initiatives and from his initial prophetic-literal hermeneutic, particularly his Petrine doctrine of the priesthood of the believer (1 Pet 2:9), radicalism found new authority to read and interpret Scripture without clerical authority.

It will also provide evidence that early twentieth-century Pentecostalism's manifestation of the charismata was not as uncommon historically as some would suggest.[12] The concepts of ecclesiological restitution versus reformation, conflicting interpretations of the relationship between word and Spirit, the efficacy of an experiential pneumatology based on New Testament descriptions, the debates over the Sacraments, and finally the differences concerning ecclesiological praxis, were all sources of contention during the early Reformation. They were also similar issues with which early Pentecostalism would struggle as well.

10. Pauck, *Luther*, xxx.

11. Brecht, "Luther's Reformation," 131.

12. Anderson, *Introduction to Pentecostalism*, 19. Early twentieth-century Pentecostalism will be defined by using the term "classic" and include those religious movements that believed in the manifestation of the gifts of the Holy Spirit as described by Luke in the Acts of the Apostles and by the apostle Paul throughout his New Testament writings, particularly 1 Corinthians 12–14. This necessarily will incorporate all of those idiosyncratic doctrines and praxes that evolved from those beliefs and practices globally during the late nineteenth century through 1935.

A successful analysis of early Pentecostalism's ostensible acceptance of similar theologies and praxes of early sixteenth-century radicalism, particularly its pneumatology, requires identification of those radical antecedents. The early approbation of a more literal Pauline New Testament hermeneutic by Martin Luther and the impact that Rhenish mysticism as expressed in the *Theologica Germanica* and the sermons of Tauler had, when combined with the influence of Erasmian Humanism on him, were the primary catalysts for the emergence of radicalism within Lutheranism. This resulted in two fundamental Lutheran positions: first, the rejection of Catholicism's two-source concept of the Word of God (written Scripture plus the traditions of the church as arbitrated by the pope), and second, the declaration that Scripture alone was the only true arbiter of the faith, *sola scriptura*.[13] From these two concepts, Luther initially developed a prophetic-literal ecclesiology and pneumatology which, when accepted by his radical adherents, resulted in a highly charismatic view of the primitive church that he did not anticipate. When coupled with the priesthood of the believer these two positions opened the door to the Christian laity to read and interpret Scripture.

The reform *(reformatio)* that Luther sought created a clear juxtaposition between reforming Catholicism and developing a radical objective of the restitution of a literal charismatic primitive church. The idea of restitution required a complete restoration of the church to its initial New Testament elements of unimpaired purity, *restitutio in integrum,* perhaps the Full Gospel in early twentieth-century Pentecostal terms.[14] This required maintaining and developing the original, more literal hermeneutic of Luther within which the concepts of *ecclesia* and *pneuma* were understood in prophetic-literal Pauline terms.[15] Radical elements began to emerge when it was understood that major aspects of Roman Catholicism were in fact being maintained by Luther. They realized that these doctrines and praxes were neither supported by Scripture nor conducive to the restitution of primitive Christianity. They were thought to be political and social accommodations to respective magistracies necessary to ensure the success of his reformation of the church.[16] With this newly

13. Goertz, "Scriptural Interpretation among Radical Reformers," 578.

14. Friedman, "Restitutionism," 145; Littell, *Origins of Sectarian Protestantism*, 79–82. *Restitutio in Integrum* "restored in its unimpaired condition, soundness, purity, and correctness" (Blumhofer, *Restoring the Faith*, 3–5).

15. Stayer, "Radical Reformation," 252–56.

16. Littell, *Origins of Sectarian Protestantism*, 3–4.

found freedom to read and interpret the Bible without papal arbitration, *sola scriptura*, radicalism increasingly pursued the restitution of primitive Christianity.

The core of Luther's reform effort will be listed in the order in which they influenced his protest as follows: anticlericalism, s*ola scriptura*, s*ola fide*, the priesthood of the believer (the right of P. 253-every Christian to read and interpret the Bible and preach the gospel), infant baptism, the real presence of Christ in the Eucharist, the word has priority over the Spirit, cessation of the manifestation of the charismata, marriage of priests, bondage of the will, and inclusion of the "magistracy in the propagation of the gospel. These core beliefs will be compared to those of the Lutheran *Schwärmer* and subsequently to those of the Anabaptists.

One source of Luther's initial theology of reform can be attributed to the significant influence of Rhenish mysticism.[17] The *Theologia* had been published anonymously in 1350, but edited and republished by Luther (who believed that Tauler was its author) in 1518. It is charismatically Christocentric in terms of the personal enablement of the Holy Spirit in encouraging obedient Christlikeness aimed at the deified union of one's soul with Christ, both in the present and in the hereafter. The idea of a deifying union is typical of medieval mysticism, particularly among the Rhenish and Dutch mystics. Bernard McGinn points out, however, that the birth of Christ in the soul (perhaps a type of the early twentieth-century Pentecostal new birth theology) and deification are often used interchangeably.[18] Tauler's theology, having been introduced by Luther, also had great influence on many radicals. Tauler's ideas concerning the role of the Holy Spirit in the life of the common Christian would influence and even be incorporated into many radical theologies. His idea of practical and personal spiritual yieldedness to Christ (*Gelassenheit*) first found its way into the theologies of Karlstadt, Müntzer, and Schwenckfeld, all ardent Lutherans.[19] Tauler's attractiveness may have been captured in his very Pentecostal-like comparison of the infilling of the Holy Spirit, described as follows:

> This precious Holy Spirit entered the disciples and all those who were open to him, bringing such wealth, such abundance and

17. Luther, "Concerning the Ministry," 32–36.

18. McGinn, *Essential Writings of Christian Mysticism*, 422; Sanders, *William Seymour Papers*, 113, 44.

19. Rupp, *Patterns of Reformation*, 120, 128, 257. "Gelassenheit" is the resignation of the self and total commitment to God.

superfluity and overflowed them inwardly. It was as if we were to allow the Rhine River its way, removing from its path all hindrances. As if it were to break its banks with its mass of flooding waters, roaring and threatening to submerge all things, filling all the valleys and inclines. So too did the Holy Spirit come upon the disciples and all those who were open to him. And so he still does today unceasingly: he fills and floods the grounds of our souls, our hearts, and minds, wherever he finds. These he fills with great wealth, graces, love and indescribable gifts. And he fills the valleys and depths which are open to him.[20]

Theologia Germanica and Tauler's sermons were classified by the church as mystical, but only in a devotional sense.

Luther's attraction to Rhenish mysticism stands as evidence of the spiritual experience that he yearned for as an ascetic Augustinian monk, or as Bengt Hoffman described it, "*sapientia experimentalis*," experiential Christian knowledge in a Pauline sense.[21] Both works emphasized a Christian spirituality based on New Testament concepts that developed subsequent to the day of Pentecost regarding the efficacious work of the Holy Spirit. The first Christians believed and taught that successful Christian living was made possible first by the indwelling of the Holy Spirit at salvation through faith alone (Acts 2:38; 4:23–31).[22] Tauler and the *Theologia* made Luther acutely aware of those aspects of the tension between the word and the Spirit in practical Christian living that were absent, or at least unaddressed by the contemporary church. However, he would eventually reject medieval mysticism as being too oriented toward the human intellect, such as that of Tauler's teacher, Meister Eckhart (1260–1328). He did, however, recognize the efficacy of the infilling of the Holy Spirit who made Christian living possible as a practical matter.[23]

DESIDERIUS ERASMUS (1469–1536)

Erasmus was a major antecedent of the Reformation efforts of Luther, Zwingli, and others, including many Anabaptist radicals. He was probably the most influential humanist of the Reformation era. The illegitimate

20. Davies, *God Within*, 84.

21. Hoffman in Luther, *Theologia Germanica of Martin Luther*, 14–20.

22. For a similar early Pentecostal perspective, see Wondey, "Pentecostalism and the Reformation," 116.

23. McGinn, *Harvest of Mysticism*, 96–97.

son of a Catholic priest, Erasmus was educated under the auspices of the previously mentioned *devotio moderna*. Thomas a Kempis's *Imitatio Christi*, the sermons of Tauler, and the *Theologia Germanica* are examples of *devotio moderna*'s theology of the immanence of God. In 1492, Erasmus was ordained an Augustinian priest, but would further his education at the University of Paris. There he engaged with humanists of the time and embarked on a humanistic writing career as an at-large scholar that would influence myriads of scholars, religious leaders, and monarchs for centuries.[24]

Among Erasmus's treatises that are important to our purposes are the *Philosophi Christi, Enchiridion militas Christiani: Hand Book of the Christian Soldier (1501), Moriae encomium: In Praise of Folly (1511)*, and his Greek and Latin translations of the New Testament (1516) including the *Paraclesis*. In these works, he was to have a most significant impact on the Reformation and its protagonists. He wrote the *Enchiridion* at the request of an anonymous woman who wished to improve her husband's morals. The tract is a moral how-to book in the Italian Renaissance-manual style, but was written according to Erasmus, "in order to counteract the error of those who make religion in general consist of rituals and observances...but who are astonishingly indifferent to matters that have to do with true goodness."[25] His handbook warned the reader that the common body of Christians—by implication the church—was corrupt in its affections as well as its ideas. Furthermore, its pastors and doctors misused these titles, which belonged to Christ, for their own advantage.[26] The text is divided into a series of rules, the fifth of which best expresses Erasmus's theological emphasis on the internal and spiritual nature of the Christian faith. It is clear that he saw the key to such faith as the correct interpretation of the word:

> For all Holy Scripture was divinely inspired and perfected by God its author. What is small is the lowliest of the Word, hiding under almost sordid words the greatest mysteries...What is inflexible and rough expresses the mystery clothed in the letter...Pluck out the spiritual sense: now nothing is sweeter, nothing more succulent...For what is the water concealed in the earth but the mystical meaning imprisoned in the letter?[27]

24. Radice, "Biographical Note," ix–x.
25. Erasmus, in Rummel, *Erasmus Reader*, 138.
26. Erasmus, in Rummel, *Erasmus Reader*, 138–51.
27. Erasmus, in Baille, *Advocates of Reform*, 303–4.

This hermeneutic method would be adopted by Luther with some nuance, but the essence was the same, the spiritual meaning of the word had to be garnered from the literal text but not violate its practical biblical meaning.[28] Luther could very well have been influenced as well, as it is also broached briefly by Tauler in his twenty-third sermon: "Note how the eternal Son of God, the Wisdom of the Father, always hid the ineffable brilliance of His wisdom in simple everyday parables."[29]

He describes a Christian as one who, if not separated from the world is at least differentiated from it in thought life and perspective. The source of this faith and world view he identified as the word:

> Just as nothing is more like the Father than the Son, the Word of the Father emanating from the inner most recesses of His spirit, so nothing is more like Christ than the word of Christ uttered in the inner most sanctuary of his most holy mind.[30]

In "Folly" he speaks out against the abuses of the clergy in such a vehement manner that the tract was placed on the church's *Index of Prohibited Books*.[31] His Latin New Testament translated many traditional Vulgate passages of Scripture that subtly but effectively gave them new meaning. By using the humanist linguistic method *ad fontes* and avoiding eisegetic scholasticism, Erasmus had John the Baptist cry out, "Repent! (Greek *metanoeite*)" in Matthew 3:2, whereas Jerome's Vulgate had him cry out, "Do penance!" This carried great implications for the medieval church which used this Scripture to support the sacrament of penance. He also presented a different perspective of the Virgin Mary as being gracious *(gratiosa)* and not, as did Jerome, full of grace *(gratia plena)* in Luke 1. This brought into question the church's tradition of quoting the Scripture devotionally in the recitation of "Hail Mary Full of Grace," theologically referring to her as being full of merit in God's sight.[32]

Erasmus made it very clear that he recognized the apostasy and corruption of the church and its clergy, and the superficiality of its ceremonies and rituals relative to the word. Luther was very much aware of Erasmus's position on the matter and was influenced to the point that he felt there was an affinity there which was conducive to collaboration.

---

28. Oberman, *Luther*, 168–72. See also McGrath, *Reformation Thought*, 159–60.
29. Tauler, in Farina, *Johannes Tauler*, 82.
30. Erasmus, in Rummel, *Erasmus Reader*, 145.
31. Erasmus, in Rummel, *Erasmus Reader*, 155.
32. MacCulloch, *Reformation*, 96–97.

Erasmus had spoken out against the effrontery of a clergy, including the pope, that had become formidable even to royalty. They were those

> Who for gain and despotic power, were leaving Christ out and preaching impudent dogmas so repugnant, such as the sale of indulgences, that even unlettered men couldn't stomach it.[33]

Erasmus also observed that this problem had been a catalyst for Luther's Reformation.

Luther and Erasmus corresponded briefly, Erasmus trying to avoid what he saw as a cataclysmic rupture in the church and Luther seeing a co-belligerent and ally against the pope and the church. However, Erasmus was quite careful; although identifying with Luther's protest, even understanding what he was attempting to reform, he avoided alienating Pope Leo while still admitting the obvious flaws of the church that Luther was protesting against.[34] In spite of his attempt to distance himself from Luther, Erasmus was still accused of being the source of Luther's Protestant theology. The catalyst for the rift between the two was a disagreement over the nature of the human will. Luther averred that human will is something in name only while Erasmus took the position that a person could, in fact, of their own free will, turn away from God, a concept considered to be a semi-Pelagian principle of medieval Ockhamism.[35] Luther recognized that Erasmus's desire for peace in the church was greater than his own urgent sense of truth and justice, and accused him of sacrificing his principles for self-preservation.[36]

LUTHER'S THREE GREAT WRITINGS OF 1520

In 1520, Luther set out his agenda for reformation in three writings: *To the Christian Nobility of the German Nation*, *The Babylonian Captivity of the Church*, and *The Freedom of a Christian Man*.[37] He wrote twenty-five other works in the same year, but it was these three in particular that captured the heart of the direction in which the Reformation would

---

33. Erasmus, in Rummel, *Erasmus Reader*, 201.
34. Bainton, *Here I Stand*, 265–70.
35. McGrath, *Christian Theology*, 24, 38.
36. Ozment, *Age of Reform*, 294–301; Oberman, *Luther*, 211–15.
37. Pettegree, *Brand Luther*, 117.

proceed.[38] All three carried the same message, the priesthood of the believer, a response to his prevailing anticlericalism, *sola scriptura,* and *sola fide.*[39]

The *Schwärmer* rejected Luther's protest, but continued to give these elements of his initial theology a literal spiritual-prophetic interpretation. They proceeded to develop appropriate praxes that followed their understanding of Luther's initial spiritual inclinations, although what resulted was not what he had intended. His experiences with the *Schwärmer* and the Anabaptists are cases in point.

Alister McGrath has observed that the tendency of Luther's medieval Augustinian tradition, the *schola Augustaniana moderna,* emphasized the basis of Christian theology as being *scriptura sola,* minimizing other aspects of theology. Luther's early views upheld the sufficiency of Scripture as interpreted by the fathers and doctors of the church, but insisted that the final arbiter was Scripture alone. Augustinian theologians appear to have affirmed that method until, at least in Luther's case, it became clear that a more radical application of *sola scriptura* was required.[40] Bernhard Lohse has correctly argued that Luther's earlier position of accepting the teachings of the church fathers, the councils, and *ratio,* along with Scripture, was mitigated as he continued to debate with the church. He realized that many traditional and doctrinal positions were in conflict with Scripture. He believed that Scripture and the church should be considered together, but as Scripture existed prior to the church, it ranked higher. Luther learned that faith, *sola fide,* was due to the Bible alone, *sola scriptura.* Lohse also asserts that after 1517/1518, Luther's application of scriptural authority to the church first began pointing the way to an inevitable breach that lends some credence to Timothy George's opinion that it was his declaration of the priority of the word over pope and council at the Leipzig Debate in 1519 that pushed him beyond reconciliation is an accurate observation.[41] Luther recognized the disparity between the church and the prescribed scriptural mandates for its spiritual character and mission, within the Pauline concepts of *ecclesia* and *pneuma,* as the

---

38. Pettegree, *Brand Luther,* 117.

39. Luther, "Freedom of the Christian," 394, 98; "To the Christian Nobility," 127–29; "Babylonian Captivity," 210–11, 394–95. See also, Goertz, *Anabaptists,* 37–39.

40. McGrath, *Intellectual Origins,* 148–51.

41. Lohse, *Martin Luther's Theology,* 187–88, 264. See also, George, *Theology of the Reformers,* 80.

body of Christ and the immanence of God respectively.[42] Luther was initially influenced by Erasmus because he had written critically about the need of the church to reform within the context of conforming to Scripture. But Erasmus rejected Luther's confrontational style and his theology of the bondage of the will.[43]

Luther understood the work of the Holy Spirit as enabling every Christian to read and interpret Scripture, as it interpreted itself. He acknowledged the efficacy of the scriptural concept of the priesthood of the believer. He promoted the idea of local congregations choosing their own pastors without ecclesiastical authority or qualification, considering them to be more suited to administer the word than the Catholic clergy.[44] In 1523, Luther would write,

> We must act according to Scripture and call and institute from among ourselves those who are found to be qualified and whom God has enlightened with reason and endowed with gifts to do so. "These fellows are the Christians, Christ's brethren, who with him are consecrated priests, as Peter says so too, 1 Peter 2 [9], you are a royal priesthood so that you may declare the virtue of him who called you into his marvellous light."[45]

Here is an early indication of Luther's intent regarding who was eligible to read and interpret Scripture and who was qualified. His initial intent was misunderstood, as Anabaptists and other radical reformers and spiritualists rejected the whole idea of a single priest because it was too much like the Roman Catholic model they were trying to reform.

In 1520, Luther had quoted the same Scripture to the German nobility declaring that consecration by a pope or bishop would never make a priest. For all who are baptized can already boast that the have been consecrated as priests. But he went on to say that no one should push himself forward without the congregation's consent or election, to do that which they have all have the authority to do.[46] Richard Marius opines that in 1520, in *The Freedom of a Christian*, Luther delineates between

---

42. I Cor 12:27.
43. Oberman, *Luther*, 294–301; Rummel, *Erasmus Reader*, 195–215.
44. Oberman, *Luther*, 309.
45. Luther, "That a Christian Assembly," 309.
46. Luther, "To the Christian Nobility," 127–29.

those Christians who might count themselves priests before God, but not understand the Bible required a class of priests who did.[47]

Nevertheless, he still considered the efficacy and work of the Holy Spirit as critical to faith. On this point he probably was influenced by the Erasmian *Philosophi Christi*, the internal and spiritual nature of faith in every Christian, Erasmus's concept of the importance of every Christian's responsibility to read Scripture, to be directly imbued with the teachings of Christ from birth, and in their respective vernaculars.[48] For Erasmus, every Christian, educated or not, could and should be a theologian.[49] Luther's theology also reflected the influence of Erasmus's emphasis on spirituality, rejection of the overemphasis on the externals of medieval religion, openness to philosophy and reason, and disdain for mysticism.[50]

THE HERMENEUTICS OF LUTHER AND ZWINGLI

Notwithstanding the independence of the reformations of Luther and Zwingli, they each adopted the same principles of reform, particularly *sola scriptura*. This gave their reformation efforts a recognizable common denominator. Both were trained scholastics and used the tools of that hermeneutical method. How Luther negotiated his way around the scholastic hermeneutic style has already been discussed. Where Luther was initially influenced by Rhenish mysticism, Zwingli was initially influenced by Erasmian humanism, which will be discussed in chapter two. Jerome's Latin Vulgate was the primary Bible in use as well as the *Glossa Ordinaria*, the accumulation of various glosses of the Bible. Similar works such as *The Catenae* (patristic interpretations) and *Liber Sententiarium*, a compilation of the interpretations of other scholastics, were also much-used tools for interpreting Scripture.[51] This compendium of biblical commentaries inserted filters between the reader of Scripture and Scripture itself, and therefore the Bible was being read indirectly.[52] The methodology of using the fourfold sense of Scripture, the *Quadriga*, had been developed as a way of distinguishing between the literal and

---

47. Marius, *Luther*, 270.
48. Olin, *Erasmus*, 97–108.
49. McConica, *Erasmus*, 45–47.
50. George, *Theology of the Reformers*, 112–13.
51. Berkhof, *Principles of Biblical Interpretation*, 24.
52. McGrath, *Intellectual Origins*, 125.

spiritual interpretation of the word. The method was taught in the following format;

> *Littera gesta docet, quid credas allegoria, moralis quid agas, quo tendas anagogia:*
>
> The letter teaches what happened; the allegory what you have to believe; the morality, how you have to act; and the anagogia, what you have to strive to.[53]

Scholasticism was greatly enhanced by the advent of printing, which enabled the publication and circulation of the linguistic tools mentioned above.[54] It reached its zenith, however, in the *opus magnus* of Thomas Aquinas (1225–1274), *Summa Theologica*. Thomism held that humans had the capacity of reason that enabled them to comprehend at least some of the truths of God, particularly those classified as natural theology, a synthesis of Aristotelian natural reason and the supernatural truth of faith.[55]

As they began studying Scripture, a transition between medieval scholasticism and a more nuanced approach was developing, particularly the increasing use of the literal prophetic-spiritual sense of the word. But Luther remained dedicated to the spiritual sense as he, "was deeply rooted in the traditional monastic approach to Scripture as the *sacra pagina*."[56] Charlotte Methuen points out, however, that although early-modern exegetes rejected the scholastic method, they, at the same time, contributed to its continued development in that they concentrated on new literal meanings of Scripture. They persisted in using spiritual readings which were only subsumed under an expanded definition of literal.[57] But the Roman Catholic Church continued to insist on a two-source definition of the word, thus establishing the concept of apostolic succession.[58] This created an indispensable clergy without whom none of the elements critical to salvation were accessible to the common Christian.[59] The Pauline concept of the body of Christ on earth as the gathering of believers which

---

53. Raeder, "Exegetical and Hermeneutical Work," 367.
54. Berkhof, *Principles of Biblical Interpretation*, 26.
55. Oberman, *Dawn of the Reformation*, 6.
56. Hagen, "Omnis Homo Mendax," 85.
57. Methuen, "Interpreting the Books of Nature," 2.
58. George, *Theology of the Reformers*, 81.
59. MacCulloch, *Reformation*, 10–11.

forms the *ecclesia* (Col 1:24) was lost in the clerical usurpation of the priesthood of the believer (1 Pet 2:9), a concept derived from personal application of *sola scriptura* by Luther and Zwingli and embraced, *en toto*, by radicalism in general.[60]

The acceptance by both Zwingli and Luther of Erasmus's declaration that Scripture was the final arbiter of the faith, *sola scriptura*, became the foundation of their respective Protestant Reformations. Just as it opened the doors to a popular Christian confession which enabled Christians to read and interpret Scripture through the power of the Holy Spirit, it also opened the same doors to Pentecostals in the early twentieth century. *Sola scriptura* was Luther's ultimate answer to an apostate church, not unlike the apostasy of the early twentieth-century church as perceived by Pentecostalism. In both instances, the Scripture began to be read and understood more literally. This in turn highlighted the Pauline spirituality of 1 Corinthians 12–14, which in both movements began to be expressed with manifestations of the charismata.

THE INDULGENCE CONTROVERSY

The Catholic theology of sin, contrition, confession, absolution, penance, and purgatory had been inextricably linked together by the church. One sinned, contritely confessed to a priest, was granted absolution, and penance was demanded for satisfaction to occur. If one should die in God's grace, but is still imperfectly purified, they are assured of their salvation, but must after death be purified in order to enter heaven. Purification at that point occurs in Purgatory, the final but temporary place for the purification for the elect once they achieve the holiness to enter heaven.[61] Indulgences were lucrative monetary devices sold by the church to buy a remission before God either partially or totally.[62] What were actually being sold were the merits of Christ, Mary, and saints who had avoided Purgatory by dying totally purified. These merits were under the control of the pope. The larger the payment for the indulgence, the more merits received. It became an embarrassment of riches to many protesting

---

60. Eph 1:23. *Ecclesia* is used throughout the book of Acts and the Pauline Epistles.

61. Rupp and Drewery, *Martin Luther*, 11. See also, Ratzinger, *Catechism of the Catholic Church*, 268–69.

62. Ratzinger, *Catechism of the Catholic Church*, 370.

churchmen, such as Jan Hus (1371–1415), Erasmus (1466–1536), and not the least of whom was Martin Luther.[63]

Richard Marius has pointed out that indulgences, although costly, were popular. Everyone wanted to limit or escape their time in Purgatory. The church would periodically issue Jubilee Indulgences which became a very lucrative source of funds for various building projects and growing the Vatican treasury in general. Various German rulers objected to the Vatican taking indulgence funds from their respective lands and taking them to Italy. In 1515, the infamous Dominican friar, Johann Tetzel, who is said to have coined the legendary phrase, "When the coin in the coffer rings, a soul from purgatory springs," came to Saxony where Luther was teaching and preaching, to sell indulgences. Frederick the Wise, Elector of Saxony and Luther's patron, refused to allow the sale. He objected to the Vatican taking funds from Saxony back to Italy.[64]

SOLA FIDE AND SOLA SCRIPTURA

On October 31, 1517, Luther decided to challenge the practice of selling indulgences based on his new literal spiritual-prophetic hermeneutic method which had rendered many church practices, such as the sale of indulgences, scripturally invalid. He challenged the practice by submitting for disputation his *Ninety-Five Theses* that challenged the church not only on indulgences and Purgatory, but on the two primary fundamentals of his new theology that would render Catholic, works-related salvation unbiblical. The theses were sent to Cardinal Albrecht of Mainz for consideration. He may have also posted them on the Wittenberg castle church door as was the custom for such disputations. Heiko Oberman observed that in theses 62 to 66 he argued that indulgences can only commute punishments of the church, only the gospel can remove the consequences of sin. Simple repentance was all that God required for his grace and forgiveness. Luther in effect had now combined two of the three principles of the Reformation, "unmerited grace and pure Scripture."[65] It cannot be overlooked that Luther also had challenged the authority of the pope as well as a lucrative source of income, neither of which would be tolerated. The theses were soon printed and distributed in German to the

---

63. Baille, *Advocates of Reform*, 11–12.
64. Marius, *Luther*, 132–35.
65. Oberman, *Luther*, 190–92.

public where they were received with great acclaim.⁶⁶ This would be the catalyst of the Reformation that was to come.

TWO KINDS OF RIGHTEOUSNESS

In 1519, Luther penned a sermon, "Two Kinds of Righteous," which set out his theology of how the righteousness of God was manifested in Christ. William Russell explained that the first kind was alien or external righteousness which is non-existent in humans because of their sinful nature. It is made available to them only as a free gift from Jesus. This righteousness is given in baptism and repentance and allows humans to claim all the benefits Christ accomplished on the cross as Christians. The second kind of righteousness (proper) is that which flourishes in Christians after they have found justification in Jesus. This righteousness is what enables a Christian to live pious lives, do good works, love their neighbour, and live as Christians in the world. It is not, however, due to any inherent goodness, but is only possible as a response to the gift of alien righteousness from Jesus.⁶⁷ Paul Althaus and Bernard Lohse concur with Russell's synopsis.⁶⁸ Proper righteousness is also justification through Christ for the forgiveness of sin upon repentance, but not for any future sin; therefore one is simultaneously righteous and sinful, *simul peccaor et iustus*. Luther compared the sinner to a sick man wherein recovery depended upon the doctor's regimen of treatment, but complete healing was not possible until the regimen was finished. One's sins are forgiven, but one is not completely redeemed (healed) until one dies in Christ. The perspective is of one living a pious life, but needing daily forgiveness for frequent lapses and failures which God provides in grace. This perception appears very much like the idea of progressive sanctification.⁶⁹ Luther wrote:

> This alien righteousness, instilled in us without our works by grace alone—while the Father, to be sure, inwardly draws us to Christ...Christ drives out the old Adam more and more in

---

66. Pettegree, *Brand Luther*, 174–76.

67. Russell, "Introduction," 134.

68. Althaus, *Theology of Martin Luther*, 232. See also, Lohse, *Martin Luther's Theology*, 76–77.

69. Althaus, *Theology of Martin Luther*, 242–243; Lohse, *Martin Luther's Theology*, 76.

accordance with the extent to which faith and knowledge of Christ grow. For alien righteousness is not instilled all at once, but it begins, makes progress, and is finally perfected at the end through death. The second kind of righteousness is our proper righteousness, not because we alone work it, but because we work with the first and alien righteousness. This is that manner of life spent in good works, in the first place. In the second place, this righteousness consists of love of one's neighbour, and in the third place, in meekness and fear toward God.[70]

LUTHER'S SCHWÄRMER

The three Lutheran adherents discussed below—Karlstadt, Müntzer, and Schwenckfeld—became the core of what Snyder has identified as the first "evangelical radical reformers." Although they are not considered to be Anabaptists by a strict definition of the term, they did indeed lay a foundation for radical reform which included the restitution of the primitive New Testament church which had some influence on the emergence of Anabaptism.[71] Their collective rejection of Luther's turn away from his initial reform theology, particularly the Petrine doctrine of the priesthood of the believer and a Pauline pneumatology combined with his inclusion of the magistracy, had a definite influence on the emerging Anabaptist movement.

ANDREAS BODENSTEIN VON KARLSTADT

The tension between Luther and Karlstadt, who was the first to abandon Luther, can be characterized as a conflict between their developing perspectives on the nature of the Reformation in its broadest terms. Luther and Karlstadt were colleagues at the University of Wittenberg from 1511 to 1522, during which time Luther challenged Karlstadt's Aristotelian theology, suggesting he reevaluate Augustinianism as more biblically valid.[72] Karlstadt's study resulted in his rejection of the Pelagian tendencies of Aristotelian scholasticism and his firm theological alignment with Luther. He would also become a seminal radical and vanguard of

---

70. Luther, "Two Kinds of Righteousness," 136.
71. Snyder, *Anabaptist History and Theology*, 26.
72. Sider, *Andreas Bodenstein Von Karlstadt*, 9–10.

anti-Lutheran radicalism, if not a precursor of Anabaptism, before their relationship would end.

By Karlstadt's own admission, both Luther and Johannes Staupitz (1460–1524) were extremely influential in his conversion to Augustianism.[73] Moreover, his Augustinian studies intensified his awareness of the problem of satisfying the requirement of fulfilling the law of God in the absence of good works as merits of congruity. His solution was to transpose the dilemma into one of word and Spirit, with the Spirit having precedence. This ultimately led to his devaluation of religious externalities such as the Bible, preaching, and the Sacraments. Scripture was not exactly the word of God but a witness to the word, an outward visible sign of an internal spiritual reality.[74] "Right living is from charity infused in the hearts, not from the written law."[75] Gordon Rupp observed that this idea foreshadowed Karlstadt's future mystical spirituality,[76] although it is most likely that both Luther's and Staupitz's early interests in the mysticism of Johannes Tauler and the *Theologia Germanica* were quite influential as well.[77] It should be further noted that Rupp's identification of Karlstadt's spirituality as mystical is also an indication of his transition to a more primitive Pauline pneumatology wherein the Spirit indwells and empowers the believer as the third person of the Trinity.[78]

Luther, having posted his *Ninety-Five Theses* in 1517, was the subject of a papal bull issued on June 15, 1520, which threatened both him and Karlstadt with excommunication.[79] By March 1521, Luther had been excommunicated and placed under an imperial ban for refusing to recant at the Diet of Worms. He was secretly taken incognito to Wartburg Castle, on the orders of Frederick the Wise, Elector of Saxony (1463–1525), where he remained in hiding until March 1522.[80] Karlstadt found himself

73. Steinmetz, *Reformers in the Wings*, 124–25.
74. Rupp, *Reformers in the Wings*, 125.
75. Sider, *Andreas Bodenstein Von Karlstadt*, 28.
76. Rupp, *Patterns of Reformation*, 59.
77. Rupp, *Patterns of Reformation*, 57.
78. Fee, *Pauline Christology*, 587–88. It should be noted that Paul was not introducing new pneumatological concepts, but simply describing the experiences and practices of the first Christian converts. His ensuing revelations and illuminations were solidly based on those early experiences as well as the Old Testament Scripture.
79. Sider, *Andreas Bodenstein Von Karlstadt*, 98–99.
80. Brecht, "Martin Luther," 463.

in the position of having to take a stand with Luther and his new theology of reform, notwithstanding Luther's absence.[81] He published a tract in October 1520 entitled, *Tract on the Supreme Virtue of Gelassenheit*, a Taulerian concept which allows for one's inner detachment from the world, abandoning self-will, and yielding completely to God in preparation by, not for, in some mystical sense, the Holy Spirit to manifest His gifts[82]:

> Even if I should burn in the midst of flames, but if I have no detachment [*gelassenheit*] my suffering would be of no merit to me [1 Cor. 13:1].[83]

From May 1521 to December 1522, Karlstadt encouraged the Wittenberg town council to proceed with Luther's reforms and denounced, from Luther's pulpit, without authority, images, organs and music, and choirs.[84] He had indeed assumed sole leadership and responsibility for most aspects of the reform in Luther's absence. Philipp Melanchthon (1487–1560) and others close to Luther had withdrawn in the face of such traumatic reforms. On December 4, Luther made a clandestine visit to Wittenberg and advised Georg Spalatin (1484–1545), Prince Frederick's secretary and spiritual advisor, that everything taking place was acceptable with the exception of the improper conduct of some, most likely referring to Karlstadt.[85]

On December 22, Karlstadt announced his intention to celebrate an evangelical mass at All Saints Church on the first day of January; however, Elector Frederick requested that he refrain. But on Christmas Day, a week earlier than proposed, Karlstadt celebrated a public mass in laymen's clothes, in German, and served the elements in both kinds to the communicants in defiance of the authority of the Elector.[86]

Two days later, three prophets, preaching within the context of 1 Corinthians 12–14, from Zwickau, and known to Thomas Müntzer, appeared in Wittenberg, preaching special spiritual insights received directly from the Holy Spirit through dreams and visions.[87] Melanchthon's

---

81. Sider, *Andreas Bodenstein Von Karlstadt*, 103.
82. Davies, *God Within*, 83–84.
83. Sider, *Andreas Bodenstein Von Karlstadt*, 37; Davies, *God Within*.
84. Rupp, "Andreas Karlstadt and Reformation Puritanism," 215
85. Luther, "Letter to George Spalatin," 350–51.
86. Preus, "Carlstadt's *Ordinaciones* and Luther's Liberty," 10.
87. Rupp, *Patterns of Reformation*, 171, 84; Gritsch, *Reformer without a Church*, 24–26.

encounter with them caused him to request Frederick to recall Luther to deal with their highly spiritualistic teachings.[88] There is little evidence that they had much influence on Karlstadt, as they left within a few days, but the incident may be seen as a portent of his future relationship with Müntzer and the development of his perceived mysticism, at least in the mind of Gordon Rupp. But it was more likely to have been Karlstadt's attempt to conform to a more Pauline pneumatology.[89] On February 3, Frederick ordered Karlstadt to stop preaching and writing and held him responsible for the distressing reforms instituted in Wittenberg. On March 6, 1522, Luther returned to Wittenberg and immediately preached the eight *Invocavit Sermons*, attired as an Augustinian monk and thus restoring the city's confidence in him and the Reformation. He preached that what had been done was correct, but done without consideration for weaker Christians or in love.

Karlstadt decided to leave Wittenberg in 1523 for Saxony to pastor the church in Orlamünde where he continued to gradually acquiesce to a more Tauleresque and Pauline spirituality and wrote another tract on *Gelassenheit*. He reverted to the life of a lay preacher working in the fields with other laymen and refrained from wearing clerical vestments. He instituted many reforms that he had started in Wittenberg and also began to encourage his congregants to prophesy in services according to 1 Corinthians 14, and gave some credence to dreams and visions, which were early Pentecostal-like practices.[90] In 1523, he encouraged his congregation to step out and function as the priesthood of believers that Luther had recognized as the legitimate priesthood of all Christians. He would write the following paraphrase of 1 Corinthians 12:29–31:

> Accordingly, we must reveal God's name to each other and proclaim the name of God to our brothers-not in some corner, but in the midst of the congregation so that they may be enticed to accept and praise God's clear words. For it is the gracious will of God that everyone ought to trade with and humor others with his talent. For the Lord's sake I should handle his goods faithfully not only toward myself by returning a profit on the main

---

88. "Spiritualistic" describes those who rejected all physical aspects of Christian ritual and ceremonial worship, including the Bible.

89. Preus, "Carlstadt's *Ordinaciones* and Luther's Liberty," 10; Rupp, "Andreas Karlstadt and Reformation Puritanism," 315.

90. Preus, "Carlstadt's *Ordinaciones* and Luther's Liberty," 9. See also, Corum, *Like as of Fire*, 1, 3; Anderson, *Introduction to Pentecostalism*, 43.

gift, but also toward my fellow brothers whom I ought to love as myself. Everyone needs the other, especially since God's gifts are diverse and since no one has them all.[91]

THE EUCHARIST DISPUTE

Karlstadt was ultimately expelled from Saxony in September 1524.[92] In the fall of that year, he wrote seven pamphlets on the Lord's Supper which brought responses from both Luther and Zwingli, perhaps even precipitating the eucharistic controversy that engaged Protestantism for the remainder of the decade.[93] Later he would side with Zwingli against Luther by interpreting the Eucharist as a memorial act of faith, without salvific efficacy or substance. In 1524, he would write a discussion with Gemser entitled *Dialogue or Discussion Booklet on the Infamous Abuse of the Most High Blessed Sacrament of Jesus Christ*:

> Pet: Confess the truth and [48] say that Christ's body is not in the bread and his blood not in the cup. Yet we ought to eat the bread of the Lord in remembrance or knowledge of his body which he surrendered for us into the hands of the unrighteous, and drink of the cup in the knowledge of the blood which Christ shed for us. To sum up, we are to eat and drink in the knowledge of the death of Christ.[94]

Rupp correctly suggested that Karlstadt's commentary (1517–1519?) on Augustine's *Spirit and Letter* delineated his Augustinianism from that of Luther in terms of the contrast between his letter (law) and spirit and Luther's arguments concerning law and gospel. Karlstadt stressed the inwardness of the work of the Spirit, or the inner word, whereas Luther had evolved to proclaim the critical precedence of the outward word, Scripture, preaching, and the sacraments, which he felt must precede the Spirit.[95] Ronald Sider rightly observed that Karlstadt interpreted the law in its spiritual sense, using the New Testament, rather than the literal spiritual-prophetic sense of Old Testament sacrifices. Whereas the literal law demanded the physical, the spirit of the law demanded purification

---

91. Furcha, *Essential Carlstadt*, 182. See also, 1 Pet 2:9 and 1 Cor 12:29; 14.
92. Furcha, *Essential Carlstadt*, 247–67.
93. Hillerbrand, "Andreas Bodenstein Von Carlstadt," 390.
94. Furcha, *Essential Carlstadt*, 315.
95. Rupp, *Patterns of Reformation*, 59.

of the heart through faith. Christians fulfill the law because of their faith in Christ. The Scripture does not lose its importance and must be read, studied, and interpreted, but it is the Spirit which reveals the truth of the secrets of the law.[96] Karlstadt certainly continued to hold on to Luther's initial idea of the priesthood of the believer and the efficacy of the Holy Spirit to enable all Christians to interpret Scripture. He believed that the inner word and its presence in the inner man was not only necessary, but possible in order to compensate for the insufficiency of *sola scriptura* as a spiritual catalyst.

In the sermon he preached on Christmas Day 1521, the first Protestant Eucharist in Wittenberg, Karlstadt proclaimed, "Faith makes God's Word useful only to those who receive the divine promise in faith (Heb.4 [:2]). God's Word purifies all who receive it in faith."[97] Here Karlstadt linked the word with preaching, hearing the word, and the sacraments. Although he saw the word as insufficient without the Spirit, he did affirm the need for external proclamation, very much like both Luther and Zwingli. Preaching of the word was based on the true call on the preacher's life by the Spirit as he said in 1523 in *Reasons Why Carlstadt Remained Silent:* "No one can truly write or preach about God, unless the spirit of God has first led him into truth and has compelled him to write, speak or testify."[98]

However, for him, preachers and prophets were only a conduit through which the word flows; one must not add anything, thus reiterating the authority of *sola scriptura*.[99] His opinion of the word and Spirit, although at variance with Luther, did not result in an invalidation of *sola scriptura*.[100] Sider appropriately suggests that he adapted Luther's idea that eternal life was obtained through faith alone. On the other hand, Rupp argues that Karlstadt's and Luther's concepts of faith were not necessarily the same; Karlstadt placed greater emphasis on the inward work of the Spirit which provided another glimpse, in his opinion, of his mystical spirituality.[101] But here, once again, it was more an indication of his continued embrace of Luther's initial idea of the Pauline description

---

96. Sider, *Andreas Bodenstein Von Karlstadt*, 112–17.
97. Sider, *Karlstadt's Battle with Luther*, 11.
98. Furcha, *Essential Carlstadt*, 174.
99. Sider, *Andreas Bodenstein Von Karlstadt*, 105.
100. Lohse, *Martin Luther's Theology*, 190–91.
101. Rupp, *Patterns of Reformation*, 59.

of the meaning, purpose, and value of the role of the Holy Spirit and may have been only his continued turn toward Paul's concept of the efficacy of the indwelling of the Holy Spirit (Rom 12:6–7).

Luther found Karlstadt's decision to proceed with the Wittenberg reform in spite of Luther's absence to be precipitous and entirely inappropriate. His actions were based on his commitment to Luther's reform and his willingness to precisely execute it rather than wait for his reappearance. Luther responded by stopping him and his efforts, viewing them as untimely and too rapid for weaker Christians.

Consequently, Luther ostracized him, which ultimately brought into focus their long-standing disagreement over some theological issues, particularly regarding the Eucharist and the spiritual tension between the word and the Spirit, the Spirit having precedence in Karlstadt's understanding. His subsequent pastorate in Orlamünde was indicative of a similar Pentecostal-like pneumatology and ecclesiology in praxis. He encouraged the laity in psalm-singing and allowed up to three members to prophesy during services in accordance with 1 Corinthians 12–14, reinforcing the Lutheran concept of the priesthood of the believer.[102] Eventually he would come to criticize Luther regarding the continued practice of pedobaptism, the baptism of infants who could not understand their desires toward Christ thus precluding any informed decision to follow him.[103] Although there is no evidence that he continued or discontinued the practice himself, there is also no evidence that it became important to his ministry doctrinally. In 1561, Heinrich Bullinger (1504–1575), Huldrych Zwingli's successor in Zurich, published a history of the *Origins of Anabaptism* and claimed that Karlstadt was the founder of the movement.[104]

Karlstadt's precipitous reformation of Wittenberg in Luther's absence reflected his tendency toward the restitution (*restitutio*) of the primitive New Testament church, not just the reform of Catholicism. His actions were indicative of his concern for the laity and enabling their participation in Christian worship juxtaposed against sole ecclesiastic control by a privileged and corrupt Catholic clergy. He would opt to circumvent Frederick's order to cease and desist by conducting the Christmas Mass in German without wearing the liturgical vestments. On

---

102. Williams, *Radical Reformation*, 117; Rupp, *Patterns of Reformation*, 114–16.
103. Karlstadt, in Furcha, *Essential Carlstadt*, 366.
104. Bullinger, *Widertoeufferen Ursprungen/Secten*.

the other hand, Luther's response to Karlstadt's initiative was an early indication of Luther's evolving consideration of the magistracy as a critical and active entity in the reformation *(reformatio)* of the church.[105] Luther, unlike Karlstadt, complied with Frederick's command and restored those aspects of Karlstadt's reform (e.g., the Mass) that he and Frederick considered much too fast without the involvement of a more authoritative ecclesiastical body. Karlstadt was unwilling to allow any human tradition that was not commanded by Scripture to remain in the church, an extremely restitutional position regarding the primitive church.[106] His insistence on biblical authority, the priesthood of the believer, and the precedence of the Spirit over the word, were core beliefs for him. However, Luther was probably already retreating from the idea of the priesthood of the believer and was beginning to strengthen his word-over-Spirit position as indicated in his letters to Almsdorf and Melanchthon. He would even state that the gifts of the Spirit were in a state of cessation since the establishment of the institutional church and clergy in his commentary on Galatians.[107] Karlstadt's experience in Wittenberg may have marked both his inclination for the complete restitution of the primitive church in conformity with 1 Corinthians 12–14, and Luther's migration toward a reformation of the Roman Catholic Church with a strong and highly involved magistracy.

Two things became apparent that would cause Luther to eventually declare Karlstadt a *Schwärmer*. First, Karlstadt's insistence, not so much on the reform of the church, but on the restitution of the primitive New Testament church, complete with the manifestation of the gifts of the Spirit; and second, Luther's own choice not to go against the magisterial authority of Elector Frederick, indicative of his predilection toward giving the magistracy some role in spreading the gospel. Both would be signs pointing toward the dissolution of their relationship. Luther would classify him as a dreamer and visionary, a conclusion supported by Karlstadt's future influence on Anabaptists and other radical elements.

---

105. Preus, "Carlstadt's *Ordinaciones* and Luther's Liberty," 10. Sider, *Karlstadt's Battle with Luther*, 5.

106. Snyder, *Anabaptist History and Theology*, 25.

107. Luther, "Lectures on Galatians," 374–75. Luther quotes 1 Corinthians 14:22, but states that when the church had been gathered and confirmed, "it was not necessary for this visible sending forth of the Holy Spirit to continue." See also, "Letters to Almsdorf and Melancthon," 364–67.

Karlstadt was the first to act on Luther's theology of reform. His attempts to put the Petrine doctrine of the priesthood of the believer, and Pauline pneumatology into practice in Wittenberg, however, although accepted by parishioners, were rejected by Luther. What Karlstadt demonstrated was an unwillingness to leave those principles behind while Luther began to cooperate with the magistracy. This was to become a prevalent breaking point for the emerging radicalism of the Reformation.

THOMAS MÜNTZER

Müntzer would become the next and most radical of Luther's *Schwärmer*, developing into a highly charismatic apocalyptic preacher who had significant influence on the radical Anabaptist movement emerging in Switzerland. Stanley Burgess has singled out Müntzer as the most Pentecostal-like of the radical reformers. Burgess points out that Müntzer's acceptance of a literal Biblicist interpretation of Joel 2:27–32 was an indication that he believed that the parousia was imminent.[108] For Müntzer, the efficacy of dreams and visions validated the idea that Paul espoused in 1 Corinthians 14:26 of any believer sharing a prophecy or revelation in a meeting, but only as long as it was confirmed by Scripture.[109] Burgess is correct in observing that the above-listed biblical interpretations and admonitions to praxis of Müntzer were similar to those of early Pentecostalism. He wrote to Luther in 1523:

> Nor should those who boast about Christ be believed unless they have his spirit, Romans 8. This assurance enables him to distinguish by divine revelation between the work of God and that of malignant spirits; here he draws quite legitimately on really genuine appearances and hidden portents, discerning profound mysteries from the mouth of God Corinthians chapter 2, Isaiah 8: "The people will demand from their God a vision on behalf of the living and the dead for a law and a testimony greater etc."[110]

He was not of the Wittenberg school, but it was on Luther's recommendation in 1520 that Müntzer received a position as supply preacher

---

108. Burgess, *Holy Spirit: Medieval Roman Catholic and Reformation Traditions*, 203–9.

109. Matheson, *Collected Works of Thomas Müntzer*, 57–58, 240–41, 44, 360.

110. Matheson, *Collected Works of Thomas Müntzer*, 57–58.

at St. Mary's in Zwickau.[111] His notoriety, however, is based primarily on his involvement as a leader of the German Peasants' War (1524–1526), rather than his theology. It was the prophetic and apocalyptic nature of Müntzer's theology that brought him to the place of acting out his beliefs in rebellion. When he was appointed rector of St. Mary's in Mühlhausen he formed a local militia, and in May 1525 led peasant farmers in a battle at Frankenhausen. The peasants lost six thousand combatants and suffered Müntzer's capture and execution.

Müntzer's theology of the word of God and Scripture may best be defined within the context of a letter he wrote to Luther on July 13, 1520, shortly after his assignment as supply preacher in Zwickau. He had immediately begun to preach against the local Franciscans. Seeking Luther's advice on the matter, he revealed a personal core belief regarding Scripture, "I know the word of the Lord does not return empty (Isaiah 55:11). I will combat them with unceasing groans and with the trumpet of the word of God."[112]

He did not hesitate to declare Scripture to be the word of God and in fact made consistent and prolific use of it to support his position.[113] A further and perhaps more critical assessment of the word by Müntzer is discovered when he wrote in his *Prague Manifesto* of 1521, "But if we learn the real living word of God we will win over the unbeliever and speak with obvious authority."[114] There were two aspects to Müntzer's theology of the word: the authority of Scripture, *sola scriptura*, and its nature as the living word.

For Müntzer, the spoken word of God was directly related to Scripture. In his *German Church Service Book* of 1523, he explained that for the edification of poor people he translated the psalms into German under the leading of the Holy Spirit so that all the elect might be instructed by God.[115] In the *German Evangelical Mass* of 1524 he further explained that,

> My aim and intention, which is to people's poor, pitiable, blind consciences by producing a shortened form of what the devious, false priests, monks, and nuns had previously chanted and read

---

111. Rupp, *Patterns of Reformation*, 159–60.
112. Matheson, *Collected Works of Thomas Müntzer*, 18–20, 192.
113. Gritsch, *Thomas Muntzer*, 20.
114. Matheson, *Collected Works of Thomas Müntzer*, 359.
115. Matheson, *Collected Works of Thomas Müntzer*, 168.

> in the churches and monasteries in Latin, thus withholding it from the masses of the poor laity, to the destruction of the faith, the gospel, the word of God, and contrary to the clear, lucid teaching of apostle Paul in 1 Cor. 14.
>
> The psalms are sung and read properly for the poor layman; for it is in them that the working of the Holy Spirit can be clearly discerned.[116]

The reading and singing of the word was paramount for Müntzer, for it was in the singing of the word that the Spirit moved, witnessing to the truth of the Scripture. Müntzer believed that it was the Spirit that brought life to Scripture, transforming it into the living word. Again in the *Prague Manifesto, 1521*, Müntzer wrote that it is within the heart of man that God has written his word;

> God has done this for his elect from the very beginning, so that the testimony they are given is not uncertain, but an invincible one from the holy spirit, which then gives our spirit ample testimony that we are the children of God.[117]

Like Luther and Karlstadt, he felt that Scripture was critical to faith, but agreed with Karlstadt that it was insufficient as the source. It was the Spirit who brought faith and understanding to the word, as he stated in 1524 in *Protestation or Proposition*: "For you will never have faith unless God himself gives it to you, and instructs you in it."[118] Scripture was to interpret Scripture, but it was the role of the Spirit to confirm any interpretation, "For the knowledge of God to which the books of the Bible testify requires a careful comparison of all the clear statements to be found in both Testaments, 1 Corinthians 2."[119]

In the *Prague Manifesto, 1521*, he wrote that the accursed priests preached from mere Scripture that which they had stolen from the Bible, lacked any personal experience of, and therefore were distributing only the letter of the word and not breaking the bread of life for the people.[120]

---

116. Matheson, *Collected Works of Thomas Müntzer*, 180, 182. See also, Brandt, *Thomas Muntzer*, 114–17.

117. Matheson, *Collected Works of Thomas Müntzer*, 358.

118. Matheson, *Collected Works of Thomas Müntzer*, 199.

119. Matheson, *Collected Works of Thomas Müntzer*, 192.

120. Matheson, *Collected Works of Thomas Müntzer*, 357–58.

The prophetic word for him fell primarily within Paul's teachings in 1 Corinthians 14. He wrote that in the contemporary church, the word was not being made alive by the Spirit because priests talked as if God had become silent, perhaps a reference to Luther's theory of cessation of the gifts after the institutional church and clergy had been established. The result, he said, was the distribution of undigested food, "like storks vomiting frogs to her young." It is unrealistic to assume that the world would be receptive to such assertions as, "It is written here, it is written there."[121] He paraphrased 1 Corinthians 14:23–24 in the *Prague Manifesto, 1521*:

> If a simple man or an unbeliever was to come into one of our gatherings, and we tried to bowl him over with our chatter he would say: "Are you mad or stupid? What is your scripture to me?" But if we learn the real living word of God we will win over the unbeliever and speak with obvious authority when the secret places of his heart are revealed so that he has to confess humbly that God is in us. Look, Paul testifies to all this in the first epistle to the Corinthians, chapter 14, saying there that a preacher needs revelation; without it he should not preach the word. The devil believes in the truth of the Christian faith. If the servants of Antichrist deny all this, then God must be mad and stupid, since he has said that his word will never pass away. Would that not be the case if God had ceased to speak?[122]

Müntzer—clearly agreeing, literally, with Pauline doctrine as opposed to a mystical understanding—was convinced that God was still prophetically speaking to Christians just as he had in the primitive church. In *Vindication and Refutation* of 1524, he wrote, in response to Luther's *Letter to the Princes of Saxony* of 1524, "In 1 Corinthians 14, Paul says this about prophets: A true preacher has to be a prophet and indeed—though the world may laugh this to scorn—the whole world must become prophetic if it is to judge who the false prophets are."[123]

Williams characterizes Müntzer's *Sermon to the Princes*, delivered on July 13, 1524, as his most extraordinary public utterance and "possibly the most remarkable sermon of the whole Reformation era."[124] It is a description of his deeply held convictions concerning the apocalyptic and

---

121. Matheson, *Collected Works of Thomas Müntzer*, 359.
122. Matheson, *Collected Works of Thomas Müntzer*, 359.
123. Matheson, *Collected Works of Thomas Müntzer*, 347.
124. Williams, *Radical Reformation*, 130.

spiritual nature of his theology and earthly ministry within the context of the Peasants' War. Müntzer took Daniel 2 as his text and equated German princes with King Nebuchadnezzar, rulers faced with the reality of the teleological hand of God directing the destiny of the German people and the Christian church within their domains. His sermon was reminiscent of Joachim de Fiore (1130–1202) who had divided history into the ages of the Father, Son, and the last age of the Holy Spirit, which had just arrived. This parallel had become apparent to Müntzer's contemporaries as well.[125]

The German princes were living in the age of the Holy Spirit and therefore had an opportunity to participate in the restitution of Christianity to its original and final form. Nebuchadnezzar's visionary image represented corrupted Christianity. In Müntzer's mind, its smashing was imminent, therefore it was the duty of the princes to be the sword of justice protecting and restoring true Christianity. Strength for such efforts was to be obtained by the wisdom of God through the Holy Spirit. Everyone had to become conscious of the everyday revelation of God. Dreams, visions, and direct words from God—prophecy—were the instruments of the revelation of the divine will as in Joel 2 and 1 Corinthians 14. He emphasized that these (Pentecostal-like) phenomena must be subject to corroboration by the Scripture. But, they are nevertheless the source of power and confirmation that enabled confident participation in the destructive effort. In this way, the princes could and should proceed to participate in ushering in the last age of history in Joachim's de Fiore's terms.[126] Because of the problems created by the lack of documentation of Müntzer's early life and theological development, there is a debate as to how he managed to arrive at the theological place he did.

Müntzer was attracted to Luther's Reformation theology, particularly the anticlerical aspects aimed at the reform of church corruption of Scripture. He was not a Wittenberger, but his affinity for Luther's theology and willingness to propagate it made him an asset to the growing Lutheran movement. He would not come under any direct influence of Zwingli. Nevertheless, he attracted the attention of those radicals who rebelled against Zwingli to become the Swiss Brethren of the early Anabaptist movement. Although he pointed out the error of infant baptism, as Karlstadt did, there is no evidence that he made adult baptism a doctrinal

---

125. Matheson, *Collected Works of Thomas Müntzer*, 71–72.
126. Matheson, *Collected Works of Thomas Müntzer*, 230–52.

practice.[127] When he became the pastor of St. Catherine's Church in Zwickau, he realized that he had inherited as parishioners, the infamous Zwickau Prophets, who had previously appeared in Wittenberg during Karlstadt's reform effort. This highly spiritualistic sect, later referred to as Storchians, appeared to have been influenced by a profusion of late-medieval radical, mystical, and oft-heretical religious beliefs peculiar to the Zwickau and Bohemian regions.[128] One debate regarding Müntzer's theology revolves around the question of whether or not the Storchians influenced him or he influenced them. The Zwickau Prophets—Nicolaus Storch, Marcus Stübner, and Thomas Drechsel—were already present and active at St. Catherine's under the leadership of Storch. However, by April 16, 1521, Müntzer had been forced to leave the city, leaving the prophets to their own devices.

Not unlike Karlstadt, Müntzer was much influenced by the Taulerian doctrine of reception of the Holy Spirit in the innermost depths of the soul as a precondition of faith, in that it became one of the cornerstones of his theology.[129] As the spirituality of Tauler and the *Theologia Germanica* were first broached by Luther, this makes him at least a catalyst in Müntzer's and Karlstadt's exploration of the possibilities of a more Pauline pneumatology, most often confused with mysticism, in the development of their individual theologies.[130] Notwithstanding Luther's emphasis on the centrality of *sola scriptura* and its influence on Müntzer, once in Zwickau, other influences of theological extreme came to bear on his thought. Prior to his arrival at St. Catherine's, the Zwickau Prophets were already convening private conventicles for the purpose of promulgating their radical spiritualism. As reported by Nicholas Hausman, Müntzer's successor at St. Catherine's, to Duke John of Saxony on December 18, 1521, Storch taught, "the advent of the millennium, polygamy, adult baptism, economic communism, and the violent overthrow of all political and ecclesiastical governments."[131] In addition, Storch dismissed the external and divine word and the Eucharist as nonsense and said:

---

127. Müntzer, in Matheson,

128. Karant-Nun, *Zwickau in Transition, 1500–1540*, 106.

129. Goertz, *Thomas Muntzer*, 45–46; Gritsch, *Reformer without a Church*, 30; Scott, *Thomas Muntzer*, 11.

130. Gritsch, *Reformer without a Church*, 25.

131. Gritsch, *Reformer without a Church*, 25.

> You can receive the forgiveness of sins without all this nonsense, in your own quiet home or wherever you are if you believe in the revelation of the spirit...Don't you believe that God has another word which he will reveal to you through the spirit? Thus the external, audible word of the priests is not the word of God but their own.[132]

Thomas Scott, Eric Gritsch, and Hans Jurgern Goertz all concur that Müntzer was initially influenced by Tauler and the *Theologia Germanica* as introduced by Luther.[133] However, Scott argues that Storch may have been a pupil of Müntzer notwithstanding any radical predisposition of his own.[134] Gritsch favors the idea that Müntzer developed his own theology as influenced by Luther and Tauler, but felt no need to preach it exclusively from his pulpit which left the door open to Storch's influence as well.[135] Goertz proposes that Storch and Müntzer found themselves in mutual spiritual and theological agreement, with both taking advantage of the coincidence.[136] Karant-Nun admits to the doctrinal similarities between the Zwickau Prophets and earlier Bohemian radicals such as the Hussites, Taborites, and even the Waldensians, but suspects the evidence used by others to support this is weak.[137] Rupp takes the position, given what is known of Müntzer's formidable personality and disposition as a theologian, apocalyptic pastor, and revolutionary leader, that the Storchian influence was not a prevailing issue for him. However, one must not minimize the influence that the Bible had on him within every aspect in which he considered it to exist, whether it was written or God-breathed, that is, spiritually revealed. His mind was saturated in Scripture, as evidenced by the prolific citations throughout all of his writings.[138] Once again this debate leaves the door open for consideration of the possibility of Müntzer's proclivity to rely on Scripture in a literal sense, particularly in this case, Paul's pneumatology.[139] As to the Zwickau Prophets, in a

---

132. Gritsch, *Reformer without a Church*, 25.
133. Gritsch, *Reformer without a Church*, 25.
134. Scott, *Thomas Muntzer*, 11.
135. Goertz, *Thomas Muntzer*, 13–17.
136. Goertz, *Thomas Muntzer*, 65–66.
137. Karant-Nun, *Zwickau in Transition*, 178–79.
138. Rupp, *Patterns of Reformation*, 259–60.
139. Burgess, *Holy Spirit: Medieval Roman Catholic and Reformation Traditions*, 203–9.

letter dated July 9, 1523, he denied knowing what they had said when they met with Luther:

> You raise objections about Markus [Stübner] and Nicholas [Storch]. What manner of men they are is up to them, Galatians 2. I fear and tremble before the divine judgements. As to what they said to you, or what they have done, I know nothing about it. You objected that certain things sickened you. I do not know which they are, but surmise; perseverance, tribulation, gifts of the spirit etc.[140]

Müntzer, again not unlike Karlstadt, struggled with the theological tension between the word and the Spirit. But he interpreted that tension in a more prophetically apocalyptic perspective which, although lending more credence to the Spirit, emphasized the imminence of Christ's return and the responsibility of all Christians to participate in making that return possible in a practical and profound way.[141] After Müntzer tried to enlist the Orlamünde congregation into the Peasants' War, Karlstadt warned him, as a friend, not to get involved, but he saw the war not as a social rebellion but an integral part of the second coming of Christ.[142] His concept of reform revolved around his sense that the Peasants' War, the current restitution of the church, and the current outpouring of the Holy Spirit in New Testament praxis all pointed to the reality of the genuine parousia. His acceptance, or perhaps indulgence, of the Zwickau Prophets was demonstrated by his willingness to uncritically allow the manifestation of the gifts of the Spirit at St. Catherine's. Müntzer's openness to the manifestation of the charismata and adult baptism was attractive to the Zwinglian radicals that would eventually be called the Anabaptists. Conrad Grebel, one considered to be the founder of Swiss Anabaptism, and a group of his followers corresponded with Müntzer in reference to his reform theology in mostly approving terms.[143]

---

140. Matheson, *Collected Works of Thomas Müntzer*, 58–59. See also, Vogler, *Thomas Muntzer*, 137–39.

141. Anderson, *Introduction to Pentecostalism*, 217; Corum, *Like as of Fire*, 25–26.

142. Matheson, *Collected Works of Thomas Müntzer*, 91–92. See also, Barge, *Andreas Bodenstein Von Karlstadt*, 115.

143. Harder, *Sources of Swiss Anabaptism*, 284–92.

CASPAR SCHWENCKFELD

Last in the line of Luther's *Schwärmer,* was Schwenckfeld. The influence of this Silisian courtier on the emerging radicalism was significant, particularly as he became involved in a polemic regarding adult baptism with Pilgram Marpeck, a future leader and theologian of the Anabaptists of Austria and Southern Germany.

Silesia was fertile ground for, and perhaps even anticipated, Luther's reforms in that by 1518, the Reformation had permeated Junker, usually Hussite, towns and villages with much success. The Silesian Reformation was a more rural phenomena having support from the landed nobility as opposed to the more urban reform efforts elsewhere in the Empire.[144] Duke Friederick II of Liegnitz (1499–1547), the most powerful of the Silesian princes[145] and gate keeper of Lutheranism in Silesia, managed this without getting embroiled in the Peasants' War, as in Saxony, or the iconoclasm of Karlstadt's Wittenberg movement.[146]

In 1519, Schwenckfeld was a lower-level diplomat at Duke Friederick's court and is credited with Friedrich II, Duke of Liegnitz's conversion to Lutheranism in 1521.[147] Schwenckfeld had been an avid reader of Luther's works and eventually experienced a *heimsuchung,* a divine visitation, which resulted in his traumatic conversion to Lutheranism in 1519. He began to read the Bible faithfully and formed study groups (conventicles) that would become the platform for future evangelical efforts. In his role as courtier, he established himself as the impetus behind the Silesian Reformation.[148] Although inspired by Luther's writings, he was not a contemplative man, but saw the Reformation as something to be done in praxis, not polemics. As an active lay preacher, he initiated a series of missionary campaigns that included instruction, preaching, admonition, and consolation. Wittenberg apparently approved of his reform efforts in that preaching the pure word of God with nothing added was Luther's conception of what reformation intended.[149]

---

144. McLaughlin, *Caspar Schwenckfeld,* 19.

145. Steinmetz, *Reformers in the Wings,* 131–32; McLaughlin, "Radical Reformation," 42–43.

146. Fleischer, "Silesia," 60.

147. McLaughlin, *Caspar Schwenckfeld,* 28.

148. Spinka, *Advocates of Reform,* 161.

149. McLaughlin, *Caspar Schwenckfeld,* 22–23.

The Reformation had proceeded quickly and fervently under the leadership of Karlstadt in Wittenberg in 1521 and 1522. Nevertheless, the disappearance of Luther fomented rumors of his kidnapping which, combined with the exigency of the reform there, served as a catalyst for an expeditious reformation in Silesia as well.[150] By this time, Friedrich, totally committed to the reformation of Breslau and Liegnitz, began appointing Protestant preachers to local churches. Valentin Crautwald (1465–1545), a trilingual humanist and Lutheran, was made canon at Liegnitz.[151] By 1524, Friedrich had declared the Holy Scripture to be the rule of faith in Breslau and Liegnitz.[152]

Schwenckfeld's attention then turned from the practical side of reformation to its theological aspects and published his first two tracts. In 1524, he wrote an open letter to the new Catholic Bishop of Breslau soliciting his approval and participation in the Reformation movement, which he refused.[153] The second tract, *Admonition Concerning Abuse of Certain Important Articles of the Gospel*, was also directed at the recently empowered Protestant clergy, as well as Friederick.[154] He thought that an intervention had become necessary to prevent Lutheran *sola fide* (justification by faith alone) from evolving into antinomianism in the same way Catholicism's works righteousness became bondage of conscience.[155] His intent was to find a *via media* between a sociopolitical revolution and ecclesiastical reform, including preaching the gospel as mandated by Friederick.[156] *Admonition* was directed toward Catholic and Protestant clergy alike, regarding the abuses being committed by both on their respective congregations. Typical of magisterial Lutheranism was the increase of secular power in coercing and propagating the gospel. Schwenckfeld encouraged Friederick, in reference to this practice, to protect his subjects from Catholic error and teach them the pure New Testament gospel as he believed it was the Duke's duty. Agreeing, Friederick empowered congregations to choose their own pastors and permitted Protestant

---

150. McLaughlin, *Caspar Schwenckfeld*, 24.
151. McLaughlin, *Caspar Schwenckfeld*, 29.
152. Fleischer, "Silesia," 60.
153. McLaughlin, *Caspar Schwenckfeld*, 29–34.
154. Schwenckfeld, "Ermanung Des Missbrauchs," 40.
155. McLaughlin, *Caspar Schwenckfeld*, 30.
156. McLaughlin, *Caspar Schwenckfeld*, 31.

preaching.[157] Thus he enabled Luther's initial concept of the priesthood of the believer. But Schwenckfeld made it clear that the duke had no power over anyone's soul. Schwenckfeld's Reformation had three goals: proclaiming the word of God, correct worship of God, and Christian piety. Reform was to be accomplished by prioritizing the inner substance of faith over the outer forms with which it was expressed. The Silesian Reformation was to be determined by his ultimate goals of reform and the precedence of inner spiritual change over formal external change.[158]

Recognizing the weakness of attempting to reform the Roman Catholic Church, he held Scripture in high regard and as a key to restitution of the primitive church, and blamed the decay of Catholicism on the biblical ignorance of the clergy. He also considered the poorly educated and deceitful clergy responsible for oppressing simple peasants with superstitions out of greed and ignorance. His *Admonition* demanded vernacular liturgy for prayers, psalms, baptismal rites, receiving the Eucharist in both kinds, preaching the gospel, and the right of priests to marry.[159]

Schwenckfeld had initially accepted Luther's five core doctrines of the Reformation, *"Das alleine der gloube uns rectfertige, Das wir keine frehen willen haben, Das wir gottis gebot nicht halten mogen, Das unsere werk nichts sehn, und Das Christus habe fur uns genug gethon,"*[160] but Williams observed that his major eucharistic concern was the absence of personal piety after communicants took the elements of the Sacrament, particularly among the peasants, which resulted in the antinomianism that he feared.[161] If a Christian was filled with the Holy Spirit at salvation, then there must be some physical evidence of the infilling. Williams also observed that he differed from Luther in that he perceived forensic justification as progressive sanctification and not a moment in time. He therefore expected a Christian life of pious living based on the knowledge of Christ, "Justification derives from the knowledge of Christ through faith."[162] This knowledge was based on partaking of the

157. McLaughlin, *Caspar Schwenckfeld*, 34.
158. McLaughlin, *Caspar Schwenckfeld*, 35.
159. McLaughlin, *Caspar Schwenckfeld*, 36–37.
160. Schwenckfeld, "Ermanung Des Missbrauchs," 42. This translates to: "Faith justifies us, We have no free will, We cannot obey god's commands, Our works are nothing, and Christ has paid our debt." See also, McLaughlin, *Caspar Schwenckfeld*, 40.
161. Seguenny, "Schwenckfeld," 351–62; Williams, *Radical Reformation*, 201–9.
162. Williams, *Radical Reformation*, 201–9.

elements of the Eucharist, both physically and spiritually through faith. The elements provided inward spiritual nourishment that enabled the will, which Luther considered bound, to be free. Now Christians were enabled to act freely by the knowledge of Christ through the Eucharist and able to keep the commands of Christ: "It is not impossible for the new regenerate man that is, for all Christians who believe in Christ, to keep them."[163] Schwenckfeld would eventually adopt Crautwald's theology of the *"Nouus homo."* Crautwald posited that a Christian was "new" in Christ because only Christ gives the Spirit, and faith in him is the sole source of spiritualization, which demands ministry that is dependent upon the preached word. Although water baptism is essential to initiation into the spiritual life, he makes no mention of the Eucharist. Finally, he says the infilling of the Holy Spirit is evidenced by the good works manifested in Christian living.[164]

The will of a Christian could now achieve sanctification by growing in the knowledge of Christ through the power of the Spirit, thus solving Schwenckfeld's dilemma over the lack of piety, notwithstanding participation in the Eucharist. Unlike Luther, who saw regeneration as a moment in time of passing from law to grace, he saw it as a progressive experience. He blamed the lack of piety among the peasants on the failure of Lutheranism, and saw sanctification as the solution, the *koniglichen strosse gewandert sein und das mitel zwischen,* or the royal way between Catholicism and Lutheranism. He thought that Christians were humanly unable to keep the commandments but, empowered by the Holy Spirit, could obey them in faith.[165] Whereas Williams seemed to blame Schwenckfeld's alteration of Luther's doctrine of justification by faith alone with narrow interpretation, while giving a higher priority to solving the issue of the continuing immorality among Christians,[166] Séguenny argued that Schwenckfeld believed people simply did not understand what Luther was saying about his five tenets of reformation; this is perhaps the more logical explanation.[167] Schwenckfeld commenced to apply an Erasmian solution, perhaps blinded by the incessant lack of piety in the people, notwithstanding participation in the Lord's Supper. He agreed faith alone

163. Williams, *Radical Reformation*, 203.

164. Backus, "Valentine Crautwald's *Nouus Homo*," 330–31; Shantz, "Role of Valentine Crautwald," 296–97.

165. Schwenckfeld, "Ermanung Des Missbrauchs," 62.

166. Williams, *Radical Reformation*, 203.

167. Seguenny, "Schwenckfeld," 353.

justifies, but faith is evidenced by moral change demonstrated by good works. It is true that one can regain their freedom, but it is a gift of God. Works have no salvific value, but without them there is no evidence of faith. Works must be seen, therefore, as an act of God only.[168] He then opposed the idea of passive justification by saying a Christian must follow Christ by way of the cross: "If we are to be conformed to God, we must first be conformed to Christ, otherwise we clearly come to nothing." Séguenny points out that the idea of being conformed to Christ in this sense is found in Erasmus's *Enchiridion*: "It is Christ alone who establishes the person."[169]

EUCHARISTIC CONTROVERSY

Schwenckfeld collaborated with Valentin Crautwald (1465–1545), Duke Friedrich's court theologian and newly appointed canon at Liegnitz, in developing a scripturally based theology to support his concept of a more efficacious Eucharist.[170] He approached Crautwald in 1525 with the idea that John 6 implied that the preservation of Christ's body must be predicated upon its inseparable union with the word, and further that salvation through his body was received by faith only and not by the elements of the sacrament. Initially, Crautwald was not impressed.[171] The idea opposed the traditional Catholic theology of impanation which Luther would cling to against Karlstadt, Johannes Oecolampadius (1482–1531), and Zwingli at the Marburg Colloquy of 1529.[172]

After reconsideration, Crautwald applied his knowledge of Hebrew and had what he described as an inspired revelation. He determined that the words of institution, "This is my body," were a Hebraism wherein pronouns initiate statements which are clarified when the statement is reversed; "This is my body which is given for you" should read "My body which is given for you is this, namely bread." This would render John 6:55 to mean that Christ's body and blood were the true spiritual food of believers, but received by faith alone. Schwenckfeld recognized Crautwald for his hermeneutic and immediately facilitated its teaching in

168. Seguenny, "Schwenckfeld," 351–62.
169. Seguenny, "Schwenckfeld," 352–53.
170. Seguenny, "Schwenckfeld," 352–53.
171. Shantz, *Crautwald and Erasmus*, 28.
172. Schmid, "Marburg Colloquy," 2–3.

the Silesian churches. He also submitted it to Luther in Wittenberg who rejected it and admonished him to abstain from its teaching, calling him a "culprit (who) increases the plague on the church."[173]

Schwenckfeld eventually tried to convince Luther in person, paying him a visit, but Luther rejected his theology and identified him as a Zwinglian sacramentarian. This was the final break with the Wittenberg movement. On April 26, 1526, Schwenckfeld and other Silesian reformers declared a *Stillstand* (suspension) of the Eucharist (and eventually baptism).[174] He was already predisposed to adult baptism in that pedobaptism had no meaning without "inner baptism," but he was opposed to Anabaptists' baptismal theology because it placed too much emphasis on the physical ritual itself.[175] Schwenckfeld would write concerning the reasons for instituting *Stillstand*:

> I have felt for a long time since the sacraments have been distributed and promoted . . .very little certain improvement has followed, but rather a whole lot more destruction, division, and disunity.[176]

It became obvious, however, that Silesia was going to remain a Lutheran state as Duke Friederick distanced himself from Schwenckfeld ,who had decided to go into a self-imposed exile in April of 1529, over the eucharistic controversy. Crautwald, using his contacts, made arrangements for him to stay in Strasbourg where he would come into contact with many other radical reformers, particularly Anabaptist Pilgram Marpeck (1495–1556). By the end of 1530, Friedrich had successfully suppressed Schwenckfeldianism.[177] Schwenckfeld would go on to develop a highly spiritualistic theology of the Eucharist wherein the human nature of Jesus was denied in favor of what he referred to as his "Celestial Flesh," denying the distinction between Christ's earthly nature and his divine nature.[178]

In 1531, while a resident in Strasbourg, Marpeck had written a response to Schwenckfeld's *Stillstand* and "Celestial Flesh" theology entitled, *Verantwortung* (Response), a near systematic theology which

173. Shantz, *Crautwald and Erasmus*, 4:30–31.
174. McLaughlin, "Spiritualism," 127.
175. Williams, *Radical Reformation*, 717.
176. Williams, *Caspar Schwenckfeld*, 127.
177. McLaughlin, *Caspar Schwenckfeld*, 114.
178. Williams, *Radical Reformation*, 496–500.

repudiated Schwenckfeldian spiritualism in its broadest sense. Schwenckfeld's encounter with Marpeck in Strasbourg would incite him to write the *Judicium* in 1542, a harsh critique of the Marpeck's *Vermanung, 1542* (Admonition), an exposition of Anabaptism's position on the sacraments of baptism and the Lord's Supper.[179] As a result of this polemic, Marpeck was inspired to expound and publish a theology of Anabaptism that would provide a *via media* between radical separatist factions such as Schwenckfeld, the spiritualists, and Anabaptist adherents.

Schwenckfeld was a very pragmatic man in that he believed that if a reformation of the church was to be effective, there should be some obvious evidence of that effectiveness. His unwillingness to accept what he perceived as Luther's Catholic explanation of the Lord's Supper, due to the lack of any derived piety, caused him to seek a theology with a more pious outcome.[180] His reticence, in Luther's mind, was dangerously antithetical to the Reformation and caused him to classify Schwenckfeld as a *Schwärmer*, along with Karlstadt and Müntzer. Schwenckfeld, like the others, believed the Spirit to precede the word and therefore understood by the Spirit, a position that Luther vehemently opposed as a direct threat to his concept of *sola scriptura*. Consequently, he would try to convince Luther of the spiritual nature of the Eucharist juxtaposed against its physicality. Ultimately, Luther would reject his theology and Schwenckfeld would call for a suspension (*Stillstand*) of the Sacraments. He would also be a major catalyst in the development of the theology of Pilgram Marpeck, which consequently would reflect an early Pentecostal-like pneumatology.

CONCLUSION

It can be concluded that Luther's initial regard for the theology of the *devotio modern*, the *Theologica Germanica*, Tauler, and Rhenish mysticism played a significant role in the development of his theological thoughts of how the reformation of the church should proceed. His acceptance of *sola scriptura* as an Augustinian monk, the influence of Erasmus, and

---

179. Hartranft, *Schwenckfeld's Juditium, 1542,* 1542</style>, 1911 ed., vol. ll, Study of the Earliest Letters of Schwenckfeld (Norristown, Pa.: Board of Publkication of the Schwenckfelder Church, 1907159.

180. Luther, "Confessions Concerning Christ's Supper, 1528," 216.

biblical Christianity as described by Paul, completed the first elements he would apply to his reform effort. For him, the reformation of the church was paramount, but could only succeed within the bounds of a pneumatology and an ecclesiology that conformed to these influences. Karlstadt, Müntzer, and Schwenckfeld, the *Schwärmer*, were initially in agreement with his five tenets of reform, but their understanding of the tenets differed significantly as he gravitated toward a more magisterial-supported reform that enlisted the state into propagation and coercion of the gospel. As Luther's Reformation progressed, the *Schwärmer* would become Lutheran radical reformers, the first radicals to reject his reform, and influence an emerging non-Lutheran radicalism that would continue to embrace and develop his initial theological experiments.

Initially, the doctrine of *sola fide* forced radical recognition of the lack of personal piety and antinomianism among the reformed in comparison with the Pauline description and teaching of what the infilling of the Holy Spirit accomplished at salvation in the believer's life in a practical sense. This incited these radicals to question the efficacy of a reformation of Catholicism and opt for the restitution of primitive New Testament Christianity. Although they never focused on "speaking in tongues" as the initial evidence of being filled with the Spirit as Pentecostals would, they insisted that if one became a Christian, a life of piety as described by Paul's definition of the "fruit of the Spirit" in Galatians 5 should be in evidence. This is not to preclude the emerging differences among them concerning the interpretation of what that church consisted, of as there were many, but in a broader view they were in agreement, perhaps only separated by degrees of application and praxis.

Luther believed in a forensic justification, a one-time act of faith alone through grace without any human participation or merit, because one's will was bound.[181] The *Schwärmer* believed the same thing but not the same way. Christians did in fact have free will and participated in their own salvation, but not with works of merit. Instead, they did so through acts of piety enabled by the Holy Spirit, as evidence of the inner spiritual experience of salvation. Although they embraced *sola fide,* they saw it as the work of the Spirit first in every Christian and not through any intellectual endeavor, and thus all Christians were capable of interpreting the Scripture as a priesthood of believers. Luther's concept of human sin and depravation requiring salvation without works of merit

---

181. Althaus, *Theology of Martin Luther*, 129. See also, McGrath, *Reformation Thought*, 126–28.

was also accepted, but they saw a Christian's pious works as a process of continuing sanctification made possible by the work of the Holy Spirit. They believed one to have a free will with the possibility of a conscious response, either positively or negatively, which necessarily precluded pedobaptism, as an informed response was not possible from an infant.

Sacramentally, Luther believed in the real presence of Christ in the Eucharist, but not transubstantiation of the elements as the church did. For him Jesus' words of institution established his real presence, and not the priestly elevation of the host. He arrived at this position by a metamorphic process over several years. But the *Schwärmer* considered the efficacy of the elements, only in a spiritual sense, received by faith in memoriam. Once again, both appear to believe in the same thing but not in the same way.[182]

In regard to pneumatology, Luther evolved into a cessationist who believed that the efficacy of the gifts of the Holy Spirit were for the primitive church only and had ceased to be of use. They believed that the Spirit was still active and present in the church, empowering the *ecclesia* as a priesthood of believers to live changed lives, interpret Scripture, and give evidence of their inner transformation by being able to live new lives regenerated by the Holy Spirit. This also became a tenet of Anabaptist faith.[183]

The evangelical *Schwärmer*—Karlstadt, Müntzer, and Schwenckfeld—acted out their differences by seeking a measured efficacy in people in terms of personal piety. They understood the manifestation of the gifts of the Holy Spirit according to 1 Corinthians 12–14 by every Christian to be a prophetic fulfillment of the idea of the priesthood of the believer. Each had a definite impact on the development of future Reformation radicalism, particularly within the Swiss Reformation from which Anabaptism emerged. They set spiritual precedents and presented restitution of the primitive church as an alternative to Lutheran reform, thus establishing a new liminality beyond the magisterial Reformation that emphasized the viability of the restitution of the New Testament church based on Paulinism. The impact of the Lutheran radicalism, played out first in Zwingli's Reformation of the church in Switzerland as evidenced by the emergence of Anabaptism, will be discussed in chapter two.

182. Althaus, *Theology of Martin Luther*, 380–82. See also, Luther, " Babylonian Captivity," 224–25; Luther, "Treatise on the New Testament," 77, 86–87.

183. Snyder, *Anabaptist History and Theology*, 87–88.

Chapter 2

Zwingli's Reformation and Anabaptist Radicalism

In 1519, two years after Luther had posted his *Ninety-Five Theses*, Huldrych Zwingli was elected stipendiary priest of the Grössmunster in Zurich. By 1522, he began to take advantage of his position within the church to petition for grievances regarding the abuses and non-biblical practices of the pope and the church's hierarchical priesthood. The acceptance of his anti-clericalism by civic leaders and local congregations persuaded him to actively engage in an effort to reform the church to a more biblical model. Thus the Swiss Reformation was initiated.[1] However, as he abandoned some of his initial theological premises for reform, some of his staunchest adherents rejected the new positions as being pro-Catholic, compromising any real attempt at a reformation. These adherents would become known initially as Swiss Brethren and subsequently Anabaptists. Zwingli was aware of Luther's Reformation activities, but he saw the reform of the Swiss Catholic Church as something apart. An examination of the Swiss Reformation will emphasize that although the Swiss did act autonomously, radical elements emerged, just the same as in Germany. This chapter will argue that the emergence and development of Swiss radicalism and the resultant Anabaptist movement was predicated upon Zwingli's initial reform theology which established his early goals and objectives. Zwingli's rejection of a corrupt Catholic priesthood, acceptance of *sola scriptura, sola fide,*

---

1. Gordon, *Swiss Reformation*, 51.

Luther's Petrine doctrine of the priesthood of the believer, and initial agreement with anti-pedobaptism all contributed to and encouraged the emergence of Anabaptism.

BIOGRAPHY

Zwingli was a young Swiss student of Erasmian humanism who felt a call to the priesthood. He was ordained in Constance in 1506 after a typical education and training for those already possessing a master's degree. Although this did not approach the education of the Augustinian Luther, it sufficed for the regular priesthood.[2] His first pastorate was in the province of Glarus where he remained from 1506 to 1516. It was there that he accepted the role of chaplain to the Swiss mercenaries from Glarus. In that role he became appalled at the lucrative practice of the mercenary conscription of young Swiss men between the ages of eighteen and thirty by the Cantons for the Imperial armies of Europe, including those of Pope Julius II (1503–1513).[3] As he witnessed the ravages of war and carnage inflicted on Swiss youth, and when he noted that even the pope would involve himself to further his personal political agendas, as well as those of the church, he ultimately proclaimed that it was un-Christian. Based on this, he began his protest and call for the reformation of the church.[4] From 1516 to 1518, he held the position of people's priest at the Benedictine monastery in Einsiedeln. Here he would immerse himself in the study and application of Erasmian biblical humanism and patristics, eventually settling for the Bible alone, *sola scriptura*, as the key to the true Christian faith.[5]

The catalysts for Luther's Reformation did not occur in a vacuum. The influences and antecedents that prevailed upon him were also prevalent throughout Western Europe, impacting many other churchmen. Not the least of these was Zwingli. In 1506, he was in Basel under the tutelage of Thomas Wyttenbach (1472–1526) who, along with Erasmus, decried the practice of selling indulgences. Both had seen the apostasy

---

2. Gaebler, *Huldrych Zwingli*, 25–25, 29. He had previously studied in Vienna and Basel from 1498–1506. A regular priest was ordained for the work of pastoring, whereas a secular priest was ordained for the monastic life.

3. Gordon, *Swiss Reformation*, 27.

4. Stephens, *Theology of Huldrych Zwingli*, 10.

5. Gaebler, *Huldrych Zwingli*, 32–40.

of the practice years before Luther.⁶ However, Zwingli would not begin to speak out against the practice in writing until 1524. At that time, he would say that Christians were free from all laws meant to make them pious, including indulgences, and further it was only false shepherds who enriched themselves and their relatives by selling the unscriptural instruments.⁷

The early influence of Erasmian biblical humanism, the study of the church fathers, the Erasmian/Lutheran-like literal spiritual-prophetic interpretation of Scripture as *sola scriptura,* and Zwingli's initial position of being anti-pedobaptism set the stage for a primitive Pauline New Testament pneumatology that strongly inferred the restitution of the early church for the Swiss Brethren Anabaptists and not the reformation of the church.⁸ The development of the foundation upon which the Anabaptist movement was established was unwittingly laid by the combination of the initial reform theology of Zwingli and Luther alike.

ZWINGLI'S HERMENEUTICS

After Zwingli assumed his duties as the people's priest at the Grossmünster in Zurich, he began a careful but insistent opposition to the Catholic Church, based primarily on his conviction that the Bible, the word of God, and its apparent contradiction of church practice and tradition, was and should be the only rule of faith. In a retrospective sermon he preached in September 1522 entitled *Of the Clarity and Certainty of the Word of God,* which may have marked his transition from Erasmian humanism to Augustinian biblicism, he said:

> I under took to devote myself entirely to the Scriptures I was always prevented by philosophy and theology. But eventually I came to the point where led by the Word and Spirit of God I saw the need to set aside all these things and to learn the doctrine of God direct from his own Word.⁹

---

6. Rilliet, *Zwingli.*

7. Zwingli, "Short Christian Instruction (1523)," 65–66; Zwingli, "Shepherd (1524)," 112–14.

8. Zwingli, "On Baptism 1525," 139.

9. Zwingli, "Clarity and Certainty," 90–91. An obvious commitment to *sola scriptura.*

Alister McGrath observes that Zwingli adopted Erasmus's hermeneutic method where the interpreter adopts a natural sense of the Scripture. This is very much like Luther's idea that one must look for the spiritual meaning without doing any harm to the literal meaning, a literal spiritual-prophetic style. Zwingli's early admission that he abandoned theology and philosophy to be led only by the word and Spirit of God was a commitment to this spiritual method of hermeneutics.[10]

Like Luther, Zwingli was a radical, as previously defined, an advocate of extreme and fundamental innovations to church doctrine and theology. His *Sixty-Seven Articles,* published in Zurich in 1523, began an initial systematic attempt to reform the church.[11] It would be from Zwingli's protest that Swiss Reformation radicalism would find its incentive, resulting in the emergence of Anabaptism, the most prevalent and lasting of the radical reform efforts of the sixteenth century. The **archetypical Lutheran** radicalism of Karlstadt, Müntzer, and Schwenckfeld, the *Schwärmer,* has already been discussed. Based most likely on his experiences with this triumvirate, Luther made it very clear that he would tolerate no deviation from his position of the word having precedence over the Spirit.[12] He rejected what he considered their extreme spiritualism and charismatic pneumatology, stating that the manifestations of the gifts of Holy Spirit had been relegated to the primitive church and were in cessation, no longer necessary, since the church had become established institutionally.[13] Zwingli's initial hermeneutic—again much like that of Luther, and combined with some influence from the *Schwärmer*—became the threshold through which Anabaptist radicalism would emerge. Zwingli's experience as a reformer began separate from, and was initially uninfluenced by, Luther's efforts in Germany. He refused to be labeled a Lutheran and would state in 1523, "I did not learn my doctrine from Luther, but from God's Word itself."[14] It should also be mentioned that the initial influence of Rhenish mysticism on Luther, as previously noted, was not an issue for Zwingli.

---

10. McGrath, *Reformation Thought,* 160.
11. Zwingli, "Exposition and Basis," 371–73.
12. Luther, "Against the Heavenly Prophets 1525," 146.
13. Luther, *Lectures on Galatians 1535,* 374–75.
14. George, *Theology of the Reformers,* 113.

SUPERIORITY OF THE WORD

On January 29, 1523, the first Zurich Disputation was called to challenge Bishop Hugo of Constance, the presiding ecclesiastic authority over Zurich. Zwingli had written the articles specifically for the anticipated dispute, but the Bishop's delegation refused to attend and debate such important theological matters in a nonacademic environment.[15] Zwingli proceeded to present his arguments to the disputants who did attend, with an introduction to the articles which informed them of how important Scripture was to his arguments:

> The Articles and opinions below, I, Ulrich Zwingli, confess to have preached in the worthy city of Zurich as based upon the Scriptures which are called inspired by God, and I offer to protect and conquer with said articles, and where I have not correctly understood Scriptures I shall allow myself to be taught better, but only from said Scriptures.[16]

Most pertinent of the articles to his consideration of the apostasy of the church and this study are:

> "The Eighteenth Article, That Christ who offered himself up once as a sacrifice, is a perpetual and valid payment for the sin of all believers; from this it follows that the mass is not a sacrifice, but a memorial of the sacrifice and a seal of the redemption which Christ has manifested to us,
>
> The Fifty-Seventh Article, The true Holy Scriptures know nothing of Purgatory after this life,"
>
> "The Sixty-First Article, Of an [indelible] character which priests have appropriated to themselves in recent times, scripture knows nothing at all;"

and

> "The Sixty-Second Article, It [scripture] knows of no priests other than those who proclaim the word of God."[17]

In summation he said;

---

15. Zwingli, "First Zurich Disputation," 111–17.
16. Zwingli, "First Zurich Disputation," 111.
17. Zwingli, "First Zurich Disputation," 335, 355, 357.

> Let no one undertake here to argue with sophistry or human
> foolishness, but come to the Scriptures to accept them as the
> judge *foras cares!* the Scriptures breathe the Spirit of God, so
> that the truth may be found, or if found, as I hope, retained.
> Amen.[18]

Subsequently he was not accused of heresy and the Zurich City Council, which was sitting in judgement at the disputation, ruled that

> Master Ulrich Zwingli continue and keep on as before to proclaim the holy Gospel and the correct divine Scriptures with the Spirit of God in accordance with his capabilities so long and so frequently until something better is made known to him.[19]

The City Council had been convinced by Zwingli as early as 1520 of the validity of *sola scriptura*; their decision was more of a reiteration of previous support given for the doctrine as well as a vote of confidence in Zwingli.[20] This was a clear indication of how Zwingli, again like Luther, was to utilize the magistracy in reforming and protecting the church. Ultimately, he decided to use the coercive action of the state against radical elements and enlisted the magisterial authorities for the propagation of the gospel and his reform.[21]

The superiority of the word of God to Zwingli cannot be overstated, but it needed to be defined with specificity within the context of *sola scriptura*. For Luther, the word was that which inculcated Christ into the hearts of Christians whether written, preached, or through the sacraments. How that occurred was dependent upon the Holy Spirit.[22] Walter Klaassen has argued that at best Zwingli was reticent to claim that preaching was the word of God.[23] He based his conclusion on a statement made by Zwingli;

> I recall that it was once imputed to me as wrong that I had said
> that God spake by my mouth when I was setting forth His word.
> But that I did, that the crowd might not think I spoke of myself and give me the credit that belonged to Christ. I even gave

---

18. Zwingli, "First Zurich Disputation," 117. Take care! Be careful!
19. Zwingli, "First Zurich Disputation," 93.
20. George, *Theology of the Reformers*, 116–17; McGrath, *Intellectual Origins*, 43.
21. Williams, *Radical Reformation*, xxix.
22. Lohse, *Martin Luther's Theology*, 189–90.
23. Klaassen, "Word, Spirit, and Scripture," 66.

distinct warning that no one must make a mistake about that point.²⁴

In 1522, Zwingli had already published *Of the Clarity and Certainty of the Word of God*, in which, G. W. Bromiley has noted that Zwingli only implies that the spoken word of the gospel equates with the written word of the Bible. However, in the absence of any clear differentiation between the spoken and written word, in his opinion, Zwingli proceeded to enumerate an exhaustive list of biblical illustrations, from both Testaments, of instances where the word of God was spoken. Zwingli differentiated between the creative words of God, the redemptive words of Christ, and the written record of each.²⁵ Moreover, he prefaced the list with, "The Word of God is so sure and strong that if he wills all things are done the moment that he speaks his Word."²⁶ In the same year, he preached a sermon and wrote an exhortation at the request of Joachim von Watt (1484–1551), known as Vadian, for the benefit of bishops, shepherds, and guardians of the reform entitled, "The Shepherd," wherein he listed the pastor and priest among those who spoke the word of God when they preached:²⁷

> Thus in the first place we want to consider the word of God out of the mouth and activity of Christ, true God, and thereafter from the prophets and apostles, in order to see what and how big the office of shepherd is which we call bishop, pastor, people's priest, prophet, evangelist or preacher.²⁸

Zwingli consistently maintained that the written words of the Bible contained the word, but not exclusively. He took the position that prior to the recorded word, the spoken word existed in a larger, more generic context. God's creative words, the words of Annunciation to Mary, and of course the living Word, Christ himself, were all examples of that broader context.²⁹ Again he wrote in *Of the Clarity and Certainty or Power of the Word of God*,

---

24. Zwingli, in Klaassen, "Word, Spirit, and Scripture," 41. See also, Zwingli, "Preaching Office, 156–57.
25. Zwingli, "Clarity and Certainty," 54, 68–72.
26. Zwingli, "Clarity and Certainty," 68.
27. Zwingli, "Shepherd (1524)," 81.
28. Zwingli, "Shepherd (1524)," 86.
29. George, *Theology of the Reformers*, 128.

> In the first place, by the Gospel we do not mean only the writings of Matthew, Mark Luke, and John. But as we have said, all that God has revealed to man in order that he may instruct him and give him a sure knowledge of his will.[30]

W. P. Stephens argues that Zwingli understood preaching to be the outer word, but only seen in the context of the sovereignty of God, in that it is not a matter of personal charisma, but a combination of Spirit and word made effective by God alone.[31] Peter Opitz observes that not only did Zwingli consider the Bible as the sole source of the divine word and sufficient for the liberation of the soul, but that hearing the word served in the same capacity.[32] Gottfried Locher more correctly agrees that Zwingli considered preaching to be the word of God, as he believed that it was through the preacher that the Bible began to speak again. Scripture was not to be separated from its proclamation or its interpretation.[33] It appears then that both Klaassen and Bromiley may have been premature in their conclusions. Zwingli himself, as noted above, is probably the best witness to his conviction that preaching was the word of God. But more importantly, he allowed space for the efficacy of the Pauline concept of the enabling role of the Holy Spirit, both in proclamation and interpretation of the word.

PNEUMATOLOGY

Zwingli's hermeneutics reflected the influence of biblical humanism. His emphasis on spirituality, rejection of the externals of medieval religion, openness to philosophy and reason, and disdain for the mysterious and sacramental all point to Erasmian influence.[34] When Erasmus's Greek New Testament appeared, Zwingli all the more pursued his studies of the biblical languages and made the Bible the central text to his thinking.[35] However, as pointed out above, he would eventually eschew humanism for a more spiritual hermeneutical lens.

---

30. Zwingli, "Clarity and Certainty," 86.
31. Stephens, *Theology of Huldrych Zwingli*, 135.
32. Opitz, "Exegetical and Hermeneutical Work," 415.
33. Locher, *Zwingli's Thought*, 10–11.
34. George, *Theology of the Reformers*, 112–13.
35. Potter, *Huldrych Zwingli*, 1–5, 19, 39.

Peter Opitz describes Zwingli's exegetical method for interpreting the Old Testament as consisting of three steps: the literal meaning, the practical or present meaning, and the allegorical meaning pointing to Christ, an apparent contraction of the medieval *Quadriga* mentioned earlier.[36] Zwingli was not a doctor of theology and by his own confession a self-taught theologian. Alister McGrath suggests that although it appears that medieval exegetical methods such as the *Quadriga* had little if any influence on him, the effect of Erasmus on his hermeneutics was significant. He consistently used humanist methods, employing the use of the original languages as aids in interpretation, as well as humanist rhetorical theory to distinguish between various misuses of tropes, including catachresis and synecdoche, which were of theological importance.[37] He also emphasized the philological-historical method in his exegeses.[38] Timothy George characterizes Zwingli's use of the church fathers as a humanist trait, but notes that he made a distinction between them and the medieval "sophistic" theologians.[39] Charlotte Methuen and Gregory Miller rightly conclude that scholasticism and humanism were not necessarily mutually exclusive.[40] It appears then that Zwingli was, in many ways, a pragmatic theologian as he incorporated those hermeneutic aspects of both medieval and humanistic methodologies which he felt to be either compatible with his understanding or conducive to his own interpretation regarding the meaning of the word.

A critical variable for the foundation of his hermeneutics was the role of the Holy Spirit. Reference has been made as to how Zwingli believed he had been personally led by the Spirit to learn the doctrine of God directly from God's word. As he began to teach this theory, he wrote in *Of the Clarity and Certainty or Power of the Word of God*:

> God can never be learned with greater certainty than when it is taught by God himself, for it comes from God, and he alone is truthful, indeed, he is truth itself. We do not need human

---

36. Opitz, "Exegetical and Hermeneutical Work," 423.

37. Catachresis is the abuse and misuse of metaphor; synecdoche is defining the whole using one part.

38. McGrath, *Intellectual Origins*, 167–68.

39. George, *Theology of the Reformers*, 126; Stephens, *Theology of Huldrych Zwingli*, 52–54.

40. Miller, "Huldrych Zwingli (1484–1531)," 1–2; Methuen, "Interpreting Nature and Scripture," 159.

> interpreters but his anointing, which is the Spirit, teaches us of all things-all things, notice-and therefore it is truth and is no lie.[41]

This was tantamount to confirmation of the concept of the priesthood of the believer.[42]

Unlike Luther, for him, the Spirit was first in priority relative to Scripture, for without the Spirit, human intelligence misunderstands the word. It is beyond human capacity to bring others to faith, for that is the purview of God alone. However, according to Zwingli's understanding of Paulinism, "Faith comes from what is heard, and what is heard comes by the preaching of Christ" (Rom 10:17), understood as the word.[43] This did not mean that preaching the external word could accomplish much without the internal working of the Spirit.[44] The Spirit and word are not exclusive, but inclusive, notwithstanding the Spirit's precedence, a contradiction of Luther's theme that the Spirit cannot be present without the word.[45] The combination of the two,[46]

> [Shows] conclusively that God's Word can be understood by a man without any human direction: not that this is due to man's own understanding, but to the light and Spirit of God, illuminating and inspiring the words in such a way that the light of divine content is seen in his own light.[47]

This was another confirmation of the doctrine of the priesthood of the believer.

Here, Luther and Zwingli agreed that it is God who makes the word effective, but it was a case of congruence of the word and the Spirit for Zwingli, which made interpretation and understanding possible. Zwingli addressed the practical aspects of applying the process of interpreting the word with the following methodology that is remarkably similar to early Pentecostalism:

---

41. Zwingli, "Clarity and Certainty," 87–88.
42. Zwingli, "Clarity and Certainty," 82–83. See also 1 Pet 2:9.
43. Stephens, *Theology of Huldrych Zwingli*, 58n49. Here Zwingli references testing everything by the gospel and the "fire of Paul."
44. Zwingli, "Of the Upbringing and Education," 104.
45. Klaassen, "Word, Spirit, and Scripture," 49.
46. Stephens, *Theology of Huldrych Zwingli*, 135.
47. Zwingli, "Clarity and Certainty," 78.

> Before I say anything or listen to the teaching of man, I will first consult the mind of the Spirit of God, Psalm 84, (A. V. 85): . . . Then you should reverently ask God for His grace, that he may give you his mind and Spirit, so that you will not lay hold of your own opinion but of his. . . . And then go to the written word of the Gospel. . . . You must be *theodidacti* that is taught of God, not of men that is what the truth itself said (John 6), and it cannot lie.[48]

Grant Wacker has pointed out that early Pentecostals considered the Holy Spirit to be the final arbiter and interpreter of the word. Although understanding that the Spirit worked through the lips of the teacher, "The Teacher recognized above all others is the divine author the Text Book [the Bible] -the Holy Spirit."[49]

Zwingli's consideration of the relationship between the Old and New Testaments is important background for understanding his concept of the prophetic word. W. P. Stephens observes that Zwingli considered both Testaments to be in continuity with each other, and in the context of 1 Corinthians 10:11, a source of prophetic word, referring to Christ in symbols and types for the instruction of Christians, an idea similar to that of Luther. The Old Testament was therefore to be read in the light of the New Testament, and particularly in the light of Christ.[50]

Alister McGrath accuses Zwingli of falling into the conundrum of indulging in eisegesis of Scripture, rather than exegesis, by reading his own theology back into the typological illustrations of Christ he believed to be within the Old Testament.[51] Walter Klaassen understands Zwingli to treat both testaments for the most part as God's whole revelation, but with the definite distinction that the New Testament was clearer and more complete in that it revealed Christ, another similarity to Luther. This was the most probable of Zwingli's hermeneutics. It was also a praxis that early Pentecostals developed in their biblical hermeneutic, commonly referred to as preaching "the full gospel." Early Pentecostalism "heard and longed for themes in Scripture which were being ignored or were deemed as unacceptable" in the contemporary church.[52] There is no evidence,

48. Zwingli, "Clarity and Certainty," 88–89.
49. Wacker, *Heaven Below*, 150.
50. Stephens, *Theology of Huldrych Zwingli*, 71–72.
51. McGrath, *Intellectual Origins*, 170.
52. Archer, *Pentecostal Hermeneutic*, 28–29. See also, Warrington, *Pentecostal Theology*, 184–88.

however, that they were following any historic Anabaptist examples. They both were simply reading and interpreting the same Scriptures the same way.

Most likely to reinforce his sense of the importance of Scripture, Zwingli founded a theological college in the Grossmünster in September of 1523. He began teaching both testaments in Latin, Greek, and Hebrew using the Vulgate Bible and Erasmus's New Testament, much in the humanistic style.[53] The school was known as the *Prophezei*, from its emphasis on preaching as prophetic forthtelling as well as foretelling, and was significant in terms of his definition of the prophetic word.[54] The term was taken from 1 Corinthians 14 and referred to the charismatic gift of prophecy. According to Peter Opitz, Zwingli thought of prophecy as the exposition of Scripture with the "office of prophet" having three purposes: prophesying as in 1 Corinthians 14, understood much like early Pentecostalism,[55] the responsibility entrusted to Old Testament prophets, and the exposition of the tradition according to 1 Corinthians 11 and Luke 2. All were joined together for the purpose of expounding Scripture, announcing God's work of salvation, and the transmission of warnings and threats.[56]

Zwingli defined "apostle" as another term for "messenger," quoting Luke 6:13. The office of apostle was to preach the gospel; however, preachers differed from prophets, evangelists, and teachers, and are, indeed above them because they were the first to go to an alien, unbelieving world and spread God's word. Zwingli's exposition of Ephesians 4 defined the role of prophet as one who predicts what the future will hold, but goes on to equate it with the role of evangelists, bishops, and ministers of religion, the very offices listed in 1 Corinthians 12–14. According to Jeremiah 1:9–10, it is the role of the prophet to pluck up, tear down, and destroy whatever is set against God and begin to build and plant what God desires.[57] Zwingli rejected the manifestation of the gift of prophesy by Anabaptists, because they maintained that any Christian could

---

53. Potter, *Zwingli*, 221.
54. Zwingli, "Preaching Office," 158–60.
55. Warrington, *Pentecostal Theology*, 81–84.
56. Opitz, " Exegetical and Hermeneutical Work," 421.
57. Zwingli, "Preaching Office," 156–58.

prophesy—not just those who were literate—according to 1 Corinthians 14:30–33.[58]

He also counted New Testament prophets as those who were contemporaries of the apostles, such as Agabus (Acts 21:10) and those mentioned in 1 Corinthians 14, who, in the absence of the New Testament, proclaimed the word through preaching. "From this we learn that those, too, were called prophets at the time of the apostles who expounded the writings of the Old Testament for the entire congregation."[59] In a similar Pentecostal sense, he equated them with those referred to by Paul in 1 Corinthians 14:26–33, where Paul lists the charismatic gifts of the Spirit to include speaking in tongues, speaking in tongues with interpretation, and revelation. In the passage Paul also explains the praxis and administration of the gifts. Zwingli comments and emphasizes that only one person speaks to the edification of the church, while speaking in tongues is to be done by two or three at most, speaking in turn with one interpreter. If there is no interpreter, the speaker should be silent in the church, speaking only to God and one's self. If there are prophets, two or three are to speak and others are to judge what is said against the word. It is at this point that Zwingli described more precisely the prophet's role in "The Preaching Office":

> Now this is the meaning of Paul's words: when you come together to hear psalms or Scripture, some of you are learned, some know languages, to some God has given a special revelation, some are capable interpreters, translating Hebrew into Greek or some such. You are to undertake everything in a way that will enable you to upbuild therewith.[60]

Zwingli obviously considered the concept of the gifts of tongues, tongues and interpretation, and revelation as the ability to understand biblical languages, and clearly valued the intellectual ability to translate the original languages into the vernacular. This did not mean however that the congregation was prohibited from participation at this level:

> Prophets then must have been well versed in languages, for all other gifts served to the end of attaining to the highest, i.e. to prophesy which means to interpret, 1 Cor. 14:1 "Seek after spiritual gifts, above all, to prophesy, which is to be able to interpret

58. Zwingli, "Preaching Office," 160–61.
59. Zwingli, "Preaching Office," 158.
60. Zwingli, "Preaching Office," 159.

the writings of God's word." "Does not Paul say in 1 Cor. 14:31, You are all to prophesy, one after another? Which, in other words, is to speak on the meaning of Scripture before the gathered congregation." The entire community, i.e. everyone else, judges whether or not the prophet does justice to the word.[61]

This statement seems to contradict Zwingli's first understanding of 1 Peter 2:9 when he said, "all prophets must be well versed in languages," but then quotes 1 Corinthians 14:31: "you are all to prophesy." Nevertheless, he provided a clarification for his position. There was a difference, however, between translating the scriptural language and interpreting it. The prophet would interpret the translation, giving it meaning. Although the translator and interpreter could be one and the same person, no one else could speak in judgment until after interpreters, prophets, and those with language abilities had spoken. The prophetic word then for Zwingli was Scripture translated from the original languages, interpreted by the prophets who were the preachers, bishops, evangelists, ministers, or pastors.[62]

ECCLESIOLOGY

In 1531, after his seeming reformation success and overcoming the Anabaptists, Zwingli penned his definitive description of the body of Christ, the church, in *An Exposition of the Faith*. In it he made a clear statement that the Roman Catholic Church was not the visible church on earth.

He believed the church to be one, holy, universal church and it is either visible or invisible (or better said both). The invisible church is the one which comes from God to those who believe and know his embraces by the power of the Holy Spirit. It is not invisible because believers are invisible, but because it is not seen by nonbelievers. The visible church is that which consists of all who profess faith in Christ the world over. It consists of those who are called Christians, but who actually are not because they have not embraced the power of the Holy Spirit. They have no inward faith and are not members of the invisible elect church. Though their brethren cannot identify them, as they take the Communion to their own detriment, this church consists of the insolent and hostile. This

---

61 Zwingli, "Preaching Office," 159.
62. Zwingli, "Preaching Office," 180–81.

situation creates the need for governments to provide for the safety and security of society at large, the residence of the church at large.[63]

Zwingli did see the government much like Paul described it in Romans 13, as did Luther: necessary for the well-being of society, Christian or not. It was not responsible for the inward righteousness of the church, but it was to be held accountable for the promotion of outward righteousness resulting from individuals being constrained to obey the law. This was considered by the Anabaptists as using coercion to propagate the gospel using the magistracy.[64]

Although starting from a different theological point, and a disparate geographic location than Luther, Zwingli recognized that the church had been corrupted by an avaricious clergy led by the pope, who presided over a church that did not model, conform, or even hold any pretence to *sola scriptura* in a primitive New Testament sense. In turn he saw the desperate need for a reformation of the church. Notwithstanding his wanting to distance himself and his Swiss Reformation from Luther, Zwingli no doubt was aware of the ongoing events in the Holy Roman Empire and Luther's plight. He had no compunction about his preference for Erasmian humanism over Lutheranism, but eventually rejected both for a more biblically literal ecclesiology. A study of the one hundred volumes of Zwingli's library still in existence revealed that he had collected and studied the church fathers, Latin classics, Luther, and Christian humanists, not the least of whom was Erasmus, but his marginalia was found to be overwhelmingly concentrated in Erasmus's work.[65]

It was from a position of magisterial support that Zwingli began to reform the church in practical ways similar to Karlstadt's activism in the Wittenberg movement of 1521. The ensuing disputations and writings of Zwingli from 1522 to 1525 challenged the church's positions on the Mass, images in worship, the meaning of baptism, the nature of salvation, and ecclesiology. The Zurich City Council would declare the Ave Maria to be nonbinding, the breviary was to be simplified, and very much like the concerns of the *Schwärmer*, the issue of Christian impiety was addressed with legal measures to control immorality and violent behavior. Zwingli would also challenge the church's teachings on fasting, images,

---

63. Zwingli, *Zwingli and Bullinger*, 24, 265–66.

64. McGrath, *Reformation Thought*, 228–29.

65 Gaebler, *Huldrych Zwingli*, 33–40; McGrath, *Intellectual Origins*, 48–49; Peters, "Introduction," xviii.

clerical marriage, and the growing theology of Marian intercession.[66] For Zwingli, Christian freedom was found in love, not law. The tension, however, was between inner and outer piety, spirit and flesh, the efficacy of the word as revealed by the Holy Spirit that could be interpreted and understood by all Christians in the power of the Spirit only.[67]

Zwingli's political power and control over the Zurich City Council grew out of his charismatic personality and his forceful, but articulate vernacular preaching. He was also careful not to usurp any of the council's authority in the name of the church.[68] Without the approval and enforcement of the council, his reformation was inconceivable to him. However, his more radical followers, believing that the state should not be involved in any way with the affairs of the church, would object most vehemently and began to increase pressure on him to apply his initial ideas for reformation. Not even his acceptance of Karlstadt's symbolic Eucharist, his initial opposition to pedobaptism, or even his emphasis on the Spirit's precedence over the word, would dissuade radical detractors.[69] His blatant use of the magistracy to coerce religious reform and continue to practice many Catholic traditions that he had previously spoken out against, would disqualify him from any restitution of the New Testament primitive church.[70] However, it was his willingness to accept pedobaptism in acquiescence to the Zurich City Council's concern for social unity that would be the cause of a major radical schism.

THEOLOGY

In the beginning, Zwingli accepted *sola scriptura* as the foundation of the Christian faith, understood the work of the Holy Spirit as enabling every Christian to read and interpret Scripture, depending upon the self-interpreting nature of the Holy Writ, all of which acknowledged the efficacy of the Petrine doctrine of the priesthood of the believer.[71] He accepted the idea of local pastors being chosen by their own congregations without

66. Wandel, "Zwingli," 321–22.
67. Gordon, *Swiss Reformation*, 53–56.
68. Gordon, *Swiss Reformation*, 54.
69. Harder, *Sources of Swiss Anabaptism*, 314; Bender, "Infant Baptism."
70. Stayer, "Radical Reformation," 255.
71. Luther, "Christian Assembly has the Right," 305–14. See also, Zwingli, "Preaching Office," 179–82; 1 Pet 2:5, 9; Muller, *Dictionary of Latin and Greek*, 277. *Scripturam ex Scriptura explicandam esse* ("Scripture is to be explained from Scripture").

ecclesiastical authority or qualification. He considered the efficacy and work of the Holy Spirit as being critical to faith. He was influenced by the Erasmian *philosophia Christi,* the internal and spiritual nature of faith for every Christian, as well as Erasmus's concept of the importance of every Christian's responsibility to read Scripture, to be directly imbued with the teachings of Christ from birth and in their respective vernaculars.[72] Although there were many similarities to Luther's theology, Zwingli would attribute them to the Holy Spirit first, whereas Luther would attribute them to the word first.[73] Zwingli's soteriology was within the context of Erasmus's humanistic vision of the regeneration and perhaps the restitution of Christianity, *Christianismus Renascens,* and the *philosophia Christi*.[74] His theology also reflected the influence of Erasmus's emphasis on spirituality, rejection of the externals of medieval religion, openness to philosophy and reason, and disdain for the mysterious and sacramental as mentioned above.[75] Zwingli believed that a Christian should focus on internal spirituality rather than external piety, an idea found in *Rule Five* of Erasmus's *Enchiridion*.[76] Where Luther initially had been influenced by Rhenish mysticism, Zwingli opted for a more biblically literal spiritual-prophetic and Pauline spirituality after Erasmus. Their disagreement over the nature of the Holy Spirit and the word of God and which had precedence over the other was never settled. Luther held onto his premise that if the Spirit was given precedence it would diminish the value and efficacy of the word, but Zwingli insisted that the Spirit was as efficacious in the absence of the word as he was in its presence.[77] Charlotte Methuen has pointed out that although early modern exegetes rejected scholastic hermeneutics, they, at the same time, contributed to its development. As reformers, they concentrated on new spiritual meanings, they were only being subsumed under an expanding definition of literal which was to include "spiritual-prophetic."[78] Whereas Luther would rely first on the literal spiritual-prophetic word, *sola scriptura,* depending on the Spirit only after its presentation, for understanding and interpretation, Zwingli

---

72. Olin, *Erasmus,* 97–108. *Paraclesis Novuum Testamentum 1516.*
73. Pipkin, *Huldrych Zwingli Writings,* 116–20.
74. McGrath, *Intellectual Origins,* 48–49.
75. George, *Theology of the Reformers,* 112–13.
76. Rummel, *Erasmus Reader,* 140–54.
77. Zwingli, *Zwingli and Bullinger,* 24, 78.
78. Methuen, "Interpreting Nature and Scripture," 2.

insisted that the word was only effective when interpreted by the Spirit and that this could be accomplished by all Christians under the spiritual discernment of the congregation. This gave precedence to the spiritual interpretations that included acceptance of that which was rationally logical and rejecting that which was not, but still held to the inerrancy of the word, *sola scriptura*.

Initially, Zwingli had doubts about infant baptism, which first attracted those radical adherents who were so inclined, but he had second thoughts that were influenced by the magistracy. He would write:

> Just as some have so rashly supposed that signs strengthen faith, so some have felt obliged to oppose child baptism, for faith cannot be strengthened in children who cannot yet believe. This mistake had misled me some years ago so that I thought it was much better that children should have their first baptism when they reached an appropriate age, although I did not act so presumptuously that I put myself arrogantly forward, as some now do.[79]

THE ANABAPTISTS EMERGE

By 1524, Zwingli, realizing the negative cultural and social impact that opposing infant baptism had on his coveted support of the city council, distanced himself from anti-pedobaptism and began to teach that, not unlike the Old Testament practice of circumcision—a symbol of God's choice and setting apart of the Israelites—infant baptism was in effect the same kind of sacramental ritual.[80] However, the nature of the theological question for radicals went directly to the heart of their protest against official ecclesial rituals and laws that demanded obedience for salvation. In their minds, if salvation was by faith through grace and not a function of sacramental practice, what was the value of baptizing an infant who could not participate in a conscious decision to accept Christ?

Zwingli had surrounded himself with men who had already been recognized in Zurich as respected academics, politicians, churchmen, and businessmen, many of whom were anti-pedobaptist. They included academic and theologian Heinrich Bullinger (1504–1575); priest and

---

79. Potter, *Huldrych Zwingli*, 37.

80. Williams, *Radical Reformation*, 149. See also, Snyder, *Anabaptist History and Theology*, 53.

academic Leo Jud (1482–1542); Joachim von Watt; Vadian (1484–1551), humanist and Bürgomeister of St. Gall; Conrad Grebel (1498–1526), a humanist patrician whose father was a member of the City Council; Felix Mantz (1498–1527), a canon at the Zurich Grossmünster; Andreas Castelberger (d.1528), a bookseller; Johannes Brötli and Wilhelm Reublin (1482–1560), both of whom were priests in the local villages of Zollikon and Witikon, respectively.[81] Of course there was a larger cast of characters who would contribute in supporting roles. There were other men of significance who supported Zwingli's Swiss reform, such as Wittenberger Karlstadt, Swiss-born Johannes Oecolampadius (1482–1531) of Basel, and Balthasar Hubmaier (1480/85–1528) of Waldshut. It was from this group of adherents that a radical element would emerge to challenge Zwingli, first upon his insistence on incorporating the state into the propagation of the gospel, and second, his willingness to use it to coerce the acceptance of his reformation.

At the end of 1522, Zwingli had resigned his post as priest at the Grossmünster and been appointed preacher under the direct control of the city council. At the first Zurich Disputation, January 1523, the city council supported Zwingli and his *Sixty-Seven Articles* against Bishop Hugo and the church at large, particularly accepting the idea of *sola scriptura*. They further authorized him to continue preaching in the same biblical vein, as long as he deemed it appropriate. They did not, however, decide the means for adopting such preaching in church praxis.[82] In the interim period of developing a carefully considered plan for reformation and the second Disputation in October of 1523, the council and Zwingli continued to practice the traditional Catholic Mass and rituals of the church. This made it very clear to the emerging radical elements that Zwingli was going to use the enforcing power of the council to coerce the reformation effort. The Mass was continued as before, as well as infant baptism. Attempts by the radicals to remove images from the church were rebuffed, but the council's authorization to continue the practice of collecting the tithe and sending it to the city coffers was a particularly grievous action, for it maintained a Catholic act of "monkish" avarice against the local congregations.[83]

---

81. Stayer, "Radical Reformation," 255.

82. Blanke, *Brothers in Christ*, 7–11.

83. Snyder, *Anabaptist History and Theology*, 51–53; Stayer, "Radical Reformation," 255.

The Disputation of October 1523 was called to debate Catholic imagery and the Mass. Much to the chagrin of Conrad Grebel, the most outspoken of the radical leaders, the council decided that it was not time for a radical departure from the Catholic practices in question, much like Luther's dilemma in Wittenberg under Karlstadt.[84] Another prominent radical, Balthasar Hubmaier, participated in the Disputation in support of Zwingli's opinion that the Mass had no salvific efficacy, but in fact was only a memorial to be celebrated in the vernacular with the distribution of both elements to the communicants.[85] This sacramentarian position would be maintained by all future Anabaptists.[86] The city council was also in agreement with Zwingli, et. al., but once again fearful of the social and cultural implications of moving to reform too fast. So they mitigated the conclusions of the disputation by allowing images to remain and the Mass to proceed as before.[87] The postponement of the reformation and Zwingli's acquiescence became another critical sign to the radicals that he was in the process of compromising many of his initial biblically supported theological positions, which had been expressed both in public and private. The council further authorized him to continue preaching in the same vein as long as he deemed it appropriate.

Throughout 1524, those who opposed Zwingli, led by Grebel and Mantz, had become disruptive in Zwinglian Reformed churches, specifically in the nearby villages of Zollikon and Witikon, where the congregations of Brötli and Reublin refused to baptize infant children. Subsequently, in January 1525, the city council called for a disputation regarding the matter. The council confirmed Zwingli's position and mandated the baptism of all infants within eight days as a civic duty. Three days later all unauthorized assemblies were forbidden; Grebel and Mantz were ordered to cease their teachings and disputations regarding infant baptism and obey the council's orders. Further, Reublin, Brötli, Ludwig Hätzer (1500–1529), and Castelberger were ostracized from Zurich.[88]

---

84. Snyder, *Anabaptist History and Theology*, 53. Harder, *Sources of Swiss Anabaptism*, 275–76. A letter from Grebel to Vadian, December 18, 1523.

85. Harder, *Sources of Swiss Anabaptism*, 234–50. A translation of an excerpt from Ludwig Haetzer's notes.

86. Snyder, *Anabaptist History and Theology*, 53.

87. Harder, *Sources of Swiss Anabaptism*, 251. Council's mandate after Disputation, October 1523.

88. Harder, *Sources of Swiss Anabaptism*, 337–38. Decree Against Anabaptists, January 21, 1525.

Shortly thereafter, the first adult baptism was performed when Grebel baptized Georg Blaurock (martyred 1529) in Zurich. Blaurock in turn baptized the rest of those present.[89] The council's actions did not deter the movement which proceeded to begin an evangelistic effort that would reach numerous surrounding communities and came to be known as the Swiss Brethren, the first early Anabaptist adherents.

The Anabaptists' position concerning Christian initiation, insisting on adult baptism and rejecting infant baptism, went unaddressed by both the council and Zwingli, and remained unresolved until January of 1525. Until that time, Zwingli's radical adherents rapidly distanced themselves from him and the council's reticence to proceed quickly with church reform. They continued to preach the Pauline concepts according to 1 Corinthians 12–14, as initially encouraged by Zwingli and Luther, within their respective congregations, but most notably disobeyed all the council's mandates for continuing the Catholic forms of the Mass, veneration of images, and infant baptism. The critical nature of an informed confession of faith in Christ to the radicals was paramount to being a Christian and thus precluded infant baptism as inconceivable and a threat to a biblical understanding of the faith. This logically demanded adult or believer's baptism, or rebaptism, thus beginning the formation of a believer's church as opposed to a state church.[90] It was also a prelude to the establishment of local radical Anabaptist conventicles, house church prayer and study meetings much like those initiated by Luther and Zwingli to propagate their reforms, which fomented discussions of forming an alternative church. According to a Latin tract, *Catabaptistarum Strophas Elenchus (Refutation of the Tricks of Anabaptists)*, written by Zwingli in July 1527, Grebel and Simon Stumpf, a Franconian monk and radical supporter, submitted a plan to him in December 1523 for establishing a new church—what became known as the Swiss Brethren (Anabaptists). The new sect was being designed to incorporate all of the disputed aspects that the Zurich Council had denied to the radical disputants.[91] It also reflects the influence of the *Schwärmer*, the unequivocal adherence to *sola scriptura*, and a Pauline pneumatology of inner spiritual empowerment. Franklin Littell contends that for them, only the

89. Hutterite Brethren, *Chronicle of the Hutterite Brethren*, 45.

90. Harder, *Sources of Swiss Anabaptism*, 335. Translation of Bullinger's notes, January 17, 1525.

91. Harder, *Sources of Swiss Anabaptism*, 276–79, 300–1. Zwingli's account of the Grebel-Stumpf plan.

restitution of the New Testament church would satisfy these criteria.[92] Hans Schlaffer (martyred 1528) would write in 1527:

> Through [Christ's] grace he has given us this understanding and it does not matter that the popes, church fathers or councils have ordered and decided something different. It is a much surer and more true foundation to build upon Christ and his teaching than to rely upon church fathers and councils.[93]

What ensued from the above-described events was the marginalization and diaspora of Anabaptism, a movement determined to see the restitution of primitive Christianity, throughout Western Europe. It would not be long before they were criminalized, persecuted, and martyred. By 1528, Zwingli had been excommunicated under the Edict of Worms, which excommunicated Luther in 1521. Both proceeded, however, with their respective reformation efforts and continuing disputes with each other.[94]

THE EUCHARISTIC CONTROVERSY

By 1529, Zwingli's reform appeared to be unstoppable, but there was a major split within the Protestant Reformation at large over the Eucharist. Luther had rejected the Catholic concept of transubstantiation, but he insisted on the validity of the real presence of the body and blood of Christ in the elements. His theology focused on the premise that the word of God and the sacraments were inseparable. Moreover, the word was capable of creating and supporting faith. Therefore, Jesus's words of institution, Matthew 28:27–30, "*This is my body*" (*Hoc est corpus meum*), literally established his real presence in the elements, not the priestly elevation of the host. He did not believe that the Eucharist was another sacrifice of Christ with salvific efficacy. Any other interpretation of the words of institution was thought by Luther to be a threat to the foundation of *sola scriptura*. Karlstadt and Müntzer took exception to Luther's eucharistic theology and perhaps should be seen as the catalysts for ensuing disputations regarding the issue. Both considered the Eucharist as a non-salvific memorial, and not another corporeal sacrifice. Each thought that the Eucharist, the Lord's Supper, was received through faith only by

---

92. Littell, *Origins of Sectarian Protestantism*, 80–82.
93. Schlaffer, "Instruction on Beginning," 107.
94. Gordon, *Swiss Reformation*, 70.

the Spirit.[95] Schwenckfeld, however, in agreement with Crautwald, also thought the Eucharist to be a memorial, but the real presence of Christ could not be in the elements in any form actually or spiritually, as this would demand the ubiquity of Christ, requiring him to be at the right hand of the Father and on earth at the elevation of the host at the same time. For Schwenckfeld, this would preclude the human nature of the risen Christ. However, he took the position that the Spirit could not be connected to the physical body of Christ, or even the believer's body. It was through the Holy Spirit that the elements really were the presence of the Lord in the Lord's Supper. "Therefore, the believing guests truly eat the precious body of our Lord and drink his holiest blood."[96]

Zwingli and his followers also insisted that the Eucharist was a memorial without salvific value, accepted by the communicant by faith alone. Zwingli would write in *True and False Religion* in 1525,

> By faith we believe that the physical and perceptible body of Christ is here. Things are believed by faith that is completely alien from perception. All physical things, indeed, are perceptible; if they are not perceptible then they are not physical. Hence believing and experiencing are different. Now, if it is bodily, there is no need for faith. The theologians have asserted here something that the senses cannot perceive, namely that the bread is flesh.[97]

Phillip of Hesse, who supported the Reformation—both that of Luther and Zwingli—sought to resolve the dispute by calling for a disputation in Marburg in 1529. The disputants who attended represented a significant number of Reformation leaders who had varying degrees of theological perspectives on the Eucharist in particular. But on the majority of those issues debated they were in general agreement. This was not the case regarding the Lord's Supper. Out of fifteen articles discussed, only one—the fifteenth—was undecided, and that was even after all agreed that both the bread and the wine was to be used, the Mass has no salvific value, the Sacrament of the Altar is a sacrament of the true body and blood of Jesus Christ, and that the spiritual taking of it is necessary for every Christian, the use of the sacrament, like the word, has been

---

95. Harder, *Sources of Swiss Anabaptism*, 271. See also, McGrath, *Reformation Thought*, 188–89.

96. Williams, *Caspar Schwenckfeld*, 126.

97. Potter, *Huldrych Zwingli*, 99.

given and ordained by God to excite faith by the Holy Spirit, but they agreed to disagree on whether or not the true body and blood of Christ are physically present in the bread and wine.[98] The issue was not settled and Lutherans and Zwingli agreed to disagree.[99] For Zwingli, the disputation outcome ultimately thwarted his efforts to establish his reform in Germany and Austria, as they were firmly entrenched in the Lutheran reform camp. As for the Anabaptists, they were solidly ensconced in Zwingli's memorial theology.[100]

ZWINGLI'S DEATH

Zwingli's highly successful campaign to convince the Zurich city fathers to accept his religious reform of the Catholic Church ultimately resulted in his demise. His success emboldened him to attempt evangelizing other Swiss cities and cantons, as well as South German and Austrian territories, which he did with some success.

Zwingli proceeded to solicit the authority of various canton magistracies to coerce compliance and acceptance of his reforms in those cantons that refused to leave the Catholic faith. The result was a willingness of those who refused to go to war to protect the Catholic Church. A war was eventually precipitated by a Swiss Reformed Protestant economic blockade which only served to exacerbate the situation, as even some of those who followed Zwingli could not justify such dire coercion. The Catholic cantons armed for war and proceeded to battle against their adversaries. During the battle of Kappel in 1531, the Catholic forces were victorious; Zwingli was killed acting as a military chaplain for the Protestants.[101]

Heinrich Bullinger replaced Zwingli in Zurich as the recriminations over the defeat began. Some suggested that the battle was lost for trying to coerce a heresy on the Catholic Church. Others claimed that the loss was due to the lack of fighting on the part of Reformed Protestants for the true religion of the reform. In effect, Zwingli's confrontation with the political reality of how coercion of the new theology would impact its adoption by recalcitrant cantons had not been carefully considered.[102]

98. Luther, "Marburg Colloquy," 88–89.
99. Luther, "Confessions Concerning Christ's Supper, 1528," 367.
100. Snyder, *Anabaptist History and Theology*, 85–86.
101. Gordon, *Swiss Reformation*, 132–34.
102. Gordon, *Swiss Reformation*, 142.

Bruce Gordon surmised that, "The Reformation barely survived, but the bill had to be paid, and the price was full subordination to the state."[103]

CONCLUSION

Anabaptist radicalism can be attributed in part to its early exposure to Erasmian humanism and Lutheranism, particularly the *Schwärmer*. However, it was Zwingli's initial theology of *sola scriputura, sola fide*, the priesthood of the believer, the power of the Spirit over the word, anti-pedobaptism, the efficacy of Pauline pneumatology, and the restitution of the New Testament primitive church that set in motion those same ideas, but from radical, literal biblicist perspectives. The Swiss radicals first emphasized the critical importance of abandoning infant baptism and being for adult re-baptism in order to restore the primitive church, thus the term "Anabaptist" was assigned to them and their movement. As Zwingli saw the necessity of incorporating the Zurich magistracy into his reform, if it was to be successful, the Anabaptists realized that the Catholic rituals, particularly infant baptism and the Mass, were not going to be discontinued. They saw the need, not to reform the church, but to form a new church which insisted on the restitution on the primitive New Testament church. Their biblicist approach to Scripture, under the authority of the Petrine priesthood of the believer doctrine, gave rise to a literal prophetic-spiritual understanding of Paul's pneumatology according to 1 Corinthians 12–14. This in turn saw the advent of many Pentecostal-like manifestations of the gifts of the Holy Spirit and an exigent sense of evangelization. Another critical element that was gathered from their Zwinglian experience was the necessity of the separation of the church from the state, an idea that has been generally embraced today by Christianity at large. Chapter three will discuss the development of Anabaptism's appropriation of Zwingli's and Luther's early theological and spiritual tenets, but with a literal, spiritual-prophetic, biblicist hermeneutic that attempted to restore primitive Christianity.

103. Gordon, *Swiss Reformation*, .

CHAPTER 3

Restitutio in Integrum: Restoring the Fallen Church

> "Ah Constantine! To how much ill gave birth, not to your conversion but that dower which the first rich Father took from thee"[1]

THE EFFECT OF ADOPTING the initial Reformation theologies of Erasmus, Luther, and Zwingli by the radical elements of the Swiss Reformation cannot be overestimated. What follows is a discussion regarding the impact of the adoption of the ongoing Protestant reform efforts and the ensuing realization by radical adherents that the restitution of the church was not being seriously considered. It was particularly disconcerting that pedobaptism, as well as the incorporation of the magistracy in the propagation of the gospel, was being maintained by both Luther and Zwingli. The present chapter will examine Anabaptists' efforts to restore the primitive church and argue that, very similar to early Pentecostalism's "full gospel," the full restitution of the New Testament church, *restitutio in integrum,* would at least require active and effective evangelism, the reappropriation of the gifts of the Holy Spirit according to 1 Corinthians 12–14, the institution of adult rebaptism replacing infant baptism, the separation of church and state, and the principle of pacifism. It will call attention to the idea that the Roman Catholic Church was directly related to the belief, by many reformers, that the church held its political power and ecclesiastical ascendency because of a fraudulent proclamation attributed to Emperor Constantine in the

1. Alighieri, *Inferno*, Canto xix st. 115.

fourth century, referred to as the *Donation of Constantine*. Once the proclamation was proven to be fraudulent, reformers were convinced that the church needed restitution to the biblical principles of the New Testament primitive church, as reformation was no longer possible.[2] By maintaining and developing the initial theology of the priesthood of the believer of Luther and Zwingli, radical reformers dismissed the idea of reforming Roman Catholicism and opted for the restitution of the primitive New Testament church. An examination of the radical Anabaptist evangelization within Switzerland, South Germany, Austria, and the Netherlands from 1524 to 1527 will be undertaken, thus marking the transition of the radical Swiss Brethren Zwinglians to missional Anabaptists. This will validate a Pentecostal-like missiology that confirms several scholarly observations mentioned above that Anabaptism was similar to Pentecostalism in that regard. The means used for their respective separation and denomination from Luther and Zwingli, as well as from each other in some cases, will be discussed. A brief examination of the religious, social, economic, and cultural demographics of the Peasants War of 1524 to 1526, juxtaposed with the reformation efforts in both Germany and Switzerland, will provide the first evidence that the theology of the Reformation was beginning to have a significant impact not only on the religious life of the people, but their social, cultural, and economic lives as well.

The spiritual condition of the sixteenth-century church did not go unnoticed or ignored by those who, in addition to the major protagonists of the Reformation, recognized the disparity between the existing institution and the prescribed scriptural mandates for its spiritual character, nature, and mission, especially within the Pauline concept of the body of Christ as the *ecclesia*.[3] The long but intermittent suspicion that the church was developing into something other than that depicted in Scripture had been recognized as early as the Montanist movement of 157–

2. John Wycliffe (1328–1384) would accuse Constantine in his anti-papal rhetoric of poisoning the church when he gave Pope Sylvester I sweeping powers over all of Christendom for healing him in sickness. He saw the *Donation of Constantine* as the secularization of the church. Although he believed the fourth-century document rediscovered in the eighth century was legitimate, it was proven to be a forgery by humanists Nicholas Cusa in 1432–33, Lorenzo Valla in 1440, and Reginald Peacock in 1450, thus destroying any sense of validity concerning the preeminence of the Roman Bishop. Dante had referred to the Donation in his *Inferno*. See also, Kerry, *Wyclif*, 77; MacCulloch, *Reformation*, 78–82; Alighieri, *Inferno*, Canto xix st. 115.

3. I Cor 12:27.

172. But the conversion and involvement of Emperor Constantine in 315, particularly with regard to his "Donation" to Pope Sylvester, seemed profoundly prophetic to many in regard to the perceived fall of the church into an apostate condition. This idea would loom large in regard to its future reformation, particularly among radical reform movements.[4]

ANABAPTIST SEPARATION AND DIASPORA

In 1525, the radical Anabaptist elements of Zwingli's reform effort, led by Conrad Grebel, Simon Stumpf, and George Blaurock, finally concluded that Zwingli was not willing to proceed with reforming the church as intended. This left them with no acceptable alternative but to proceed with forming a new church on the model of New Testament primitive Christianity. By 1527, Anabaptists had decided that the new church would be identified as the gathered congregation of believers who had entered it by baptism upon confession of faith. Only those who were obedient to Christ could be members and love was the chief mark of this new church. Such love demanded a community of material self-denial and mutual aid. It was to be a gospel light to those living in the darkness of the world.[5]

Acting as believer priests, various Anabaptist confessions of faith were written attempting to unify the movement after the emergence of a myriad of groups holding a multiplicity of beliefs and practices; however, they achieved limited and varying degrees of success. In spite of a seeming consensus regarding the restitution of the New Testament church, there would be great internal controversy as to what that church should look like. These confessions, their sources, and their impact on Anabaptism will be examined within the context of the developing spirituality and theology of, as well as their similarities to, early Pentecostalism.

During the tumultuous year of 1524, amidst the official disputations called by existing magistracies and churches to consider the radical ideas concerning anti-pedobaptism, the Mass, and images, Grebel and his associates wrote a letter to Thomas Müntzer in hopes of gaining his support. The letter, dated September 5, presented twenty-five theological propositions held by the Swiss Brethren, the Anabaptists. Each was presented as either a question for affirmation or a challenge to Müntzer's purported positions either from his writings or hearsay. In effect, they

---

4. Robeck, "Montanism and Present Day Prophets," 418–19.
5. Klaassen, *Anabaptism in Outline*, 101.

basically outlined current Anabaptist theology and praxes. There were three specific areas of concern on their part, believer's baptism, the separation of church and state, and pacifism. The letter confirmed the relationship between Müntzer and Karstadt, the rejection of pedobaptism by both, and Anabaptist respect for both men. It also confirmed Anabaptist correspondence, or attempts thereto, with Karlstadt.[6] Unfortunately, there is no evidence extant that Müntzer received the letter or that there was a response to it.[7] It did, however, confirm Swiss Brethren attempts to contact Luther's *Schwärmer* and the degree of influence they had on the Swiss Brethren. The letter was signed by the Anabaptist leadership of Zurich: Conrad Grebel, Andrew Castelberg, Felix Mantz, John Ockenfuss, Bartolomew Pur, and Henry Alberli. A postscript to the letter was signed by the same, plus Johannes Pannicellus, Hans Brötli, and John Hujuff from Halle.[8] The Zurich City Council's decision to order the radical Anabaptists, particularly Grebel and Mantz, to cease and desist from their anti-pedobaptist teaching and begin baptizing their children as a civic duty, was no deterrent. Not only did both continue their teaching clandestinely, but they immediately began to evangelize the surrounding areas as missionaries, understanding evangelism to be critical to the restitution of the New Testament church.

Zwingli's relationship with Erasmus has already been discussed as well as the initial closeness of Zwingli and Grebel in Zurich. But it should be noted that Grebel had matriculated at the University of Basel under the tutelage of the humanist Heinrich Loriti, called Glarean (1488–1563), a friend and colleague of Erasmus. The certainty of Erasmus's influence on the leader of the Swiss Brethren remains doubtful, but he was certainly exposed to Erasmian Christian humanism.[9]

The significant influence that Erasmus had on both Luther and Zwingli was derived from their concurrence with his recognition of the disparity between how the Bible described Christianity and the praxes of the church.[10] His application of humanistic methods to translate early Greek biblical manuscripts and the Latin Vulgate of Jerome into two new texts, Greek and Latin, reinforced the validity of the Augustinian idea of

6. Grebel, "Letters to Thomas Muntzer 1524," 71–85.
7. Williams, *Radical Reformation*, 192.
8. Grebel, "Letters to Thomas Muntzer 1524," 84–85 and footnote 47.
9. Bender, "Conrad Grebel, the Founder," 9–16.
10. Spinka, *Advocates of Reform*, 282.

sola scriptura as the sole arbiter of the faith. Erasmus's work also presented theological problems regarding many accepted Catholic tenets, such as Purgatory and Mary. At the same time, his Paulinism inspired all three of our protagonists to attempt reforming the church on the foundations of *sola scriptura*. Erasmus would write:

> Just as Paul wrote that the law of Moses was not full of glory compared with the glory of the Gospel succeeding it, so may all Christians hold the Gospels and the Letters of the Apostles as so holy that in comparison with them these other writings do not seem holy.[11]

His Pauline perspective comes through clearly in the "Paraclesis" as he used the inclusive language, "Let all those. . . pledged in baptism," and is also indicative of his perspective concerning the priesthood of Scripture:

> Why spend nearly all of life on the ordinances of men and on opinions in contradiction with themselves? The latter, in fact, may now be the views of the more eminent theologians, if you please; but certainly the first steps of the great theologian in the days to come will be in these authors [of Holy Scripture].
>
> Indeed, I disagree very much with those who are unwilling that Holy Scripture, translated into the vulgar tongue, be read by the uneducated, as if Christ taught such intricate doctrines that they could scarcely be understood by very few theologians, or as if the strength of the Christian religion consisted in men's ignorance of it.
>
> Would that, as a result the farmer sings some portion of them at the plow, the weaver hum some parts of them to the movement of the shuttle, the traveller lighten the weariness of the journey with stories of this kind. And if anyone under the inspiration of the spirit of Christ preaches this kind of doctrine, inculcates it, exhorts, incites, and encourages men to it, he indeed is truly a theologian, even if he should be a common labourer or weaver.[12]
>
> Let all those of us who have pledged in baptism in the words prescribed by Christ, if we have pledged sincerely, be directly

---

11. Erasmus, "Paraclesis," 103.
12. Olin, *Erasmus*, 96–98.

imbued with the teachings of Christ in the midst of the very embraces of parents and the caresses of nurses.[13]

Both Luther and Zwingli saw in Erasmus one who was at least a co-belligerent, if not a supporter of great reform within the church. However, it was not to be, as Erasmus was more a man of peace who opted against Luther's confrontational style. Zwingli, on the other hand, chose to abandon sophistry and philosophy in favour of *sola scriptura* as interpreted by the Holy Spirit himself, thus marginalizing any proclivity on his part toward Erasmianism.

Luther's insistence on *sola scriptura* as the final arbiter of the faith also pushed the boundaries of heterodoxy in the minds of the defenders of Catholicism. In his suspicion regarding the impotence of his personal faith, careful examination of Scripture led him to the conclusion that a Christian was saved by faith alone, *sola fide*, a Pauline concept realized from Romans 5:1. He also developed an interest in the inner spirituality of Rhenish mysticism, particularly that in Tauler's sermons and the *Theologia Germanica*. He incorporated many aspects of these *devotio moderna* writings into his early teachings. He emphasized the inner spirituality of these works and believed in the priesthood of the believer as empowered by the Spirit also expounded in the Epistles of Paul.

In order to gain the political support he thought he needed from the magistracy for a successful reformation, he opted to move gradually away from mystical spirituality and acquiesce to the preservation of many Catholic rituals and traditions, including the Mass and infant baptism. His radical adherents, who had embraced his initial attempts at reform, based on a more biblically based spirituality, saw this as an unacceptable compromise of conviction. Luther's *Schwärmer*—Karstadt, Müntzer, and Schwenckfeld, all strong Lutheran leaders within their respective areas of ministry—took issue with him on several matters, particularly his insistence on maintaining those Catholic traditions. The *Schwärmer* would become radical catalysts in their own right as they continued to develop Luther's original theological positions.[14] Much like Luther, Zwingli was challenged, not only by the church, but by radical reformers from among his own followers, particularly those opposed to pedobaptism. Zwingli's relationship with Karlstadt was brief and related primarily to his agreement with him that the Eucharist was a commemorative rite without sal-

---

13. Erasmus, "Paraclesis," 104–5.
14. See chapter two.

vific efficacy in the disputations with the Lutherans from 1524 to 1529.[15] There was no direct relationship between himself and Müntzer. However, both became important to him inasmuch as they had influenced the anti-pedobaptist contingent, particularly Conrad Grebel and his circle of adherents.[16]

The Zurich Council's actions approving Zwingli's reform and mandating infant baptism did not deter the movement which proceeded to begin an evangelistic effort that would reach numerous surrounding communities and towns, becoming known as the Swiss Brethren, the initial Anabaptists, *der Wiedertaufer*.[17] Under the leadership of the core of the Zurich followers of Grebel, Anabaptism quickly spread into the Rhine Valley, west to Basel and Bern, east to St. Gallen and Appenzell, and north to Schaffenhausen, Hallau, and Waldshut. It was at Waldshut that the movement came into direct contact with the evolvin, Peasants' War. Alister McGrath names him as one of the three most important theologians of the Radical Reformation[18]

ANABAPTIST PACIFISM

Hubmaier's Theology of Resistance

The intersection of Anabaptism and the Peasants' War was important on many levels. Balthasar Hubmaier (1480/85–1528), the Catholic pastor at Waldshut, involved himself in propagating many Anabaptist beliefs within the context of the revolt. He would be the only trained and educated theologian who would join the emerging radical leaders, the Swiss Brethren, out of Zwingli's Reformation. He was not one of the initial radical Zurichers, who preached more than they wrote; Hubmaier became the most prolific writer of the developing Anabaptist theology and author of its first confession of faith.[19] An important consequence of the Peasants' War was the development of the idea of pacifism as a core Anabaptist

---

15. Luther, "Marburg Colloquy and the Marburg Articles, 1529."

16. Goertz, *Anabaptists*, 70.

17. "Anabaptist" means rebaptized or baptized again. Zwingli would call them catabaptizers, those against baptism (Zwingli, "Refutation of the Tricks," 123).

18. Snyder, *Anabaptist History and Theology*, 55; Stayer, "Swiss Anabaptism," 65–69.

19. Pipkin, *Balthasar Hubmaier*, 15.

belief.[20] Having studied with Urbanus Rhegius (1489–1541) and Wolfgang Capito (1478–1541), Lutheran reformers from Augsburg and Strasbourg respectively, Hubmaier would develop an affinity for Erasmian Humanism and Zwinglianism after arriving in Waldshut. He would be counted as a friend and ally of Zwingli and Oecolampadius (1482–1531), a Zwingli sympathizer in nearby Basel.[21] By 1523, he had solidified his relationship with Zwingli and one of his allies, the humanist Vadian of St. Gallen, supporting him in the October dispute over the Mass and images in the church.[22] Within the same timeframe, he had apparently agreed with Zwingli, while visiting Zurich, that children should not be baptized before coming of age.[23] He effectively managed Waldshut's defection to the Lutheran Reformation, to the point where Austrian Habsburg officials appeared in the spring of 1524 and demanded the city council arrest him, but they refused, having been convinced of the efficacy of Hubmaier's reform teachings. He published his first article in May 1524, *Achtzehn Slussreden*,[24] in which he set out eighteen theses upon which the Christian life is based. The following is a paraphrase of his article which was generally accepted as Anabaptist tenets of faith[25]:

1. "Faith alone makes us righteous before God."
2. This faith is the knowledge of God's mercy, which he has shown by offering his only begotten Son.

---

20. The situation was very much like early Pentecostalism's initial dilemma juxtaposing biblical tenets of peace against war when the United States entered World War I in 1918, twelve short years after the Azusa Street revival began and only four years after the organization of the Pentecostal Assemblies of God in 1914.

First, a more detailed review of the evolution of Hubmaier's theology as a radical Anabaptist will be followed by an assessment of the demographics of his time and their relative similarity to that of early Pentecostal theology.

21. Pipkin, *Balthasar Hubmaier*.

22. Williams, *Radical Reformation*, 222. Hubmaier would introduce Zwinglian evangelicalism to St. Gallen by preaching open-air sermons there in 1523.

23. Armour, *Anabaptist and Baptism*, 19–20; "Zwing. Der Jrrtumb hat auch mich vor etwas Jaren verfurt, das ich maint,es wer vil weger, man taufft die Kindlen erst so sy zu gutem alter kummen weren" (Bergsten and Westin, *Balthasar Hubmaier*, 186); "Many years ago this error misled me too so that I thought it would be better if one baptized children only when they had come to good age" (Pipkin, *Balthasar Hubmaier*, 194).

24. Eighteen Theses, my translation.

25. The paraphrase is mine.

3. Faith cannot be idle, but must be shown in works of brotherly love toward others. This negates "candles, palm branches, and holy water."
4. Works are good which God has commanded, and evil when he has forbidden them. Thus denying "fish, cowl, and tonsure."
5. "The mass is not a sacrifice but memorial of the death of Christ." It cannot be offered for the dead or the living as such.
6. As often as this memorial is held, the death of Christ will be proclaimed. The mass is dead.
7. "Images are good for nothing."
8. Every Christian believes and is baptized for himself so the pastors shall be judged by Scripture as to whether they are feeding and watering the congregation (the priesthood of the believer).
9. "Christ alone died for our sin…only he [can] be appealed to as our sole intercessor and mediator. Here all pilgrimages fall away."
10. It is better to translate psalms into the vernacular, than to sing them in a foreign language.
11. "All teachings, which God himself did not plant, are in vain." The teachings of Aristotle and the scholastics such as Thomas, Scotus, Bonaventure, and Occam, and all others that are not scriptural are invalid.
12. "No one will be counted a priest except he preach the word of God. Here fall away early masses, votive, requiem, and middle masses."
13. The members of the church cooperative "are obligated to maintain with appropriate food and clothing and to protect those who exposit to them the pure, clear, and unmixed word of God. This destroys courtesans, pensioners, members of collegia, absentees, and babblers of lies and dreams."
14. Purgatory does not exist.
15. "To forbid marriage to priests and then tolerate their carnal immorality is … to kill Christ."
16. "To promise chastity in human strength is nothing other than to promise to fly over the sea without wings."

17. "He who denies or silences the word of God for temporal gain . . . Christ will also deny him."

18. He who doesn't earn his bread by the sweat of his brow is banned.[26]

Hubmaier's theses are very similar to Zwingli's *Sixty-Seven Articles* presented at the first Zurich disputation in January 1523, which were not particularly Anabaptist at the time. But they did maintain some Lutheran concepts, such as salvation by faith alone, priestly marriage, and article number seventeen, the consequence of denying Scripture as God's word. He did participate in the second Zurich disputation in October 1523, in support of Zwingli's position that the Mass and images were not supported by Scripture. He was now completely dedicated to the idea of reforming the church, but at the time the most radical elements of Zwingli's inner circle had yet to separate themselves as Anabaptists.[27]

The Habsburg pressure placed on Hubmaier in 1524 for his adoption of Lutheran church reforms, such as removing images and relics, and celebrating the mass in German in 1523, caused him to flee to neighboring Schaffhausen as the authorities continued to pressure the Waldshut City Council to arrest him.[28] He returned in October, but the authorities increased their pressure to coerce the Waldshut council to comply. In response, peasant volunteer soldiers from Zurich reinforced the defenses of Waldshut. The Peasants' War became a military reality for Hubmaier for the next two years. Many of the peasant volunteers who responded to Waldshut were the emerging radical elements of Zwingli's reform movement in Zurich.[29] The Peasants' War would be important to Hubmaier for several reasons, including his imminent adoption of Anabaptism, realization of the social and economic plight of the rural commoner in the midst of a religious reformation, as well as the dilemma of whether or not Christians should take up arms against oppression or be pacifists.

---

26. Hubmaier, "Eighteen Theses," 30–34. My paraphrase.

27. Pipkin, *Balthasar Hubmaier*, 21–22.

28. Hubmaier established a relationship with Sebastian Hofmeister, the Zwinglian reformer for Schaffhausen at the time and participant with him and Zwingli at the Zurich Disputation in October 1523 (Pipkin, *Balthasar Hubmaier: Theologian of Anabaptism*, 35).

29. Snyder, *Anabaptist History and Theology*, 56.

THE PEASANTS' WAR, SOCIETY, AND RELIGION

It was a time when social issues directly reflected the religious concerns of the ongoing Reformation. Examination of how the Peasants' War influenced Hubmaier's resistance theology will reveal the challenge early Anabaptism faced concerning what they would consider to be a correct biblical response to war and peace. The war did not occur in a vacuum, but in the midst of a turbulent evolution of social, economic, and cultural conditions that had been in progress since the dissipation of the plague at the end of the fourteenth century, which killed approximately one-third of the Western European population. The Malthusian effect of this catastrophe left vast amounts of land under agrarian development abandoned due to the diminution of the work force. The tremendous population migration that resulted from this economic contraction caused an increase in wages, but depressed food prices, which favored the town and urban manufacturing of consumer goods over rural agricultural pursuits.[30] The advent of Anabaptism coincided with the emergence of these very traumatic events, and in some minds was a contributor in a religious sense.

A peasant in the feudal socioeconomic system of sixteenth-century Germany was forced to grapple with an emerging urban middle class of artisans, craftsmen, and entrenched, landed nobility. Additionally, the anti-clerical church reformation efforts that had begun in earnest in 1517 contributed to a bloody rebellion by German commoners against the entire system, as it had been corrupted at all levels of their lives, including socially, culturally, and religiously. They rebeled against the diminution of their means of subsistence, increased rents, services, dues, fees, taxes, and tithes which originated from feudal lords, rulers, or the church, all of which impacted their survival. Serfdom, as idealized by the peasants, was the feudal contract which exacted services and dues from them in exchange for the lord's protection. They felt this had been violated by the land owners, as no protection was provided and perhaps little needed. The tithe, which was collected by the church in addition to that which was demanded by the lords, was a biblically based tax for the maintenance and care of local church property and sustenance for its clergy. However, the tithe was being sent out of the local parish to support the hierarchy of the Roman Catholic Church that was rarely present ,and was in fact the source of much church corruption. This contributed to a decided anticlericalism that forced socioeconomic grievances into juxtaposition

---

30. Rowan, "Urban Communities," 197.

with religious complaints, which caused the rebellion to look like the two were inextricably bound together.[31] The war also tended to focus on those regions where the Roman Catholic Church was a significant land holder.[32] Peter Blickle correctly describes the initial causes of the war as economic. But he also contends that social tensions between the poor and the rich grew as the increasing economic pressures on the peasant population increased. The significant growth of political expectations on the part of the poor must also be taken into account. For as the economy deteriorated, peasants, whose population was increasing, became more attracted to urban life. This in turn caused the lords to restore serfdom to prevent an urban migration. Political expectations also increased among the peasantry as the towns' administrative competences expanded to include areas with the parliaments and other corporate bodies that represented them.[33] Religiously, the Peasants' War was at least partly precipitated by the peasantry's understanding of what Luther and Zwingli both demanded of the Catholic clergy, to preach the pure gospel plus nothing. Moreover, Blickle further opines that that was understood as the "godly law" which controlled how one lived in society. Godly law applied to the daily lives of all, both spiritually and naturally.

THE SWABIAN LEAGUE AND THE "TWELVE ARTICLES"

According to Thomas Brady, the Swabian League was formed in 1488 as a deterrent against Bavarian expansion by the smaller powers of the Habsburg's realm in Upper Swabia. An army was formed to enforce the laws of the league and guarantee its security. The league successfully accomplished its mission. By 1525, it had become a significant military force in the region. But the Peasants' War, at that time, was in full bloom. The 10,000 Swiss mercenaries deserted the league force and met with other peasant rebel fighters in Memmingen, a free city of Swabia. But the league forces engaged and defeated several of the rebel factions and punished them, including noble supporters.[34] Peter Blickle points out that apparently during the peasant rebel meeting at Memmingen, a list

---

31. Scribner, "Peasants' War."
32. Stayer, *German Peasants' War*, 35; Goertz, *Anabaptists*, 10–13.
33. Blickle, "Popular Reformation," 175–76.
34. Brady, "Swabian League."

of grievances was drafted against landed nobility and first published in Ulm. The grievances were the same as those that had been presented to the Memmingen city council days earlier. Blickle believes that a local pastor, Christoph Schappeler, wrote them in collaboration with peasant supporter Sebastian Lotzer.[35] George Williams supports the Schappeler/Lotzer theory, but also cites the debate involving Martin Brecht, Georg Seebass, and Blickle, which is unresolved.[36]

The peasants had organized themselves enough to draft the "Twelve Articles" in March 1525, which attempted to codify their grievances for presentation to the nobility as a new legal basis for the peasant-lord relationship. This was the first application of some Reformation theological principles to a sociopolitical issue. The "Twelve Articles" (paraphrased);

1. The community must have the right to elect and dismiss clergy, because only in this way can the proclamation of the word of God necessary for salvation be assured.
2. The small tithe (fruits, vegetables, etc.) is to be abolished; the large tithe (grains) is to be administered by the community for the maintenance of the clergy, for the poor, and for taxes for defense.
3. Serfdom is to be abolished even though the lord's authority is expressly not to be eliminated.
4. Free hunting and fishing are demanded.
5. Forests and woodlands will be returned . . . to the communities and administered by communal forest officials so that the peasants are properly supplied with wood for burning and construction.
6. Services to the lords reduced to a tolerable level.
7. The determination of the bills of enfeoffment with regard to labor must be strictly adhered to so that the peasants . . . earn a reasonable return.
8. Farms must be reevaluated by honorable people according to their productivity.
9. The penalties for crimes must not be increased and arbitrarily passed, but set according to traditional written statutes.

---

35. Blickle, "Twelve Articles."
36. Williams, *Radical Reformation*, 153–55.

10. Communal fields and arable lands will be claimed by the communities in accordance with the provision for tithes, fisheries, and forests.

11. The death tax on inheritance must be abolished since it is an unjust burden on the heirs.

12. We (peasants) are ready to submit all the articles to a test of compatibility with Scripture.[37]

There is some conjecture and debate as to who drafted the articles. James Stayer claims that Hubmaier is universally accepted as the author, based on the record of his trial in Vienna wherein he confessed to writing them.[38] This conclusion, however, places an Anabaptist in the position of being clearly involved in and promoting the Peasants' War. Stayer cites the work of Gottfried Seebass, who has presented convincing evidence that Hubmaier was not the sole author of the "Twelve Articles." It appears that there may have been many regional editors of the document. Thus any significant connection between the Anabaptists and the war has been greatly diminished by the preclusion of Hubmaier.[39] This is supported by Hubmaier's confession, in that he only admitted to expanding the articles, expositing them, and declaring them reasonable.[40]

The Peasants' War began in May 1524 as an act of civil disobedience when subjects (peasants) of the abbey of St. Blasien in the Black Forest and Franconian Forchheim refused to render feudal dues and services to their overlord. In June, the peasants of Lupfen and Stühlingen also rebelled, followed by rebellions in Klettgau and Hegau. Locations all along the Swiss-German border north of the Rhine between Schaffhausen and Waldshut became involved. The area also contains the Black Forest (*Schwartzwald*) of Southwestern Germany east of Freiberg, the site of St. Peter's monastery, Michael Sattler's residence. Leaders such as Hans Müller from Bulgenbach were able to quickly organize the peasantry into regional bands *(Bundschuh)* and local assemblies, and negotiate with the lords about joint grievances. They also sought to establish alliances with large towns like Waldshut and Zurich. The rebellion extended from Upper Swabia, the Rhine, Franconia, Württemberg, Alsace, Thuringia, Saxony, and the Tyrol. James Stayer divides the conflict into two time

---

37. Blickle, "Twelve Articles," 195–201.
38. Stayer, *German Peasants' War*, 66. See also, Pipkin, *Balthasar Hubmaier*, 564.
39. Stayer, *German Peasants' War*, 68.
40. Pipkin, *Balthasar Hubmaier*, 564.

periods, May–March 1524 and April 1524—June 1525. The first period was primarily an armed mass movement aimed at the landed nobility, the clergy and their cathedral chapters, and monasteries, but also establishing binding negotiations for redress. Only after April was the term "war" actually appropriate, for it was then that the princes and their mercenary armies, led by the Swabian League,[41] began to disperse or destroy the large bands of peasants. Most battles were one-sided slaughters of the commoners. At their height, the rebels numbered 300,000, but 100,000 would eventually lose their lives. The war was not an Anabaptist event, for it would not ultimately separate itself from Zwingli until January of 1525 with the first adult baptisms at Zollikon as mentioned earlier.[42] But it was in part a religious rebellion spawned by the ongoing reformations.[43] Luther attempted to achieve peace in April 1525 by recognizing some validity in the "Twelve Articles" and pleading with all parties to cease and desist.[44] But his castigation of the peasants in a pamphlet entitled *Against the Robbing and Murdering Hordes of Peasants*, published in May 1525, wherein he called for the lords to end the peasants' resistance, "Stab, smite, slay, whoever can. If you die in doing it, well for you! A more blessed death can never be yours," seriously alienated the peasantry, particularly those who were already looking to abandon Luther and Zwingli for Anabaptism.[45]

The role of Thomas Müntzer has already been discussed above, as well as his influence on Swiss Brethren. The peasants' failure to consolidate battle victories in Franconia and Thuringia, particularly their failure to seize the garrison at Würtzburg or capitalize on the victory at Freiberg in Breisgau on May 24, 1525 resulted in the ultimate failure of the rebellion.[46] By 1526, the war was over and the rebellion crushed, but this tended to further solidify Anabaptism, particularly concerning whether or not it was to be a separatist-and-pacifist movement.

The dilemma that the war presented regarding whether a Christian could or should take up arms in defense of the gospel, or for that matter any reason, was answered in the positive by Hubmaier. At Waldshut,

41. Brady, "Swabian League."

42. Gordon, *Swiss Reformation*, 66. There were some isolated events that occurred in northern Switzerland, but nothing as significant as in southern Germany.

43. Stayer, "Peasants' War 1524–1525," 4.

44. Luther, "Friendly Admonition to Peace," 67.

45. Luther, "Against the Robbing and Murdering," 121–26.

46. Scribner, "Peasants' War."

he took the position of both Luther and Zwingli, stating, that it was a Christian duty to support the local government with armed resistance as the protecting entity provided by God for the church, the body of Christ (Romans 13), and that necessarily entailed the use of the sword.[47]

However, Anabaptists were not all of one mind on this matter. In the letter that Grebel and his Swiss Brethren had written to Müntzer in September 1524, when the war had just begun, they informed him:

> The gospel and its adherents are not to be protected by the sword, nor themselves, which as we have heard . . . is what you believe and maintain. True believing Christians . . . must be baptized in anguish and tribulation, suffering, and death, tried in fire, and must reach the fatherland of eternal rest not by slaying the physical, but the spiritual. They use neither worldly sword nor war.[48]

As pointed out above, when Zwingli first responded to the call to the priesthood he was greatly influenced by Erasmus and denied being influenced by Luther. Eventually he would also move away from his relationship with Erasmus, claiming his reform was based solely on the word of God as revealed by the Holy Spirit.[49] This very well may be counted as another significant antecedent to Anabaptism. It can also be argued that the development of the myriad of disparate radical and Anabaptist groups and individuals that emerged after the Zurich City Council's decision to outlaw the most important Anabaptist theological positions, was a result of the initial theological concept of the priesthood of the believer, what Brad Gregory appropriately contends fomented an unintended reformation.[50]

The Anabaptist evangelization effort soon began making inroads in an increasingly larger geographic area as they began baptizing converts and establishing congregations throughout Switzerland, Germany, Alsace, Eastern Europe, and the Netherlands. The aggressive evangelistic nature of Anabaptism was believed to be a biblical command from Acts

---

47. Zwingli, "Sermon on Divine and Human Justice," 218; Luther, "Against the Robbing and Murdering."
48. Grebel, "Grebel Letter to Muntzer," 290.
49. Hillerbrand, *Reformation*, 125–26.
50. Gregory, *Unintended Reformation*, 24.

1:8. Pilgram Marpeck would become an influential proponent of this belief.[51]

Johannes Kessler (1502–1574), a school *meister* in St. Gallen, located forty miles east of Zurich, chronicled his impression of Anabaptist evangelistic fervor in his city when he wrote in *Sabata* July of 1525:

> Our Anabaptists assumed the apostolic office as the first in the newly established church, believing that it was their obligation to follow Christ's command when he said, "Go ye into the world, etc." [Mark 16:15]. They ran beyond the city gate into outlying villages, regions, and market towns to preach.[52]

HUBMAIER AND THE ANABAPTIST DIASPORA

Anabaptists began to evangelize surrounding towns and villages. For instance, Grebel and Reublin both traveled to Schaffhausen and engaged Sebastian Hofmeister (1476–1532), an Anabaptist sympathizer and Zwinglian associate of Hubmaier. From Schaffhausen, Reublin traveled on to Waldshut.[53] Hubmaier, encouraged by Johannes Oecolampadius's seeming acceptance of Anabaptism and Hofmeister's tacit acceptance as well, published a call for a public disputation on February 2, 1525[54]:

> Whoever wishes to do so, let him prove that infants should be baptized, and do it with German, plain, clear, and unambiguous Scriptures that deal only with baptisms, without any addition. Balthasar Fridberger [Hubmaier] offers in his turn to prove that the baptism of infants is a work without any basis in the divine Word.[55]

Reublin had just arrived in Waldshut and had begun baptizing the consenting adults. He and Hubmaier agreed to conduct a larger baptism on Easter Sunday, at which time Hubmaier and sixty others were baptized

---

51. Klaassen and Klassen, *Writings of Pilgram Marpeck*, 458. Rempel, *Jorg Maler's Kunstbuch*, 606.

52. Kessler, "Sabata," 607; Harder, *Sources of Swiss Anabaptism*, 423; Littell, *Origins of Sectarian Protestantism*, 111–15.

53. Harder, *Sources of Swiss Anabaptism*, 350–51. In a letter written by Johann Brötli to the brethren at Zollikon in February 1525, he stated that, "Dr. Sabastian was of one mind with us regarding baptism," but implied he was not quite committed yet.

54. Hubmaier, "Letter to Oecolampadius, January 1525," 68–72.

55. Hubmaier, "Public Challenge," 80.

by Reublin. Hubmaier himself baptized over three hundred in the few days that followed.[56] In spite of his agreement with Anabaptist positions on infant and adult baptism, Hubmaier would maintain his theology of armed resistance, but just as important for the purposes of this thesis was his pneumatology.

PNEUMATOLOGY

Hubmaier's pneumatology was much like that of Zwingli with the exception of glossolalia, which Zwingli interpreted as biblical languages that should be learned by those gifted by the Spirit to do so, whereas Hubmaier seems to have a more Pentecostal-like understanding of speaking in tongues. Concerning prophecy, he invoked 1 Corinthians 14:29–33 in his *An Earnest Appeal to Schaffhausen*, 1524 and his *Theses against Eck*, November 1524.[57] Concerning the baptism in the Holy Spirit he described in *On the Christian Baptism of Believers*, 1525, five different kinds of Christian baptisms: water, water for or unto a change of life, baptism in the Spirit and fire, baptism to be born out of water and Spirit, and baptism in water in the name of the Father, Son, and Holy Spirit, or in the name of our Lord Jesus Christ.[58] Most pertinent to his pneumatology for this study was the baptism in the Spirit and fire. He explains this baptism as that which

> make[s] alive and whole again the confessing sinner with the fire of the divine Word by the Spirit of God. This takes place when the pardon of his sins has already been granted by the life-giving Word of God. The Spirit of God makes and effects this enlivening internally in the human being. Outside of the same all teaching of the Word is a killing letter, Matt. 3:11; Luke 3:16; 2 Cor. 3:6.[59]

To prove his point, he quoted from Acts 19, where Paul baptized the disciples of John the Baptist he found at Ephesus in the name of Jesus Christ. Then he laid hands on them and they spoke with tongues

---

56. Bergsten and Westin, *Balthasar Hubmaier*, 27; Williams, *Radical Reformation*, 231.

57. Pipkin, *Balthasar Hubmaier*, 45, 49.

58. Pipkin, *Balthasar Hubmaier*, 121.

59. Pipkin, *Balthasar Hubmaier*, 100.

(glossolalia) and prophesied.[60] Hubmaier was writing about Christian baptism in the Spirit and fire, emphasizing water baptism and the difference between that of John and that of Jesus; however, he does go on to observe that when the men "spoke in tongues (glossolalia) and prophesied, these are works that are in general given to the new believers and the newly baptized."[61] It appears from these two statements that Hubmaier considered the baptism in the Holy Spirit and fire as a separate event subsequent to water baptism that was generally accompanied by glossolalia and prophecy, an observation similar to early Pentecostalism's initial evidence doctrine.[62]

This is not only an early Pentecostal belief, but one held by the primitive apostolic church according to Cyril (315?–386?), Archbishop of Jerusalem (351?–357?).[63] In his *Brief Apologia*, 1526, Hubmaier objects to the singing and reading in church by the Roman clergy according to the approved liturgy. But he defends that which is done in the "spirit and from the heart and with understanding of the words to the edification of the congregation, as Paul teaches in 1 Corinthians 14:26."[64] This is where Paul describes an early New Testament church meeting where each attendee, "has a psalm, has a teaching, has a tongue, has a revelation, has a interpretation"[65] for the edification of everyone there. In answer to the question, what is the baptism of the Holy Spirit?, Hubmaier responds in his *Christian Catechism* of 1526, "It is an inner illumination of our hearts that takes place by the Holy Spirit through the living Word of God."[66]

This is similar to what William Seymour wrote in November 1906. As pastor of the Pentecostal Azusa Street revival, he wrote of the illumination one receives when baptized with the Holy Spirit. He couched his thoughts within the context of a sermon from John 4 where Jesus confronts and convinces the Samaritan woman at the well that he, (the Living Word of God), was the gift of God that supplies rivers of living

---

60. Pipkin, *Balthasar Hubmaier*, 111, 131. Here the German reads as follows: "Paulus die hand auff sye legt, kam der heylig geyst auff sey, und redten mit zungen."

61. Bergsten and Westin, *Balthasar Hubmaier*, 132; Pipkin, *Balthasar Hubmaier*, 113. Once again the German here is *redten mit zungen*, glossolalia.

62. Gohr, "Historical Development of the Statement," 63.

63. McDonnell, *Christian Initiation and Baptism*, 183–85; Cyril of Jerusalem, "Catechetical Lectures," 115–33.

64. Pipkin, *Balthasar Hubmaier*, 300.

65. 1 Cor 14:26.

66. Pipkin, *Balthasar Hubmaier*, 438.

waters of everlasting life. She immediately went to tell others that Jesus had identified himself as the Messiah and asked them to come a see him. Seymour preached:

> How true it is in this a day when we get baptized with the Holy Spirit, we have something to tell, and it is the blood of Jesus Christ cleanseth from all sin. The baptism with the Holy Ghost gives us power to testify to a risen, resurrected saviour. Our affections are in Jesus Christ, the Lamb of God that takes away the sin of the world.[67]

By Easter of 1525, the Anabaptist diaspora was successfully proceeding. Hubmaier had been baptized in Waldshut and was fully committed to Anabaptism. In 1526, the Peasants' War ended in ignominious defeat for the peasants, but the armed resistance position of Hubmaier concerning Christians and war became untenable for Anabaptists, not only according to their developing biblical pacifism, but in a very practical sense of military and political incapability. Tenacious in his unwillingness to acquiesce to the others, Hubmaier maintained his belief in armed resistance until his death. However, pacifism would become the accepted belief regarding the relationship between Anabaptism and governments. This demanded separation between them and not only secular governments, but the world—nonbelievers—in general. At the same time, the Anabaptist congregations that emerged realized the need for some clarity of confession and praxis.

Hubmaier, the theologian, would have great influence on Anabaptist pneumatology as they proceeded to restore the apostolic church. Much of his hermeneutic appears in the early ecclesiology and spiritual praxes of local Anabaptist congregations. However, his armed resistance doctrine, which had to include a strong Anabaptist magistracy, did not gain many followers after the Peasants' War. He continued to preach a baptism in the Holy Spirit while in Nikolsburg, Moravia, but he was arrested by the Austrians, who had hounded him since Waldshut. His early martyrdom by burning at the stake by the Habsburg regime in Vienna in 1528 precluded a life of prolific writing and ministry.[68] In 1527, after the failure of the peasant rebellion, Michael Sattler would write another Anabaptist

---

67. Sanders, *William Seymour Papers*, 40.
68. Stayer, "Hubmaier, Balthasar."

confession of faith attempting once again to unite the Anabaptist movement which included pacifism as a tenet of faith.[69]

The Peasants' War may not have been primarily a religious war, but Reformation theology had its influence so much so that at the end of the war many disaffected veterans would look to Anabaptism and its more spiritual perspective to continue to seek redress from existing religious, spiritual, and social oppression. Luther's diatribe against them certainly encouraged them to avoid Lutheranism. The obvious inclusion of many of the initial theological positions of Luther and Zwingli in the peasant "Twelve Articles," the priesthood of the believer as scriptural support for the ability of local congregations to choose or remove their own priest, *sola scriptura* as the sole arbiter of the faith, anticlericalism, and the importance of the assurance of salvation and its propagation, are all indicative of the incorporation of scriptural principles from a reform perspective into everyday life in peasant thinking.

ANABAPTIST SPIRITUALITY AND PRAXES 1521–1527

A large number of disparate radical and Anabaptist groups began to appear due to their rapidly expanding evangelistic efforts after the City of Zurich ordered the ostracism and execution of radicals. As the congregations multiplied they also began to alienate themselves from each other, primarily over theological issues that rarely challenged the perceived and traditional Christian orthodoxy in any critical sense. But it was indicative of the struggle to define a restored New Testament church. The groups have been variously and correctly classified by Stuart Murray as Anabaptists of various types who were Christocentric, denied scriptural support for infant baptism, required adult rebaptism upon confession of faith, born again, believed in evangelism/discipleship as empowered by the Holy Spirit, a church free of state control, a community of goods, and the restitution of the New Testament primitive church.[70] Others, including the spiritualists, however, pushed the limits of traditional Christian orthodoxy when they would variously deny the rational efficacy of the physical nature of the Scripture, the Sacraments, and other external ceremonial rites, in favor of internal spiritual or mystical experiences

---

69. For details on Sattler's confession of faith, see below. It should be noted that pacifism was set aside during the Melchiorite Münster debacle. See chapter 6.

70. Murray, "Biblical Interpretation," 403.

exclusively.[71] Evangelical Rationalists of Italian origin embraced *sola scriptura*, but only in the sense that reason was paramount to correct interpretation. Theocentrists would go to the point of antitrinitarianism, and psychopannychism (soul sleep).[72] Anabaptists have been characterized as diverse, but still sharing several central convictions notwithstanding these divergent views that sometimes led to sharp disagreements.[73] It should be noted that it was a minority who were variously antitrinitarian, universalist, who denied such things as the idea of a visible church, the external validity of the Sacraments or Scripture, and perhaps overemphasized apocalyptic chiliasm and the parousia, but they never gained a significant following as did the Anabaptist Swiss Brethren, the Marpeckan South German/Austrians, Moravian Hutterites, or Dutch Mennonites.[74] C. Arnold Snyder brings some clarity to the definition of Anabaptism by describing it as church movement that insisted that the biblical way of forming the body of Christ was through the baptism of adult believers who freely confessed Christ.[75] What is also an important pneumatological aspect of early Anabaptism, and a critical part of the definition, was an inner charismatic spiritual experience.[76] Early Pentecostalism was fraught with the same issue of the multiplication of many varied renditions of the faith based on differences that did not alter the importance of the spiritual experience of being baptized in the Holy Spirit and speaking in tongues. Allan Anderson suggests that defining Pentecostalism should include those groups that have a "family resemblance" common to the variations which allows for the "blurred edges" of difference, but still is inclusive enough to be meaningful. In the case of Pentecostalism. it would be "churches concerned with the experience of the working of the Holy Spirit and the practice of the spiritual gifts."[77] This description is very applicable to the Anabaptist phenomena of the sixteenth century, as they also incorporated the experiential nature of the efficacy of the Holy

---

71. Packull, *Mysticism and the Early South*, 20.

72. Williams, *Radical Reformation*, xxix–xxx, 837–49; Hillerbrand, "Renato, Camillo (1500–1575)"; Szczucki, "Socianism."

73. Williams, *Radical Reformation*, xxx–xxxi; Murray, "Biblical Interpretation," 403–6.

74. Klaassen, *Anabaptism*, 2.

75. Snyder, *Anabaptist History and Theology*, 1.

76. Snyder, *Anabaptist History and Theology*, 368–69.

77. Anderson, "Varieties, Taxonomies, and Definitions," 15–17.

Spirit, the manifestation of the gifts of the Spirit, and adult baptism into their own definition of who they were.

MANIFESTATION OF THE GIFTS OF THE SPIRIT

George Williams describes the Anabaptist situation in St. Gallen as swiftly degenerating into "rank spiritualism of charismatic vagaries," where burning of the New Testament became indicative of a rejection of all but the leading of the Holy Spirit. However, his observations must be considered as prejudiced in some sense, perhaps owing to his lack of knowledge and experience concerning Pentecostal and charismatic manifestations. He admittedly relies heavily on Johannes Kessler for his information concerning instances of glossolalia, people simulating death with Christ, children laying in comas for hours (slain in the Spirit?), and an incident of fratricide allegedly committed as the will of God. Williams finally avers instances of lewdness and unchastity and the declaration by a woman who believed she was to give birth to the Antichrist.[78] Snyder has stated that manifestations of glossolalia (described as ecstatic spiritual utterances), prophecy, and "outlandish behaviour" took on the appearance of a charismatic revival between 1525 and 1526, particularly in St. Gallen and Appenzell.[79] Kenneth Davis has observed that within Anabaptism, "the gifts of the Holy Spirit to each believer," were operative for the edification of all. He further states that an interest in the works of Tertullian, as indicated by Grebel in a letter to his brother-in-law Vadian in January 1522, implied that Tertullian was an approved early-church father who not only advocated against infant baptism, but expressed strong charismatic sentiments.[80]

One of the most supportive contemporary documents for Anabaptist, Pentecostal, or charismatic manifestations of the gifts of the Spirit, particularly speaking in tongues and prophecy, is Kessler's *Sabata*. Although written from a perspective of Zwingli's Reformation, he recorded many aspects of Anabaptist spiritual praxis and theology as well as the tension between it, Lutheranism, and Zwinglianism. An analysis and

---

78. Williams, *Radical Reformation*, 228.

79. Snyder, *Profiles of Anabaptist Women*, 19.

80. Davis, *Anabaptism and Asceticism*, 72–73, 211. See also, Harder, *Sources of Swiss Anabaptism*, 155–56, 60–61.

careful translation of copies of the original manuscript will confirm the charismatic nature of early Anabaptism.

The *Sabata* documented the various activities of the Protestant Reformation as well as the rise of Anabaptism in St. Gallen, Switzerland from 1523 to 1539. The journal provides an eyewitness account of the results of a typical Anabaptist evangelistic effort in a Swiss city. In his chronicle, Kessler reported many Pentecostal-like activities among the Anabaptists, particularly the manifestations of the pneumatic gifts of the Spirit. One such entry included a description of the charismatic ministry of Margret Hottinger (martyred 1530) who had been imprisoned in Zurich in 1525 for Anabaptism, along with several major Anabaptist leaders, not the least of whom were Grebel and Sattler. She had been a member of the congregation meeting in Zollikon and had apparently exercised prophetic gifts there. After six months, she was released upon her recantation at which time she traveled to St. Gallen where she resumed her Anabaptist and charismatic activities.[81]

Writing with more than a modicum of hostility, Kessler described Margret Hottinger as a young woman greatly loved and respected among the Anabaptists for her piety, spiritual insight, and disciplined life, but also associated her with other Anabaptist women of St. Gallen who were proclaiming great theological errors. According to Kessler, she had announced that she was God, but according to a review of the record, it appears that she was simply quoting Christ's words from John 10:33–38 and 15:10. She was also accused of forgiving people of their sins, but again just quoting scripture [Gal 3:13]. She was also known for speaking in tongues, and prophesying.[82]

---

81. Snyder, *Profiles of Anabaptist Women*, 43–53.

82. Kessler, "Sabata," 618–19. *Margarita Hattingere von Zollica: Darnach sind grusame und vermessenliche irthum entstanden durch wibsbilder der widertouften, als von ainer junkfrowen von Zollica in der landschaft* Zürich, Margarita Hattinger. . .*Die kam dahin, das sy sprach, sy were Gott. Und der anderen widertoufer vil globend söllichs und wöltends gegen denen widerfochtend, beschmiren und erhalten, namlich mit dem spruch Christi, so er spricht: Hand ir nit gelesen im gesatz,ir sind götter etc. Und: Wer min bott halt, der blibt in mir und ich in im etc. Witer hat dise Margarita fürgeben und gesprochen, wer bette, der sünde, und hat niemat witer darvon sagen wellen nach kainen bschaid geben, sunder by den worten lassen bliben. Demnach hat sy so tief in Gott erhocht, das ir zungen und sprache in Gott niemat dann sy können verston, und begund also sprechen: Stat nit geschriben, verflüct sy der, so am Crüz gehanget. Und aber iemat nit witer darvon sagen wellen. Darby an strengs leben gefürt und vil ansechens überkommen; also dsas by vilen irens anhangs entstünd: Welcher am moisten reden oder sunst etwas seltens thün kund, das niemat verston nach ussrechnen mocht, den heil*

Notwithstanding William's pejorative selection of differing Anabaptist characterizations from Kessler's journal, Kessler described the Anabaptists in other places as being respected by non-Anabaptists, being truthful, and speaking only that which was from God. However, he noted that they "boasted of heavenly voices and revelations." He went on to characterize them at the same time as follows:

> Their conduct and attitude seemed quite pious, holy, and blameless. They avoided costly clothing, despised costly food and drink, dressed in coarse material, covered their heads with broad felt hats, their walk and life very humble. They carried no gun or sword or dagger, except a broken off bread knife. They said the former were wolves clothing which the sheep should not wear. They did not swear, not even the obligatory civil oath to the government. And if one transgressed herein, he was banned by them, for there was daily excommunication among them. In speaking and arguing they were hard and sullen and so unyielding that they would rather have died.[83]

CHURCH PRAXES

There was still no written liturgy for an Anabaptist conventicle. However, there was order and structure patterned to emulate Paul's instructions to the Corinthians, in an effort to facilitate the reinstitution of the apostolic church. In the conventicle setting, a reader or preacher would either preach a sermon or lead a group discussion based on a biblical passage. In either case, time would be allowed for participation by the attendees. The preachers and leaders were not necessarily trained theologians by any means, but were literate, students of the Bible, and generally respected in the community. The practice of open participation also encouraged the exercising of the gifts of the Spirit, as outlined in 1 Corinthians 12–14, in an appropriate scriptural manner. Paul's instruction in 1 Corinthians 14:29–32 regarding the gift of prophecy allowed a time for others to judge what was spoken. The practice was referred to as the *Lex Sedentium* or in German, *Sitzerrecht*, the right to speak out in the face

---

sy am höchsten vergottet und in Gott vertieft. See also, Snyder, *Profiles of Anabaptist Women*, 43–53. The idiomatic paraphrase in the text is mine.

83. Harder, *Sources of Swiss Anabaptism*, 381–82; Kessler, "Sabata," 45–46.

of the opened Scripture.[84] An excellent description of a conventicle was written in 1576 by Elias Schad, a Lutheran vicar from Strasbourg, who had followed several Anabaptists into a local forest where they gathered for prayer and teaching;

> [We] followed along behind approximately 200 men and women . . . apostles of the Anabaptist brood in that land are sent annually to this area and to a meeting like this. After [the] sermons . . . they scattered, all knelt, each usually before an oak tree as if he were worshiping it. There was great murmuring as if a nest of hornets were swarming; they waved their arms and beat their breasts almost like priests when they read mass. They sighed and moaned . . . for the Spirit. After this . . . the elder called out in a loud voice, "Now dear brothers you have heard and understood the Word of God and have prayed earnestly. If the Spirit of God reveals anything to someone to edify the brethren, let him come here and we will hear him in a friendly manner.[85]

This account falls outside the parameters of early Anabaptism for this dissertation, but is most likely an accurate description of an Anabaptist conventicle.

Unfortunately, during these same meetings, while the gifts of the Holy Spirit were being manifested properly, aberrant and less than edifying events occurred. Kessler, Vadian, and other chroniclers as well, including the city records of St. Gallen, critically recorded the most outrageous of incidents.[86] Accusations of sexual misconduct[87] and even a fratricide[88] became identified with Anabaptist conventicles along with the manifestations of the gifts of the Spirit. These records are very questionable, of a less than objective nature, and must be read with caution, but they have provided negative examples of the abuse, misuse, and aberrant behavior during Anabaptist conventicles in St. Gallen.[89] But they also document the prolific nature of Pentecostal-like behavior such as speaking in tongues (glossolalia) described as ecstatic language, prophecy, private conventicles or prayer meetings where these things occurred, as well as the occurrence of confession of sins with much contrition and weeping.

84. Williams, *Radical Reformation*, 518–19.
85. Schad, "True Account of an Anabaptist," 292–95.
86. Gamper, "Liebe Und Zorn," 41–63.
87. Snyder, *Profiles of Anabaptist Women*, 50.
88. Kessler, *Sabata*, 54–57.
89. Kessler, *Sabata*, 523–26.

They also describe a people that were living upright, holy, morally clean, ethical, and Christ-like lives in their communities.[90]

THE SCHLEIHEIM CONFESSION OF FAITH

Perhaps in response to the tragedy of the devastating loss in the Peasants' War, the failure of Hubmaier's efforts at encouraging armed resistance, and combined with the developing lack of uniformity of belief and praxis, Michael Sattler wrote a second confession of faith in a continued effort to unify Anabaptism. In 1527, the Anabaptists themselves began to understand that spiritual extremists within the movement were becoming a serious threat to any considered legitimacy. Sattler, a former monk and Anabaptist leader from St. Peter's Monastery in Freiberg in Breisgau, Germany, authored the *Schleitheim Confession*, a statement of fundamental beliefs for the Anabaptists.

The confession was entitled *Brotherly Union of a Number of Children of God Concerning Seven Articles,* and was circulated with a cover letter addressed to Sattler's congregation in Horb am Neckar. Its primary purpose was to document the tenets of Anabaptist faith as agreed upon up to that time: adult baptism, the ban (church discipline), communion, separation, election of pastors, pacifism, and no oath taking. However, the confession was not addressed to the magisterial reformers, Lutheran or Zwinglian, but to the free-thinking or libertine[91] Anabaptists, specifically to "certain false brethren among us . . . in the way they intend to practice and observe the freedom of the Spirit and of Christ."[92] The "false brethren" was a reference to those in St. Gallen and similar places who had obviously misunderstood the freedom of the Spirit, not unlike the Corinthian church of the New Testament. They had given themselves over to self-indulgence, thinking that faith and love permitted all kinds of behavior.[93] Sattler made reference to this abuse in the cover letter he wrote while awaiting execution in Rothenburg am Tauber, having been convicted of being an Anabaptist. He stated that the love Paul spoke of in 1 Corinthians 13 had been

---

90. Kessler, in Harder, *Sources of Swiss Anabaptism*, 382.
91. Yoder, *Anabaptism and Reformation in Switzerland*, 70.
92. Williams, *Radical Reformation*, 291.
93. Williams, *Radical Reformation*.

adulterated by some of the brethren (I know who they are); they have not been willing to edify one another by love, but are puffed up and unprofitable with the vain knowledge and understanding of things which God would have remain hidden to all, but Himself alone, I Corinthians 8:1. I do not censure or reject the grace and revelation of God, but the puffed up make use of this revelation. What would it profit, says Paul, if I should speak with the tongues of men and angels, and understand all mysteries and knowledge, and have all faith, tell me, what profit is all this, if love be not exercised? You have experienced what such presumptuous speaking and ignorance has produced; you still daily see their false fruits, though they have given themselves to God.[94]

Sattler went on to exhort his beloved brethren not to forget to assemble themselves together, for that is where they would uncover the hearts of the false brethren. It is evident that he was referring to the *Sitzerrecht (lex sedentium)* and Pauline instructions for the proper manifestation of the gifts of the Holy Spirit. His reference to speaking in tongues, and an unwillingness to reject the grace and revelation of God, referring to the gift of prophecy in all probability, as well as his insistence that the believers at Horb continue to assemble themselves together in order to continue to edify and correct each other in love, all confirm the manifestation of the pneumatic gifts of the Holy Spirit in Anabaptist meetings.[95] The seven articles of the *Schleitheim Confession* are as follows:

> *Article 1* Baptism shall be given to all those who have been taught repentance and who believe that their sins have been taken away through Christ.
>
> *Article 2* The Ban shall be employed with all those who have given themselves over to the Lord, been baptized into the Body of Christ, and let themselves be called brothers and sisters and still somehow fall into error and sin. They shall be warned twice privately and on the third time be publically admonished before the congregation (Matt. 18).
>
> *Article 3* Concerning the breaking of bread (the Lord's Supper), all those who desire to break the one bread in remembrance of the broken body of Christ and to drink of one drink in

---

94. Sattler, "Letter to the Church," 418–20.
95. Byrd, "Pentecostalism's Anabaptist Heritage," 10–13.

remembrance of the shed blood of Christ must be united beforehand in the Body of Christ (the congregation) and that be baptism.

Article 4 We have been united concerning the separation from evil and wickedness of the world and have no fellowship with them in the confusion of their abominations. By this are meant popish and repopish works and idolatry, gatherings, church attendance, winehouses, guarantees and commitments of unbelief, and other things of the kind, which the world regards highly. From all this we shall be separated.

Thereby shall also fall away from us the diabolical weapons of violence-such as sword, armor, and the like, and all of their use to protect friends or against enemies-by virtue of the word of Christ: "you shall not resist evil."

Article 5 The shepherd of the church shall be a person according to Paul, fully and completely, who has a good report of those outside the faith. The shepherd shall read, exhort, teach, warn, admonish, or ban in the congregation and preside over the brothers and sisters in prayer, and in the breaking of bread (the Lord's Supper) and the general edification of the Body of Christ. The shepherd is to be supported so that he who serves the gospel can live therefrom. If the shepherd should be replaced for cause, another shall be ordained to his place (by the congregation).

Article 6 The sword is an ordering of God outside the perfection of Christ. It protects the good. But within the perfection of Christ only the ban is used for the admonition and exclusion of the one who has sinned, without death, simply a warning and the command to sin no more. It does not befit a Christian to be a magistrate as the rule of government is of the flesh. The rule of a Christian is according to the spirit. The weapons of the flesh are carnal whereas those of a Christian are spiritual.

Article 7 We have been united as follows concerning the oath. Christ . . . forbids His followers all swearing, whether true or false; neither by heaven nor by earth, neither by Jerusalem nor by our head; and for the reason which He goes on to give: "For you cannot make one hair white or black."[96]

---

96. Snyder, *Life and Thought*, 114–27; Yoder, *Legacy of Michael Sattler*, 34–43.

The *Schleitheim Confession* would not be the unifying panacea it was meant to be. It was more of a praxis-oriented treatise than doctrinal or theological, and did not address such issues specifically. Although the practical "how to" of pacifism was gaining support, it was yet to be universally accepted. The idea of a separatist church was also controversial on a biblical basis. Things that were not considered in the document such as communitarianism, whether the church was a visible or invisible body, whether or not the written Scripture, the Bible, was a mere symbol having been replaced by the inner word or the Holy Spirit, and adult baptism in danger of becoming a legalistic symbol required by the church for membership. These were the complaints of many, particularly the spiritualists, and spiritualist Anabaptists, who believed that each Christian had been filled with the Spirit, rendering all the material symbols of Christianity moot, in that one could now depend on the Spirit to " lead them into all truth" without such help. The "inner word" superseded the "outer word." Much was left to be considered in future efforts to unify the Anabaptists. Additionally, there were no eschatological references which many of the spiritualists believed were the primary point to the radical effort to restore the New Testament church in what they considered the last days of time.

CONFESSIONS OF FAITH COMPARED

Hubmaier's confession of faith was very similar to that of Zwingli's *Sixty-Seven Articles,* including the commemorative nature of the Lord's Supper, the magisterial cooperation and support of the propagation of the gospel, and eschewing pacifism in cooperation with the magistracy to resist evil. He did, however, part ways with him regarding infant baptism and the rebaptism of adults. The "Twelve Articles" of the Peasants' War included many aspects of Luther's and Zwingli's Reformation theology which could also be identified as being consistent with Hubmaier. The authors of the "Twelve Articles"—Hubmaier, Luther, and Zwingli—had no problem with involving the magistracy in resisting enemies of the church with violence. Sattler's *Schleitheim Cconfession*, although accepting much of everyone's traditional orthodox theology, rejected the whole concept of violence and, like Grebel, thought the visible church was to be nonresistant, separated from the magistracy, accepting persecution and martyrdom as a prerequisite for membership in the true church of Christ.

Hubmaier initially accepted and preached Luther's reform in Waldshut, but as Zwingli's reform developed in Zurich he felt greater affinity for him. But even the Swiss reform became less attractive than the Anabaptist's anti-pedobaptism and adult baptism. Notwithstanding his anti-pacifism theology, he continued to try to persuade the Anabaptists otherwise. Eddie L. Mabry surmises that the difference between Hubmaier and the Anabaptist perception of the church was primarily: the separation of church and state; although infants were precluded from baptism, informed children were not; the Anabaptist Ban occurred often and excommunication was not the restorative process he supported; and whereas both believed in believer's baptism, Anabaptists saw it as a way of assuring the restitution of a sinless church, a community of saints, while Hubmaier saw it as a sign of a covenant between the believer and the church.[97]

Many Pentecostal-like aspects of early Anabaptism have been noted above, particularly the manifestation of the pneumatic gifts of the Spirit according to 1 Corinthians 12–14, evangelism, adult baptism, pacifism, the parousia, and the restoration of the primitive New Testament church for example. These were all things that the founders of at least American Pentecostalism embraced as well. In 1906, William Seymour published the first of *The Apostolic Faith* in Los Angeles wherein he described the movement as standing for, "The restoration of the faith once delivered unto the saints—the old time religion, camp meetings, revivals, missions, street and prison work and Christian Unity everywhere."[98] The foundation of early American Pentecostal movements such as the Assemblies of God, the Church of God (Cleveland), and the Church of God in Christ invariably reflected the same high priority for a Pauline pneumatology.[99] The same can be said for the early Western European Pentecostals, particularly those of Britain, Germany and Scandinavia.[100]

---

97. Mabry, *Balthasar Hubmaier's Doctrine*, 52–57, 94–95.
98. Seymour, "Apostolic Faith Movement," 12–15.
99. Conn, *Like a Mighty Army*, 145–61; Menzies, *Anointed to Serve*, 242–43.
100. McGee, "Missions Overseas (North American)." See also, Hollenweger, *Pentecostals*, 184–85.

CONCLUSION

The Swiss Brethren, Marpeckan South German/Austrians, Moravian Hutterites, and Dutch Mennonites shared several theological concepts which, while not strictly a systematic theology, was certainly a praxis. Snyder observes that there were many similarities between the Anabaptists and the Lutheran radical archetypes, Karstadt, Müntzer, and Schwenckfeld. Foremost was their mutual doctrinal position of anti-pedobaptism. Although the *Schwärmer* were not as dogmatic about infant baptism, they preached a strong biblical spirituality, the interpretive and regenerating work of the Spirit, a pneumatology which demanded a life of discipleship, visible signs of an inner-working grace or evidence of the infilling of the Holy Spirit in a Pentecostal sense, a soteriology based on salvation by grace through faith alone, but evidenced by good works, and a sacramentarian view of the Eucharist. *Sola scriptura* was thoroughly embraced, as was the concept of the priesthood of the believer.[101]

A major difference with Luther, however, was the Anabaptist rejection of forensic justification, perhaps influenced by Erasmus, in favor of a justification of inner/outer transformation that approached early Pentecostal progressive sanctification,[102] and a freedom of the will that would allow for human participation in terms of good works as evidence of faith. Just as significant were differences which included the exclusion of predestination as believers made conscious choices to accept Christ, pacifism, communitarianism, and the Ban, all of which made the church a visible community of believers.[103] Early manifestation of the gifts of the Holy Spirit according to 1 Corinthians 12–14, particularly speaking in tongues and prophecy, as well as other Pentecostal-type phenomena such as being slain in the spirit, were prevalent.[104] Snyder accurately posits that Anabaptist pneumatology is probably the most underestimated part of their core theology and ecclesiology, agreeing with Karl Holl and James Stayer that they placed greater weight on the efficacy of the Spirit for ethics, conversion leading to baptism, and biblical hermeneutics, than on learning and literal understanding.[105] The catalysts for these theological concepts can be attributed primarily to Anabaptists' continued

---

101. Snyder, *Anabaptist History and Theology*, 43–49; Menzies, *Anointed to Serve*.
102. Hollenweger, *Pentecostals* 24–26; Klaassen, *Anabaptism in Outline*, 41–42.
103. Snyder, *Anabaptist History and Theology*, 94–95.
104. Williams, *Radical Reformation*, 228.
105. Snyder, *Anabaptist History and Theology*, 96.

adherence to the initial theological positions and praxis of both Luther and Zwingli as noted above. Anabaptism conceived a practical theological basis for a free believer's church beginning with *sola scriptura*, a pneumatology which saw the work of the Holy Spirit as efficacious in every Christian's life, a literal biblicism that embraced the Petrine position of the priesthood of the believer, utilization of the theological essence of the *schwärmer* rebellion, and the incorporation of the initial hermeneutics and pneumatology of Luther and Zwingli. The result was the emergence of radical congregations that were neither Roman Catholic, Lutheran, nor Swiss Reformed Protestant, but free believers' churches in a primitive New Testament sense. Their initial composition included biblical literalists, biblical spiritualist charismatics, mystics, spiritualists, and an assorted conglomeration of those who fell into some synthesis or antithesis of all the above. Under such a large and eclectic tent, however, they held one thing in common: anti-pedobaptism succeeded by adult baptism, thus qualifying each for the title of Anabaptist.[106] Moreover, although baptism became a common characteristic, it did not preclude a very dominant praxis of Pauline pneumatology wherein the manifestation of the gifts of the Spirit, particularly prophecy and speaking in tongues, was viewed as being critical to a true church.[107] Furthermore, this emerged in the face of Luther's subsequent distancing himself from his initial acceptance of Rhenish mysticism and Pauline pneumatology when he voiced opposition to the *schwärmer*, that the gifts of the Spirit, as described by Paul in 1 Corinthians 12–14, were in cessation and had only been necessary to institutionalize the primitive church and establish a hierarchical clergy.[108] In 1531, he would lecture from Galatians that

> as Luke witnessed in Acts 10:44–46, Peter and Paul had only to preach and the Holy Spirit came upon those who heard their message, and through him they also received various gifts, so that they spoke in tongues.[109]

---

106. Murray, "Biblical Interpretation," 404; Snyder, *Anabaptist History and Theology*, 83; Williams, *Radical Reformation*, 1256–57.

107. Williams, *Radical Reformation*, 228; Byrd, "Pentecostalism's Anabaptist Heritage."

108. Pelikan, *Lectures on Galatians 1535*, 374–75; Hoffman, *Theologia Germanica of Martin Luther*, 14–20, 27–28.

109. McGrath, *Galatians by Martin Luther*, 122.

In a marginal note written in 1 Corinthians in his personal Bible, Luther interpreted speaking in tongues as plain reading or singing biblical texts.[110] In 1525, he wrote that speaking in tongues is not forbidden, but interpretation must take place when it occurs, although he was most likely referring to the practice of reading the gospel in Latin before the sermon, "which Paul calls speaking in tongues in the congregation."[111]

Although Zwingli, as opposed to Luther, had acknowledged the validity of the current manifestation of the gifts by every Christian and encouraged the practice, he understood the gifts of tongues and interpretation and prophecy only within the context of rational biblical study and hermeneutics. The gift of speaking in tongues, for him, like Luther, was the study and learning of the biblical languages, their utilization, and exposition in compliance with Paul's instructions to the Corinthians. Neither, it appears, accepted the Pentecostal and charismatic phenomena that developed under the aegis of their previously taught doctrine of the priesthood of the believer. However, notwithstanding both being accomplished biblical translators, they used the Greek and Latin translations of Erasmus as sources for their respective New Testament German translations, but they obviously did not translate Erasmus's word "glossolalia," which referred to unknown or unlearned languages in the Greek in reference to 1 Corinthians 12–14 as such, but simply to learned biblical languages.[112] Both recognized the difficulty in maintaining any magisterial control over the charismatic or errant prophets, teachers, and evangelists, without ecclesiastic and clerical standards, much in the same way that the *Didache* attempted in the first century.[113] This was critical in their minds to the development of an institutional clergy-led church that would be acceptable to the existing magistracies if they were going to be

---

110. Foller, "Martin Luther on Miracles," 350.

111. Luther, "Against the Heavenly Prophets 1525," 142–43.

112. It should be noted that the German terms *zungen* and *zungen reden* are indicative of the biblical terms from the Greek γλωσσα, *glossa*, and Latin, *loquitor ligua*, respectively defined as the gift of tongues, speaking a language naturally unlearned, and in need of explanation as in 1 Corinthians 12–14 (OED). *Zungen rede (t)* is also the phrase that Luther used to translate γλωσσα from the Greek in 1 Corinthians 12–14. Zwingli translated it the same way in the Zurich Bibel. Contemporary sixteenth-century German dictionaries also used *glossa* to define *Zungen*, tongues talking or tongues speaking. See also, de Smit, *Die Teutsch Spraach*. For known and learned languages the German word is *Sprache*,

113. Kleist, "Didache," 22–23.

recognized as legitimate religious institutions, juxtaposed against Roman Catholicism and the Anabaptists.

Anabaptists repeatedly insisted on the efficacy of the Spirit in the absence of the word, but yet the word remained critical to any manifestation of the gifts in terms of confirmation.[114] Johannes Kessler gives clarity to this perspective in *Sabata*. The emergence of the radical elements of Zwinglian reform in the guise of the Swiss Brethren, the Anabaptists, was the liminal fruition of Lutheran and Zwinglian biblical spirituality as they introduced it at the inception of their respective reformations. Upon their ostracism from Zurich in 1525, the Anabaptists began an intensive evangelization effort that spread rapidly throughout the region. At the same time, it gave rise to many renditions of radical Anabaptism which varied ecclesiologically, pneumatologically, and theologically in belief and praxes that, although remaining within the common denominator of "family resemblance," still created much havoc in terms of unification efforts meant to create an agreed-upon statement of faith. Both the confessions of Hubmaier and Sattler were a step forward, but neither was acceptable to all. In the midst of the disunity, the increased pressure from the local and imperial magistracies that continued to criminalize Anabaptism enhanced the threat of their very survival not only as a church, but as a people. The loss of property, vocation, and the threat of incarceration, and martyrdom became an expected recompense for their faith.

Within that paradigm, religious and spiritual individualism appeared, as the spiritualists began to preach their respective gospels. Schwenckfeld began to attack the Anabaptists for their legalistic approach to baptism, something he had suspended due to its failure to produce spiritual piety. Hans Hut (1485–1527), a follower of Müntzer in the Peasants' War, Hans Denck (1500–1527) and the Austrian Anabaptists, who were focused on the Eschaton, Hans Bünderlin (1499–1544?), Christian Entfelder, and Sebastian Franck (1499–1542), are among the more significant spiritualists that emerged. But the most important character for this argument is Pilgram Marpeck, the South Austrian civil engineer and lay theologian who wrote many apologies against the spiritualists and attempted to develop a *via media* between them and the Anabaptists. Marpeck would also align himself with Jakob Hutter of Moravia (1500–1536), founder of the Hutterite Movement, and attempt to unify Western European Anabaptism. Chapter four will examine Pilgram Marpeck's

---

114. Byrd, "Pentecostalism's Anabaptist Heritage," 49–61.

efforts against the various arguments that spiritualists made against the Anabaptists. It will also provide an analysis of the Anabaptists' perspectives regarding pacifism, the charismata, ecclesiology, evangelism, persecution, and how they compare with the same issues as handled by early Pentecostalism.

Chapter 4

Evangelism, Persecution, and Pacifism

THIS CHAPTER FOCUSES ON the importance that both Anabaptism and Pentecostalism placed on evangelism being critical to the restitution of the apostolic church, the persecution that it precipitated, and the development of pacifism. The consequences of magisterial intervention in the sixteenth century, both at the local and imperial levels, and the traumatic effect it had on the Anabaptist diaspora that ensued, only encouraged evangelistic efforts. An examination of the magisterial persecution that took place, including the enforcement of various laws and mandates passed to control, suppress, and eliminate Anabaptism, will reveal what effect it had on the movements, both negative and positive. In addition, a comparison will be made between the two regarding the issues of evangelism, persecution, and pacifism. Finally, a description of the dilemma faced by American and European Pentecostals regarding pacifism will be addressed. The experiences each had to deal with concerning evangelism, persecution, and pacifism will be explained and compared.

The ostracism of the Swiss Brethren from Zurich in 1525 and consequent spread of Anabaptism throughout Western Europe resulted in the criminalization of the movement. The coincidence of their criminalization with their strongly held belief in the highest priority of Christ's mandate to "go into all the world and preach the [gospel],[1] became a mechanism, first to fulfill this "Great Commission," and then to seek

---

1. Mark 16:15 NIV

asylum to do so in safety. Peter Riedemann (1506–1556) would write in the early 1540s:

> Just as John could not be a forerunner of Christ without teaching and preaching, so water baptism cannot happen without being preceded by preaching.[2]

It was also within the context of evangelism that manifestations of the charismata began to appear in Anabaptist conventicles.

John Bossy contends that Luther's theology of "two kingdoms," one divine and one secular, both having exclusive responsibilities, contributed significantly to the secularization of many former ecclesiastic responsibilities during the Reformation. This resulted in an individualism that polarized church and community. He argues that the word religion," a religious rule and those who adhere to it, became defined as a worshipful attitude toward God or respect for holy things.[3] "Christian Religion, for John Calvin, meant the primary posture of the Christian community, or the individuals who composed it, towards God."[4] For the more radical elements of the Reformation, Bossy asserts that the impetus toward restitution of the New Testament church was initially driven by Karlstadt in Wittenberg during Luther's absence. Although Luther was able to restore magisterial order, Zwingli had more difficulty with the Anabaptists in Zurich. They had struck at the very foundations of Christian society by opposing infant baptism. Although Bossy agrees that the advent of printing was a great catalyst for a myriad of reformation ideas, theologies, and spiritual concepts, he carefully describes its real effect as only being the transition from an exclusive scholarly function to one practiced by preachers, but also anyone who could read. Effectively the written word had become a "hearable" sign within the control of the reader, preacher, and interpreter.[5] However, Bossy does not make the connection between the Anabaptists' adoption of the priesthood of the believer doctrine and every Christian's ability to interpret Scripture through the power of the Spirit. He recognized the evangelistic propensities of the movement, driven by the desire for the restitution of primitive Christianity, in that this calling sent them "along the life lines of the Empire." Moreover, he

---

2. Riedemann, *Peter Riedemann's Hutterite Confession*, 108. See also, Littell, *Origins of Sectarian Protestantism*, 109; Marpeck, "Admonition of 1542," 180.

3. Bossy, *Christianity in the West*, 153–54,60.

4. Bossy, *Christianity in the West*, 170.

5. Bossy, *Christianity in the West*, 100.

also does not mention the emergence of the numerous sectarian movements that appeared because of this phenomenon, although he does name several of their leaders.[6]

ANABAPTIST EVANGELISM

The trauma of life-threatening persecution was catastrophically devastating to the Anabaptists. This was not considered as anything, but what was to be expected, in that they thought they were living in the last days before the second coming of Christ, as Grebel pointed out in the letter to Müntzer in 1524.[7] At the same time, persecution of the Anabaptists became a great catalyst for the evangelization of the Protestant and Catholic regions to which they would flee. Pedobaptism had rendered evangelism relatively moot within the Western European Catholic Church, in that every newborn child was involuntarily baptized into the church as a Christian.[8] Upon reaching the age of majority, there was no need for any further confession of faith, only contrition and participation in the Mass, confession, and penance. Anabaptists believed that Scripture demanded informed confession and contrition from adults before being baptized. Children were not intellectually capable of such a confession, therefore everyone who had been baptized as a child had to be rebaptized upon a confession of faith: a believer's baptism. Conrad Grebel also wrote to Thomas Müntzer in 1524:

> Baptism . . . signifies the washing away of sins by faith and the blood of Christ . . . it signifies one has died and shall (die) to sin and walks in newness of life and Spirit. We hold that all children who have not attained the knowledge to discern between good and evil . . . are surely saved through the suffering of Christ. We hope that you will not act contrary to God's eternal Word . . . according to which only believers should be baptized and will not baptize children.[9]

---

6. Bossy, *Christianity in the West*, 106–11.

7. Harder, *Sources of Swiss Anabaptism*, 290. See also, Friedmann, *Theology of Anabaptism*, 56.

8. Evangelism was more prominent and effective in Asia and the Americas. See, Hsia, *World of Catholic Renewal*, 178–93.

9. Harder, *Sources of Swiss Anabaptism*, 290–91.

Therein was the impetus for the unrepentant attitude concerning the critical nature of evangelism and the restitution of the apostolic church for Anabaptists.

The failure of the Peasants' War, the alliance of Lutheran and Catholic forces against the peasants, successfully and finally separated the Anabaptists from the Reformations of Luther and Zwingli. The evangelization that ensued resulted in the establishment of congregations throughout the Rhine Valley from Worms to Schaffhausen, the Main River Valley from Frankfurt to Regensburg, and the Danube Valley from Ulm to Vienna. Claus-Peter Clasen documented the effectiveness of the initial Anabaptist evangelism in south and central Germany, Switzerland, and Austria by attempting to demographically quantify the movement over the ensuing ninety-three years. He documented, for example, the appearance of no fewer than 257 new Anabaptist leaders between the first adult baptism in Zurich in 1525 and 1529. During the same time period 3,617 Anabaptists were documented as living in over 500 cities and towns in the same geographic area. Three thousand six hundred eighty-seven more adherents were documented as active in the same region from 1530 to 1549, for a total of 7,304. His impressive sociological study documents an additional 3,871 from 1550 to 1618, for a total of 11,175. However, he does offer the caveat that there were many more Anabaptists who he did not or was not able to document, such as the Hutterites who emigrated from south and central Germany, Switzerland, and Austria, and numbered themselves at more than 10,000.[10] Also not included in his study were the Anabaptist populations of Belgium, France, Spain, Italy, and the Netherlands. Claus-Peter Clasen's study dramatically demonstrates the priority that Anabaptists placed on evangelism in addition to its effectiveness. At the core of Anabaptist desire for the restitution of the New Testament church was the evangelization of the "world" within the context of the Great Commission of Christ.[11] Their missionary zeal was further entrenched in their belief in the imminence of the parousia.

---

10. Clasen, *Anabaptism*, 15–29. It should be noted that Clasen challenges George H. Williams's description of Anabaptism as "a tremendous movement at the core of Christendom" based on his limited but important statistical study which, to his mind, did not numerically support such a conclusion (28). See also, Finger, *Contemporary Anabaptist Theology*, 257–59.

11. Littell, *Origins of Sectarian Protestantism*, 109. See also, Marpeck, "Admonition of 1542," 250–51.

PERSECUTION OF THE ANABAPTISTS

In 1531, as the persecution of Anabaptists increased, Pilgram Marpeck would write *Clare Verantwortung*, arguing with the Lutherans and the spiritualists against the cessation of miracles, signs, and wonders after the time of the apostles, and that God still had a free hand and still performed miracles. He argued that there were individuals (Anabaptists) who currently testified to this with their "death and blood."[12] He would go on to say:

> They do so uncoerced-freely, deliberately, and joyfully through the abundant comfort and power of the Holy Spirit of Christ. Many of them have remained constant, enduring tortures inflicted by the sword, rope, fire, and water, and suffering terrible, tyrannical, unheard-of deaths and martyrdoms, all of which they could have easily avoided by recantation. Moreover, one also marvels when one sees how the faithful God ... raises from the dead several such brothers and sisters of Christ after they were hanged, drowned, or killed in other ways. Even today, they are found alive and we can hear their own testimony.[13]

It is also difficult to determine the exact number of Anabaptist martyrs due to the haphazard preservation efforts of pertinent documentary evidence during that time. Some records were partially preserved while others were destroyed intentionally, and still in many cases no records were made at all. Historiographical difficulties occur, such as confessional, prejudicial, and limited studies' failure to deal with the realities of the lack of accurate documentation.[14] However, there have been attempts at estimating the number of Anabaptists actually executed in the various manners described above. Paul Schowalter states that the total number probably exceeds 4,000 executions.[15]

Claus-Peter Clasen's highly respected, but limited, demographic study of Anabaptism suggests that as many as 845 documented, certain, and probable, executions were carried out in South Germany,

---

12. Marpeck, "Clear Refutation," 50.

13. Marpeck, "Clear Refutation" 50. This is an Anabaptist position that is comparable to that of early Pentecostalism regarding raising the dead. See Seymour, "Apostolic Faith Movement," 6; Horton, *Gifts of the Spirit*, 128; Yong, *Who Is the Holy Spirit*, 110–11.

14. Yong, *Who Is the Holy Spirit*, 110–11.

15. Schowalter, "Numbers of Anabaptists Martyred," 5.

Switzerland, and Austria. However, he mentions 2,246 from contemporary, but unverified, chronicles, 950 from Ensisheim and Heidelberg were not included, and neither were an additional 2,300 which he believed the records of which had been lost. His final estimated total was 4,341 martyred Anabaptists between 1525 and 1618.[16] Schowalter reported that records indicate that there were 1,500 executions in the Netherlands and an estimated 2,500 in Belgium. An additional 800 are listed in the *Martyr's Mirror*. The Hutterite *Geschict-Buch* lists between 600 and 1,386 martyrdoms in the Tyrol. There are some records that are contradictory of each other, which again demonstrates how difficult it is to obtain accurate death estimates.[17] However, it can be accurately stated that thousands of Anabaptists and other radicals were executed for crimes defined as violations of Catholic, Lutheran, and Swiss magisterial mandates based on confessions they accepted as Christian doctrines and practices by their respective magistracies.[18] Over a period of ninethy-three years, from 1525 to 1618, according to those statistics reported above, 11,127 Anabaptists were martyred. It is also noted that these executions were limited geographically to Western Europe. Those suffering corporeal punishment not resulting in death and the various other punishments for being Anabaptists have not been included here.

PERSECUTION OF THE AMERICAN AND EUROPEAN PENTECOSTALS

Early sixteenth-century Anabaptism was limited geographically to propagation within Western Europe. This makes it difficult to compare it with the persecution suffered by early Pentecostalism. This is due to the technological advances in travel, communications, and global population growth over the last 500 years. A general global recognition in the twentieth century of the value of Francis Fukuyama's argument that, "Liberal democracy may constitute the end point of mankind's ideological evolution and the final form of human government," has seen mankind come

---

16. Clasen, *Anabaptism*, 370–74. For corroboration, see also, Gregory, *Salvation at Stake*, 203, and Scribner and Grell, *Tolerance and Intolerance*, 50, 55, 57.

17. Schowalter, "Numbers of Anabaptists Martyred." See also, van Braght, *Martyr's Mirror*; and Stayer, "Anabaptists."

18. Klaassen, *Anabaptism*, 1. Klaassen uses this description arguing that Anabaptism "overcame the perversions of the church of Rome that Luther and Zwingli failed to reach."

to recognize the validity of this thesis by the establishment and pursuit of the idea of the United Nations. His argument is significant, yet still to be globally accomplished. Significant aspects of the theory, for this thesis, are the ideas of the separation of church and state and government by consent of the people as opposed to monarchy, fascism, and communism.[19] Hereditary despotism was commonplace in the sixteenth century, including that of the church, but then there was no other choice than to submit or protest.

Notwithstanding those important global developments, the persecution of early Pentecostals can be compared when limited geographically to North America and Western Europe. Any larger geographic consideration goes beyond the scope of this thesis.

Persecution and discrimination against early Pentecostals within the context of twentieth-century society's adaptation of the separation of church and state, a sixteenth-century Anabaptist concept, was significant.[20] They suffered racial and religious discrimination. In the American movement, racial discrimination was legal. Moreover, it was primarily legal discrimination and social marginalization. But illegal acts, sometimes ignored by authorities, were also committed. The movement was predominantly African-American at its inception, and legal racial discrimination took a significant toll on its adherents.[21] It is problematic to compare the persecutions, incarcerations, and martyrdoms of sixteenth-century Anabaptists with the issues early twentieth-century Pentecostals faced. The unfortunate truth is that both faced persecution primarily from other Christian denominations, both Protestant and Catholic. The fortunate thing is that by the early twentieth century, the Anabaptist concept of a "free church," i.e., the separation of church and state, had been adopted by the majority of Western nations.[22] The American Constitution's first amendment, adopted in 1791, guaranteed the freedom of and from religion by prohibiting the federal government from making any law respecting the establishment of any religion or abridging the exercise thereof. Those nations that had not incorporated the concept of a free church into practice had at least legislated religious toleration into law, as

---

19. Fukuyama, *End of History*, xi.

20. Troeltsch, *Social Teaching*, 2:704–5. See also, Bainton, "Anabaptist Contribution to History," 317.

21. Hollenweger, *Pentecostals*, 26.

22. See FN 3 of ch. 1.

did the English Parliament with the Toleration Act of 1689.[23] However, there were still many governments worldwide that continued to embrace the incorporation of religion and government, where religions foreign to the government were illegal and subject to civil and criminal actions to control and even exclude them. Many Muslim nations of North Africa, the Middle East, and Central Asia have adopted such laws.[24]

In the case of American Pentecostalism, persecution was initially more on the level of extralegal actions of vigilante-type groups who would use violence, but later would also use the judicial enforcement of the new Jim Crow laws prohibiting racial integration.[25] Accusations of social noncompliance and racial integration were employed by the public media as well as by traditional nonintegrated Christian denominations that used passive-aggressive acts of discrimination, exclusion, and accusations of heresy. Moreover, these were the parameters of persecution against American Pentecostalism at its inception.

The initial early German Pentecostal experience occurred within the context of a resurgence of seventeenth-century Lutheran Pietism that coincided with the rise of the Evangelical (Holiness) Movement, known as the *Gemienshaftsbewegung* (GB). The GB appeared within the structure of German Evangelical Protestantism, the *Gnadauer Verband* (GV).[26] Heinrich Dallmyer (1870–1925), an evangelist with the GB, was acquainted with Emil Meyer (1869–1950) and Jonathan Paul, also adherents of the Pietist Holiness resurgence who introduced him to two female Pentecostal followers of T. B. Barratt in the Oslo revival in 1907. Paul and Meyer had attended Barratt's meetings in Oslo. There Meyer became acquainted with two sisters, Dagmar Gregersen and Agnes Thelle, with whom he would share Pentecostal meetings in Hamburg in June of 1907. Meyer also invited Dallmyer to share in the meetings as well, whereupon he received the Spirit baptism, evidenced by glossolalia, and was healed of a heart condition. Dallmyer then invited the two sisters to join him in meetings he was holding in Kassel in August.[27] Manifestations

---

23. Stephenson, *Sources of English Constitutional History*, 599–605. See also, Tucker, *History of English Civilization*, 416.

24. Booze, "Africa, North."

25. Brown and Harlan, "Plessy V. Ferguson," 92–100. U. S. Supreme Court, Justice Brown for the majority.

26. Macchia, *Spirituality and Social Liberation*, 21–23. See also, Adogame, "Germany."

27. Simpson, "Development of the Pentecostal," 62–63.

of glossolalia and healings were prolific, but unfortunately certain aberrant behavior went unchecked and after several days the meetings were declared a threat to public order and closed down by the German police on orders from the city government.[28]

Within days of the termination of the Kassel meetings, in December 1907, the Barmen conference of the GB was convened in which it was decided to suspend the publication of matters concerning the spiritual gifts in all church publications for one year.[29] Notwithstanding Jonathan Paul's continued advocacy of Pentecostalism, there was growing resistance within the broader GV, including accusations of Pentecostalism being of the devil or demonic derivation.[30] But, there was division within the GV with some maintaining a position of neutrality and willingness to engage in dialogue.[31] In December 1908, the European Pentecostal movement began to solidify itself at the Hamburg conference. It was an international event in that Boddy, Barratt, Gerrit R. Polman (1868–1932), founder of Dutch Pentecostalism, Jonathan Paul, and two men who had attended the Azusa Street revival—Cecil Polhill (1860–1938) and Andrew Johnson from Sweden—were all in attendance. This conference decided to publish a new periodical edited by Paul, *Pentecostal Greetings (Pfingstgrüsse)*.[32] Nevertheless, the ultimate decision of the GV and the GB concerning the validity of Pentecostalism as a Christian movement was rendered in September 1909 as the *Berlin Declaration*. The declaration stated that the movement was *"nicht von oben, sondern von unten,"* (not from on high, but from below), it was "satanic" in origin and of a lying spirit. Cited as evidence for the condemnation were allegations of human error, dogmatic error, arrogance, pride, Pharisaism, confusion of worthless utterances with the inspiration of the Holy Spirit, and a litany of other vices.[33] The larger GV party, who supported the declaration, refused all association with Pentecostals, thus initiating a discriminatory position that would marginalize the movement within German Protestant Christianity that

28. Simpson, "Jonathan Paul and the German," 171–72. See also, Bundy, "Early European Perspectives on Pentecostalism," 8–12; Hollenweger, *Pentecostals*, 223.

29. Simpson, "Development of the Pentecostal," 63–64. See also, Bundy, "Early European Perspectives on Pentecostalism," 8.

30. Bundy, "Early European Perspectives on Pentecostalism," 8.

31. Hochen, "Berlin Declaration."

32. Simpson, "Development of the Pentecostal," 64.

33. Simpson, "Development of the Pentecostal." See also, Hollenweger, *Pentecostals*, 225.

P. D. Hochen says was, "both fiercer and more theologically sustained in Germany than in any other country."[34] The marginalization of, and discrimination against, Pentecostals would go unimpeded until 1995 when the *Berlin Declaration* was declared irrelevant by representatives of German Pietists and Lutheran evangelicals in agreement with Pentecostals and charismatics.[35]

ANABAPTIST SECTARIANISM

Very soon after Anabaptism was criminalized, ostracism ensued. Various sects began to materialize and spread throughout Western Europe. Following the concept of the priesthood of the believer, a variety of Pentecostal-like manifestations of the gifts of the Spirit after 1 Corinthians 12–14 started to appear, unfortunately including aberrant behavior much like that experienced in early Pentecostalism. What follows is a description from various contemporary sources of the multitude of those sects that emerged.

In 1527, Zwingli published a refutation of Anabaptist *(Catabaptists)* beliefs and practices wherein he categorically refutes each theological tenet of their confession one by one.[36] In doing so, he described some of their conventicle practices and behavior such as that of being slain in the Spirit, and prophecy:

> At Appenzell they use the following tricks: Some Catabaptist throws himself down just as though he were an epileptic; as long as he can he holds his breath and pretends to be in ecstasy. Those who have seen it say he presents a horrible appearance. Finally, like one waking up, he begins to testify about what he has heard and seen in ecstasy. They have all seen especially that Zwingli is in error about catabaptism, and this opinion one pronounces gently and another violently. They saw that the day of judgment was at hand two years ago, and that catabaptism was a righteous and holy thing, and all that kind of foolishness.[37]

---

34. Hochen, "Berlin Declaration." Berlin Declaration.
35. Hochen, "Berlin Declaration."
36. *Catabaptist* is a Latin term meaning, "opposed to the traditional Catholic sacrament of water baptism."
37. Zwingli, "Refutation of the Tricks," 216. See also, Zwingli, *Catabaptistarum Strophas Elenchus*, 130.

He went on to describe a similar incident of glossolalia, involving a young girl in St. Gallen who experienced a similar phenomenon where she also, "babbled out those empty ravings of theirs."[38] Zwingli was not ostensibly a witness to either incident, but only reporting what he had been told. Similar experiences in early Pentecostalism were referred to as being slain in the Spirit, accompanied by gifts of prophecy and speaking in tongues and interpretation.[39] He, however, did not associate such stories with his understanding of being able to speak in other tongues, interpretation, or prophecy (1 Corinthians 12–14), which for him was an intellectual exercise in biblical languages and inspired preaching, as he taught in his school of prophecy, the *Prophezei*.

Consequent to the persecution and diaspora of Anabaptism from 1525 to 1531 was perhaps the inevitable appearance of a myriad of radical sects. In 1531, Sebastian Franck (1499–1542), a former Catholic priest and a spiritualist who rejected all four contemporary religious confessions—Catholic, Lutheran, Zwinglian, and Anabaptist—would write a critical but important and authentic analysis of Anabaptism based on his personal experience.[40] Franck observed that the foremost leaders of Anabaptism in 1526 were Hubmaier, Melchior Rinck (1493–1553), Hut, Denck, and Hätzer, and described them in his *Chronica of 1531* as follows:

> These men moved about so rapidly that their teaching spread quickly and secretly throughout the whole land. They obtained a large following, baptized many thousands. They did this with their appearance of piety and also with the letter of Scripture to which they adhered rigidly. For, apparently, they taught nothing but love, faith, and the cross. They proved themselves patient and humble in much suffering. They broke bread with one another as a sign of unity and love. They conscientiously helped each other, faithfully lending, borrowing, and giving. They taught that all things should be held in common, and called

---

38. Zwingli, "Refutation of the Tricks," 217. See also, Zwingli, *Catabaptistarum Strophas Elenchus*, 131.

39. Cecil Robeck describes the manifestation of Azusa Street adherents going into "trances" during prayer and worship, including William Seymour's experience of being baptized in the Spirit and speaking in tongues, having fallen to the floor "as though dead." Zwingli uses the Latin word *ecstasia* in his Catabaptist pamphlet which is also translated "trance" as well as "ecstasy" (Robeck, *Azusa Street Mission and Revival*, 12, 69).

40. Snyder, "Sebastian Franck on the Anabaptists," 228–30.

each other brother. But they hardly greeted nor helped anyone who was not of their sect, and kept to themselves.[41]

Franck went on to say that the Anabaptists were so disunited that he could not write anything definite or final as to their beliefs or praxes. Some considered rebaptism essential to becoming a Christian, while a minority did not. Some considered infant baptism an abomination, while others thought it to be a matter of choice for the parents. Some considered themselves sanctified and pure and separated from the others, "holding all things in common . . . all personal property being a sin with them."[42] Others held all things in common, but only to the extent that no one suffers need. In the case of need, everyone shared what was theirs willingly, but there was no claim by anyone to another's property. However, "at this point there is much hypocrisy, unfaithfulness, and very much of Ananias as they themselves will know."[43]

Franck described some phenomena that reflected similar divisive activities, not only like those described by Zwingli above, but also to those of early twentieth-century Pentecostal behavior described by William Seymour in his *Apostolic Address of 1915*.[44] Franck would write:

> Some tell of new commands of God revealed daily to evangelize both their brothers as well as strangers. Some go into a trance, distort their faces, and lie prone up to an hour. Some shake, some lie still, some as much as two or three days. Afterwards, when they again come to themselves, they prophesy and tell of wonders as though they had been in a different world. They think they have this in common with Paul, 2 Corinthians 11[:12], who was caught up into the third heaven. Many cannot tell the mysteries which they saw in this trance.[45]

Franck made no attempt to classify the myriad of Anabaptist sects as noted above, but he did mention a few by name: "The Apostolic Brethren, the Silent Brethren, and brethren who experienced ecstasies, visions and dreams."[46]

---

41. Franck, "Sebastian Franck on the Anabaptists," 231.

42. Franck, "Sebastian Franck on the Anabaptists," 233.

43. Franck, "Sebastian Franck on the Anabaptists," 233.

44. Sanders, *William Seymour Papers*, 117–18.

45. Sanders, *William Seymour Papers*, 236. See also, Franck, *Chronica*, 987, cxciiii–cxcv.

46. Franck, in Clasen, *Anabaptism*, 30.

Independent of Franck, but describing the same sectarian events, also in 1531, was English clergyman William Barlowe, Bishop of St. David's, Bath and Wells, and Chichester. He first published an anti-Lutheran treatise in the midst of Henry VIII's dispute with the pope, wherein he described his personal continental experience of witnessing the development of three factions of the Protestant Reformation firsthand, i.e., the Lutherans, the Zwinglians, and the Anabaptists. However, after the accession of Catholic Queen Mary, he republished the treatise in 1553, apparently for self-preservation, and lost favor with Archbishop Cranmer.[47] He first characterized Luther as the chief of the heretics, but would classify Zwingli as likewise heretical and also the source of Anabaptism. He declared that there were no less than forty sects of Anabaptists in addition to those of the Lutherans and Zwinglians.[48] He described the various sects of the Anabaptists as follows:

> The third faction is called Anabaptists, because they are twice christened and will admit no one as their faithful brethren except they be baptized again. They suffer not their children to be christened until they are of great age, and have many strange opinions. They affirm that it is impossible for Kings, princes, justices, and other governors of the commonweal, to be Christian men. They say that Christian men ought to make no provision against their enemies, but freely suffer them to do their will. Also they show holy perfection outwardly, observing vigils, fastings, with continual reading of scripture, ready to help their needy brethren using their goods in common. I have heard them dispraise much the lying of the Lutherans and Oecolampadians [Zwinglians], saying as I have heard them my self-report, that they are worse than the clergy, whom they call Papists, because they have the gospel in their mouths and frame their lives nothing thereafter, showing no amendment of their lewd conversation, but continue still in vicious excesses after the common rate of misbelievers. And therefore they be in grievous hatred and suffer much persecution of the other, as excommunication, exile, imprisonment, and often cruel execution of death.[49]

47. Lunn, *Bishop Barlowe's Dialogue*, 4–5.

48. Lunn, *Bishop Barlowe's Dialogue*, 43–57. See also, Barlow, *Dyaloge Descrybyng the Orygyinall*, and MacCulloch, *Reformation*, 631. Barlowe did caveat his information as also having come from trusted reliable sources.

49. Lunn, *Bishop Barlowe's Dialogue*, 57–58.

Barlowe continued by pointing out the many excesses and aberrations of the movement that he had either witnessed or acquired via hearsay:

> There are some which hold opinion that all devils and damned souls shall be saved at the day of doom. Some persuade that the Serpent which deceived Eve was Christ. Some grant to every man and woman two souls. Some affirm lechery to be no sin and one may use another man's wife without offence. Some take it upon themselves to be soothsayers and Prophets of wonderful things to come, and have prophesied the day of judgment to be at hand. Some of them both men and women at their congregations for a mystery show themselves naked, affirming that they are in a state of innocence. And some hold that no man ought to be punished, or suffer execution for any crime or trespass be it ever so horrible.[50]

Barlowe's last reference to Anabaptists believing that no man should be held accountable for criminal activities was in all probability a reference to the fratricide committed by Thomas Schuggers in St. Gallen in 1526, as reported in Kessler's *Sabata*.[51] Joachim von Watt, Vadian, the Burgomaster of St. Gallen at the time, adjudicated the case and declared Schuggers insane and had him executed with the acquiescence of the Schuggers' Anabaptist family. Notwithstanding Kessler's account which indicated that the crime was committed during an Anabaptist conventicle, Vadian's report couched the incident in terms of a nonreligious eruption of insanity.[52] Barlowe's report should be considered spurious in many respects as it tends to rely on hearsay rather than fact for the more fanatical descriptions of Anabaptist behavior. His descriptions are like those of some early Pentecostal aberrant antics recorded by William Seymour while at Azusa Street.[53]

In 1538, Caspar Hedio (1494/95–1552), the main preacher at the Strasbourg cathedral from 1523 to 1552, presented a list of thirteen groups: Müntzerites, Silent Brethren, Praying Brethren, Dreamers, Childlike, the Sinless Baptized Children, Binderites, Sabbatarians, Maderani, Hofmanites, and Newly Circumcised.[54] In 1544, Johannes Gast

50. Lunn, *Bishop Barlowe's Dialogue*, 59–60.
51. Kessler, *Sabata*, 54–56.
52. Horsch, "An Inquiry into the Truth," 26–31.
53. Sanders, *William Seymour Papers*, 12–13.
54. Clasen, *Anabaptism*, 443n2. My translation from the Latin.

listed seven groups, and in 1566, Wendel Artz also listed seven, including Silent Anabaptists, Praying Anabaptists, etc.[55]

In 1561, Bullinger would name a number of groups and divisions in his history of the origins of the Anabaptists, but distinguish them from the General Anabaptists who he thought to be of the original Swiss Brethren and those who ascribed to their confession.[56] He singled out the Apostolic Anabaptist, Secluded and Spiritual Anabaptists, Holy, Pure, and Sinless Anabaptists, the Taciturn Anabaptists, the Praying and Quiescent Anabaptists, two groups of Free Anabaptists, followers of Hans Hut, the Augustinian Brethren, the Munsterites, and the Abominable Anabaptists, Servetus, Melchior Hoffman, David Georgians, Libertines, Universalists, and those who believed that Christ had abolished the Old Testament.[57]

Georg Eder (1523–1587), a prominent citizen of Vienna and officer of the Habsburg court, wrote extensively as a defender of the Catholic faith in the face of the success of Protestantism. In 1573, he penned his *Evangelische Inquisition* in which he identified those heretical groups who posed the greatest threat to the Roman Catholic Church. They were the Lutherans, the Calvinist [Zwinglian Reformed], the Schwenckfeldians, the Anabaptists, and the Muslims.[58] He identified more than thirty-eight Anabaptist groups some of which are as follows: the followers of Müntzer, the naked-running Adamites, those of the Staff, those who worshiped on Saturday rather than Sunday, the Secret or Garden brothers, the Open Witnesses, those who believed the devil would be saved, the Libertines, the Cohabiters, the Grübenhaimers, the Weeping Brethren who held emotional prayer meetings, the Silent Ones, the followers of David Georg, the Mennonites, the Cathari, the Apostles who left their families, and the Augustinian soul sleep Psychopannychists. The list is indicative of the tendency of various Anabaptist groups to overemphasize specific aspects of the Bible and isolate them out of their Protestant contexts in support of independent ecclesiologies.[59] Such was the state of secular radicalism in 1528. The Swiss Brethren and Pilgram Marpeck would be the leaders that chose to accept the task of solving the problem.

55. Clasen, *Anabaptism*, 30–31.
56. Clasen, *Anabaptism*, 30–31.
57. Bullinger, *Der Widertoufferen*, 1–66. See also, Clasen, *Anabaptism*, 31.
58. Fulton, *Catholic Belief and Survival*, 12, 92.
59. Eder, *Evangelische Inquisition*, 58–59. See also, Williams, *Radical Reformation*, 1069.

IMPERIAL FREE CITY TOLERATION

The persecution of early sixteenth-century Anabaptists forced adherents to begin meeting in clandestine conventicles, but more importantly encouraged their emigration to those regions which were religiously tolerant and either not enforcing the mandates against them or simply ignoring them. At the Diet of Worms in 1521, a list of eighty-five cities under the title of Free Imperial Cities was drawn up. Sixty-five of them were directly subject to the empire. More than fifty of these cities officially recognized the Reformation, an indication that free imperial cities were initially more involved in Protestantism than other estates of the empire.[60] The growth of these urban centers can be attributed to the trade and industry developed from the transition from an agrarian labor economy to a capitalistic currency economy after the devastation of the plagues and famines of the Late Middle Ages. The appearance of merchant bankers and venture capitalists, and their ability to fund not only traditional businesses, but the political aspirations of royalty, caused ever-increasing taxes on the local nobility. As the nobility became resistant to these importunate financial demands, royalty began to co-opt them by selling royal offices thus diminishing the effectiveness of the local legislative bodies formed by the nobility. Even the popes began to participate in this effective way to maximize revenues, thus creating positions such as prince–bishops.[61] Yet imperial cities could still align themselves, in the feudal sense of protection and benefit, with the royalty of the larger empire. Such was the case with the Swabian League. These urban centers developed a more communal character in the late medieval period and operated with annual elections and typical communal responsibilities.

Bernd Moeller points out that along with civic duties went religious responsibilities, for each citizen embraced the idea that town law was God's law and violation was in fact disobedience of him. Natural catastrophes were seen as God's punishment and oaths of allegiance to the town were seen as pledging spiritual obedience. The local priest would lead the whole town in processions of repentance with relics of the town's patron saint. Whoever incited communal discord courted the wrath of God and was treated like a Judas. Therefore, every citizen was convinced that the church was both the center of the civic as well as the religious life of the town. This effectively made the town also responsible for spiritual and

60. Moeller, "Imperial Cities and the Reformation," 41.
61. Ozment, *Age of Reform*, 190–97.

ecclesiastical matters. The concurrence of religious life and secular life of a city was not unique. When radical reformers, like the Anabaptists, appeared, if they were seen as Judases, sowing religious and therefore civic discord in the community, they made themselves subject to the criminal penalties of the local and imperial mandates.[62] Moeller also observed that the above-described sociopolitical situation was in place at the time of Luther's Reformation; furthermore, the idea of the equality of all community members fit quite well with his priesthood of the believer theology.[63]

STRASBOURG

Strasbourg was one of the Free Imperial cities which attracted and tolerated the residence of many Anabaptists, spiritualists, and various other types of religious radicals who rejected Catholicism, Luther, and Zwingli. This meant that the city had garnered independence and formed a constitutional government with councils and a mayor.[64] It had wrested political control from the local prince-bishop and was responsible only to the emperor, having become a republic whose nobles and guildsmen adopted their own constitution.[65] This put the city council in control of deciding who was or was not a Judas. George Williams says that Strasbourg had a reputation for penal moderation summarized by a contemporary statement: "He who would be hanged anywhere else is simply driven from Strasburg by flogging."[66]

The early development of Anabaptist theology and spirituality and their similarity to early Pentecostalism is shown by the various protagonists' interactions with one another while taking asylum in Strasbourg. The city's importance centers on the fact that many radical reformers fled from persecution and martyrdom to the relative safety of the city. There they were able to engage with the city's Lutheran reformers, as well as each other, in sharing and debating their respective positions. Michael

---

62. Moeller, "Imperial Cities and the Reformation," 44–46. See also, Ozment, *Reformation in the Cities*, 8–10.

63. Moeller, "Imperial Cities and the Reformation," 71–72. See also, Ozment, *Reformation in the Cities*, 6–7.

64. Moeller, "Imperial Cities and the Reformation," 44–46, 71–72.

65. Williams, *Radical Reformation*, 363.

66. Williams, *Radical Reformation*, 363.

Sattler, one of the first to see the need for Anabaptist unity, stayed there long enough to ingratiate himself to the Lutheran leaders of the city, Martin Bucer (1491–1551) and Wolfgang Capito (1478–1541). Followers of Thomas Müntzer, spiritualists, Hans Hut (1490–1527), and Hans Denck (1500–1527) also spent time there, as did Schwenckfeld.

It was in Strasbourg that Pilgram Marpeck and his circle began their attempt to unify Anabaptism by reconfirming traditional Christian orthodoxy, including a Pauline pneumatology, as the foundation of the movement.[67] His polemic against the spiritualists, particularly Schwenkfeld, denied their claim that since the Holy Spirit was present in every Christian, and when combined with the initial Lutheran concept of the priesthood of the believer, that the physical aspects of church liturgical and theological praxes such as reading the Bible, the Mass, and baptism were no longer necessary. Not the least of early Anabaptist leaders to appear in Strasbourg was the Dutch radical reformer Melchior Hoffman (1495–1543), the apocalyptic leader of those charismatic Anabaptists who would bring about the Münster debacle of 1534 and 1535.

Many of the Swiss Brethren and other Anabaptists also sought refuge in Moravia, a region that was also tolerant of religious diversity. That is where Jacob Hutter (1500–1536) had found sanctuary fleeing from persecutions in Austria and the Tyrol. The Hutterites were very missionary minded and would attempt to collaborate with Marpeck to find a *via media* for Anabaptist unification. It was during this time of intense and prolific Anabaptist evangelization and diaspora to more religiously tolerant regions of Europe that Anabaptist spirituality and theology began to develop.

Juxtaposed with magisterial reformers, George Williams observed that radical reformers, including Anabaptists, found a place for the ministry of prophets as forth-tellers and critics of society in general as well as apostles (gospel messengers). They considered contemporary Christendom at large anti-Christian, or at best sub-Christian. George Williams contended that they then "turned with vehemence to the pentecostal task of converting Christendom and the world to [primitive] Christianity."[68] Motivated by the belief that Christ was the soon-coming king, they were inspired to exigency concerning the "lost" of the church and the world.

67. "Orthodoxy" will be defined as "a biblicist perspective on the constitution of the primitive New Testament church as understood by the Anabaptists, very similar to that of the Pentecostals."

68. Williams, *Radical Reformation*, 1276.

The spiritual success of their conventicles attracted dynamic converts from the lower classes of society who eventually developed into leaders, much like those of the New Testament. This became an important factor which incentivized their evangelism.[69] Although he correctly characterizes Anabaptist opinion of contemporary Christianity, Williams' bias is evident as their missionary zeal is better explained as simple obedience to Christ's directive to "Go into all the world and preach the gospel," which they understood literally as being necessary for the restitution of the New Testament church as noted above. In 1525, Kessler would write of the St. Gallen Anabaptists in *Sabata*:

> [They] assumed the apostolic office as the first in the newly established church, believing that it was their obligation to follow Christ's command when he said, 'go ye into the world, etc.' [Mk. 16:15]. They ran beyond the city gate into the outlying villages, regions, and market towns to preach.[70]

The increasing pressure on local magistracies and imperial regimes to eliminate Anabaptists created a problem in terms of determining exact numbers of Anabaptists and identifying who they were. The pressure brought to bear on the Anabaptists forced them into clandestine conventicles and constant emigration to avoid persecution. Christian Hege published a list of 133 mandates issued within the Holy Roman Empire between 1525 and 1561 against Anabaptists and Mennonites.[71] Mandates were the official laws of the Holy Roman Empire, both imperial and territorial. In 1525, the Zurich City Council demanded that all infants be baptized, and by 1526 the death penalty was enacted against any adult who had been re-baptized upon a confession of their new faith. Punishments also included ostracism, imprisonment, loss of property, torture, and mutilation, including cutting off of limbs and branding, drowning, burning, hanging, beheading, and being buried alive. Crimes enumerated in the mandates included sheltering, feeding, or employing suspects. The principal violation was disagreement with the official doctrines and institutions of the established churches. Government officials hired informants to identify practicing adherents and testify against them. In 1528,

---

69. Williams, *Radical Reformation*, 1277.
70. Harder, *Sources of Swiss Anabaptism*, 423. See also, Kessler, *Sabata*, 45.
71. Hege, "Mandates."

mandates against the Anabaptists were extended by Emperor Charles V to the entire Holy Roman Empire.[72]

ANABAPTIST PACIFISM

C. Arnold Snyder states that Anabaptist pacifism, discussed in some detail in chapter four relative to Hubmaier and the Peasants' War, remained as an undecided issue among the earliest Anabaptist groups in Switzerland, South Germany, and Austria. That was the case not only for pacifism, but for biblical hermeneutics and the relationship of church to state, including issues of the oath and the sword. However, by 1530, some, but not all issues had been settled. For example, the separatist nonresistant stance of Sattler's *Schleitheim Confession* became acceptable to the Swiss Brethren. Sattler's position on the sword and oath was adopted by the Swiss Anabaptists. Yet pacifism among other issues would still remain a matter of dispute within Anabaptism at large.[73] But by 1552, Menno Simons, then the leader of the Anabaptist movement, at least in the Netherlands, wrote *The Swearing of Oaths*, wherein he provided scriptural guidance for not swearing an oath:

> We confess and heartily believe that no emperor or king may rule as superior, nor command contrary to His Word, since He is the Head of all princes, and is King of all kings. Therefore it is that through fear of God we do not swear, not dare to swear, though we must hear and suffer much on that account from the world.[74]

Swearing an oath of allegiance to the magistracy was tantamount to agreeing to take up the sword for its safety and security, a willingness to resist violence with violence. Pacifism was to become a major tenet of the Mennonite faith.

PENTECOSTAL EVANGELISM

Early twentieth-century Pentecostalism adopted missionary evangelism as a spiritual calling of the highest priority from their Holiness

---

72. Hege, "Mandates."
73. Snyder, *Anabaptist History and Theology*, 197.
74. Simons, *Complete Writings of Menno Simons*, 518.

Movement predecessors and converts. Christ, as the soon-coming king, and the quest for the restitution of the primitive church were great driving forces behind the importance they placed on evangelism, much like the early Anabaptists.[75] However, many American Pentecostals believed that speaking in tongues, in addition to being the initial evidence of the infilling of the Holy Spirit, was a genuine foreign language to be used in the foreign land one was called to evangelize.[76] Charles Fox Parham's missiology was based on the appearance of glossolalia, which he interpreted as genuine foreign languages (xenolalia) and a sign of the eschaton when an outpouring of the Holy Spirit was preparing missionaries to preach the gospel without formal training throughout the world.[77] In 1906, William Seymour would write an article in the first edition of *The Apostolic Faith* periodical entitled, *The Precious Atonement*, which concerned four things the children of God received from the atonement:

> Fourth. And we get the baptism with the Holy Ghost and fire upon the sanctified life. Christ enthroned and crowned in our hearts. Let us lift up Christ to the world in all his fullness, not only in healing and salvation from all sin, but in His power to speak all the languages of the world.[78]

Not unlike the emergence of various Anabaptist groups in the sixteenth century, Pentecostalism initially produced several variations as well. Its early evangelistic perspectives were couched in the context of their Holiness Movement origins. This was an existing network of contacts and opportunities for evangelism and missionary outreach of which they readily took advantage. They were primarily converts from movements such as Wesleyan Holiness, and therefore considered themselves as Wesleyan Pentecostals who continued to embrace the Wesleyan theology with the exception of their understanding of the new Pentecostal experience.[79] The initial theology and spirituality which caused separation and division among them can be generally divided into disagreements

---

75. See also, Parham, *Voice Crying in the Wilderness*, 25–26. Wacker, *Heaven Below*, 72.

76. Anderson, *Spreading Fires*, 24–25. See also, Karkkainen, "Missiology"; Wacker, *Heaven Below*, 48.

77. Synan, *Holiness-Pentecostal Tradition*, 89–92; Parham, *Voice Crying in the Wilderness*, 25–26. See also Wacker, *Heaven Below*, 45; Goff, *Fields White unto Harvest*, 164.

78. Seymour, "Precious Atonement," 2.

79. Blumhofer, *Restoring the Faith*, 26–29.

over five Pentecostal cardinal doctrines: justification by faith, entire sanctification, the baptism in the Holy Spirit with the evidence of speaking in tongues, divine healing provided by Christ in the atonement, and the imminent premillennial second coming of Christ.[80] Soon after the initial appearance of Pentecostalism, a number of diverse North American Pentecostal groups began to appear. Each of them held differing opinions and interpretations concerning the scriptural and theological meaning and application of the five main doctrines generally embraced by the movement. Much like the Anabaptists, their differences consisted of more personal revelation and preference than theological substance.

Here the common denominator of the priesthood of the believer, and all that it encompasses for believer priests by the power of the Spirit, is discovered. Both Anabaptists and Pentecostals began their spiritual journey into scriptural obedience by thoroughly embracing the concept. Anabaptists and Pentecostals both believed in the efficacy of the work of the Holy Spirit, whom Christ promised would empower them to be witnesses of the gospel throughout the world, and so acquitted themselves accordingly. Both believed that conforming to the charismatic biblical model for spreading the gospel was critical to the restitution of the primitive apostolic church. The evangelistic and missionary zeal of the early Pentecostals is reflected in their statements of belief that speaking in tongues was evidence of the empowerment of the Holy Spirit, primarily for preaching the gospel. Like the Anabaptists, the exigency of evangelism was likewise contingent upon the imminent second coming of Christ. Prime examples of the connection Pentecostals made between evangelism and the second coming are as follows: Parham would write after one of his students in Topeka, Kansas, spoke in tongues that "the Baptism in the Holy Spirit [evidenced by speaking in tongues] is especially given now as the sealing. Therefore the sureness of the last days."[81]

William Seymour would declare:

> Behold the Bridegroom cometh! O the time is very near. All the testimonies of his coming that have been going on for months are a witness that he is coming soon. But when the trumpet sounds, it will be too late to prepare. Those that are not ready at the rapture will be left to go through the awful tribulation.[82]

---

80. Synan, *Century of the Holy Spirit*, 111.
81. Parham, *Voice Crying in the Wilderness*, 30.
82. Seymour, "Apostolic Faith Movement," 2.

T. B. Barrett would pen a poem in 1927, toward the end of his career, that captured the urgency of his Pentecostal perspective and ministry:

> Time is short, the Day is coming,
> When our Saviour will appear;
> Words of warning daily reach us,
> Words of comfort and of cheer!
>
> Work and spread the Glorious Gospel,
> Save the dying, heal the sick;
> If you wish the lost ones rescued,
> Oh, for Christ's sake then be quick![83]

A. A. Boddy quoted from his personal diary, written in Norway on March 5, 1907: "The near coming of Christ seems to be impressed upon everyone who comes under the power of the Spirit. The message of nearly everyone is "Jesus is coming."[84]

PENTECOSTAL PACIFISM

Early Pentecostalism's struggle with pacifism was not unlike the Anabaptist experience. World War I, the Great War, caused no little consternation among Pentecostals at its inception in the summer of 1914. European Pentecostals, particularly the English and the German citizens of the two main protagonist nations in the war, had begun a close and effective relationship at the beginning of the Pentecostal outpouring. But the war forced them into having to choose between Christian peace and national patriotism. In October 1914, A. A. Boddy, leader of English Pentecostalism pastoring in Sunderland, wrote in *Confidence*, the regularly published periodical for the movement, a justification for England's involvement in the war:

> Why are we in this war? England was not prepared to go to war. Belgium had been guaranteed protection. She was cruelly invaded and ravaged, contrary to treaty. England was compelled, in honour, to do all she could. The whole country is one on this point. Many hundreds of thousands of Britain's best sons have offered their lives, and are being formed into a new army to

---

83. Barratt, *When the Fire Fell*, 166.
84. Boddy, *Pleading the Blood*, loc. 13 of 1437.

be effectively trained-keen to learn and patriotic in spirit, and longing to have an opportunity to help the oppressed. We British people should pray that "Militarism" may come to an end through this war.[85]

In the same issue he wrote, "A friend in Holland wrote that some 40 Pentecostal workers [had been imprisoned] in Germany . . . but not Pastor Paul, Pastor Voget, or Predigers Edel or Humberg."[86]

Pastor C. O. Voget wrote:

We realise not only in theory but in our hearts that God has got one holy nation upon the earth, united by the Blood of Jesus, saved from the war spirit. And this we do, though we cannot deny our national feelings. We do not hold that true Christianity and true patriotism exclude each other.[87]

The British movement wasn't absolutely pacifist as conscientious objection was permitted. Moreover, two of the national leaders of British Pentecostalism were conscientious objectors during World War I, one of whom was Donald Gee. Some were totally exempted while others were not and served time in prison.[88]

In December 1914, G. R. Polman wrote a letter justifying the Great War. It was published by the *Christian Evangel* by the Assemblies of God, in Findlay, Ohio. Boddy wrote an introduction to the letter which expressed sorrow and sympathy for the German Pentecostal brethren caught up in the war in Germany and the many Belgian wounded and German prisoners of war that were being held and cared for in England. He criticized the Germans for invading Belgium and threatening France, but excused England as not being prepared for war yet. He did couch his remarks by saying, "As awful as war is it would be worse to stand by and make no effort to protect the weak."[89] Polman justified the war as a sign of the second coming and as an evangelistic opportunity presented to preach the gospel to the wounded and the German prisoners being held in England.

---

85. Boddy, "War," 191.
86. Boddy, "War," 191.
87. Boddy, "War," 191.
88. Beaman, *Pentecostal Pacifism*, 101.
89. Polman, "European War Justifiable?," 1.

The tension between Christian peace and love and national patriotism on both sides was palpable. Notwithstanding recognition of a common Christian confession of faith, neither side seemed to be able to separate themselves completely from their respective patriotisms. The Pentecostal Anglican Church of England brethren saw the war as justified by righting an injustice and creating an opportunity to spread the gospel. British nonconformist Pentecostals tended toward pacifism.[90]

On April 28, 1916, Samuel H. Booth-Clibborn published the following statement in the Assemblies of God Weekly Evangel in response to his own question, "Should a Christian Fight?":

"No! As far as the Christian is concerned the 'eye for an eye' system has given place to the 'Turn the other cheek' Matt.5:39–44."[91]

The war had become a reality for American Pentecostals and the issue was forced into consideration. The newly organized American Pentecostal organization, the Assemblies of God (1914), published a statement written in April 1917 which decidedly proclaimed, after describing the various scriptural reasons for requesting exemption from military service which required the taking of life, that

> therefore, we as a body of Christians, while purposing to fulfil all the obligations of loyal citizenship, are nevertheless constrained to declare we cannot conscientiously participate in war and armed resistance which involves the actual destruction of human life, since this is contrary to our view of the clear teachings of the Inspired Word of God, which is the sole basis of our faith.[92]

The statement was forwarded to President Wilson on April 28, who waited until the U. S. Congress could pass legislation, not only regarding the Assemblies of God exemption request, but for many others like it. On July 25, 1917, the War Department advised that their exemption was granted.[93] Although some adherents opted to apply for conscientious objector status, ordained ministers had received a total exempt status.[94]

---

90. Alexander, *Peace to War*, 83–88.

91. Booth-Clibborn, "Christian and War," 5. See also, Anderson, *Spreading Fires*, 223–29.

92. Frodsham, "Pentecostal Movement," 6–7.

93. Frodsham, "Pentecostal Movement," 6–7.

94. Menzies, *Anointed to Serve*, 326.

Although America would enter the war three years after the European nations, the dilemma of reconciling Christian peace and love and national patriotism was common to them both. The Americans opted for conscientious objector status, which still included support for the war effort, but in noncombatant roles, as did the British and German Pentecostals. However, Germany court-martialed and executed pacifists. Nevertheless, both unequivocally pledged allegiance to their respective nations.

Compared to the Anabaptist experience of pacifism and nonresistance, the American and European Pentecostals rarely suffered such drastic consequences. Moreover, Anabaptists were routinely incarcerated, tortured, and martyred. Although Pentecostals were incarcerated, they were rarely martyred. Unless there was some intent to subvert the law, capital punishment was possible, but also rare.[95]

Early Pentecostals, like early Anabaptists, were confronted with the issue of pacifism. At the onset of World War I, most American Christians supported the war, but most Pentecostals sided with Christian pacifists, such as the Assemblies of God, who were advocating conscientious objection. Official U. S. Government prosecution, in the form of enforcing military conscription laws, resulted in the incarceration of nineteen Pentecostal Christians with sentences ranging from three to twenty-five years.[96] The U. S. had no specific laws providing for absolute pacifism, but there was a provision for religious objector status. The U. S. Congress passed an Espionage and Sedition Act in 1917, violation of which was punishable with fines and up to twenty years in prison. Jay Beamon reports that Pentecostal objectors Clarence Waldron and William Reid were sent to prison, having been convicted of violating the law. He further recounted that only 20,873 men had been inducted who claimed noncombatant status. Thirteen hundred were accepted into noncombat assignments; 1,200 were sent to farm work; and 99 to a French Reconstruction Unit.[97] The Church of God, according to Charles W. Conn, resolved in 1917, "Against members going to war." However, many of its young men served in the military without any repercussions as the church began to modify its position.[98]

95. Frodsham, "Pentecostal Movement," 6.

96. Alexander, *Peace to War*, 75, 351. See also, Hollenweger, *Pentecostalism*, 187–90. Hollenweger, *Pentecostals*, 400–1.

97. Beaman, *Pentecostal Pacifism*, 101–2.

98. Conn, *Like a Mighty Army*, 172–74.

The European Pentecostal perspective on the war was quite conflicted. There were proponents of both pacifism and war which reflected the close proximity of the conflict to those who were directly affected. This was clearly indicated by the Assemblies of God in their weekly *Christian Evangel*, when E. N. Bell (1866–1923) published various letters and opinions from some of the European Pentecostal leadership on December 12, 1914. Some saw the Germans as bullies who needed punishment, while others opted for Christian pacifism in terms of loving their enemies.[99]

The dilemma of pacifism was faced by early Anabaptism with the onset of the Peasants' War and Balthasar Hubmaier's theology of Christian resistance. They opted to disregard Hubmaier's position and adhere to the perceived biblical principle of nonviolence. Compliance would have obligated them to the physical security of their residency. They would not bear arms or swear allegiance to the government. Early Pentecostalism struggled with the theology of pacifism as well in that it conflicted with the government's mandates regarding required military service. The American and European dilemma was concerned with how to remain loyal to the nation and obedient to the biblical principle of nonviolence. The solution that both Pentecostal movements arrived at was different, with the Americans opting for conscientious objector status and Anglican Pentecostals choosing to participate in a just war, while Anabaptists refused all participation in violence of any kind. What follows is a description of how this unfolded in the European and American Pentecostal movements respectively.

EUROPEAN PERSECUTION AND WORLD WAR I

On the European stage of early Pentecostalism, discrimination was evident, but never to the level of the American racial discrimination experience. The movement in Britain was prompted primarily by Alexander Boddy (1854–1930), an Anglican pastor at All Saints' Church in Sunderland.[100] His innate spirituality had been influenced by the Holiness Keswick convention which began in 1875, and the Welsh revival of 1904 and 1905. But it was the news of the American Azusa Street Pentecostal revival from William Seymour's *The Apostolic Faith* paper in 1906, and his attendance of Thomas Ball Barratt's (1862–1940) Norwegian Pentecostal

---

99. Bell, "Is European War Justifiable?" See also, Wilson, "Pacifism."
100. Anderson, *Spreading Fires*, 28–31.

revival in Oslo in March 1907, that convinced him and a cadre of All Saints' parishioners that the Pentecostal movement was what they had been spiritually seeking. Boddy invited Barratt, an Anglo-Norwegian, to preach in Sunderland in August 1907.[101] The success of the meetings was published nationwide and resulted in Boddy inaugurating the yearly Pentecostal Sunderland Convention (1908–1914) which drew European and other adherents from around the world, although the convention elicited criticism from other Pentecostals such as George Jeffereys (1889–1962), founder of the Elim Pentecostal Church, who saw the movement as an evangelistic effort and not the ecumenism of Anglican Christianity that Boddy envisioned. It did result in some unfriendliness from other Anglican clergymen, but Boddy never intended to establish another church. He remained true to his Anglicanism and was neither reprimanded nor discriminated against by the Church of England.[102] It should also be pointed out that records do not reflect racial discrimination, in the American sense, as a factor in the early British Pentecostal movement.

Barratt's exposure to the Azusa Street revival occurred while he was visiting New York. While there, he read the first edition of Seymour's *The Apostolic Faith*. He was filled with the Holy Spirit, spoke in tongues, and sailed back to Norway with several Azusa Street missionaries on their way to Africa. Once home he became a Pentecostal zealot who would influence Anna Larssen Bjorner (1875–1955), Petrus Lewi Pethrus (1884–1974), and Jonathan Paul (1853–1931), future leaders of Pentecostalism in Denmark, Sweden, and Germany respectively.[103] William Seymour's Azusa Street periodical, *The Apostolic Faith*, was replete with numerous testimonies of successful domestic and foreign evangelistic outreaches. For example, in the first two issues there are reports of conversions from disparate places outside of Los Angeles like Salem, Oregon, Central Africa, Danville, Virginia, Houston, Texas, and the California towns of Oakland, Monrovia, Pasadena, San Pedro, Sawtelle, and Whittier.[104] One

---

101. Boddy, *Vicar's Testimony*, loc. 252 of 449.

102. Kay, "Alexander Boddy and the Outpouring," 44–56. See also, Bundy, "Barratt, Thomas Ball"; Bundy, "Boddy, Alexander Alfred."

103. Anderson, *Spreading Fires*, 50–52. See also, Bundy, "Barratt, Thomas Ball"; Anderson, *Introduction to Pentecostalism*, 84–88; Hochen, "Bjorner, Anna Larssen"; Bundy, "Pethrus, Petrus Lewi."

104. Seymour, "Apostolic Faith Movement," 2.

report states that "eight missionaries have started to the foreign field since this movement began in Los Angeles a few months ago."[105]

The European Pentecostal movements, particularly those in England and Norway as noted above, were influenced by the exposure of Boddy and Barrett to the news of the Azusa Street revival. Their subsequent baptism in the Holy Spirit, with manifestations of speaking in tongues, was the catalyst for both becoming leading proponents of Pentecostalism in their respective nations. Both also became great evangelists for the movement throughout Europe and globally. Boddy would provide a link between various groups through his periodical *Confidence*, the Whitsuntide Conventions in Sunderland, and the Pentecostal Missionary Union founded by him and Cecil Polhill (1860–1938).[106] Boddy reported in his *Confidence* periodical in February 1909 that

> the Pentecostal Missionary Union has soon born fruit, for which we praise God indeed. Our two first Missionaries sail (D. V.) for India on February 24th. Miss Kathleen Miller, of Exeter, speaks Tamil and Bengali, and has previous Indian experience. Miss Lucy James has been a worker in the Pentecostal League, and goes to Mukti to work with Pandita Ramabai.[107]

Boddy counseled those seeking the baptism in the Holy Spirit, with the evidence of speaking in tongues, to pray, "Lord it is my heart's desire to be useful to Thee in thy Kingdom on this earth. I cannot be an effective witness without the power from on high."[108]

Barratt's Norwegian Pentecostal work influenced many leaders of Western European Pentecostal movements, including those of Sweden, Denmark, England, Germany, Poland, Estonia, Iceland, and Finland.[109] He traveled extensively throughout Scandinavia and Western Europe, conducting evangelistic meetings and preaching at Pentecostal conferences. He wrote regularly for his periodical, *Byposten,* which he renamed *Korsets Seir* (The Victory of the Cross) in 1910.[110] Barratt had previously visited India and the Pentecostal work of Pandita Ramabai in Mukti, as well as Palestine in 1908. After his return to Norway, he founded "Nor-

---

105. Seymour, "Apostolic Faith Movement," 2.
106. Hollenweger, *Pentecostalism*, 343–45.
107. Boddy, "Brief Items," 38.
108. Boddy, *Pleading the Blood*, loc. 133 of 203.
109. Bundy, "Barratt, Thomas Ball." See also, Barratt, *When the Fire Fell*, 139–44.
110. Barratt, *When the Fire Fell*, 129–136, 39.

way's Free Evangelical Mission to the Heathen" and sent two missionaries to India with funds raised through the *Korsets Seir*.

CONCLUSION

There are many similarities between the praxes and experiences of early sixteenth-century Anabaptism and early Pentecostalism. For both, the primary catalysts were the Lutheran and Zwinglian ideas of *sola fide, sola scriptura*, the priesthood of the believer, and the acceptance of Pauline pneumatology; all of which encouraged evangelism, persecution, and pacifism. The belief in the imminence of the second coming of Christ stressed the pursuant exigency of bringing the gospel to an unsaved world. This in turn stimulated continuation of the existing Reformation practice of conventicles for prayer, worship, and Bible study, and preaching. It was in these types of meetings that the Anabaptists and Pentecostals alike manifested the gifts of the Spirit according to 1 Corinthians 12–14. They believed that every Christian was filled with the Holy Spirit, and therefore each one was empowered to exercise all the duties and requirements of a Roman Catholic priest including interpreting Scripture. This encouraged them to interpret the Bible with spiritual-prophetic literality and act it out as described, particularly in Pauline terms of spirituality, love, peace, and evangelistic work as commanded by the Gospels. The heightened public exposure caused by public preaching precipitated increasing persecution of early Anabaptists by Catholics, Lutherans, and Zwinglian reformers. The same can be said for the persecution suffered by early Pentecostals from denominational protestants, as well as federal, state, and local governments. This resulted in discrimination, incarceration, loss of property, and ostracism, but rarely martyrdom. A palpable spiritual freedom ensued when Anabaptists embraced the priesthood of the believer doctrine. Pentecostal rejection of the higher criticism hermeneutic brought them to a more literal biblical hermeneutic, much like the Anabaptists. Both saw this way of reading Scripture as conducive to the restitution of the New Testament primitive church. It also inspired them to act it out as described, particularly in Pauline terms of spirituality, love, peace, and evangelistic work as commanded in the Gospels. The separation of church and state was a commonly accepted governmental principal in Western Europe and North America in 1906, at least in theory. Among the early sixteenth-century Anabaptists it had become an unnegotiable principle called the free church. This particular tenet of their respective confessions of faith instituted similar interpretations of biblical teachings on nonviolence. For both, if the state and church remained connected, safety and security were every citizen's sworn duty. The Anabaptists faced this dilemma during the Peasants' War, and for Pentecostals it was World War I; both opted for pacifism. Finally, a major disadvantage to the new hermeneutics unfortunately resulted in the emergence of an embarrassment of sects and divisions within both movements.

It can be concluded that both early Anabaptism and early Pentecostalism demonstrated similar biblical interpretations of Corinthians 12–14 and put them into literal praxis. They considered evangelism to be critical to the restitution of the primitive church, suffered persecution, and had to resolve the problem of pacifism. Chapter five will discuss the development of these spiritual and theological concepts in more specific detail and provide an analytical comparison using Pilgram Marpeck as a primary example of an early Anabaptist approach similar to that of early Pentecostalism.

Chapter 5

Pilgram Marpeck and Early Pentecostalism

THE HISTORICAL DEVELOPMENT OF early Pentecostalism was similar to that of early sixteenth-century Anabaptism in that both emerged in comparable religious, social, and cultural circumstances. There was a proliferation of theological exploration by a plethora of radical groups and constituents who were seeking the restitution of the New Testament primitive church. The search was primarily reduced to the recurring theme of the importance that Scripture placed on the work and role of the Holy Spirit in the first-century church. A review of contemporary literature regarding this quest revealed that in some cases it produced an overemphasis on the role of the Holy Spirit by some, or an overemphasis on the legal aspects of Christian piety in others. It also included many heretical and heterodox ideas such as psychopannychism (soul sleep), the salvation of Satan, and anti-Trinitarianism. A disconcerting number of apocalypticists appeared as well, including Thomas Müntzer and Melchior Hoffmann.

Stanley Burgess nominated Müntzer as "one of the leading revolutionary Spiritualists" as an example of those who inclined toward a Pentecostal-like pneumatology.[1] But closer examination reveals that it was Pilgram Marpeck who attempted to develop some common ground through the morass of theological viewpoints. His middle road to the restitution of the primitive church incorporated a comparable Pauline Pentecostal-like pneumatology as being essential to a normative Christian confession.

1. Burgess, *Roman Catholic and Reformation Traditions*, 201-9.

Chapter five will argue that early Anabaptism, within the context of Pilgram Marpeck's spirituality and theology, interpreted Pauline pneumatology, particularly 1 Corinthians 12–14, as being the foundation for the restitution of the primitive New Testament church. It will confirm that 500 years later, early Pentecostalism, using the same Scriptures, interpreted in the same way, developed into a similar pneumatological movement in belief and praxis. A comparative analysis will establish that both radical confessions included parallel theological insights and opinions, based on comparable hermeneutical praxes and spiritual experiences. Essentially the argument will clarify that early Pentecostalism was not derivative of early Anabaptism, but that the spiritual truth of Paul's writings was found to be equivalent, providing a historical common denominator. The result was that both were scripturally Pauline in nature, resulting in similar Pentecostal consequences. The initial development of Anabaptism will be explained in three sections: the definition, identification, and analysis of the advent of Anabaptism and the appearance of the spiritualists; the importance of sixteenth-century Strasbourg to the progress of Anabaptist growth and development, the result of which will identify those praxes and beliefs that were similar to early Pentecostalism; and Anabaptist unification attempts in the face of growing sectarianism. This will be accomplished within the context of the life and work of Pilgram Marpeck.

Marpeck was one of very few Anabaptists who wrote prolifically regarding the critical importance of getting the theology and pneumatology biblically correct. Alister McGrath has accurately identified Marpeck as one of three of the most significant theologians in the Anabaptist movement, including Balthasar Hubmaier and Menno Simons, both of whom were trained and educated Catholic priests, while Marpeck was a layman, a mining engineer, and civil servant.[2] His life and work also serves to validate the magisterial Reformation's initial concept of the priesthood of the believer. Menno Simons would first appear after the collapse of

---

2. McGrath, *Reformation Thought*, 10. The first recovery of Marpeck Circle writings was not until 1860. However, in 1950 a codex identified as the *Kunstbuch*, or "book of understanding," a collection of the unidentified Anabaptist writings, was found, having been in a catalogue of the Burgerbibliothek in Bern, Switzerland since 1697. But it wasn't until 1956 that Heinhold Fast and J. F. G. Goeters found the same codex again and published it as the work of the Marpeck Circle that the importance of Marpeck became a growing reality in Anabaptist life and studies. Rempel, *Jorg Maler's Kunstbuch*, 4–5. See also, Klaassen, *Marpeck*, 23–24, 34.

the Münster Apocalyptic experiment of 1534 and 1535, and ultimately rescue Anabaptism from extinction.³

A comparison of the beliefs of both early Pentecostalism and early Anabaptism regarding biblical hermeneutics, the priesthood of the believer, Pauline pneumatology, pacifism, a commemorative Eucharist, the necessity of the restitution of the primitive New Testament church, rejection of Protestantism and Catholicism, and acceptance of traditional Christian orthodoxy, which eventually would enable both to obtain a position of legitimacy in the broader Christian context, will establish that early Anabaptism and early Pentecostalism shared a common spirituality and theology.⁴

ANABAPTISM AND SPIRITUALISM

Spiritualists were those who acted within the newly found freedom of a religious reformation in progress, having been persuaded by Luther's initial mystical inclinations and Zwingli's early proclivity toward humanism. They chose to reject Catholicism, Protestantism, and rapidly growing Anabaptism, which featured adult baptism as the primary tenet of their Christian confession. The difficulty in distinguishing between the spiritualists and the Anabaptists is *prima facie* evidence of the superficiality placed by some Lutheran leaders on the many similarities between their beliefs, without consideration of the many differences in their respective hermeneutics.⁵

Defining spiritualism is incumbent upon an understanding of the broader Reformation dispute over the prioritization of word and Spirit. Luther's initial encounter with the charismatic Zwickau prophets in Wittenberg inspired him to clearly declare that the word had precedence over the Spirit. For him, Scripture interpreted Scripture, but no one could interpret Scripture with his own reason. He said, "The Holy Spirit Himself must expound Scripture."⁶

3. Simons, *Complete Writings of Menno Simons*, 28–29.

4. Brumback, *Suddenly from Heaven*, 130–31. Hubmaier, "Christian Catechism, 1526," 340–65; Hubmaier, "Eine Christliche Lehrtafel, 1526," 305–26; Sanders, *William Seymour Papers*, 130–31; Snyder, *Anabaptist History and Theology*, 84–85; Gohr, "Historical Development of the Statement." Warrington, *Pentecostal Theology*, 29.

5. Stayer, "Radical Reformation," 259.

6. Luther, "Catholic Epistles," 166. See also, Luther, *Schmalkald Articles, 1537*, 29–30.

A critical variable in the foundation of Zwingli's hermeneutics was also the role of the Spirit in interpretation of the word. Zwingli believed he had been personally led by the Spirit to learn the doctrine of God directly from God's word. As he began to teach this theory he wrote in *Of the Clarity and Certainty or Power of the Word of God* that

> God can never be learned with greater certainty than when it is taught by God himself, for it comes from God, and he alone is truthful, indeed, he is truth itself. We do not need human interpreters, but his anointing, which is the Spirit, teaches us of all things-all things, notice-and therefore it is truth and is no lie.[7]

They both seemed to be saying the same thing about the role of the Holy Spirit, but the priority would be a major point of disagreement. Unlike Luther, Zwingli declared the Spirit to be first in priority relative to Scripture, for without the Spirit, human intelligence misunderstands the word. It is beyond human capacity to bring others to faith, for that is the purview of God alone. However, he says, according to St. Paul, "Faith comes from what is heard, and what is heard comes by the preaching of Christ" (Rom. 10:17), understood as the word. This did not mean that preaching the external word could accomplish much without the internal working of the Spirit. The Spirit and word are not exclusive, but inclusive, a variation on Luther's theme that the Spirit cannot be present without the word. For Zwingli it is the combination of the two that

> show conclusively that God's Word can be understood by a man without any human direction: not that this is due to man's own understanding, but to the light and Spirit of God, illuminating and inspiring the words in such a way that the light of divine content is seen in his own light.[8]

Here, Luther and Zwingli agreed that it is God who makes the word effective, but there is a sense of unity between the word and the Spirit which makes this possible. Zwingli addresses the practical aspects of applying the process of interpreting the word with the following methodology:

> Before I say anything or listen to the teaching of man, I will first consult the mind of the Spirit of God, (Psalm 84 (AV 85)): Then you should reverently ask God for His grace, that he may give

---

7. Zwingli, "Clarity and Certainty," 17.
8. Zwingli, "Clarity and Certainty," 17–18.

you his mind and Spirit, so that you will not lay hold of your own opinion but of his. And then go to the written word of the Gospel. You must be *theodidacti* that is of God, not of men that is what the truth itself said (John 6), and it cannot lie.[9]

This was the theological milieu, regarding word and Spirit, within which radicalism, particularly Anabaptism, emerged. For the radical spiritualists, only the Holy Spirit was necessary for faith, in that all Christians were filled with the Spirit. External rites, ceremonies, rituals, and even the Bible, were no longer needed by Spirit-filled Christians.

CATEGORIZING RADICAL REFORMERS

The appearance of so many radical sectarian movements, including the Anabaptists, demanded a detailed historical description and explanation of the religious situation. It was George H. Williams who coined the term "Radical Reformation," and attempted to give some order and clarity to the complicated nature of the radical sectarianism by identifying three principal groups, the Anabaptists, the spiritualists, and the Evangelical Rationalists. This not only helps to ascertain the various groups that manifested aspects of Pentecostalism, but separates those out who exceeded the bounds of traditional Christian orthodoxy. Williams's opus is a recognized scholarly work accepted by most Reformation historians, with some reservations, as an innovative and clarifying classification of the Radical movement.[10] Williams's *The Radical Reformation*, for that reason, is a valuable work for the comprehensive identification of the Pentecostal aspects of the Reformation's various radical movements.

Williams categorized the Evangelical Rationalists as those who recognized the place of natural piety and reason, both speculative and intuitive, alongside the Scripture. They are the originators of Unitarianism and Socianism as a distinct part of the Radical Reformation. But they also came to embrace anti-Trinitarianism. Representatives of this group are former Calvinist adherents Michael Servetus (1509–1553), who was martyred in Geneva under the auspices of John Calvin (1509–1564); Fausto Sozzini (1539–1604), founder of Socianism; Bernardio Ochino

---

9. Zwingli, "Clarity and Certainty," 18.

10. Hillerbrand, *Reformation*, 294; Snyder, *Anabaptist History and Theology*, 400; Yoder, *Anabaptism and Reformation in Switzerland*, xxix–xxxiii; Williams, *Radical Reformation*, xxviii–xxxiv; Stayer, *Anabaptists and the Sword*, 17–18.

(1487–1564); and Sebastian Castellio (1515–1563).[11] This group, although many of them had limited interaction with Anabaptists and spiritualists, were generally rejected for their lack of traditional Christian orthodoxy by both, therefore they will not be the primary focus in this study.

Williams characterized the Anabaptists as more orthodox in the traditional sense, looking to the past and using the Bible and the historical martyr church as a model. The spiritualists, perhaps more heterodox, focused on the future of the church, which they believed either had not yet been reestablished by revolution after the Constantinian fall of the church, or, suspending all human effort, sought comfort with the fellowship of the invisible church of the Spirit awaiting the parousia.[12] Their protests against Catholicism, Lutheranism, and Zwinglian reform Protestantism reflected a perspective of the *corpus christianum*, the institution of Christianity versus the *Corpus Christi*, the body of Christ, not unlike Paul's *ecclesia*.[13] This was derived from their acceptance of the initial Lutheran and Zwinglian theologies of *sola scriptura*, the Petrine priesthood of the believer, and Pauline pneumatology. It was also indicative of their belief in the critical nature of personal confession regarding baptisms, both in water and Spirit. Here, Williams began to set Anabaptism apart in a way that tends to identify it as falling within the same spiritual "family" with early twentieth-century Pentecostalism.

He devised three divisions each within Anabaptism and spiritualism. The Anabaptists were divided into Evangelicals, Revolutionaries, and Contemplatives. Evangelicals considered the New Testament normative for doctrine, polity, and ethics. The Old Testament was interpreted allegorically or typologically. They were pacifists, and practiced banning and shunning as church discipline which distinguished them from the Revolutionaries and Contemplatives. He stated that they eventually became sceptical of Spirit possession and prophecy, which he described as charismatic vagaries. Normative Christianity was for them strict adherence to the teachings of Christ and an imitation of his life, including discipleship, evangelism, and in the case of the Hutterites, communitarianism. The gospel became new law which hardened into legalism.[14] Ex-

11. Williams, *Spiritual and Anabaptist Writers*, 24–25. See also, Williams, *Radical Reformation*, 829, 959, Ochino and Castellio respectively.

12. Williams, *Spiritual and Anabaptist Writers*, 22–23.

13. Williams, *Spiritual and Anabaptist Writers*, 25.

14. Williams, *Spiritual and Anabaptist Writers*, 30–31.

amples of evangelical Anabaptist leaders are Jacob Hutter (1500?–1536) and Ulrich Stadler (d. 1540) of the Hutterites; Georg Blaurock; Conrad Grebel; Michael Sattler; Balthasar Hubmaier; Dirk Philips (1504–1568); and Menno Simons (1496–1561) of the Swiss Brethren.

Revolutionary Anabaptists believed, as did all Anabaptists, in the restitution of the apostolic church, but also considered both testaments to be normative for theology and ecclesiology. They even embraced the idea that the church was meant to restore God's Israel and instituted Old Testament tenets of regulation when establishing their fierce and polygamous theocracy, the New Jerusalem, in Münster (1534–35). Lead by Melchior Hoffman (1495–1543), its first prophet, the Melchiorites interpreted the Old Testament as containing types of the restored church of the Spirit. Williams asserts that they might also be called charismatic in that Spirit possession was a visible characteristic of its various leaders particularly the manifestation of the gift of prophecy.[15]

Williams called the third division—those who were closest to some of the spiritualists, but farthest from the Revolutionary Anabaptists—Contemplatives. Represented by Hans Denck (1500–1527), Louis Haetzer (1500–1529), and Adam Pastor (1510–1552), they are called contemplatives to highlight their emphasis on the inner working of the Spirit as opposed to the outer working of the word.[16] This group is also indicative of the difficult nature of trying to separate Anabaptism into distinctive categories. They were variously in and out of Anabaptist circles over their lifetimes, but ultimately stood alone in contemplative Christianity writ large.

Moving to the divisions of the spiritualists, Williams divided them into three similar groups as well: Revolutionary, Evangelical, and Rational. The Spirit was central to their life and thought, the source of their authority, the cohesive power of Christianity, the inspiration of whom was superior to the record of the work of the Spirit, whether biblical or traditional.[17]

Revolutionary, or charismatic, spiritualists experienced the Spirit as a driving power exemplified by the Zwickau Prophets, and Luther's *Schwärmer*, Müntzer and Karlstadt, as noted in chapter one. Williams used the term "charismatic" here much in the way he referred to the

15. Williams, *Spiritual and Anabaptist Writers*, 29.

16. Williams, *Spiritual and Anabaptist Writers*, 30, 86–87. See also, Furcha, *Hans Denk*, 8–9.

17. Williams, *Spiritual and Anabaptist Writers*, 31–32.

manifestations of the gifts of the Spirit by the Anabaptists of St. Gallen as Pentecostal vagaries in chapter four. The Spirit defined the word, particularly in Daniel and Revelation, juxtaposed against Luther's position of the word defining the Spirit. These examples all encouraged the manifestation of the gifts of the Spirit (Charismata) according to Paul in 1 Corinthians 12–14.[18] Each met Williams's criteria of revolutionary spiritualists in that, although they were not Anabaptists per se, they embraced anti-pedobaptism, but without insisting on adult baptism. For Müntzer, the primacy of inner baptism in the sense of martyrdom "of the cross of the bitter Christ," was paramount, thus connecting him to the Evangelical Anabaptists whom he influenced.[19] Müntzer was convinced that a theocratic kingdom of God could only be established after the physical defeat of the "ungodly" based on the prophetic and apocalyptic sources of his inspiration. Although this tends to identify him with the Melchiorite Anabaptists of Münster, at times a biblical literalist, he would prophetically read Scripture as the confirmation of his compulsive inspiration of the Spirit and not as the source of faith,[20] much like the perspective of Contemplative Anabaptist Hans Denck, whom he also influenced. However, like Evangelical spiritualist Schwenckfeld, he believed that the "Spirit speaks to man through a living prophet, the inner Christ, the preexistent Christ, the Word of God, the gospel of Christ, the Scriptures, and even the law."[21] All of which is indicative of the influence of the medieval mysticism of Johannes Tauler, the *Theologia Germanica*, the Hussites, and Joachim de Fiore (1130–1202), but very unlike the Evangelical Anabaptists.[22] Finally, Williams opines that Müntzer replaced Luther's *sola fide* with a doctrine of the experienced cross, "the bitter Christ."[23] This rejection of Luther's forensic justification, *iustificatus sola fide*, demanded the personal and progressive sanctification of every Christian. Thus Müntzer and the Revolutionary spiritualists in general were in effect "thrice born" in Williams's estimation, moving to a sanctification of society under the power of the Holy Spirit, identified as the preexistent Christ of the

---

18. For the relationship between the Zwickau prophets and Müntzer and the manifestation of the charismata, see chapter one.

19. Williams, *Spiritual and Anabaptist Writers*, 32., Spiritual and Anabaptist Writers

20. Matheson, *Collected Works of Thomas Müntzer*, 192, 99, 358–59.

21. Williams, *Spiritual and Anabaptist Writers*, 32.

22. Williams, *Spiritual and Anabaptist Writers*, 32.

23. Williams, *Spiritual and Anabaptist Writers*, 33.

Old Testament.[24] Rational spiritualism, or speculative spiritualism, was grounded more on the *spiritus humanus* than the *Spiritus sanctus*, and emphasized the universal aspects of Christianity including contemplation of the order of nature. Paracelsus (1493–1541) and Valentine Weigel (1533–1588) exemplify this category in that they both allegorized Scripture into a cosmic philosophy, mystically contemplating the celestial flesh of Christ, and "delights in the correspondences between the microcosm and the macrocosm."[25] Sebastian Franck (1499–1542), another example, stressed the seminal reason common to all men as revealed in history and contemporary society. Rational spiritualists tended to dissolve churches from within and allegorize doctrines and praxes of apostolic Christianity given that the "true church" was a fellowship of likeminded people in all ages who, like them, believed that behind fluctuating theologies is a common sense of piety and vision of the divine.[26] There was no impulse to create communities that would pass from church history into general intellectual history the moment its position was completely clarified.[27]

Evangelical spiritualism, according to Williams, is the most important of the three categories of spiritualism discussed so far. He described it as being more biblical, implying that it was influenced by a literal reading of the Gospel of John and the Epistles. It was like Rational spiritualism, but more mystical than speculative. It was based on biblical grace as understood traditionally, but with the strength to create fellowships. It stressed piety, not intellectualism, but based on the Holy Spirit as experienced and defined in patristic and medieval Christianity. Also characteristic was a "physico-realist" sense of deification through the restorative and healing power of the Holy Spirit. Although acknowledging the divine initiative in the process, according to them, sanctification and perfectionism were the goals and achievement of Christian life. Caspar Schwenckfeld and Gabriel Ascherham (d. 1545) were good examples of Evangelical spiritualists.[28]

This concludes the synopsis of Williams's categorization of Radical Reformation groups. His characterization of Anabaptism, with its ability to assimilate theological and spiritual principles, even from those groups

---

24. Williams, *Spiritual and Anabaptist Writers*, 33.
25. Williams, *Spiritual and Anabaptist Writers*, 33.
26. Williams, *Spiritual and Anabaptist Writers*, 34.
27. Williams, *Spiritual and Anabaptist Writers*, 34.
28. Williams, *Spiritual and Anabaptist Writers*, 34.

that were moving away from *sola scriptura,* tends to place it within the variegated Pentecostal family. The restitution of the apostolic church, *sola scriptura,* a Pauline *ecclesia,* a personal salvation/conversion experience, the Petrine doctrine of the priesthood of the believer, restoration of the manifestation of the charismata, including glossolalia and prophecy, evangelism, and the imminent second coming of Christ, are all tenets that early Pentecostalism embraced.

However, there are those who have attempted to fine-tune his work with moderate success, notwithstanding their continued acceptance of his prodigious and encyclopaedic accomplishment. C. Arnold Snyder observed that Williams's methodology in categorizing radicalism in all three categories was based on the development of theological and spiritual ideas, but paid little attention to social, political, and economic factors that were behind the emergence of the ideas. On occasion, historical circumstances in different locales became more or less significant depending on their respective locations than typological similarities or dissimilarities. Thus, Williams's typological approach, typologies being static, did not foster close attention to the catalysts of the ideas within the movement, therefore making developmental description difficult.[29] Snyder is right in that many theological and spiritual ideas crossover within his categories, an indication of this phenomenon.

Geoffery Dipple observed that Williams's spiritualist Anabaptists included Denck, Hätzer, Jacob Kautz, Johann Bünderline (1498–1533), and Christian Entfelder, but also Adam Pastor and Gabriel Ascherham. But he considered spiritualist Anabaptism as a recurring phenomenon in the Radical Reformation. Likewise, Dipple stated that Snyder treats them as a widespread and integral part of the movement in its initial development. He identifies the complexity of the situation as one of definition, both of spiritualism and Anabaptism, and its sustainability as distinct typologies. The issue of the initial comingling of groups and ideas prohibits anything but a general definition of both in order to facilitate any clear understanding. He points out that Walter Klaassen denied the implicit claims that spiritualism was the polar opposite of the biblical literalism of Anabaptism, and preferred instead to speak of degrees of spiritualization: "This makes the Spiritualist Anabaptists a much more common, and

---

29. Snyder, *Anabaptist History and Theology,* 402.

much more influential, occurrence."[30] Dipple concludes, however, that "what the term gains in significance, it loses in clarity and coherence."[31]

James Stayer observed that Williams had used Roland Bainton's descriptive idea, "the left wing of the Reformation," to categorize the protagonists. Bainton had proposed that the line of demarcation was the separation of church and state and the rejection of the civil arm of the church from a Catholic perspective, thus the left wing. But Williams objected to the highly political connotation of the term and opted for "Radical Reformation." Yet, Stayer continues, "he covertly used the same line of division as Bainton, when he set the term Radical over against a Magisterial Reformation." According to Stayer, Williams suggested that sanctification as opposed to justification, restitution as opposed to reformation, expression of the universal priesthood through missions and martyrdom rather than work through one's calling, the practice of rebaptism, reordination, and the belief in soul sleep prior to final resurrection, were universal, when in fact they were not.[32]

R. Emmet McLaughlin said of Reformation spiritualism:[33]

> The tendency to oppose and privilege the spiritual against the material, the soul against the body, the internal against the external, the invisible against the visible, and the direct against the mediated, at its root is a dualism that refuses to credit the material, the physical, and the external with any role in conveying the spirit, illuminating the mind, or transforming the soul. Rather it prefers to see that transfer, illumination, or transformation as unmediated, from spirit to spirit, from spirit to mind, and from spirit to soul. Spiritualism normally defines itself, at least implicitly, in opposition to "Materialism."[34]

McLaughlin's definition of materialism assumes that the physical was no obstacle to the working and presence of the Holy Spirit, thus granting a role for the Bible, baptism, the Mass, and other religious rites and ceremonies that inspire or transform the inner man. "In practice, material Christianity was the default spirituality for the vast majority of Christians throughout Antiquity and the Middle Ages."[35]

30. Dipple, "Spiritualist Anabaptists," 259.
31. Dipple, "Spiritualist Anabaptists," 257–60.
32. Stayer, *Anabaptists and the Sword*, 18.
33. Roth, "Marpeck and the Later Swiss," xix.
34. McLaughlin, "Reformation Spiritualism," 124.
35. McLaughlin, "Reformation Spiritualism," 124–25.

In spite of Williams's attempt to classify the largest groups as Anabaptists of various types, it is not very helpful in distinguishing them from each other, particularly when juxtaposed against meticulous sociological studies of the groups. He admits that "the nature of spiritualism has emerged from our narrative and analysis as variegated and complex."[36] Clasen has stated that from 1531 to 1588, various contemporary writers had identified approximately forty-two different groups of Anabaptists, some of whom constituted non-Anabaptist radicals such as the spiritualists and Evangelical Rationalists.[37] Stuart Murray, on the other hand, identifies probably a more valid list of Anabaptist groups based on their viability as a movement and their longevity: the Swiss Brethren, the Moravian Hutterites, the South German/Austrian Marpeckans, and the Dutch Mennonites, who would coalesce as a viable group after the Münster debacle of 1534 and 1535.[38]

The above-described plethora of pneumatic theologies and praxes held by various groups and persons, at various times and places initiated by the Lutheran and Zwinglian concepts of *sola scriptura*, the priesthood of the believer, and Pauline pneumatology, convinced radical Christians that they in fact were empowered by the Holy Spirit to read and interpret Scripture. This contributed significantly to an anti-clerical, anti-intellectual, and subsequently pro-laity radicalism.[39] A biblicist literalism emerged as all were now allowed to participate in their own salvation, because that is what the word said, "But when He, the Spirit of truth, comes, he will guide you into all truth."[40]

Thus was the radical religious landscape as made possible by the initial Lutheran and Zwinglian theologies of reformation, with each group convinced of the validity of their respective hermeneutic. Believer priests, now led by the Spirit, sought the asylums of political peace that would provide them the safety to practice and propagate their particular confessions of faith.

---

36. Williams, *Radical Reformation*, 2298.
37. Clasen, *Anabaptism*, 30–36.
38. Murray, "Biblical Interpretation," 404.
39. Goertz, *Anabaptists*, 66–67.
40. Stayer, "Radical Reformation," 255. See also, John 16:13.

STRASBOURG 1525–1545

As pointed out in chapter four, Strasbourg was a free Imperial City and thus able to govern itself under certain parameters allowed by the Holy Roman Empire. Therefore Martin Bucer, Wolfgang Capito, and Caspar Hedio (1494–1552) were able to initiate a Lutheran Reformation movement that initially tolerated various radical reformers within the city from 1525 to 1533. The toleration was based on seemingly common beliefs, primarily concerning anti-clericalism, the Eucharist, and *sola scriptura*.

The inability of the Strasbourg reformers to distinguish between Anabaptists and spiritualists began in 1525, as persecuted masses of radicals started to appear in the city in increasing numbers, each with a definite ecclesiology that sought the restitution of the primitive apostolic church. Although an untenable situation for Strasbourg's Lutheran reformers, for the Anabaptists it was a time of sorting out the various theologies of a myriad of Radical Reformation elements. William Klassen has called it the "Purification of Anabaptism."[41] Deppermann and Yoder have referred to it as a "time of crystallization."[42] For Reformation Radicalism, this was a time and opportunity of clarification and separation. The Swiss Brethren, emanating from Zurich, made up a majority of the Anabaptists present in Strasbourg at the time.[43] Some, while agreeing specifically with adult baptism and anti-pedobaptism, didn't actually participate by being rebaptized and therefore were not considered Anabaptists by the Swiss Brethren, men such as Karlstadt and indigenous radicals Clement Ziegler and Hans Wolff.[44] Yet other radical adherents opposed the Anabaptists as legalists, not unlike the dogmatic Catholics, Lutherans, Zwinglians, Marpeckan biblical literalists, as well as other radical spiritualists, who understood the workings of the Holy Spirit differently. This group falls into Williams's category of spiritualists as described above.

However, what developed was intolerance for the highly spiritualistic tendencies of the predominant group of radicals whom they identified generically as the "Anabaptists."[45] But the reality of the matter proved

---

41. Klassen, *Covenant and Community*, 25. Also see chapter four for Clasen's study of Anabaptist groups.

42. Snyder, *Life and Thought*, 92.

43. Clasen, "Anabptist Sects," 259–60; Musing, "Anabaptist Movement in Strasbourg," 91.

44. Snyder, *Anabaptist History and Theology*, 130–32.

45. Davis, *Anabaptism and Asceticism*, 19.

conversely to be the existence of many individuals and groups of spiritualists, as defined above, with whom the Anabaptists, as also defined above, not only disagreed with, but engaged in ongoing, complicated, and protracted theological disputes, both oral and written. The Strasbourg reformers were unable to make any clear delineation among the disputants.[46] The resolution of the problem eventually came in 1533, when Bucer was able to persuade the city council to adopt a dogmatic church order and catechism that precluded the Anabaptists and by default the spiritualists, which officially made Strasbourg a Lutheran Reformed city. Although disagreeing with the Lutheran eucharistic element of the Augsburg Confession of 1530, approved by Charles V, Bucer concurred with articles 8 and 9 and their condemnation of the Anabaptists which, for him, perhaps unwittingly, included the spiritualists.[47]

What emerges from this analysis of radical reformers active in Strasbourg beginning in 1525 is actually three groups (excluding Williams's Evangelical Rationalists); spiritualists, Anabaptists, and spiritualist Anabaptists.[48] Although none of the three can be said to consist of specifically defined and exclusive confessions, each did embrace a highly developed sense of pneumatology, the critical nature of the meaning, purpose, and value of the Holy Spirit to a Pauline *ecclesia*.[49] But it was the spiritualist Anabaptists (biblicists,[50] or biblical literalists[51]) who were most like early twentieth-century Pentecostals. They were biblical literalists, but only in the sense of Pauline pneumatology, wherein the leading of the Spirit was critical to living a Christian life.[52] Biblical concordances were circulated in manuscript form from 1529 to 1540, and eventually published by the Swiss Brethren. They were adopted and used by Anabaptists without any commentary, which was indicative of their disdain for intellectualism, in that Scripture interpreted Scripture with only the aid of the Holy Spirit, as Luther and Zwingli had initially taught. The Spirit enabled all Christians who could read could interpret the Bible

---

46. Musing, "Anabaptist Movement in Strasbourg," 106.

47. Greschat, "Bucer, Martin," 1:221–24; Kittelson, "Strasbourg," 4:115–18; Williams, *Spiritual and Anabaptist Writers*, 20–21; Kolb, "Augsburg Confession, 1530," 42–43.

48. Dipple, "Spiritualist Anabaptists," 259–60.

49. 1 Cor 14:1–4 (NIV).

50. Williams, *Radical Reformation*, 1255–60.

51. Stayer, "Radical Reformation," 255.

52. Snyder, *Biblical Concordance*, 14–16.

as believer priests. Moreover, Scripture interpreted Scripture. The Swiss Brethren commentary could be referred to as a biblical "rule of life" that provided central guidance for Anabaptist spirituality.[53]

MARPECK AND THE REFORMATION

The trauma visited on the Imperial authorities and the church, both Catholic and Protestant, by the Peasants' War and other radical religious protests resulted in the issuance of Imperial mandates criminalizing Anabaptists as heretics, which caused the martyrdom of thousands. What also followed was the emigration of these radical and Anabaptist refugees seeking asylum and safety within the free cities of the empire, such as Strasbourg. Moravia, ruled by the House of Habsburg, was also a tolerant religious safe haven.[54] The centralization of these radical groups, particularly in Strasbourg and Moravia, created an opportunity for them to define, develop, and refine their respective theological and spiritual confessions with unification as the objective. An analysis of this developmental period will identify with some specificity those spiritual and theological praxes that were held in common between early sixteenth-century Anabaptism and early twentieth-century Pentecostalism.

Before Pilgram Marpeck, an Austrian Tyrolean who was to become the leader of South German and Austrian Anabaptism, arrived in Strasbourg in October 1528, the city had already undergone a series of disruptive radical and spiritualistic religious incidents. Karlstadt had been there in October 1524, about the same time his anti-Lutheran eucharistic writings reached the city, causing great concern among the Lutheran preachers. This prompted a letter from them, probably under Bucer's leadership, to Luther, who denied Karlstadt's eucharistic theology. Zwingli, however, had given Karlstadt a more positive hearing.[55] The influence that Karlstadt may have had on Anabaptism has been discussed earlier.[56] Karlstadt teamed with Clement Ziegler, the indigenous Strasbourg citizen (mentioned above) who preached positions not unlike those Karlstadt espoused in Wittenberg and Orlamünde, such as iconoclasm, a commemorative Eucharist, and anti-pedobaptism. Ziegler,

---

53. Snyder, *Biblical Concordance*, viii–ix, xviii.
54. Klassen, "Moravia," 24–25.
55. Luther, "Letter to the Christians," 63, 65–71.
56. See also, Boyd, *Pilgram Marpeck*, 48.

described by Williams as a rational evangelical spiritualist, also stressed the priesthood of believers, and the direct leading of the Holy Spirit.[57] However, he brought into doubt the "fully God fully man" theology of traditional orthodoxy, much like Schwenckfeld and Hoffman, speaking instead of the "celestial flesh of Christ."[58]

Another radical of note was Hans Wölff from Benfeld, who was brought before the city council in May of 1526 for his teachings of pacifism, absolute obedience to Scripture, the separation of church and state, anti-pedobaptism, and the lack of piety. He implied the failure of Lutheranism to bring about an inner obedience to Scripture, a position very much like the observations of Luther's *Schwärmer*, particularly Schwenckfeld. Hans-Werner Musing declares that Wölff's ideas were reminiscent of ancient Montanism, where he believed in the immediate possession of the Holy Spirit and prophesied the end of the world on "Ascension Day at twelve o'clock,"[59] the sum of which precluded both his and Ziegler's identification as Swiss Brethren. Wölff was eventually arrested and banished from the city after interrupting a sermon being preached by Matthew Zell (1477–1548), the cathedral preacher in 1526.

In September 1526, Capito wrote to Zwingli confirming the presence of Anabaptists in the city and declared the movement to be dying out, most likely based on the declining influence of Wölff. By the end of the year, however, Wilhelm Reublin, who had baptized Balthasar Hubmaier in Waldshut, came to Strasbourg and assumed the leadership of the Swiss Brethren present in the city. Pilgram Marpeck would associate himself with Reublin and the Swiss Brethren upon his arrival in 1528.[60] Hans Denck, who, as Rector at St. Sebald School in Nürnberg, was banished from there in 1525 for his Anabaptist leanings, appeared in Strasbourg in 1526.[61] Michael Sattler, mentioned among others above, had arrived and contributed to the problems the Lutheran reformers had in deciphering the confusing issue of who exactly was an Anabaptist.[62]

---

57. Williams, *Radical Reformation*, 1250.
58. Williams, *Radical Reformation*, 490–93.
59. Musing, "Anabaptist Movement in Strasbourg," 93–96.
60. Klaassen, *Marpeck*, 44, 115.
61. Furcha, *Hans Denk*, 3.
62. Furcha, *Hans Denk*, 98–99.

In 1526, Michael Sattler had come to Strasbourg where he came to be held in high regard by Bucer, but especially by Capito.[63] He had come from the Zurich area, but probably was not part of the Swiss Brethren at the time. He had been arrested with Grebel and other Anabaptist leaders, including Reublin, while in Zurich, but was allowed to leave based on his recantation.[64] It was only after that experience that he was rebaptized and began to preach as an Anabaptist in the Strasbourg area. While in the city, he pleaded with Bucer and Capito for the release of Anabaptist prisoners. However, Sattler's uncompromising position on the separation of not only church and state, but from a sinful world in general, left no room, particularly for Bucer, for him to be allowed to stay in the city. He probably left of his own accord as he was still esteemed as a Christian brother, particularly by Capito.[65] Sattler's farewell letter to them both, framed in twenty theses, contained seven points that would later appear in his *Schleitheim Confession* in 1527, six of which had been previously been discussed with the Strasbourg reformers: baptism, the Supper, the sword, the oath, the ban, and separation. The confession was an early attempt to unify Anabaptism.[66]

Balthasar Hubmaier, although never having a role in Strasbourg, did attempt to unify Anabaptism with his *A Christian Catechism* of 1526. It wasn't successful, but not unlike Sattler's *Schleitheim Confession*, it was a genuine effort to bring unity and clarity to the movement.[67] However, by 1527, Hubmaier had been arrested in Nikolsburg, Moravia by his Waldshut nemesis, Ferdinand I of Austria. He was imprisoned in Vienna and burned at the stake there. Within a year, Tyroleans Leonhard Schiemer (d. 1528) and Hans Schlaffer (d. 1528), important influences on Pilgram Marpeck, were also executed as Anabaptists. These events would be the ultimate catalysts for Marpeck's flight to Strasbourg.[68]

Marpeck was most likely born in Rattenberg on the Inn River, the Tyrol region of Austria, to a Catholic family of nobility. His father, Heinrich Marpeck, arrived in Rattenberg in 1495 from Rosenheim. By 1509, he had become a member of the Brotherhood of Mine Workers

---

63. Snyder, "Sattler, Michael," 27.
64. Snyder, *Life and Thought*, 76–80, 86–88.
65. Yoder, *Legacy of Michael Sattler*, 19.
66. Snyder, *Life and Thought*, 93. See also chapter three of this dissertation.
67. Pipkin, *Balthasar Hubmaier*, 339–65. See also chapter three of the dissertation.
68. Klaassen, *Marpeck*, 44, 110, 14.

(Bergwerksbrüderschaft), a small corporation of propertied mining investors. In 1511, having been politically active, Heinrich was elected mayor of the town.

Pilgram Marpeck received his first city position by appointment of the council in 1518 as secretary treasurer of the local miner's guild *Brüderhaus*, a hospital for sick, injured, or retired miners. From 1518 to 1527, he would serve on city councils as *Bürgermeister* and as mining magistrate. The magistrate position required political as well as mining responsibilities that included the management of mining, smelting, and the forests of Rattenberg and the adjacent town of Kufstein. Attendant duties included administration and adjudication of mining disputes over the rights and claims of the miners, the investors, and the nobility.[69] It was within these responsibilities that Marpeck would first come into contact with the Protestant Reformation. In 1520, as a city father, he and his peers were responsible for choosing the local priest for the Church of Saint Vigil in Rattenberg. This unique privilege had been granted to the town in 1378, and in turn, the town was responsible for the clergy's subsistence.[70] Their choice of Stefan Castenbauer, aka Boius Agricola, (1491–1547), placed Marpeck in a difficult position as Castenbauer turned out to be a Lutheran. Prior to his selection he had published various works which had been critical of church abuses like those pointed out by Luther, emphasizing that the message of the Bible was a call to serve God. An excellent preacher, he attracted large numbers to his services and gained the respect and admiration of the community. By 1522, he gained the attention of Archduke Ferdinand, the brother of Charles V, the reigning emperor of the Holy Roman Empire. Ferdinand ordered the city council and the *Bürgermeister,* Pilgram Marpeck, to arrest Castenbauer for teaching Lutheranism, upon which the townsmen revolted. Marpeck and his peers unsuccessfully attempted to intervene on behalf of the priest and the community with Ferdinand. Castenbauer was eventually released, but under pressure from the miners of Rattenberg and their economic influence in the region. However, he never resumed his role as priest at the Church of Saint Vigil.[71]

It was Castenbauer who most likely introduced Marpeck to Lutheranism as he continued to act as an intermediary between Ferdinand,

---

69. Boyd, *Pilgram Marpeck*, 5–12. See also, Klaassen, *Marpeck*, 44, 55–67.
70. Klaassen, *Marpeck*, 44, 67–72.
71. Boyd, *Pilgram Marpeck*, 15–20.

the church authorities, and Castenbauer's enthusiastic parishioners.⁷² Although Jacob Strauß (1480?–1527) had been the first to bring Lutheranism to the towns of Schwaz and Hall, upriver from Rattenberg, he and Castenbauer were probably simultaneous arrivals in the valley. He, like Castenbauer, published Lutheran pamphlets that were readily available to everyone in the region. Walter Klaassen and William Klassen state that Strauß and Castenbauer preached on an Easter Sunday together to "thousands" of enthusiasts at Schwaz and Hall.⁷³ Stephen Boyd posits that Marpeck perhaps was enlightened by the Lutheran influences present in the Inn Valley, but expressed himself later as disillusioned by the lack of Lutheran piety as evidence of the "obedience of faith" as did the Anabaptists,⁷⁴ or as in the Pentecostal idiom, the "spirit-filled life." It should also be pointed out that Strauß had been influenced by Müntzer before the advent of the Peasants' War and was probably already pulling away from Luther toward a more spiritualistic radicalism, not unlike some Anabaptists, as evidenced in some of Müntzer's correspondence.⁷⁵

Another important factor in Marpeck's conversion to radicalism was the appearance of Michael Gaismaier (1491–1532) in the Inn Valley. He was the leader of a band of peasant rebels in May 1525 who were in sympathy with the Peasants' War rebels of the Black Forest of Southwestern Germany. Acting against the same principles of economic and religious abuse of the landed nobility, he unsuccessfully attempted to foment revolution and social change in the region. However, his incorporation of ideas of establishing a Christian utopia differentiated him from the majority of the broader German rebel forces. Gaismaier was arrested by Archduke Ferdinand, but managed to escape, leaving many peasants, miners, and artisans in the lurch of unfulfilled political and spiritual aspirations. Although he escaped captivity, he was eventually assassinated on the order of Ferdinand while hiding in Italy.⁷⁶ Gaismaier's impact on Marpeck was felt when, as Rattenberg's mayor and councilman, he had to supply men and material to combat the rebels upon the orders of Ferdinand. Klaassen conjectures that Marpeck had already been dealing with the religious discontent of Rattenberg, standing with the miners and citi-

72. Klaassen, *Marpeck*, 44, 72.

73. See also, Boyd, *Pilgram Marpeck*, 13–14.

74. Boyd, *Pilgram Marpeck*, 20–21. See also, Marpeck, "Expose of the Whore of Babylon, 1531," 28.

75. Matheson, *Collected Works of Thomas Müntzer*, 126, 31, 226, 434–35, 54.

76. Williams, *Radical Reformation*, 168–70.

zens of the town in the Castenbauer affair, and then having to send them to war against those who basically were trying to achieve similar goals through violence.[77] Stephen Boyd observes that Gaismaier's efforts and the Peasants' War in general were considered a Lutheran-instigated rebellion at the time and touching the war personally may have contributed to Marpeck's disaffection with the Lutheran reform's current tactics.[78]

MARPECK'S ANABAPTIST CONVERSION

Marpeck's acceptance of Anabaptist radicalism began in the midst of the religious turmoil he was witnessing, even presiding as a town politician in Rattenberg. The focus of this section will be on the people and events that influenced his decision to leave his position as politician, civil servant, and mining engineer to follow and propagate Anabaptism as an evangelist and theologian until his death. Revisiting Marpeck's conversion will lay the groundwork for his evolving, Pentecostal-like spirituality and theology.

That there were many radical elements active in the Inn Valley and Austria in general was indicative of the influence that the early teachings of Luther and Zwingli had concerning the efficacy of *sola scriptura*, the priesthood of the believer, and the work and presence of the Holy Spirit in every Christian's life. These were personally empowering ideas for cleric and layman alike, enabling and encouraging each to interpret Scripture and assume the spiritual prerogatives and responsibilities formerly reserved for the Catholic clergy only.

By January 18, 1528, Marpeck had submitted his letter of resignation, which was accepted by Ferdinand I without prejudice on the 28th.[79] It has already been pointed out that Anabaptism, at least that of the Swiss Brethren, had spread from Zurich beginning in 1525, reaching much of Western Europe, including Austria. Balthasar Hubmaier was in Nikolsburg, Moravia, on the Austrian northern border in 1526, where he published many Anabaptist pamphlets and tracts. However, he was arrested in Vienna and burned at the stake for his failure to recant by Ferdinand I in 1528. Georg Blaurock, one of the initial Anabaptist leaders in Zurich, had travelled as far as the Etsch Valley, Tyrol, in 1527, about the same

---

77. Klaassen, *Marpeck*, 44, 53–54.
78. Boyd, *Pilgram Marpeck*, 21.
79. Klaassen, *Marpeck*, 44, 102.

time Ferdinand I warned in a letter to the Innsbruck Administration of the presence of Anabaptists in the region.[80] In contrast to Western Anabaptist influence was an Eastern influence in the personages of Hans Hut and Hans Denck, proponents of Müntzer's apocalypticism. These two, having been influenced by the medieval mysticism of the *Theologia Germanica* and Tauler as introduced by Luther and mediated by Müntzer, also brought to the Inn Valley and Austria the influence of Caspar Schwenckfeld and Sebastian Franck.[81] In December 1527, Ferdinand I had issued a mandate which required the cooperation of all imperial officials in enforcing the prohibition of "Heretical sects and teaching, especially rebaptism."[82] Leonhard Schiemer (d. 1528) had come to Rattenberg after leaving a Franciscan monastery in Styria, seeking a faith without hypocrisy. He met with Hubmaier in Nikolsburg, then travelled to Vienna and met with Hut, was converted there, and was then rebaptized upon his confession of faith. From there he began preaching and baptizing many into Anabaptism throughout Bavaria and Austria, including Salzburg and the Tyrol. In November 1527, after only six months of Anabaptist evangelism, he was arrested in Rattenberg. Schiemer was convicted under provisions of the mandate, beheaded, and his body burned to ashes within sight of Marpeck's home.[83] As pastor of the Rattenberg Anabaptist congregation, Schiemer would write from his prison cell, "My brothers and sisters sealed in the Lord; each one of you must share the gift you have received from God and hold it in common (Rom. 4:1–4, 12:4–8; 1 Cor. 12:4–7)." This was in concurrence with Anabaptist teachings of the time.[84]

Hans Schlaffer (d. 1528), another disaffected Catholic priest and disciple of Hut, travelled to the Tyrolean Inn Valley to visit some relatives in Rattenberg. From there he went on to Schwatz to attend an Anabaptist meeting a short distance upriver, and] where he was arrested on December 5, 1527. Convicted of Anabaptism, he was beheaded on February 4, 1528. Primarily an advocate of Müntzer's theology as mitigated by Hans

---

80. Klaassen, *Marpeck*, 44, 54; Boyd, *Pilgram Marpeck*, 21–22.

81. Furcha, *Hans Denk*, 1; Packull, *Hutterite Beginnings*, 56–60; Packull, *Mysticism and the Early South*, 35–41; Boyd, *Pilgram Marpeck*, 22.

82. Klaassen, *Marpeck*, 44, 96.

83. Snyder, *Sources of South German*, 64–65; Klaassen, *Marpeck*, 44, 97–98.

84. Schiemer, "Letter to the Church of God at Rattenberg, 1527," 68. See also, Friedmann, "Schiemer and Schlaffer."

Hut, Schlaffer submitted in his prison epistle a pneumatic series of statements that have a similar Pentecostal-like perspective[85]:

> It is impossible to say too much in words about this new testament. For it only is the work of the Spirit in the human heart and is at the same time the baptism of the Spirit and fire with which Christ baptizes.

And:

> Not in any way do we bind salvation to external baptism, for Christ says: Whoever does not believe is condemned. He totally omits baptism. Everyone can read in the book of Acts that Peter, when he preached to the gentiles, witnessing to Christ and proving it with Scripture, all who heard the word and believed it, received the Holy Spirit; only later were they baptized. (Acts 10: 44–48)[86]

These two executions must have had a catalytic effect on Marpeck. Within weeks he refused to participate in Ferdinand's anti-Anabaptist pogrom, resigned his official position, and left Rattenberg at least as an Anabaptist sympathizer. It was within this setting that Marpeck would flee with his wife to Strasbourg, leaving his daughter and two adopted children behind.[87]

Prior to arriving in Strasbourg in 1528, Marpeck travelled north to Krumau, a Bohemian mining town where refugees from the Inn Valley fled from the persecutions and martyrdoms described above.[88] At that time, there was a large community of Anabaptists in Krumau who had apparently become Marpeck's incentive to take refuge there as Ferdinand I was still searching for him. Later that same year (1528), a significant number of the Krumau Anabaptists moved to Austerlitz. Werner Packull attributes seventy-one executions in the Tyrol to Ferdinand I by 1529.[89] Stephen Boyd conjectures that Marpeck arrived in Krumau with the Rattenberg Anabaptist Church Order authored by Schiemer.[90] Further he suggests that, according to Leupold Scharnschlager (d. 1563), he

---

85. Snyder, *Sources of South German*, 82; Friedmann, "Schiemer and Schlaffer."

86. Schlaffer, "Brief Instruction for the Beginning," 91, 93; Friedmann, "Schiemer and Schlaffer."

87. Klaassen, *Marpeck*, 44, 24–25.

88. Boyd, *Pilgram Marpeck*, 52.

89. Packull, *Hutterite Beginnings*, 135–38.

90. Packull, *Hutterite Beginnings*, 34–37, 303–15.

eventually received a commission from the Moravian congregation to go to Strasbourg and baptize new converts.[91] The identity of the person who may have baptized Marpeck is still unknown. Supposition, however, points to his appearance in Krumau and association with those Anabaptists who would eventually be associated with one of the seven congregations located at Austerlitz and environs at the time, but none of the Hutterite persuasion.[92] Nonetheless, he did leave Rattenberg in January 1528, appeared in public records in July 1528 at Krumau, and purchased his citizenship in Strasbourg in September 1528.[93] What makes the following important is that upon his arrival in Strasbourg and alignment with the Swiss Brethren there, particularly Wilhelm Reublin, he began to incorporate various aspects of the Moravian Anabaptist confession as he had experienced it, such as obtaining his citizenship, working for the city as an engineer, and necessarily taking an oath of allegiance thereto, all of which were in opposition to the Swiss Brethren Anabaptist confession. This highlights Marpeck's *via media* perspective regarding Anabaptism as he would also begin to criticize the Swiss Brethren for their developing biblicist legalism, as well as challenging the spiritualism of Hans Bünderlin and Christian Entfelder.[94]

Subsequent to his appearance in Strasbourg, he was quickly placed in a leadership role in the growing Anabaptist community. He associated himself with Wilhelm Reublin, leader of the Swiss Brethren, and became involved in the administration of the care of the poor and ministry to those in prison.[95] It wasn't long thereafter that he began a polemic with the spiritualists as well as spiritualist Anabaptist biblicists, a pursuit that would continue until his death. These disputations would unveil his *via media* plan to reconcile the more extreme elements of spiritualist Anabaptists described above. His "way between" incorporated those things which maintained the efficacy of traditional Christian creedal orthodoxy, rejected any spiritualization which denigrated the external values in orthodox creeds, yet incorporated *sola scriptura*, the priesthood of the believer, the infilling (baptism) of the Spirit, a commemorative Eucharist, water baptism, the gifts of the Holy Spirit (1 Cor 12–14), love,

---

91. Boyd, *Pilgram Marpeck*, 52.
92. Rempel, *Jorg Maler's Kunstbuch*, 371.
93. Packull, *Hutterite Beginnings*, 136.
94. Klassen, *Covenant and Community*, 98.
95. Boyd, *Pilgram Marpeck*, 54.

evangelization, and pacifism, all in what could only be described as a Pentecostal-like perspective. An important motivating and Pentecostal-like factor was the desire to see some external evidence of the internal spiritual event that Scripture described as the result of salvation upon confession of faith in Christ, including being filled with the Holy Spirit according to Acts 2:38.

In less than a year however, Anabaptism had divided itself into three groups: the spiritualists, those following the mystical spiritualism of Jacob Kautz, Hans Denck, Hans Bünderlin, Christian Entfelder, Caspar Schwenckfeld, and Sebastian Franck, who held to the condemnation of the material rites and ceremonies of the church; the Melchiorites, led by Melchior Hoffman, who was obsessed with the apocalypse, seeing faithful Christians as being chosen by God for a critical role in history's last days; and the biblicists' Swiss Brethren who, upon Reublin's expulsion in 1529, chose Marpeck as their new leader.[96] It was also at this time that Leupold Scharnschlager (d. 1563), a fellow Tyrolean then in Strasbourg, began to collaborate with Marpeck, becoming a co-author and close associate. As the theological lines of the ensuing polemic developed, Marpeck and Scharnschlager began to speak out and write against the other radical groups.

Pentecostal similarities become evident with an analysis of the theology of Marpeck and his circle of followers. The situation Marpeck was confronted with in Strasbourg in 1528 was one of spiritualists denying the efficacy of the Holy Spirit, replacing all external ecclesiastical things within the church—Catholic, Lutheran, and Reformed alike. Added to this was an Anabaptist biblical literalism that was rapidly degenerating into a legalism of dogmatic proportions bereft of Christian love. Marpeck's first two publications of 1531 began his assertion of a *via media* among the extremes of Anabaptism, were *Ain klarer/vast nützlicher unterricht, (A Clear and Useful Instruction)* and *Clare verantwortung (A Clear Refutation)*.[97] What follows is a detailed analysis of Marpeck's theology and defense of his *via media* attempt at reconciling those extremes.

---

96. Klaassen, *Marpeck*, 44, 154; Deppermann, *Melchior Hoffman*, 190–92; Klassen, *Covenant and Community*, 29–32.

97. Klaassen, *Covenant and Community*, 36, 40; Klaassen and Klassen, *Writings of Pilgram Marpeck*, 43, 69. The translators, Klassen and Klaassen, both agree that a more accurate translation of *Clare Verantwortung*, etc. would be a "defense or account," but opted for the original translation instead for the sake of consistency. See, Klaassen, *Marpeck*, 44, 137.

MARPECK'S THEOLOGY AND EARLY PENTECOSTALISM COMPARED

Marpeck's *via media* theology and spirituality is similar to that which would emerge later in early twentieth-century Pentecostalism. John Nichol has observed that Pentecostals should be placed in the "left wing" of the Reformation, a term that predates Williams's "Radical Reformation," in that "they are like their spiritual ancestors the Anabaptists."[98] He justifies his observation with five reasons:

1. The individual as well as the corporate body of believers should seek for, and submit to, the leading of the Spirit;
2. There should be a return to apostolic simplicity in worship;
3. Believers ought to separate themselves from the world;
4. Believers' baptism replaces infant baptism;
5. Believers should look for the imminent visible return of Christ who will set up his millennial reign.

John Nichol was correct in his assessment of early Pentecostalism's similarity to Anabaptism, but he could have explicitly added Anabaptism's willingness to manifest the gifts of the Spirit as well. It should be noted that the tendency of both early movements was to avoid the intellectualism that predominated Christian hermeneutics of their respective eras. Scholasticism, anticlericalism, and a general lack of biblical language expertise guided the Anabaptists away from anything more that an existential treatment of the Bible. The same holds true for early Pentecostalism's rejection of the prevailing higher textual criticism methodology of contemporary Protestant Christianity of their time.[99]

EARLY PENTECOSTALISM'S KNOWLEDGE OF ANABAPTISM

Nichol made these observations, however, in 1966 when, relative to today, not as much was known about Anabaptist theology and spirituality. It was only through the filters of Mennonite scholars looking for

---

98. Nichol, *Pentecostalism*, 3.

99. Warrington, *Pentecostal Theology*, 185. See also, Klassen, *Covenant and Community*, 12, and Friedmann, *Theology of Anabaptism*, 29.

evidence of normative Anabaptism that it was viewed at the time. The current acceptance of the idea of a polygenetic origin of Anabaptism, and the discovery of Marpeck's works, has led some to characterize him as the most Pentecostal of Anabaptist writers. There is no evidence that sixteenth-century Anabaptism had become an influence on, or a catalyst for, early Pentecostalism, although Seymour did paraphrase some of the church history he had read regarding the gift of tongues in *The Doctrines and Discipline of the Azusa Street Apostolic Faith Mission of 1915*:

> Bishop Hurst says, in his Church History, that the gift of tongues has appeared in communities under powerful religious stimulus, as among the Camisards, early Quakers, Lasare in Sweden in 1841–43, the Irish Revival in 1859, and the Catholic Apostolic (Irvingite) church (Vol. 1, page 90).[100]

In another section of the *Doctrines and Discipline* he referred to John Agricola (1492?–1566) as promoting antinomianism against Luther's preaching of the law arguing that "faith does not supersede (set aside the necessity) of holiness or good works," but "it implies both."[101] This is another example of Seymour's exposure to Bishop Hurst's church history.[102] There is no evidence or mention of Anabaptism.

A review of Bishop Hurst's church history failed to reveal any connection Seymour could have made between the Anabaptists and the manifestation of speaking in tongues. However, Hurst's characterization of the radical movement did list "Marbeck," an alternate spelling of Marpeck, as one of the "many great and noble Christians" who led the group. He described Anabaptists as being a small fanatical faction, some Unitarians, but by and large they were premillennial restorationist Protestants who emphasized the ethical teachings of Jesus, and rejected Augustinian and Calvinistic doctrines, oaths, war, the death penalty, participation in government by Christians, and infant baptism, all with a chiliastic bent that sometimes held violent and extravagant methods.[103] But, notwithstanding Hurst's failure to attribute many early Pentecostal-like theological positions and beliefs to the Anabaptists, Pentecostalism

---

100. Sanders, *William Seymour Papers*, 95. Bishop John F. Hurst (1834–1903) published several church histories in the late nineteenth century, including Hurst, *History of the Christian Church*.

101. Sanders, *William Seymour Papers*, 137. See also, Kjeldgaard-Pedersen, "Johann Agricola."

102. Hurst, *History of the Christian Church*, 2:501.

103. Hurst, *History of the Christian Church*, 2:692–93.

was still in the future when he wrote his history. Seymour's quotation of Hurst regarding historical instances of the manifestations of the gifts of the Holy Spirit without noting any Anabaptist experiences is indicative of the lack of any historical influence from that movement on early Pentecostalism. It should be noted again that the ensuing sixty years or so of Anabaptist research and scholarship has significantly advanced the historical knowledge and understanding of the radical Anabaptist aspect of the Reformation, thus revealing many Pentecostal-like aspects that were brought about by similar hermeneutical praxes of both movements as opposed to any direct or indirect inspiration.

MARPECK, ANABAPTISM, AND THE EARLY PENTECOSTAL FOURFOLD GOSPEL

Anabaptists had been schooled in Reformation anticlericalism as initiated by Erasmus, Luther, and Zwingli. However, their approach to the clerical corruption was to reject what C. Arnold Snyder called the "learned" or scholastic theology of the church.[104] If the priesthood of the believer was true, the Bible could be read and interpreted by any Christian being empowered by the Spirit, and so they proceeded. There was no initial attempt at developing a systematic theology. The goal was that, by using Scripture literally, they could respond to everyday life's typical situations from a Christian perspective, thus the development of biblical concordances without commentary, for the Bible interpreted itself.[105]

This section will identify various theological and spiritual principles that had been articulated by Marpeck. They were based on Anabaptist experiences that he considered critical to a primitive New Testament church.[106] A similar situation was faced by early Pentecostals when mainline denominational Protestant theologians embraced higher criticism as an effective methodology of biblical interpretation. Grant Wacker has emphasised the driving force of experience in early Pentecostalism that was not unlike that of the Anabaptists.[107] They will be compared to early sixteenth-century Anabaptism in a one-to-one comparative model for each similarity found.

104. Snyder, *Anabaptist History and Theology*, xvii.
105. Snyder, *Anabaptist History and Theology*, xvii. See also, viii.
106. Goertz, *Anabaptists*, 67.
107. Wacker, *Heaven Below*, 84–86.

Critical to the nature of early Pentecostalism was also the desire to restore the primitive New Testament church. The return to preaching the full gospel, meaning the restitution of the charismatic Christian confession as recorded in 1 Corinthians 12–14, was thoroughly embraced as the only way to accomplish that desire.[108] In 1906, Seymour wrote in the first issue of *The Apostolic Faith* that "The Apostolic Faith Movement stands for the restoration of the faith once delivered unto the saints."[109] Charles Parham would write in the same issue of *The Apostolic Faith*: "I desire, unless God directs to the contrary, to meet and see all who have the full Gospel when I come."[110] David W. Myland would write in 1910:

> Now by these seven steps-the Word of God, Prayer, Right Desire, Waiting with Expectation, Faith in Appropriation, God's Grace, and God's Sovereignty we may have the Latter Rain, the fullness of the Spirit and power of the Gospel of Christ restored.[111]

From this initial theological goal there developed a fourfold gospel model that initially consisted of the following five tenets; repentance, regeneration, Pentecostal baptism (speaking in tongues), divine healing, and the premillennial return of Christ. The incorporation was expressed in *The Apostolic Faith* confession of faith as justification/ sanctification, the baptism in the Holy Spirit (with speaking in tongues), divine healing, and the second coming of Jesus. The five tenets were further condensed into a fourfold statement where justification and sanctification were combined, reflecting a theological construct not unlike that of early sixteenth-century Anabaptism discussed below.[112] The fourfold gospel formula that originated with A. B. Simpson will be used to compare the theology and pneumatology of Marpeck and the early Anabaptists: salvation, baptism in the Holy Spirit with speaking in tongues, healing, and the second coming of Christ. However, this will not preclude a comparison with the fivefold gospel aspect of sanctification as a distinct experience.[113] Similar to that was the Anabaptists' theology of piety, but as a progressive experience.[114] The nature of the traditional Christian confession, Scrip-

---

108. Dayton, *Theological Roots of Pentecostalism*, 19–20.
109. Seymour, "Apostolic Faith Movement," 2.
110. Seymour, "Apostolic Faith Movement," 1.
111. Myland, *Latter Rain Covenant*, 54.
112. Dayton, *Theological Roots of Pentecostalism*, 19–23, 46.
113. Anderson, *To the Ends*, 97.
114. Snyder, *Anabaptist History and Theology*, 48–49.

ture, communion, water baptism, sanctification, and evangelism will also be considered.

MARPECK'S PNEUMATOLOGY

Anabaptist spirituality will be examined in the context of the various similarities of Marpeck's pneumatology. Marpeck's *A Clear Refutation* was a direct response to spiritualist Hans Bünderlin's *Comparison of Biblical Scripture* which argued that the New Testament ceremonies—baptism and the communion—were no longer efficacious, having been defiled by the antichrist, and so therefore should no longer be practiced.[115] The argument further posited that there was no longer a mandate for such ceremonies supported by the Bible, in that the original apostles were dead and therefore not in a position to establish an apostolic succession that could continue the ceremonies.[116] Bünderlin's work was significantly influenced by *Theologia Germanica*, Tauler via Hans Denck, Sebastian Franck, and even Schwenckfeld, which is evidence of the very complicated nature of Anabaptism in general and South German Anabaptism in particular.[117]

Marpeck saw the danger to the church in Bünderlin's theology and began by organizing his apology in *A Clear Refutation* in three stages. First he declared:

> Certain spirits (which, according to 1 John 2 "went out from us but are not of us") are advocating that the children of God should no longer use the ceremonies of the New Testament.[118]

He then proceeded to refute the spiritualists' claims by first acknowledging their observation of the abuse of the ceremonies by the antichrist, understood as the Roman Catholic Church, and retorted:

> The righteous have nothing to do with evil matters (Ezek. 18; Deut. 24) because they have not given their consent (Lk. 23; Eph. 5; 1 Tim. 5; Rev. 18; 2 Cor. 6; Ps. 26; Ex. 23). This abuse cannot invalidate them for the believer who understands, uses, practices, and promotes them in a correct and pure manner. Where, however, the Spirit of Christ is present (which those

---

115. Klaassen, *Marpeck*, 44, 137.
116. Klaassen and Klassen, *Writings of Pilgram Marpeck*, 43–44.
117. Packull, *Mysticism and the Early South*, 155–56.
118. Klaassen and Klassen, *Writings of Pilgram Marpeck*, 44.

> belonging to the Antichrist lack and, I fear, these spirits also lack) there Christ's pure ordinance is joined to it.[119]

Marpeck argued for the continued homogeneity of God's physical creation and his spiritual creation, particularly emphasizing the critical nature of Christ's incarnation and infilling of the Holy Spirit as the enigration of one only denies the validity of the other.

He then began to emphasize the critical nature of the presence and efficacy of the work of the Holy Spirit in the absence of the physical Christ:

> Just as the Israelites, rescued out of Babylonian captivity (Ezra 2), restored the ancient ceremonies, so too does Christ today, through His servants rescued out of the prison of the Antichrist, restore and renew His instituted ceremonies (Acts 3) by means of His inner command and His bestowal of the certainty of His Spirit.[120]

The Spiritualists variously declared the miracles of the New Testament, including the gifts of the Spirit, to be in cessation.[121] Marpeck responded:

> That Christ does not at this time once more in the flesh give a personal command as He did to the eleven disciples, or [that He does not] . . . perform a miracle should not deter us. Through the Spirit of Christ, there is sufficient inner command. Whoever desires more, such as miraculous signs . . . is not hungry for the truth . . . Therefore, he who in these last days desires miracles, and will not believe the truth without them, let him beware lest he be deceived and punished by those wonders and signs of deception referred to in the Scriptures (Mt. 24; Mk. 13; 2 Thess. 2; Rev. 13; Rom. 16; 1 Tim. 4.[122]

He wasn't contending that miracles and signs had been excluded from the faith, only that they were not the measure of truth, giving a warning that Scripture does not exclude them from continued manifestation:

---

119. Klaassen and Klassen, *Writings of Pilgram Marpeck*, 45–46. The idea that there are those within the church who lack the Holy Spirit appears again at the Zofingen Disputation one year later.

120. Klaassen, *Writings of Pilgram Marpeck*, 46.

121. Klassen, *Covenant and Community*, 59, 73.

122. Klaassen and Klassen, *Writings of Pilgram Marpeck*, 49.

> God has a free hand even in these last days. He has performed miracles and signs before, and even does so today for him who has eyes to see. These spirits also assert that together with ceremonies all miraculous signs ended at the time of the apostles well recognize this fact and should note how Christian baptism and the Lord's Supper are today repeated according to their original intention and institution.[123]

He then proceeded to recount that there were many instances where Anabaptists could voluntarily testify to their response to, and deliverance from, physical torture, joyfully:

> By the power of the Holy Spirit of Christ. There were even those still living once killed by the authorities.[124] Here and there one can find the same thing happening even today, it takes place among those who are powerfully moved and driven by the living Word of God and the Spirit of Christ.[125]

He pressed on to explain the efficacy of the gift of prophecy and what evidence it takes to recognize one as a prophet. It is "not by miraculous signs but by their fruits (Mt. 7). Likewise we also know the fruits of the Spirit (Gal. 5)."[126] Furthermore it is the gift of discernment which tests the spirits to determine whether or not they acknowledge Christ as having come in the flesh, according to 1 John 4. Throughout the history of the church, the polemic within which Marpeck engaged was typical of the historical apologetic that it has taken to crystalize the theology of Christianity. More importantly this is an example of Marpeckan initial evidence. It does not agree theologically with most early Pentecostal movements, but it does correspond to the early western European Pentecostal model as set out by Jonathan Paul.

Countering the idea of carnal compulsion (the call to preach) regarding a clerical vocation, he uses Philip the deacon and Apollos to argue that neither were given external commissions to preach the gospel, but were "sent inwardly by Christ's Spirit." He continues by using the ongoing Reformation, in his case Anabaptist radicalism, to argue that like his two biblical examples, "the revival and restoration of the pure

---

123. Klaassen and Klassen, *Writings of Pilgram Marpeck*, 49–50.

124. Klaassen and Klassen, *Writings of Pilgram Marpeck*, 50n503. See complete quote above in chapter 4.

125. Klaassen and Klassen, *Writings of Pilgram Marpeck*, 50n503.

126. Klaassen and Klassen, *Writings of Pilgram Marpeck*, 51.

order of Christ has occurred, and continues to occur, by the virtue of His voluntary Spirit."[127] He went on to say that these spiritualists lacked the true knowledge of Christ, an argument that would be used at the *Zofingen Disputation of 1532* against reformed theologians after Marpeck had been expelled from Strasbourg.[128] He averred that Christ still commands and directs Christians to, "preach, teach, and baptize" (Mt. 28; Mk. 16; Lk. 24), not only in Jesus' time, but throughout entire world, until his return to Earth (Mt. 24; Mk. 16; Acts 2; Rom. 15; Deut. 31; Ps. 78).[129] Christ's commands consist of the Lord's Supper (Lk. 22), Bible studies (John 5), belief in him (John 7), and foot washing (John 13),[130] a list that is perhaps a glimpse into Anabaptist church order. He goes on to say that these spiritualists deny such externalities, so judgment will fall on them: "Whoever goes ahead and does not remain in the instruction of Christ has no God (2 John 1)."[131] By comparison, in his *The Doctrines and Discipline*, "section XVI of the Sacraments," Seymour writes:

> There are three Sacraments ordained of Christ our Lord in the Gospel; that is to say Baptism and the Lord's Supper, and Feet Washing. The Sacraments were not ordained of Christ to be gazed upon, or to be carried about; but that we should duly use them. And in such only as worthily receive the same they have a wholesome effect or operation; but they that unworthily, receive, purchase to themselves condemnation, as St. Paul saith 1 Cor. xi, 20.[132]

The similarities between the two statements are obvious as both are using a biblically literal interpretation of the same Scripture, an example of Luther and Zwingli's spiritual-prophetic hermeneutic and early priesthood of the believer position, yet they were separated by more than four centuries of church history. Both supported foot washing as a Sacrament by invoking John 13.[133] Kenneth Archer and Andrew Hamilton observe that from early Pentecostal, Brethren, and Anabaptist-Pietism traditions,

---

127. Klaassen and Klassen, *Writings of Pilgram Marpeck*, 51.

128. Byrd, "Pentecostalism's Anabaptist Heritage."

129. Klaassen and Klassen, *Writings of Pilgram Marpeck*, 51.

130. Klaassen and Klassen, *Writings of Pilgram Marpeck*, 51. See also, Snyder, *Anabaptist History and Theology*, 375.

131. Klaassen and Klassen, *Writings of Pilgram Marpeck*, 51.

132. Sanders, *William Seymour Papers*, 129, 89.

133. Sanders, *Seymour Papers*, 85–87. See also, Brumback, *Suddenly from Heaven*, 279.

there is a synergistic potential for an ecumenical understanding of each other regarding the worship practice of foot washing. Admittedly, there is little evidence to connect both Pentecostalism and the Brethren to early Anabaptism, but the Brethren do have a closer connection to Anabaptist-Pietism. The common denominator, it is argued, is the common Christian metanarrative created by both interpreting John 13 the same way. The similarity to early Anabaptism then becomes clearer at that point. The Bible becomes the ecumenical link for the argument, showing similarities in all three movements.[134]

The spiritualists had accepted the gift of preaching in order to validate their theology publicly, but they could not state who commissioned them to teach, write, travel, and use Scripture to support their arguments. So Marpeck challenged them by proffering the suggestion that, if one command is "invalid then all are invalid; if one remains valid then all remain valid."[135] He again acknowledged their rejection of the rituals of the Roman Catholic Church and understood their suspicions, but accused them of desiring:

> To make the Kingdom of Christ far too spiritual, and make too great a leap, just as, on the other hand, the Antichrist has made it too physical.[136] I sense they lack the Holy Spirit dedicated to the common good (1 Cor. 12), who uses the gifts of the Holy Spirit for the edification of others (1 Cor. 14; Eph. 4), and thus serves them (1 Peter 4).[137]]

Marpeck launched into a Pauline pneumatology in that he interpreted Paul in a similar way to the early Pentecostals. In his study of the Anabaptist use of Scripture, Emmet McLaughlin observed that notwithstanding a commitment to closely following the gospel teachings, Anabaptists made good use of Paul's letters to the Romans and Galatians. But it was on 1 Corinthians that Marpeck laid his foundation.[138] Marpeck is described by McLaughlin as the most important figure of the second generation of South German Anabaptists.[139] C. Arnold Snyder noted that pneumatologically all early Anabaptism pointed to the importance of the

---

134. Archer, "Anabaptism-Pietism and Pentecostalism," 185–202.
135. Archer, "Anabaptism-Pietism and Pentecostalism," 52.
136. Archer, "Anabaptism-Pietism and Pentecostalism," 52.
137. Archer, "Anabaptism-Pietism and Pentecostalism," 52–53.
138. McLaughlin, "Paul in Early Anabaptism," 217, 24, 28.
139. McLaughlin, "Paul in Early Anabaptism," 228.

"spirit/letter" tension, but also to the necessary connection they made between the inner life of the spirit and the outer life of discipleship.[140] The focus on Marpeck's pneumatology that follows will validate both McLaughlin's and Snyder's characterizations of Anabaptist spirituality. It also reinforces the argument for the similarity between early Pentecostalism's fourfold gospel and Anabaptist theology and pneumatology.

Continuing his polemic in *A Clear Refutation* with the spiritualists, Marpeck argued against their position that they do in fact have as much faith and spirit as they need, but at the same time insisted that there is no command to use the gifts of the Spirit for others.[141] He responded:

> Their boast is nothing but a deceitful adornment of Satan. For one member to forsake another (1 Cor. 12) in spiritual matters . . . would be contrary to the faith of the Spirit, and the nature and attributes of love. The fruit of the Spirit is love and faithfulness (Gal. 5). Faith must manifest itself in witness, fruit, and work (1 Pet. 1; Jn. 7, 15; Heb. 6; Jas. 2; 1 Thess. 1). So love is faith in action (Gal. 5); it edifies and improves (1 Cor. 8). Thus, the gifts of the Spirit manifest themselves not only for private, but also common benefit, service, and improvement.[142]

Here Marpeck began to set the parameters for the evidence of the infilling of the Holy Spirit which is comparatively different than that of Charles Parham.[143] But, as noted above Marpeck's criteria for evidence was closer to that of William Seymour, F. F. Bosworth (1857–1958), Jonathan Paul (1853–1931), and many European Pentecostals.[144]

Seymour had accepted Parham's theology regarding speaking in tongues as the initial evidence of the baptism in the Holy Spirit. But, by 1914, he began to witness many contradictions of piety in the personal lives of some in his congregation who spoke in tongues, particularly that of racism. In an *Apostolic Address* included in the *Doctrines and Discipline in 1915*, Seymour declared that, due to the racism caused by divisive white men, these men would no longer qualify to serve as directors of the mission.[145] They were also held responsible for fanaticism and spreading

---

140. Snyder, *Anabaptist History and Theology*, 88.
141. Klaassen and Klassen, *Writings of Pilgram Marpeck*, 53.
142. Klaassen and Klassen, *Writings of Pilgram Marpeck*, 53.
143. Parham, *Voice Crying in the Wilderness*, 37–38.
144. Anderson, *Introduction to Pentecostalism*, 53.
145. This change was also a response to the criticism of both Parham and Durham.

wildfire, most accurately described as aberrant spiritual behavior.[146] In the preface to the *Doctrines and Discipline Faith*, Seymour wrote:

> Wherever the doctrine of the Baptism in the Holy Spirit will only being known as the evidence of speaking in tongues, that work will be an open door for witches and spiritualists, and free loveism. That work will suffer, because all kinds of spirits can come in. When we leave the word of God and begin to go by signs and voices we will wind up in Spiritualism.[147]

In the section entitled the *New Birth* he stated:

> Some people to-day cannot believe they have the Holy Ghost without some outward signs: that is Heathenism. The witness of the Holy Spirit inward is the greatest knowledge of knowing God, for he is invisible. St. John 14:17. It is all right to have the signs following, but not to pin our faith to outward manifestations.[148]

Carl Simpson stated that notwithstanding the influence of Azusa Street and North American Pentecostalism, the witness of the Holy Spirit that worked in the European movement was highly influenced by Jonathan Paul and the German Pentecostals.[149] Paul and the Germans were not adherents of Parham and classic Pentecostalism's doctrine of initial evidence, but considered, much like Marpeck, the outward manifestation of the fruit of the Spirit as the evidence of the infilling. If someone spoke in tongues, it was seen as a part of a progressive work of the Spirit.[150] This position came to bear on the meeting of the *Pentecostal Consultative Council 1912* in Amsterdam. Paul was elected to chair the council which proceeded to adopt an eight-point declaration of the European Pentecostal movement's confession of faith, wherein point three states:

> 3. The Baptism in the Holy Ghost and Fire we hold to be the coming upon and within of the Holy Spirit to indwell the believer in His fullness, and is always borne witness to by the fruit of the Spirit and the outward manifestation, so that we may receive

---

146. Sanders, *William Seymour Papers*, 117.

147. Sanders, *William Seymour Papers*, 111.

148. Sanders, *William Seymour Papers*, 113. See also Robeck, *Azusa Street Mission and Revival*, 318–19.

149. Simpson, "Development of the Pentecostal," 67.

150. Simpson, "Jonathan Paul and the German," 178–79.

> the same gift as the disciples on the Day of Pentecost (Matt. iii:11; Acts i:5–8; ii 1–4, 38, 39; 1 Cor. xii 7–13; Acts xi 15–18.
>
> We do not teach that all who have been baptized in the Holy Ghost, even if they should speak in tongues, have already received the fullness of the blessing of Christ implied in Baptism. There may be, and in most cases will be, a progressive entering of the believer into this fullness, according to the measure of faith, obedience, and knowledge of the recipient.[151]

Returning to Marpeck's argument against the spiritualists, he confronted the individualistic nature of their position. If the spiritual gifts they were exercising were not for the benefit of others, but only themselves, they were not interpreting Mark 13 correctly, where Christ said that all stewards are to watch his house and guard those within (Mk.13; Lk. 12; Mt. 24; Heb. 13) by preaching, teaching, exhortation, and the manifestation of the other gifts of the Spirit.[152] This enabled him to turn to the Christian principle of love, wherein these teachers and preachers are supposed to be watching in love in the sense mentioned above. He states that if one is to love one's neighbor according to Ephesians 6, "they are to watch for all the saints."[153] For him, salvation depended upon love for one's neighbor. If you do not love your neighbor you do not love yourself. Thus, seeking one's own profit causes great damage. The result, in effect, was neither watching over their own soul or that of others.

In 1906, Seymour would write in his *Statement of Faith and Belief*:

> We are not fighting men or churches, but seeking to displace dead forms and creeds and wild fanaticism with living, practical Christianity. "Love, Faith, Unity" are our watch words.[154]

In 1912, Jonathan Paul also would pen in the *Declaration of the International Pentecostal Consultative Council*:

---

151. Boddy, "Declaration of the International Pentecostal," 1. There were many others who did not agree with Parham's initial evidence thesis, notwithstanding the American Assemblies of God adaptation of it in 1914. Pentecostal movement leaders such as William H. Piper, pastor of the Stone Church in Chicago, F. F. Bosworth—probably the best known of the early movement leaders—and some of the African-American Pentecostal churches rejected it also. See, McGee, "Initial Evidence."

152. Klaassen and Klassen, *Writings of Pilgram Marpeck*, 54.

153. Klaassen and Klassen, *Writings of Pilgram Marpeck*, 54.

154. Sanders, *William Seymour Papers*, 17.

> Men and women who, not realizing that God has given us the spirit of power and love... dwell in things which they have seen, and delight in feelings and mystical experiences, give opportunity to the evil one to deceive them.[155]

In 1947, Carl Brumback would write in *What Meanth This?*:

> The blessed truth is that the same Spirit, who sheds abroad the love of God in our hearts, also divides severally the gifts of the Spirit! God is not impoverished when we aim at and attain love ... The Corinthians had a zeal for the gifts without love, while many today have a zeal for love without the gifts: the proper and Scriptural zeal is for love and the gifts.[156]

Love was foundational for Anabaptism, as it was for early Pentecostalism. The love for Christ, holiness, one's neighbor, and the Bible were touchstone tenets of both movements. It was this intimate Anabaptist love which Pentecostalism emulated and continued to embrace, although navigating it through the difficulties of modern Western spiritual apathy.[157]

In the third and final stage of his argument in *A Clear Refutation*, Marpeck answers the spiritualists' contention that there was no apostolic authority to create an apostolic succession in that the biblical apostles had appointed bishops to serve the flock of God in their time only. In answer to this argument, Marpeck explains that external authority doesn't make an apostle, even if the apostles themselves had made such appointments. "All is in vain if there is no inner mandate from Christ, but even that would have failed if He had not spiritually thrust the mandate into the heart of their bosom."[158] Unlike the worldly realm, the spiritual realm depends upon the inner power which Christ alone gives through his spirit.[159] Apostolic authority is not one of ruling or lordship, but one of service to the body of Christ.[160]

---

155. Boddy, "Declaration of the International Pentecostal," 277.
156. Brumback, *What Meaneth this?*, 154–57.
157. Chatfield, "Zealous for the Lord," 109.
158. Marpeck, "Clear Refutation," 55.
159. Marpeck, "Clear Refutation," 55.
160. Marpeck, "Clear Refutation," 55.

MARPECK AND PENTECOSTAL HERMENEUTICS COMPARED

Marpeck then began to emphasize the critical importance of the external Scripture. He posits that Christ left his external authority and command in the Scriptures to all his disciples, brothers, and members who had his mind and Spirit. The spiritualists sought to abolish too much of the external, including external order and the means deigned by God through which his invisible being is seen. "In Christ and in God man is led from the visible to the invisible."[161] His Christology began to take form here as he equates the physicality of the incarnate Christ with all things external as defined by the spiritualists. He believed that one cannot abolish the externality of the faith without abolishing the humanity of Jesus.

Using the Old Testament example of Joshua, who attempted to prevent Eldat and Medat from prophesying by requesting that Moses prohibit them, Marpeck appeals to Numbers 1, where Moses replied that he wished all God's people would prophesy and that God's spirit be poured out on all.[162] Moreover, he said, it was also reminiscent of Jesus' disciples forbidding someone to drive out demons because they were not of their circle, but Christ declared, "Don't forbid him or hinder him, for there is no one who does anything in my name, even if he speaks evil against me, for whoever is not against us is for us" (Mark 9; Luke 9). The spiritualists, like these examples, desired to stop up the well of the Spirit which pours from believing hearts (John 7; 2 Cor 4; Acts 2; Rom 10; Ps 115).[163] He continued:

> Christ did not restrict His command, Word, grace, Spirit, or ceremonies to the first apostles and churches. His Word and power, and the outpouring of his Spirit, have no end.[164]

Christ did not atone for the sins of part of the world, but the whole world, he argued, therefore the Scripture also is designed for those upon whom the end of the world has come (1 Cor 9, 10; Isa 30).[165] "We do not serve the Scriptures; they serve us by instruction, edification, exhortation,

---

161. Marpeck, "Clear Refutation," 56–57.
162. Marpeck, "Clear Refutation," 57.
163. Marpeck, "Clear Refutation," 57.
164. Marpeck, "Clear Refutation," 58.
165. Marpeck, "Clear Refutation," 58.

and discipline" (Rom 15; 2 Tim 1).[166] Similarly all ceremonies have been instituted for the church's service and benefit. They serve Christians in the same way that Christ the man came to serve us when they are done in faith and obedience by one who serves the body of Christ as ordered by God. When done in the Spirit and praise of God, they serve Christ and God himself. But this is not what the spiritualist scribes were doing, for Christians did them for the sake of righteousness and "with the faith of the elect in Jesus."[167] He went on:

> Therefore, moved by the Holy Spirit (2 Peter 1) and by the example of Christ through His Spirit, all messengers and teachers, should have witness of the Scriptures, but in humility and obedience to the gospel—as it has happened until now, God be praised, on many occasions.[168]

That early Pentecostalism had developed a similar position to that of Marpeck regarding the "call" to preach and teach the gospel by all, and the critical nature of the Scripture thereto is confirmed by two important examples.

William Seymour, in his *Doctrines and Discipline of the Apostolic Faith of 1915*, described the spiritual qualifications of those who were called to preach to be:

> Searching the Scriptures. First: Reading constantly some part of every day; regularly, all the Bible in order; carefully, with prayer; seriously with prayer before and after; fruitfully, immediately practicing what you learn there. Second: Meditating, at set times, by rule. Third: Hearing, at every opportunity, with prayer before [and] after. Have you a Bible always about you? Footwashing. Do you use this ordinance at every opportunity?[169]

In Alexander Boddy's *The Laying on of Hands: A Bible Ordinance 1895*, in the "Seventh Part: Bible Reading," he stresses that reading God's holy word is a Christian duty. "We speak to God in prayer, but we must also listen for His voice speaking to us. This is needed equally. There cannot be strong, helpful Christians save where there is Bible reading."[170] He then proceeded to list four different ways of reading the word:

166. Marpeck, "Clear Refutation," 59.
167. Marpeck, "Clear Refutation," 59.
168. Marpeck, "Clear Refutation," 59.
169. Sanders, *William Seymour Papers*, 147.
170. Sanders, *William Seymour Papers*, 147.

First; Reading in Church Services; Second; Private reading feeds the soul if one read it regularly and constantly listening to the "Father's voice." Third; for methodology some can use the Book of Common Prayer; some can join one of the Bible Unions and read with more structure and discipline. Fourth; Marking, underlining, highlighting, or highlighting with different colours to assist one in a more measured form of Bible study.[171]

He concludes this section of the critical nature of reading Scripture by saying;

> Oh that we were all like Apollos, mighty in the Scriptures! Our Savior says, "Search the Scriptures, for in them ye think ye have eternal life, and they are they which testify of Me" (John 5:39). If this was true of the Old Testament Scriptures, how much more of the New?"[172]

Although Seymour and Boddy were important pioneers in the Pentecostal movement in a global sense, they were by no means unique in their respective consideration of the seriousness of being scripturally prepared to respond to the "call" to preach.[173] The following examples are indicative of the similarities Marpeck had with the perspective of early Pentecostalism regarding the call to preach. Marpeck then shifted to the current efficacy of the Spirit during the lifetime of all Christian history of the church as he continued to respond to the Spiritualists:

> The pouring out of the Spirit is not as those spirits say: At the time of the apostles, the Spirit of God was poured forth over all the present and future world, until the last judgement, as if such pouring out then had ceased. The Spirit of God at that time (Acts 2) was not poured out over all, but only on the apostles and Christians. The others were unbelievers.[174]

The Spirit is poured out on believers only, but they are the product of the external hearing of the word, preaching. Referencing Joel 2 and Acts 2, "in the last days He will pour His Spirit on all flesh," Marpeck defines the "last days" as beginning with the birth of Christ.[175] Since then, he says, a richer outpouring of the Spirit has taken place, but not on all

---

171. Boddy, *Laying on of Hands*, loc. 1277 of 1438.
172. Boddy, *Laying on of Hands*, loc. 1277 of 1438.
173. Wacker, *Heaven Below*, 70–71, 153.
174. Klaassen and Klassen, *Writings of Pilgram Marpeck*, 60.
175. Klaassen and Klassen, *Writings of Pilgram Marpeck*, 61.

men—just those who are willing to suffer with Christ, that is through the genuine act of repentance. It is only those persons who

> will also participate in the suffering and discipline of the expiation of Christ and upon him God's spirit will be pour (Prov. 1) by faith (Gal. 3; Jn. 7); he will receive the rich spirit of transformation, the knowledge of Christ in his heart, indeed, the Spirit of the New Testament, in which He promised in these days to pour over all flesh.[176]

The following is a description of early Pentecostal hermeneutics compared with early Anabaptist hermeneutics. Kenneth Archer posits that

> Pentecostal reading strategy embraces a modified narrative critical methodology while simultaneously affirming the contribution of the community.[177]

This is comparable to the Anabaptist experience described below. The evolution of radical hermeneutics began with the acceptance of *sola scriptura* as open to all Christians for interpretation through the power of the Spirit. It was Luther's and Zwingli's idea to create local conventicles, *ex officio* house prayer and study meetings, in order to educate their constituents about the reform they were promoting.[178] The priesthood of the believer empowered by the Holy Spirit, as implied by Erasmus and initially taught by Zwingli and Luther, encouraged many radical Christians to continue the practice in support of their restitution efforts. Out of these groups—led primarily by the more literate, but not excluding the less educated—developed what John Roth and Stuart Murray have called communal hermeneutics or congregational theology (*Gemeindetheologie*).[179] By following Matthew 16:5–16 and 1 Corinthians 14:26–40 literally, the conventicle was confident of the leading of the Holy Spirit, a correct scriptural understanding, and thus confident in the truth of their collective interpretations. The conventicles also gave rise to the circulation of biblical concordances called guides (*Zeyger*), which served as a "Rule of Life" based on Scripture sans commentary. They were organized by various pertinent spiritual and life situations as addressed

176. Klaassen and Klassen, *Writings of Pilgram Marpeck*, 61.
177. Archer, *Pentecostal Hermeneutic*, 264.
178. Gordon, *Swiss Reformation*, 90.
179. Murray, "Biblical Interpretation," 416–19; Roth and Stayer, *Anabaptism and Spiritualism, 1521–1700*, 353.

by numerous applicable biblical citations and committed to memory by those who were less literate.[180] The conventicle movement accepted this bottom-up ecclesiastic methodology, which protracted the hermeneutic evolution but nevertheless was effective in defining basic theological commonalities among the various emergent groups of radicals. They were, however, within traditional Christian orthodoxy with a few exceptions. Noteworthy among the exceptions were the appearance of aberrant manifestations of the gifts of the Holy Spirit, particularly in the Swiss regions of St. Gallen/Appenzell and the Dutch Melchiorite movement in Münster.[181]

MARPECK'S CHRISTOLOGY

He then begins to focus on the importance of the incarnate nature of Christ which for him is the humanity of Jesus as revealed in the New Testament juxtaposed against that of the typological Messiah of the Old Testament. Once the promise of the Messiah was realized and the salvation of humanity made certain, there was no longer the necessity of looking at the Christ of the past; he had come! Speaking to the vital purpose and value of the New Testament, he states:

> How much more clearly is He known since His coming? Scriptures speak more clearly of Him after His coming than they had done before. After He came, He is clearer and more powerful than He was before, as He said Himself (Mt. 13): Many prophets and righteous men longed to see what you see, but did not see; they longed to hear what you hear, but did not hear it.[182]

Marpeck insisted that Christians must focus on the humanity of Christ. They could now know Christ better, say more about him, pattern their lives after him, and "fully partake of the divine nature and spiritual good."[183] Revenge is no longer permitted, or even necessary, as enemies are overcome by the power of the Holy Spirit, thus vengeance and resistance were forbidden by Jesus (Luke 9, 21; Matt 5) when he commanded

---

180. Snyder, *Biblical Concordance of the Swiss*, vii–xxii; Klassen, *Covenant and Community*, 51–52.

181. Deppermann, *Melchior Hoffman*, 160. Schiess, *Kessler's Sabata*, 51–52; Snyder, *Profiles of Anabaptist Women*, 273–87.

182. Deppermann, *Melchior Hoffman*, 62.

183. Deppermann, *Melchior Hoffman*, 62–63.

his children, now filled with the Holy Spirit, "to love, to bless their enemies, persecutors, and opponents, and to overcome them with patience" (Matt 5; Luke 6). This was not possible before the advent of the Holy Spirit, who could not come as long as Christ was physically here on earth with his disciples (John 12, 16):[184]

> Now we are to reflect upon Him spiritually, what kind of mind, spirit, and disposition He had and how He lived: the more we reflect upon His physical words, works, deeds, and life, the better God allows us to know His mind, and the better He teaches and instructs us (Jn. 6).[185]

For him, it was through this kind of knowledge of Christ that one came to knowledge of God and could partake of the divine nature. This is the way, through instruction, and knowledge of Jesus' mind, that God inculcates his law (Heb 8) into the minds and hearts of Christians. "All the apostles had this Spirit, receiving it only after the ascension of Christ."[186] Marpeck was referring to the day of Pentecost when, according to Acts 2, the disciples were gathered in one accord in Jerusalem, the Lord filled them with this Spirit with "a strong witness to it at the beginning, according to His will and good pleasure," something he says must be witnessed to until Jesus returns.[187] It is no longer necessary to seek or long for another beginning:

> At Pentecost, in the presence of many people, external noise, wind, and strange tongues were His witness . . . to His promise. This Spirit of promise and clarity from God is here and now in the elect an open indicator, foretaste, seal, and down payment of future glory (1 Cor. 2; Eph. 1, 4; Rom 8).[188]

MARPECK'S CONCLUSION AGAINST THE SPIRITUALISTS

Marpeck published *A Clear and Useful Instruction* in 1531 to emphasize his opposition to the spiritualists' diminution of the humanity of Christ

---

184. Deppermann, *Melchior Hoffman*, 63.
185. Deppermann, *Melchior Hoffman*, 63.
186. Deppermann, *Melchior Hoffman*, 63.
187. Deppermann, *Melchior Hoffman*, 64.
188. Deppermann, *Melchior Hoffman*, 634.

and the suspension of the Sacraments, including water baptism.[189] He wrote:

> Whoever retains, practices, or accepts baptism, the Lord's Supper, or anything else, even Scriptures, word or deed, according to the . . . example of the Antichrist . . . will inherit destruction. But whoever retains, practices, and accepts such ceremonies according to the command, attitude, form, essence, or example of Christ and the apostles, indeed according to the instruction of the free Spirit, participates without blemish, misunderstanding, or abomination in the truly reenacted spiritual apostolic order. Whoever practices or receives such ceremonies . . . without true faith . . . errs even though there is, externally, correctness of words and procedures. I admonish to believe and to genuine confession.[190]

Finally:

> Whoever has been inwardly baptized, with belief and the Spirit of Christ in his heart, will not despise the external baptism and the Lord's Supper which are performed according to Christian, apostolic order; nor will dissuade anyone from participating in them. Where they are also present in the heart, there they are also practiced externally, and practiced according to love.[191]

The similarity between early Marpeckan Anabaptism and early Pentecostalism begins to appear again in this second treatise by Marpeck, who was still attempting to find a *via media* amid the numerous spiritualistic and/or legalistic radical Anabaptist groups. By maintaining traditional orthodox Christianity as the *loci* of his attempt, he established the critical nature of Christ's physical humanity combined with the efficacy of the role of the Holy Spirit in every Christian's life in his absence, which made obedience to, and *imitatio Christi*, possible. The ordinances, or sacraments of the church as Christ commanded them, were to be followed faithfully, but only in the "free Spirit" within whom they were scripturally designed to be practiced. This praxis was only possible by those who had been "inwardly baptized" in the Holy Spirit an event that must occur in addition to the externalities of Christian ceremonies. The evidence of inner baptism was the fruit of the Spirit in a Christian's life

---

189. Klaassen and Klaassen, *Writings of Pilgram Marpeck*, 69.
190. Klaassen and Klaassen, *Writings of Pilgram Marpeck*, 65.
191. Klaassen and Klaassen, *Writings of Pilgram Marpeck*, 65.

according to Galatians 5, initiated and founded in love (1 Corinthians 13). The gifts of the Spirit were meant to be manifested for the edification of the church first, the body of Christ, and then the good of the person with the gift. This was a commonly understood position of early Pentecostalism. But all the gifts of the Spirit described in 1 Corinthians 12–14 were still to be practiced for the edification of the church. They were not in cessation as the spiritualists proposed and were to be manifested until Christ returned.

The similarity in Marpeck's pneumatology, ecclesiology, soteriology, and theology in general to early Pentecostalism's Fourfold Gospel is remarkable. Both are Christocentric, traditionally orthodox, and both emphasize the restitution of Pauline pneumatology that was classic primitive New Testament Christianity. Both accomplished this similarity by reading the Scripture in a literal spiritual-prophetic way and simply acting it out as such.

MARPECK AND SCHWENCKFELD

Many of Marpeck's writings against Schwenckfeld reflect a similar Pentecostal perspective. What follows is an examination of those viewpoints. Concurrent with *A Clear Refutation*, Marpeck, probably in cooperation with Scharnschlager, wrote *A Clear and Useful Instruction*. This treatise was directed specifically at Schwenckfeld, particularly his concept of the "Celestial flesh of Christ" theory that he and Crautwald theologized regarding the humanity of Jesus. Nothing was more critical to Marpeck than the validity of Christ's humanity, which he felt was placed in jeopardy by Schwenckfeld. In addition, Marpeck attacked Schwenckfeld's *Stillstand*, a position like that of the spiritualists wherein Schwenckfeld suspended the practice of water baptism and the Lord's Supper.[192] In spite of apparent agreement on the rejection by both of the Lutheran and Catholic theologies of the Eucharist and mutual acceptance of a faith-based belief in the efficacy of the Lord's Supper, Schwenckfeld and Marpeck parted ways as Marpeck insisted on the physical humanity of Christ.[193] He thought it critical that Christ came as a natural man to bring the gospel to natural people within their physical ability to receive his message. He explained:

---

192. Klaassen and Klassen, *Writings of Pilgram Marpeck*, 69–70. See also chapter 1 of this dissertation.

193. Klaassen, "Schwenckfeld and the Anabaptists," 395.

> The Lord Christ thus became a natural man for natural man in order that, by the natural, the destruction of his nature might be translated again into the supernatural and heavenly nature. Therefore, the Lord Christ in all His supernatural miracles permitted the natural and outward things to precede. After all, He was not here for the sake or benefit of spirits and angels, but for man's sake-who has flesh and blood and natural sensitivity. For man is here in physical life until the translation out of the natural life into the supernatural is consummated. This physical life, however, appears in, and is opened to its eternal unchangeable essence only after this fleeting, perishable time comes to an end.[194]

Later he would write in *The Humanity of Christ 1555*, regarding the flesh of Christ:

> The flesh is of a creaturely nature that is taken up into and entered into the Godhead and the Godhead is united and one essence in the flesh as the true Word which became flesh which is then the truth and life itself. To the flesh, body, and blood, I ascribe all honors which the Father has ascribed to Him that I reasonably honor Him as much as the Father.[195]

Marpeck's disputation with Schwenckfeld highlighted his concept of the critical importance of the natural physical man in appropriating the gospel through the incarnate Christ and his physical humanity. He felt that the spiritualists were separating themselves from the "Spirit of power and strength made available in the incarnation and death of Christ and mediated through the life of the gathered community."[196]

The same concept can be ascertained from Pentecostal pastor and theologian David Myland. In 1910, Myland would write the following in reference to receiving the "latter rain," a popular term for the Pentecostal baptism in the Holy Spirit with speaking in tongues at the time:

> We either serve God in a psychical way, that is, intellectual way, without the spiritual, or we serve Him in the spiritual and forget the psychical and go beyond all bounds of reason and judgment. If our service is only spiritual, it leads to fanaticism; if in the psychical only, the result is formalism. God reaches the soul through the ear-gate, the physical nature, by the voice of the

---

194. Klaassen and Klassen, *Writings of Pilgrim Marpeck*, 85–86.
195. Klaassen and Klassen, *Writings of Pilgrim Marpeck*, 509.
196. Boyd, *Pilgrim Marpeck*, 86–87.

Spirit and the Word. Then comes into the heart, the spiritual; the heart is love to Him. Heart stands for the heavenly nature, the conscience "to love your God, and to serve Him with all your heart and all your soul," because the psychical (soul) stands mid-way between the physical and the spiritual, binding them together; it is the great power of man, the center of his being.[197]

This emphasis on the physical further defined who would be the messengers of the gospel. Both in Anabaptism and Pentecostalism, the call to preach was personal, highly spiritual, and not subject to the imprimatur of any ecclesial institution. Even Luther and Zwingli agreed with this position in the initial phases of their respective reform movements.

Marpeck's natural physical man theology of preaching the gospel was a denial of the Schwenckfeld/Crautwald theology which denigrated the incarnation as being not exactly the same as human because it was sinless. Christ lived through a gradual "divinization," wherein his physical nature was spiritualized as his life was gradually deified while on Earth.[198] This thought was the derivation of the term "celestial flesh."[199]

Upon his arrival in Strasbourg, Schwenckfeld was initially attracted to the Anabaptists, identifying with their status as ostracized religious refugees like himself. When it became clear to him that the Anabaptists were not interested in his theology, particularly his Monophysite Christology of the celestial flesh of Christ, he became disaffected. The Swiss Brethren, led by Reublin and Marpeck at the time, were specifically opposed to him and his relationship with Hoffman. Schwenckfeld was critical of the Anabaptists' tendency toward accepting self-proclaimed saints and prophets, fleeting loyalties and groupings, and unbelievable associations.[200] Also, because it played no role in achieving salvation, Schwenckfeld criticized the Anabaptists for focusing too much on water baptism. He accused them of making too much of the outer symbol, and although he rejected infant baptism, he refused rebaptism for himself. Water baptism had no ecclesiological goal; it was not admission into the visible church, it was simply a confession of one's faith in Christ. Because of this perceived abuse or lack of understanding, he extended his *Stillstand*

---

197. Myland, *Latter Rain Covenant*, 10–12.

198. McLaughlin, *Caspar Schwenckfeld, Reluctant Radical*, 69. Shantz, "Role of Valentine Crautwald." See also chapter 1 of this dissertation for further details.

199. Deppermann, *Melchior Hoffman*, 190.

200. McLaughlin, *Caspar Schwenckfeld, Reluctant Radical*, 191.

from the Eucharist to include baptism.[201] Schwenckfeld expressed these objections in his treatise *Judicium*, to which Marpeck responded.[202] In direct regard to Schenckfeld's *Stillstand* of baptism and the Lord's Supper, he wrote:

> Thus you can see how both baptism and the Lord's Supper are called sacraments, namely, because both of them must take place with a commitment and sanctification which is actually what sacrament is, for merely to plunge somebody into water or to baptize them is no sacrament. You must baptize in such a manner that the one who is baptized dies to his sins in a sincere way and in the power of a living faith in Christ.[203]

Marpeck did recognize that the Anabaptist movement, particularly the Swiss Brethren, was becoming legalistic and dogmatic, and consequently a longstanding dialogue and dispute developed with Schwenckfeld that lasted until Marpeck's death in 1556. Adult baptism was becoming a litmus test for salvation and the ban was being used as an instrument of punishment instead of a restorative measure administered in patience and love. His initial response was to identify two misuses of baptism:

> First, when unwilling, innocent people who do not desire, nor are inclined to be baptized, or people who know nothing about baptism. Baptism is a mockery and is powerless for such people indeed, it is not Christian baptism. Baptism is right or wrong, good or bad, according to its usage, according to the attitude in which it is received and used. It is being misused in our day, when out of long habit and ancient practice, everywhere the innocent, unwilling, unknowing children who cannot speak, are baptized with reference to salvation. Second, baptism is also misused when someone with a false, impure heart desires to be baptized.[204]

Marpeck's observations implied a developing, but substantial problem within Anabaptism, as noted above. He made similar observations regarding the misuse of the ban. In his *Admonition of 1542*, he continued to address the issues that Schwenckfeld had with the Anabaptists

---

201. McLaughlin, *Caspar Schwenckfeld, Reluctant Radical*, 136–37.
202. Marpeck, "Admonition of 1542," 159.
203. Marpeck, "Admonition of 1542," 175–76.
204. Marpeck, "Admonition of 1542," 202–3.

as pointed out in his *Judicium*. Marpeck addressed Schwenckfeld's criticisms by specifically referring to them in the *Admonition*. The Anabaptist misuse or abuse of the ban, or excommunication, was a problem recognized by Marpeck as he was careful to answer Schwenckfeld's complaints about this Anabaptist tenet. In reference to those who would partake of the Lord's Supper unworthily, he invokes Paul from 1 Corinthians 5:13, wherein he commands that "evil doers" be rooted out of the church. However, Marpeck added a caveat:

> But we are not to be like those who maintain the ban, banning people from the face of the earth, seizing life and land forbidding place and people. Such a ban does not belong to the Christian church, nor may such a ban ever be permitted in the Kingdom of Christ, according to the words of the Lord and Paul. Paul says they shall be punished, not as enemies, but as friends (2 Thess. 3:15), for other major vices as well, but only for their improvement and repentance.[205]

Marpeck was particularly disturbed by the way the Swiss Brethren were abusing the ban. He wrote in a letter to them, *Judgement and Decision*, that the ban should not be executed based on the "leaves and blossoms" of sinfulness, but only on the fruit, or substance, of such living:

> For no one may judge the heart until the fruit appears or until an outpouring of the treasure of the heart occurs. Only God, through the Holy Spirit, may judge. Whoever therefore establishes, commands, prohibits, coerces, drives, punishes, or judges before the time the good or evil fruit is revealed, lays claim to the authority, power, and office of the Holy Spirit of the Lord Jesus Christ, and, contrary to love, goodness, and grace, runs ahead of Christ Jesus. Therefore, even if one is concerned about a lapse and sees the leaves and blossoms of evil appearance, one ought only to warn and admonish, but not judge before the time of the fruit.[206]

Marpeck's criticism of legalistic Anabaptism in his attempt to unify the movement continued until his death in 1556.

One begins to understand Marpeck's pneumatology during this period when he wrote, in *A Clear Refutation* in 1531, that the gifts of faith though Christ must be "intensively and zealously" sought after so that the

---

205. Marpeck, "Admonition of 1542," 275–76.
206. Klaassen and Klassen, *Writings of Pilgram Marpeck*, 323–25.

body of Christ can be edified.[207] Again, he writes in *A Clear and Useful Instruction*, also of 1531, "Not all are apostles, not all are prophets, not all perform miracles, not all are teachers (I Cor. 12:29). But none of these gifts of faith will be lacking to the believers in their need."[208] Both of these concepts appear as arguments in an additional work, *A New Dialogue of 1532*, as well as at the *Zofingen Disputation of 1532*, published concurrently with the *Instruction* and the *Refutation*, as reasons for Anabaptists not attending Reformed churches.

A NEW DIALOGUE AND THE ZOFINGEN DISPUTATION OF 1532

Shortly before Marpeck left Strasbourg, he published a pamphlet, a third work, entitled *A New Dialogue/Questions and Answers between a Preacher and a Baptist*.[209] Within the same timeframe, the Reformed preachers, Zwinglian theologians, summoned Anabaptist preachers to a disputation in Zofingen, Switzerland to determine why they did not attend the Reformed church services. The record of this disputation was published by Heinrich Bullinger in his history of the origins of the Anabaptist movement in 1561. An analysis of these two documents will provide additional evidence of the charismatic and Pentecostal nature of Anabaptism some five years after Sattler's *Schleitheim Confession* criticized the manifestation of the gifts of the Spirit by certain perhaps overzealous adherents. Both the *Dialogue* and the *Zofingen Disputation* also provide evidence of Marpeck's influence regarding these spiritual matters in the broader Anabaptist milieu.

A comparison of the *Dialogue* with the *Zofingen* document reveals numerous similarities with early Pentecostalism. When one includes a comparison with Marpeck's other publications, discussed above, the Pauline pneumatological perspective becomes more evident as the ground upon which he believed the primitive church stood historically. Of particular interest are the similarities between Marpeck's developing pneumatology and early Pentecostal theology and praxis, specifically in regard to Pentecostalism's perception of the fundamental charismatic nature of

---

207. Marpeck, "Clear Refutation," 73.
208. Marpeck, "Clear Refutation," 77.
209. Marpeck, "New Dialogue, 1532," 50–53.

the primitive church and the necessity of the manifestation of the gifts of the Holy Spirit.

If Werner Packull is correct, *A New Dialogue* was written contemporaneously with the *Zofingen Disputation of 1532*, and answers an identical Reformed question in the same way using the same scriptural citations: "Why don't you attend our churches?"

Marpeck was in Strasbourg from 1528 to 1532.[210] In 1531, he was accused by the authorities of composing two booklets thought to be *A Clear Refutation* and *A Clear and Useful Instruction*. One begins to understand Marpeck's pneumatology during this period when he writes in *A Clear Refutation*:

> But whoever boasts . . . of faith, he can also with a good conscience boast of and employ the presents and gifts of faith through Christ and this diversity of the gifts of grace each one must . . . intensively and zealously discover and heed for himself . . . lest they omit their function (as such spirits think).[211]

Again, he wrote in *A Clear and Useful Instruction*:

> Not all are apostles, not all are prophets, not all perform miracles, not all are teachers (I Cor. 12:29). But none of these gifts of faith will be lacking to the believers in their need.[212]

Both of these concepts appear as arguments in the *Dialogue* and in the *Zofingen Disputation* as reasons for not attending Reformed churches. The purpose of these two works was an apology for the continuation of the ordinances and sacraments of the church against the spiritualists who advocated their cessation as noted above. However, Marpeck's response not only addressed the sacraments, but included the observations also noted above regarding the current efficacy of the gifts and work of the Holy Spirit as being necessary to the restitution of a primitive New Testament church, thus insisting on restoring its charismatic nature. *A New Dialogue* consists of a conversation between a Reformed preacher and an Anabaptist and begins with the Preacher asking, "Why do you not come to hear my preaching nor celebrate the Lord's Supper with me?"[213]

The Baptist responds:

---

210. Klassen, *Covenant and Community*, 26; Klassen and Klaassen, *Marpeck*, 122.
211. Marpeck, "A Clear Refutation," 73.
212. Marpeck, "A Clear Refutation," 77.
213. Marpeck, "A New Dialogue, 1532," 54.

The proper order would have called for us to speak first of inner matters before dealing with outward things. I cannot applaud you for not wanting to hear about inner matters first. You preach and teach that one should keep the will and commandments of God and Christ but you are the first to break them.

You can neither prove (child baptism) from the Scriptures nor defend it in good conscience.

Preacher:

I consider child baptism an old custom.

Baptist:

Furthermore, you do not hold the Christian order in your congregation.

You do not exercise brotherly discipline either in terms of inclusion or exclusion (neither baptism nor the ban). . .but break the bread with everyone.

Furthermore, if someone in your congregation receives a revelation, finds a failing in you or is annoyed by your sermon and wants to bring this to public notice, (to the congregation) or discuss it according to Christian order, as outlined in the First Epistle to the Corinthians chapter 14, you will not tolerate it . . . you call on the temporal sword. You lack your own sword (the word of God), otherwise you would not need a borrowed sword. Does the temporal authority have to judge your teaching? I thought it should be your lambs and listeners who judge, according to the word of Paul, 1 Cor. 14. You do not keep the Christian order but the opposite. Individual members are not permitted to exercise their gifts for the edification of the congregation, as if you had all the gifts.

Preacher:

You say I have depraved people in my congregation. Friend point them out.

Baptist:

If you had the love of God you would consider His commandment and the order in regard to inner and outer baptism. You would investigate and test everyone's spirit personally and not year after year talk or shout into the wind.

Preacher:

Yes, but the authorities do not permit the baptism of adults. Therefore, we will keep child baptism as an ancient custom.

Baptist:

I had planned to ask you about the inner [baptism] and whether you are a Christian. But it has been revealed to me without asking that you are still far from Christian.[214]

The Anabaptist disputants at Zofingen articulated a very similar pneumatology within an ecclesiological context describing what a primitive New Testament church should look like. They answered a very similar question: "Those called Lutheran and Zwinglian . . . repeatedly ask us why we oppose the above mentioned attendance at their meetings."[215] They responded with nine reasons, the following being the first:

> The *first reason* is that they do not observe the Christian order as taught in the gospel or the word of God in I Cor. 14, namely, that a listener is bound by Christian love (if something to edification is given or revealed to him) that he should and may speak of it also in the congregation, and again thereupon be silent, according to the text which reads: "How is it then brethren? When ye come together, every one of you hath a psalm, hath a doctrine, hath a tongue, hath a revelation, hath an interpretation. Let all things be done unto edifying," etc. And again, "Let one or another prophet speak (that is prophesying), and the other judge. If anything be revealed to another that sitteth by, let the first hold his peace. For ye may all prophesy one by one, that all may learn, and all may be comforted. And the spirits of the prophets are subject to the prophets. For God is not the author of confusion, but of peace, as in all churches of the saints," etc. It thus further appears that Paul spoke to the church of God, yea to all Christians whom he in the beginning of the chapter admonished to seek after spiritual gifts, yet most of all, that they may prophesy, prophesying meaning that they receive the meaning from God to share with others (for edification, exhortation and comfort)."[216]

Anabaptists' understanding of Paul was that conventicle attendees were bound by love to speak out to edify the church using psalms, doctrine, speaking in tongues (*zungen reden*), interpretation, revelations, and prophesies. Paul encouraged Christians to seek after spiritual gifts, and especially hoped that all would prophesy, meaning that anyone who

---

214. Marpeck, "New Dialogue, 1532," 54–59. See also, Marpeck, "Ein Neu Gesprache."

215. Peachy, "Answer of Some," 10; Byrd, "Pentecostalism's Anabaptist Heritage," 58. My paraphrase.

216. Peachy, "Answer of Some," 10; italics are the author's.

had received understanding from God on some matter should share it with the others including the leader "(for edification, exhortation and comfort)"[217] and then allow it to be judged. This was to be done in a seemly, convenient, and orderly manner, for when the congregation assembles it is a temple of the Holy Spirit where the gifts or the inner operation of the Spirit in each one serves the common good.[218]

The disputants continued:

> So Paul in the end of the chapter commands that they shall not forbid speaking in tongues, which, according to the beginning of the chapter serves to the edification of the congregation. How much less authority has one to forbid prophesying, teaching, interpreting, or admonition to the edification of the congregation?[219]

The Anabaptists specifically objected to the Reformed practice of only allowing one person to speak in worship services. If only one speaks and no one else is speaking or prophesying, how could anyone confess that the congregation was spiritual according to 1 Corinthians 14 and that God was dwelling and operating through his Holy Spirit with his gifts? Forbidding others to exercise the gifts was tantamount to frustrating and impeding the work of the Holy Spirit whose role it was to edify the church, "so that men might recognize the congregation as spiritual."[220] It is interesting to note that the first reason for not attending the Reformed churches was their lack of spirituality based on Paul's instructions in 1 Corinthians 14. It would appear that to the Anabaptists the presence of the Holy Spirit, as evidenced initially through the working of his gifts within the congregation, was the mark of any true Christian church, not just an Anabaptist church.[221]

The *second reason* accused the Reformed of falling away from their former position of resisting the rulers and constrainers of the evangelical faith, such as authorities, popes, emperors, and princes in matters of faith.[222]

---

217. Peachy, "Answer of Some," 10.
218. Peachy, "Answer of Some," 11.
219. Peachy, "Answer of Some," 11.
220. Peachy, "Answer of Some," 12.
221. Byrd, "Pentecostalism's Anabaptist Heritage," 58–59.
222. Peachy, "Answer of Some," 14.

The *third reason* indicts the Reformed for using the magisterial system of justice to defend themselves and their faith with the use of violence as opposed to the sword of the Spirit and other weapons described in Ephesians 6.[223]

The *fourth reason* for not attending points out that by using the magisterial system of justice in matters of faith, the Reformed provide evidence that they do not have sword of the Spirit, "and because they do not have it, it is manifest that they also lack the Holy Spirit as he who should wield that sword in and through them."[224]

The *fifth reason* was they did not use the Christian spiritual ban to maintain spiritual order within the church because they lacked the Holy Spirit (John 20).[225]

The *sixth reason* was, lacking the Holy Spirit, "they were no established, separate church of God, nor body of Christ . . . baptized of Christ, I Cor. 12; Matt. 3."[226] This was a reference to the qualifications for those participating in the communion. First Corinthians 12 and Matthew 3 both refer to Christians being baptized in the Holy Spirit, not water.

In the *seventh reason*, they accuse the Reformed preachers of not maintaining the evangelical order as written about in Matthew 28 and Acts 2. In those Scriptures, they believed that Christians were instructed to teach the unbeliever first and then baptize them in water after a confession of faith.[227]

The *eighth reason* refers to early Reformed teachings which instructed Christians to forsake all for the cause of Christ. But now they were teaching the opposite in that they were trying to compel Anabaptists to abandon their beliefs for the sake of family, farm, and home. The Anabaptists claimed that they were holding to the original teachings of Luther and Zwingli and now were being killed for it.[228]

The *ninth and final reason* stated that, apart from sin, Christians were not forbidden to have fellowship with the world for the sake of

---

223. Peachy, "Answer of Some," 15.
224. Peachy, "Answer of Some," 16.
225. Peachy, "Answer of Some," 18.
226. Peachy, "Answer of Some," 20.
227. Peachy, "Answer of Some," 23.
228. Peachy, "Answer of Some," 24.

bodily nourishment. "This does not mean that we have fellowship in their matters of faith."[229]

SUMMARY

In summary, Marpeck's conclusion against the spiritualists is recounted in the substance of his *A New Dialogue 1532*, portions of *A Clear Refutation*, and *A Clear and Useful Instruction* and the *Zofingen Disputation of 1532*. His arguments in these writings are indicative of the perception within Marpeck's circle, and by inference Anabaptism in general, that the primitive New Testament church was first and fundamentally charismatic in nature and needed *restitutio in integrum* in that way. A comparison of the *Zofingen* document with the *Dialogue* reveals numerous similarities. Since the Anabaptist disputants at Zofingen were led by Martin Weniger, an acquaintance of many of the Swiss Brethren leaders from Zurich, including Wilhelm Reublin, Marpeck's associate in Strasbourg, it can be inferred that Marpeck's teaching played a significant role in the dispute.[230] When one includes a comparison of the spiritual positions cited in Marpeck's other two documents, his Pentecostal charismatic pneumatological perspective becomes more evident as the ground upon which the primitive church stood historically. The three works of Marpeck are typical of a broad range of Anabaptist belief and practice, including the Swiss Brethren and the Hutterites. They also are reflective of the initial influences of Erasmian humanism and Rhenish mysticism. The Anabaptist approbation of spiritual-prophetic literalism, particularly regarding 1 Corinthians 12–14, which Luther and Zwingli had initially promoted, insisted that biblical interpretation did not deny the contemporary efficacy of the manifestation of the gifts of the Holy Spirit. These factors resulted in a type of early Pentecostalism. The influence of Marpeck on the disputants at Zofingen was apparent as they had developed and argued for his Pauline Pentecostal charismatic models of the primitive church during the disputation.

---

229. Peachy, "Answer of Some," 25.

230. Yoder, *Anabaptism and Reformation in Switzerland*, 104, 353n8. See also, Harder, *Sources of Swiss Anabaptism*, 520, 57.

MELCHIOR HOFFMANN: MÜNSTER AND THE ARRIVAL OF MENNO SIMONS

The Melchiorite movement that took political control of Münster in 1534 and 1535 precipitated events that almost brought Anabaptism to dissolution. This section will speak to the aberrant misuse and abuse of the charismata, particularly the gift of prophecy, by Melchiorite Anabaptists that brought this about. It will also point out how Menno Simons was able to save Anabaptism, but in doing so, for all intents and purposes, inhibited the continued manifestation of the charismata, particularly the gift of prophecy.

After Marpeck's departure from Strasbourg in 1532, the development of the Melchiorite movement ultimately brought a significant portion of Anabaptism to an almost fatal end due to their apocalyptic and bellicose resistance theology as acted out during the Münster debacle. It was also the demise of the Melchiorities at Münster that occasioned the introduction of Menno Simons as the ultimate leader of the remnants of that movement, and the establishment of a more biblicist Anabaptist sect: the Mennonites.

Hoffman will be the last spiritualist to be discussed who was present during Marpeck's sojourn in Strasbourg. He appeared in Strasbourg, initially from 1529 to 1530.[231] He had come from Emden, East Frisia, where he and Karlstadt had participated in the disputations the Lutherans and the radical reformers had there. Hoffman's apocalypticism and Karlstadt's sacramentarianism were both embraced by radical elements there, including Anabaptists. Hoffmann was an Anabaptist and sacramentarian based on his *The Ordinance of God, 1530*, where he wrote, concerning baptism:

> It is the sign of the covenant of God, instituted solely for the old, the mature, and the rational . . . not for the immature, uncomprehending . . . who cannot understand . . . such are immature children.[232]

And of his sacramentarianism, he wrote that the apostles understood

> That he [Jesus] did not for this reason corporally exist in the bread, and that the physical bread was not himself, and that his

---

231. Deppermann, *Melchior Hoffman*, 160–61.
232. Williams, *Spiritual and Anabaptist Writers*, 192.

blood was not in the wine, nor did the wine become his physical blood.[233]

He believed that Christ had a heavenly or celestial body as opposed to human, much like Schwenckfeld had taught. Hoffman initially preached an imminent apocalypse wherein the church was to be nonresistant until the event actually occurred, at which time the secular authorities would protect the true believers with the sword, precluding any vengeful resistant acts by Christians who were not part of those authorities.[234] As to church polity, he divided it into four groups: the "Throng of apostolic messengers" who were unable to sin, the "first born" who were prophets (the office of prophet), the "Whole troop of pastors" who led the congregations, and the "simple congregants." The apostolic messengers controlled the prophets as they could only interpret the prophecies by dreams and visions.[235] Considered by some to be the "Father of Dutch Anabaptism,"[236] Hoffmann was responsible for the development of a significant Anabaptist group in North Germany and the Netherlands referred to as Melchiorites.

THE STRASBOURG PROPHETS

Facing the opposition of the Lutheran-influenced authorities in East Frisia, Hoffman and Karlstadt both left the region.[237] Arriving in Strasbourg, Hoffman discovered a substantial radical movement among the laity manifesting the gifts of the Spirit, particularly prophecy. It was particularly prevalent among radical spiritualist groups, but also within Anabaptist sects. Of twenty known and active "prophets" in the city, nine were women. The most influential in Hoffman's case were Lienhard Jost and his wife Ursula, Barbara Rebstock, Gertrude Lorenz, Agnes Jost, Elizabeth Jost, Katherine Seid, Margaret, and Appolonia.[238]

There are many perspectives as to the equality of women participating in the Radical Reformation. One argument is that within the more spiritual Anabaptist movements they were considered "companions in

233. Williams, *Spiritual and Anabaptist Writers*, 195.
234. Stayer, *Anabaptists and the Sword*, 222–23.
235. Deppermann, *Melchior Hoffman*, 263–65.
236. Williams, *Radical Reformation*, 539.
237. Deppermann, *Melchior Hoffman*, 157–58, 315–17.
238. Derksen, "Voice, Leadership, and Influence," 431–33.

faith, mission, and martyrdom."[239] In the context of new religious movements, apocalypticism, and visionary and ecstatic experiences, women preached and felt free to redefine social relationships.[240] The Anabaptist Concordance of 1540 cites Joel 2 as well as Acts 2:38-39, wherein Peter quotes Joel, making no gender exceptions regarding those who repented and were baptized in water in the name of Jesus Christ, saying they all would receive the Holy Spirit.[241] This was born out in a very charismatic and Pentecostal-like way during Hoffman's experience in Strasbourg.

Hoffman was convinced that he was the second Elijah of the Apocalypse and that he had the prophetic gift for interpreting Scripture. He was particularly impressed with the prophecies of Ursula Jost, her husband Lienhard, and Barbara Rebstock. They seemed to confirm his own apocalyptic insights regarding the coming of the apocalyptic "New Jerusalem" to Strasbourg. He was so convinced of this, that he published some of their prophecies in 1530.[242] However, about the same time, Bucer and the city council had had their fill of Hoffman's apocalyptic prophecies and sought his arrest; nonetheless he was able to escape, fleeing back to East Frisia where he baptized 300 more adults.[243] Many of Hoffman's converts in Emden made their way into the Netherlands and were successful in converting many to an apocalyptic Anabaptism.[244] Having been banished from Emden again, he returned to Strasbourg where, subsequent to a series of city council synods examining various radical reformers, he was imprisoned for life.[245] The circle of adherents Hoffman acquired in Strasbourg and the Netherlands migrated to Münster, believing that it now was to be the New Jerusalem and not Strasbourg.[246]

---

239. Derksen, "Voice, Leadership, and Influence," 428.

240. Derksen, "Voice, Leadership, and Influence," 428-29.

241. Snyder, *Biblical Concordance of the Swiss*, 16.

242. Snyder, *Profiles of Anabaptist Women*, 273-75. See also, Bakker, *Bernhard Rothmann and the Reformation*, 49-50; Deppermann, *Melchior Hoffman*, 204-6.

243. Deppermann, *Melchior Hoffman*, 316-17.

244. Deppermann, *Melchior Hoffman*, 328-29. See also Williams, *Radical Reformation*, 539-47.

245. Deppermann, *Melchior Hoffman*, 422-25.

246. Bakker, *Bernhard Rothmann and the Reformation*, 50-51.

MÜNSTER DEBACLE

The Melchiorite movement legally gained political control of the city and formed a theocratic government that considered the charismatic gift of prophecy—the main criteria for guidance. Bernhard Rothmann (1495–1535?) led the initial reform in Münster as the Catholic priest who established the first Lutheran congregation in 1532.[247] Subsequently he embraced sacramentarianism, and eventually accepted rebaptism by Melchiorite adherents of Jan Matthijs (d. 1534) from the Netherlands. Matthijs, a more resistance-oriented convert of Hoffman, claimed to be the second Enoch of the Apocalypse where he had gained many Dutch converts.[248] Also in 1532, Phillip of Hesse (1504–1567), the Habsburg landgrave governing Münster, approved the selection of his brother, Franz von Waldeck, to be the Catholic bishop of Münster. Bishop Waldeck initially supported his brother's Lutheran sympathies, thus facilitating the cause of the reform. However, by 1534, the conflict among the Catholics, Lutherans, and Melchiorites in Münster had grown exponentially. During January that year, about twenty percent of the population had been baptized by Rothmann and his followers.[249] Shortly thereafter, Matthijs sent Jan van Leiden (d. 1535) to Münster as his emissary to give further instructions to the radical reform in progress. Once van Leiden had established himself in the city, he sent for Matthijs and proceeded to send his own emissaries to neighboring cities with a call to Anabaptists to gather in Münster.[250] Large groups of Melchiorites began to arrive, including a contingent from the Netherlands that followed Matthijs, and it was not long before radical sacramentarians became Melchiorite Anabaptists. The city council was caught between enforcing the law against adult baptism and the perceived violent reaction of the Anabaptists. Consequently, they did nothing.[251] This was compounded by a rumor that Bishop Waldeck was marshalling forces to arrest the Anabaptists for baptizing adults. Catholics and Lutherans on the city council quelled the rumor, but the rift between the factions had been exacerbated. Rothmann had previously declared a position of nonresistance, but the council doubted the Anabaptist commitment to it based on their response

---

247. Klotzer, "Melchiorites and Munster," 225.
248. Bakker, *Bernhard Rothmann and the Reformation*, 3–4, 89.
249. Klotzer, "Melchiorites and Munster," 230.
250. Bakker, *Bernhard Rothmann and the Reformation*, 148.
251. Bakker, *Bernhard Rothmann and the Reformation*, 148.

to previous attempts to rid the city of them. However, the radical non-resistance stance would soon change. A growing danger was perceived by the Anabaptists which precipitated a surge in apocalyptic prophecies and end-time preaching for repentance.[252] The bishop then conscripted his own force and united with Lutheran forces in preparation for a siege of the city.[253] As the city prepared for the assault, the internal factions of the city armed themselves against the siege, but also against each other. All this coincided with the annual election of the city council, which was won by the Anabaptists, who chose Jan van Leiden as the new leader over the violent apocalyptic prophet Matthijs.[254] As the bishop began to blockade the city, van Leiden ordered anyone who refused baptism to leave the city. Approximately 2,000 people either left of their own free will or were driven out before the siege began. At the same time, numerous Anabaptists flocked to the city seeing it as a holy refuge, the "New Jerusalem."[255] Rothmann understood the history of the world to be divided into three ages: Creation to the flood, from Noah to the restitution of Christianity at Münster, and the physical temporal reign of the returned Christ and his saints. He believed that he was living at the end of the second age and Münster was the place for the ushering in of the third and final age, but it needed the Anabaptists to take up arms against the attacking heathen governments to ensure the restitution of the church in Münster and hasten the appearance of Christ.[256] He wrote in 1534, at the beginning of the coming siege of Münster:

> There may be those think that God himself will come down from heaven with the angels to avenge himself on the godless, and who confidently wait for it. No, dear brother. He will come, that is true. But the vengeance must be first carried out by God's servants who will properly repay the unrighteous godless as God commanded them. God will be with his people and will give them iron horns and bronze claws against their enemies.[257]

The bishop had established a perimeter around Münster necessary for a successful siege. In the meantime, the leadership of the city,

---

252. Bakker, *Bernhard Rothmann and the Reformation*, 150–51.
253. Kirschoff, "Munster," 98.
254. Bakker, *Bernhard Rothmann and the Reformation*, 157.
255. Stayer, *Anabaptists and the Sword*, 234.
256. Stayer, *Anabaptists and the Sword*, 241, 44–48
257. Klaassen, *Anabaptism in Outline*, 335.

Matthijs, and van Leiden were being influenced by lay prophets and pastors of the city who caused much internal strife. On Easter Sunday, 1534, Christ had not appeared, so Matthijs sallied forth from the city and attacked the siege line, only to be slaughtered.[258] This left van Leiden with the dilemma of no longer having either the second Enoch or Hoffmann, the second Elijah—imprisoned for life in Strasbourg—available for Christ's return. In the absence of the two "witnesses" as prophesied in the Bible, van Leiden postponed the imminent return of Christ by declaring that Münster was no longer the "New Jerusalem," but meant to be a model Christian community responsible for punishment of nonbelievers in preparation for his return.[259] The city responded positively to the idea and prepared to go to battle. Van Leiden decreed the establishment of a community of goods for all in the city and legalized polygamy, both with Rothmann's support. Capital punishment was used to enforce the new laws and maintain order. In the summer of 1534, a lay prophet declared that van Leiden should be made king in the role of the second David of the Bible. During this reorganization of the city, the citizens of Münster managed to thwart two assaults by the bishop's forces.[260] However, in June 1535, after months of siege and the effects of its aftermath, Münster was taken. What ensued was a bloodbath which took the lives of all but a few citizens. Jan van Leiden and his military commanders were executed, and their bodies were butchered and hung, standing in cages from St. Lambert's tower on the city square.[261]

MEDIEVAL AND EARLY MODERN PROPHECY

The charismatic gift of prophecy became an important piece of evidence for the presence of the Holy Spirit within the Anabaptist movement. A literal biblicist reading of 1 Corinthians 12–14 had convinced them that there was no true church without the manifestation of the gifts in general, but prophecy was the most effective for evangelization and edification of the church. Speaking in tongues, miracles, and healing were attested to as well, but prophecy became the most frequently manifested, and was authenticated as the true word of God.

258. Klotzer, "Melchiorites and Munster," 236–37.
259. Klotzer, "Melchiorites and Munster," 238–40.
260. Klotzer, "Melchiorites and Munster," 239–46.
261. Klotzer, "Melchiorites and Munster," 249–50.

Jon Balserak, in his study concerning John Calvin's approach to the gift of prophecy, sheds some light on what happened in Münster. Balserak identified two broad streams of thought. First, there was the Medieval tradition; the broadest definition of prophecy here is supernatural knowledge conferred divinely on the prophet, but variously further distinguished as ecstasy; vision; dreams through a cloud; a voice from heaven; the receiving of an oracle; and being filled with the Holy Spirit.[262] And then there was the Early Modern tradition, where the prophet was thought of as more of an interpreter of Scripture. This was based on what was exactly expected of the prophet. Some thought it was to reveal the mysteries of the Scripture, while others thought it to be proclamation and application.[263] Balserak does admit that these two traditions left much to be desired regarding any hard-and-fast definitions or rules. He then observes that when one moves from tradition one to tradition two, there seems to occur a synthesis, particularly in regard to Zwingli and his contemporaries.[264] It is within this genre of prophecy that Anabaptists raised its head. The Anabaptists simply began to speak out, prophetically, against the preacher during a reformed church service, challenging his right to be the exclusive speaker of the meeting. Balserak asserts that they seemed to be acting on Paul's references to prophecy, exploiting (according Zwingli) what they believed to be the proper church format for the manifestation of prophecy.[265] They were excoriated for attempting to usurp the authority of the duly appointed clergy, in the Catholic sense, but, although not mentioned by Balserak, were most likely to have been acting on the doctrine of the priesthood of the believer, initially taught by Zwingli. Anabaptists embraced the idea that every Christian was empowered by the Spirit to read and interpret Scripture and should do so for the edification of the church, something that Zwingli would have appropriated from Erasmus. For Zwingli and his contemporaries, the Anabaptists were destroying church order, not obeying 1 Corinthians 12–14. On the other hand, the Anabaptists believed that the reformed church was continuing to maintain the Catholic Church order, not reform it according to Scripture.[266] Early Pentecostalism embraced a similar interpretation

262. Balserak, *John Calvin as Sixteenth-century Prophet*, 18–24.
263. Balserak, *John Calvin as Sixteenth-century Prophet*, 25.
264. Balserak, *John Calvin as Sixteenth-century Prophet*, 32.
265. Balserak, *John Calvin as Sixteenth-century Prophet*, 51.
266. Balserak, *John Calvin as Sixteenth-century Prophet*, 51.

of the gift of prophecy. Azusa Street contemporary Frank Batrtleman, prophesied in 1906 concerning the shortness of time left for anyone to respond to God's last call to salvation. He warned of the imminence of death without Christ by using the contemporary examples of the Johnstown Flood and the 1906 San Francisco Earthquake.[267] Donald Dayton points out that initially prophecy was interpreted naturalistically as preaching or testifying, but evolved into a more supernatural ecstatic experience.[268] Keith Warrington observed that Pentecostals identify prophecies as those occasions when an individual, inspired by God, speak spontaneously and extemporarily."[269] This would also be considered a New Testament norm according to 1 Corinthians 14:3–5.

If the Anabaptist experience in Strasbourg was crystallizing, as Yoder suggested, or purifying as Deppermann surmised, their ordeal in Melchiorite Münster, if nothing else, was denominating. The vestiges of the movement broke into two primary opposing groups, those who continued to maintain an apocalyptic and bellicose resistance stance regarding their role in the second coming of Christ, and those who were also apocalyptic, but pacifists, turning to a more biblicist understanding and position.

The first group, called Batenburgers, thrived under the leadership of Jan van Batenburg (d. 1538) rampaged against the ungodly with the sword, looted churches, and destroyed the property thereof throughout Holland for three years. Batenburg was eventually arrested and executed in 1538.[270] The second group were pacifists and sought a more peaceful alternative while still holding the second coming as an imminent priority. They were initially led by David Joris (1501–1556), who sought to reunite the Melchiorite Anabaptists by distancing himself from the violent Batenburgers, who sought to establish the kingdom of God on earth by human agency. Joris declared that God would establish the kingdom in his own time and way. However, his unifying attempt failed to convince the Strasbourg Melchiorites, then led by Leinhard Jost, which left him without a strong following of former Münsterites.[271] His movement eventually gave way to that of Menno Simons.

267. Bartleman, *My Story*, 43–48, 49–52.
268. Dayton, *Theological Roots of Pentecostalism*, 93.
269. Warrington, *Pentecostal Theology*, 82.
270. Snyder, *Anabaptist History and Theology*, 150–51. See also, Williams, *Radical Reformation*, 582–83.
271. Williams *Radical Reformation*, 583–88. See also, Green, "Last Book."

The two most important leaders of the Melchiorites who had not been in Münster were Obbe Philips (1500–1568) and his brother Dirk (1504–1568). Menno Simons was to follow these two, also as one who had not been a participant in Münster. Although all three were Melchiorites, they rejected the Münster experience as being the result of false prophecies and prophets. They were Melchiorites in that they embraced the apocalyptic expectation as prophesied in the Bible, but rejected the self-proclaimed prophets, particularly van Leiden. They believed in the heavenly or celestial flesh of Christ as a confessional fundamental and preached adult rebaptism, but thoroughly rejected polygamy and the violent preparation for the coming of Christ and his kingdom. C. Arnold Snyder refers to them as the Melchiorite "pacifist" wing.[272]

This pacifist group also brought a more biblicist hermeneutic to the movement. They were not spiritualists in the sense of Hoffmann, Denck, Hut, or Schwenckfeld, but did believe that the word and Spirit were held in simultaneous tension. Thus, they did not give primacy to the manifestations of the gifts of the Spirit, as in Münster, but held them subject to the word for confirmation. When Simons assumed the leadership of the Melchiorite movement as chief among the bishops in 1542,[273] he wrote against the "Blasphemy of Jan van Leyden" and the many mistakes made in Münster, including violence and the use of Old Testament ethics.[274] He would eventually do away with Hoffmann's "Office of Prophet" for both men and women, and declare in the *Foundation of Christian Doctrine, 1539–1540*, that it is men who are called to preach:

> You see, worthy reader, with such and similar glorious figures and comparisons all pious preachers and teachers are honoured in the Scriptures, men whom the Holy Ghost has ordained bishops and overseers in His church, congregation, and house.[275]

One cannot help but conclude that this was a reaction to the number of female prophets that were active in the years prior to, during, and after Münster. Simons' perspective concerning women is captured in his *The True Christian Faith, 1541*:

---

272. Snyder, *Anabaptist History and Theology*, 151–52. See also, Stayer, *Anabaptists and the Sword*, 309–10.
273. Simons, *Complete Writings of Menno Simons*, 22.
274. Stayer, *Anabaptists and the Sword*, 310–11.
275. Snyder, *Anabaptist History and Theology*, 267.

> Be obedient to your husbands in all reasonable things so that those who do not believe may be gained by your upright, pious conversation without the Word, as Peter says.[276]

Menno Simons cannot be considered a cessationist by any means, but his marginalization of the role of women concerning the manifestation of the gifts of the Spirit, particularly prophecy, had a significant impact on Anabaptism writ large. "True apostles, bishops, preachers, and pastors,"[277] were first of all men, called by the Holy Spirit or by the congregation of a true church.[278] These two elements were brought together in his biblicist interpretation of Scripture that resulted in a more traditional orthodox Christianity as perceived by Lutheran and Zwinglian opponents of Anabaptism. A third casualty of Simons's pacifist position was evangelism. No longer was there a priority to evangelize the biblical 144,000 of the Apocalypse. In order to avoid continued hostilities, persecutions, and martyrdom, Anabaptists agreed to become the "Quiet of the Land."[279] Stuart Murray describes this hermeneutical confluence as the transition of the charismatic (Pentecostal) phase of Anabaptism into a tradition wherein the accepted communal hermeneutic was replaced by the authority of a recognized clergy and acknowledged interpretations.[280] Notwithstanding Simons's abolition of the Office of Prophet and identifying those called to ministry as male only, he did not deny the operation of the gifts of the Spirit when he quoted Ephesians 4:11 in his *Foundation of Christian Doctrine*:

> Paul says, Some he appointed apostles; some prophets; some evangelists; some pastors and teachers. Let everyone be mindful that he boast not of what is, has, or possesses for it all is the grace and gift of God. Let everyone attend to his duty, for the perfecting of the saints, for the work of the ministry, for the edifying of the body of Christ.[281]

However, this attempt to control manifestations of the charismata is reminiscent of the *Didache* of the second century, also known as the *Teaching of the Twelve Apostles*. This early Christian teaching was an

276. Simons, *Complete Writings of Menno Simons*, 383.
277. Simons, *Complete Writings of Menno Simons*, 169.
278. Simons, *Complete Writings of Menno Simons*, 161.
279. Snyder, *Anabaptist History and Theology*, 375.
280. Murray, "Biblical Interpretation," 423.
281. Simons, *Complete Writings of Menno Simons*, 146.

attempt to instruct the various congregations in how to manage the ministries of itinerant charismatic prophets and teachers. Although attempting to protect the integrity of the congregations by setting up certain ground rules, there was no intent to prohibit them. However, there were those who attempted to insert themselves into roles not conformed to, or supported by, Scripture. There was also the jeopardy of personal profit motives. Arthur Cleveland Coxe references the prevalence of incipient fanaticism in the second-century church requiring stricter rules of conduct for such transients. Thomas O'Loughlin agrees that the church had been attracted to such charlatans.[282] Simons took similar actions to avoid the same types of people and problems that were encountered during the Münster debacle. His decision also paved the way for a more acceptable Anabaptist sect as it began to appear more traditionally orthodox, at least to the more tolerant of Protestants. This precluded Anabaptism from developing into a charismatic movement similar to early twentieth-century Pentecostalism.

CONCLUSION PART 1

In 1527, Michael Sattler was insistent that the aberrant behaviour, particularly activities like those documented by Johannes Kessler in St. Gallen and Appenzell, and like those which would occur in Münster as described above, were beyond the pale of an acceptable primitive New Testament church. He made reference to this abuse in the letter he wrote to the believers at Horb while he was awaiting execution in Rottenburg. His *Schleitheim Articles* was an early attempt to unite the Anabaptists. It consisted of seven confessions of faith: baptism, the ban, the commemorative communion, separation the world, pastors chosen from the congregation, pacifism, and not taking the government oath, all indicative of the historical perspective mentioned above.[283] But there was nothing specific regarding the church order as described in the *Zofingen Disputation* and *A New Dialogue,* particularly in reference to the pneumatological work of the Holy Spirit as being fundamental to the truth. Sattler was emphatic in identifying and rejecting false brothers, whose behavior he described as lascivious and given over to license, yet he still did not reject,

---

282. Coxe, "Teaching of the Twelve Apostles," 372–83, 83. Elucidation III. See also, O'Loughlin, *Didache*, 115.

283. Yoder, *Legacy of Michael Sattler*, 34–45.

the grace and revelation of God, mentioned in his letter to the congregation at Horb. What also was quite clear at Schleitheim was the church's separation from the world.

However, it was within five years of the *Schleitheim Confession* that the *Zofingen Disputation* occurred and the *New Dialogue* appeared. A period of time in which the Anabaptist movement was defining itself, making decisions about what their theology and praxis would be and how that reconciled with their perception of what the charismatic primitive church should look like after its restitution. As C. Arnold Snyder observes, it is also an indication that not all Anabaptists, such as Marpeck, saw the church and the world from the same apocalyptic worldview.[284] William Klassen and Walter Klaassen have observed that Marpeck was perhaps developing a *via media* between the legalism of Schleitheim and the license of the spiritualists and law and liberty.[285] Marpeck spoke out against false prophets, as did Sattler, yet insisted on the validity of including the charismata as essential to the life and identity of a New Testament church. C. Arnold Snyder's analysis of the *Frankenthal Protocol of 1571* supports this conclusion: "The Holy Spirit proclaims God's glory, calls those who are to be believers, and gives them manifold gifts and graces."[286] Even though the debacle at Münster provided many reasons to curtail or control the manifestations of the charismata by many Anabaptist leaders, Marpeck chose to republish Rothmann's *Bekentnisse van beyden Sacramenten of 1533* (Confession Concerning Both Sacraments) in which Rothmann wrote prior to gaining control of Münster:

> When Scripture says in John 7 that the Holy Spirit is not yet there because Christ has not yet been glorified, John only refers to the gifts of the Spirit, such as the apostolic office, and other services and benefits for the common good, like performing miracles, healing, speaking in tongues, and so on. It was after the ascension that his promised spirit was realized. Only [after His death] then were the indivisible spirit of prophecy, the gifts, and purification attained and achieved altogether.[287]

---

284. Snyder, "Simple Confession," 121.
285. Klaassen, *Marpeck*, 44, 18, 283–84.
286. Snyder, "Simple Confession," 115–17.
287. Klaassen and Klassen, *Writings of Pilgram Marpeck*, 231–32. Marpeck's "Admonition of 1542" contained two-thirds of Rothmann's work and "stood passionately behind it" (Klaassen and Klassen, *Writings of Pilgram Marpeck*, 159). See also, Rempel, *Jorg Maler's Kuntsbuch*, 27–28.

Anabaptist spirituality and theology as outlined above, particularly that of Marpeck, is a type of Pentecostalism that emerged in the early twentieth century. The manifestations of the gifts of the Holy Spirit began to appear in both instances within the context of private prayer meetings in homes, small Bible studies and schools, or in the case of the Anabaptists' conventicles. The primary gifts manifested in Pentecostalism were speaking in tongues and prophecy, and although speaking in tongues was known and encouraged by many, the primary gift for the Anabaptists appears to have been prophecy. For both in the absence of charismata, there was no evidence of the indwelling of the Holy Spirit. They both believed that a Christian was bound by love to share their spiritual gift for the edification of the whole body notwithstanding who might be the designated leader. The idea of a separate people and church is another shared principle. They both conceived the church as being separate from any political institution, government, or the unsaved world in general.[288] The manifestation of the gifts of the Spirit was seen by both as confirmation that they were indeed facilitating the restitution of the apostolic church of the New Testament. There is much in the way of contemporary literature that provides a picture as to where and how these beliefs were derived, not the least of which are the early theological works of Luther and Zwingli. Many Radical Reformation leaders were former priests, monks, and theologians in their own right. They had studied the church fathers, particularly Tertullian, whom Stanley Burgess has called the first Pentecostal theologian.[289] The influence of Müntzer and Karlstadt, in regard to their insights into the indwelling of the Holy Spirit in the individual Christian and the difference between being baptized in the Holy Spirit and being baptized in water, cannot be overestimated. However, the impact of aberrant behavior, misuse, and abuse of the gifts took its toll as the reactions of the magisterial reformers and Anabaptists themselves at Schleitheim attest. Notwithstanding these reactions, five years after the Schleitheim Confession the Anabaptists still insisted that the manifestation of the gifts of the Holy Spirit defined a true Christian church. Focusing on the theology of South Austrian Anabaptist Pilgram Marpeck has provided some clarity to the argument as he is considered by Martin Rothkegel and John Roth to have established a great affinity with both

288. Wacker, *Heaven Below*, 217.
289. Burgess, *Holy Spirit*, 63.

the Swiss Brethren and the Hutterites, thus becoming representative of Anabaptism in general.[290]

Early Pentecostalism, particularly that which began to manifest itself in Los Angeles in 1906, was generally characterized by contemporary non-Pentecostal churches as heretical in the mildest of criticism to the "last vomit of Satan" in the most vitriolic.[291] Probably the more important of the characterizations was promulgated by the local newspapers reporting eyewitness accounts of the Pentecostal church services in progress at Azusa Street, the scene of William Seymour's revival. Of all that was reported as occurring, the most noted were the interracial nature of the congregation, the kerygmatic proclamation of the gospel, loud praying, rolling in prostration, and demonstrations of "enthusiastic festive celebration, with singing, shouting, clapping, leaping, and dancing."[292] The manifestation of dreams, visions, being slain in the Spirit, and prophecies were also experienced. But the most important phenomenon reported was various participants "speaking in tongues" (glossolalia), the evidence that was believed to prove one was "filled with the Holy Spirit."[293] Notwithstanding subsequent, more modern definitions of Pentecostalism that have developed since Azusa Street, and which incorporate a more inclusive list of the gifts of the Holy Spirit as enumerated in 1 Corinthians 12–14, speaking in tongues still remains the most delineating of the gifts. That can be attributed to the fact that many Pentecostal movements have adopted a position wherein the initial evidence of the infilling of the Holy Spirit is speaking in tongues.[294] These were the elements that identified early behavior or praxis of Pentecostalism. Early Anabaptism was accused by Zwingli of similar behavior, including the manifestation of the charismata such as speaking in tongues, speaking in tongues with interpretation, being slain in the Spirit, and prophecy accompanied by dreams and visions. This similitude of praxis supports the argument for Anabaptist similarities to Pentecostalism and points to a similar interpretation of 1 Corinthians 12–14.

It has already been noted that very early in the sixteenth century, radical movements' attempts to identify or define what the primitive

---

290. Roth, "Marpeck and the Later Swiss," 362–63. See also Rothkegel, "Anabaptism in Moravia and Silesia," 186–89.

291. Anderson, *Introduction to Pentecostalism*, 62.

292. Robeck, *Azusa Street Mission and Revival*, 129–38.

293. Robeck, *Azusa Street Mission and Revival*, 89, 135, 73–77, 87.

294. Menzies, *Bible Doctrines*, 133–43; Conn, *Like a Mighty Army*, 541.

church consisted of resulted in many and varied theologies and practices. The spiritualists thought that the fall of the New Testament church was precipitated with the advent of Constantine. They rejected all externals, including the liturgies, rituals, and ceremonies such as the Eucharist, water baptism, clergy, and even the charismata. All of these church practices were to be discontinued in a *Stillstand*. Others thought the exact opposite and practiced the gifts of the Spirit in a manner where there was only the spontaneous leadership of the Spirit, disregarding the Bible as the final arbiter of the faith. They considered the Bible to have been superseded by the pneumatic work of the Holy Spirit. Radicalism in general rejected the idea of a professional clergy in the Roman Catholic sense, but which appeared to be the same system being maintained by Luther and Zwingli.[295]

There are many similarities between twentieth-century Pentecostalism's ideas of the role and praxis of the gifts of the Holy Spirit and his work within the church and Anabaptism's ideas as revealed in the *New Dialogue*, the *Zofingen Disputation*, and the other writings mentioned above. Similar concepts of the manifestation of all the gifts including the charismata, the idea of scriptural hermeneutics by a priesthood of believers empowered by the Spirit, and a general reinvigoration of the laity as opposed to a professional clergy, to list a few, are all present and encouraged by both movements. But the catalytic essence of these concepts is a desire for the restitution of primitive New Testament Christianity as characterized by a spiritual-prophetic literal interpretation of the Bible. Both movements saw that church as charismatic, missional, communal, personal, selfless, pacifist, and worshipful among other things.

An early example of the Pentecostal concept of restitution was voiced by William Seymour in 1915:

> The Apostolic Faith stands for the restoration of the faith once delivered to the saints—the old time religion of camp meetings, revivals, missions, street mission work, and Christian unity everywhere. According to God's word, John 17:21–22.[296]

Aimee Semple McPherson (1890–1944), one of the many female leaders of early Pentecostalism, announced in 1917 a divine revelation that proclaimed the restoration of apostolic standards beginning with

---

295. Goertz, *Anabaptists*, 43, 134.
296. Sanders, *William Seymour Papers*, 196.

the Reformation and culminating in the Pentecostal movement and its restoration of the Gifts of the Spirit.[297]

Anabaptist spirituality, particularly as described in the *New Dialogue* and the *Zofingen Disputation of 1532*, was typical of early Pentecostalism of the early twentieth century. The manifestations of the gifts of the Holy Spirit began to appear in both instances within the context of private prayer meetings, small Bible studies and schools, as in the case of the Anabaptists, and conventicles. It appears that the most obvious gifts manifested in both movements were speaking in tongues, speaking in tongues with interpretation, and prophecy, and in the absence of such, Anabaptism and Pentecostalism both thought that there was no evidence of the indwelling of the Holy Spirit, and thus no true church. They both believed that a Christian was bound by love to share their spiritual gifts for the edification of the whole church, notwithstanding who might be the designated leader. The idea of a separated people and church is another shared principle. They both conceived the church as being separate from any political institution, government, and the unregenerate world in general.[298] The manifestation of the gifts of the Spirit was seen by both as confirmation of the restitution of the primitive apostolic church.

The impact of aberrant behavior, misuse, and abuse of the gifts of the Spirit took its toll on Anabaptism regarding the reactions of the magisterial reformers, as well as Anabaptists themselves, as attested to in the *Schleitheim Articles* and Marpeck's appraisal. The same aberrant phenomena had to be dealt with in early Pentecostalism as William Seymour would write in 1915:

> When we leave the word of God and begin to go by signs and voices we will wind up in spiritualism. The Holy Spirit came to give us power to stand on the infallible word and overcome false prophets.[299]

It appears that at least Marpeck was searching for mitigating ground between the efficacy of the charismata in edifying the church and aberrant spiritual selfishness as expressed by Sattler. From 1531 to 1532, Marpeck rejected spiritualists, as well as those who misused and abused the charismata. He insisted on a theology that conformed to the writings of Paul in 1 Corinthians 12–14. The founders of the early Pentecostal

---

297. Ware, "Restorationism in Classical Pentecostalism," 1019.
298. Wacker, *Heaven Below*, 217.
299. Sanders, *William Seymour Papers*, 111.

movement, not unlike Marpeck, thought that any restitution of the primitive church must incorporate the manifestation of the gifts of the Spirit for the edification of the congregation as described by Paul.

CONCLUSION PART 2

John Bossy saw the appearance of many sects of radical Christianity during the Reformation as an inevitable result of the printing press, the transition of society from ecclesiastic to secular, and the growth of individualism.[300] Brad Gregory assigned responsibility more directly to the acceptance of *sola scriptura* which obviated the necessity of a trained and educated clergy.[301] A more accurate analysis of what caused both Anabaptists and Pentecostals to resort to a less ecclesiastical church and move to a Pauline pneumatological form of faith and practice was the total acceptance and belief in the doctrine of the priesthood of the believer. Both believed that they had been empowered by the Holy Spirit to read and interpret Scripture. This resulted in general acceptance of the literality, or natural sense, of Scripture, but in a variously defined tension between the letter and the Spirit, much like Luther's spiritual-prophetic hermeneutic, the courage to put what they read into practice, and to aspire to the restitution of the primitive New Testament church as described therein.

Gregory, however, describes the situation differently. He argues that all dissent that rejected the Roman Catholic Church's teachings, rejected the authority of God's caretaker of the saving truth "for more than a millennium"[302] which is what happened in the Reformation. One of the most critical aspects of Roman Catholicism to be rejected by Lutherans, Zwinglians, and radicals, including the Anabaptists, was the definition of the word of God as Scripture plus tradition as arbitrated by the pope. Thus the word of God was established among most Protestants as *sola scriptura*, the Bible as the sole arbiter of the faith.[303] He goes on to attribute the fissiparous nature of Anabaptism to the failure of the Peasants' War and the aspiration of remaking Christendom and dismantling the feudal system. What took the place of the dream was a host of doctrinally

---

300. Bossy, *Christianity in the West*, 97–104.
301. Gregory, *Unintended Reformation*, 87–89.
302. Gregory, *Unintended Reformation*, 86.
303. Gregory, *Unintended Reformation*, 86.

and socially divisive models.[304] Gregory stipulates that for the majority of Protestants, including Anabaptists, "the shared commitment to *sola scriptura* entailed a hermeneutical heterogeneity that proved doctrinally contentious, socially divisive, and sometimes... politically subversive."[305] However, what Gregory overlooks is the biblical role of the Holy Spirit as described by Jesus in John 6. The Spirit was sent to lead all Christians into the truth of the word, confirming the Petrine doctrine of the priesthood of the believer. In 1 Corinthians 12–14, Paul described how that concept would work in the church. Both Anabaptism and Pentecostalism put those doctrines into praxis for the same reasons, the Bible said so literally.

Many historians and theologians of Reformation Anabaptism have observed the similarities between early Pentecostalism and early Anabaptism. However, this thesis provides a sustained focus on the development of theology and a chronological and geographical breadth of synthesis that has heretofore been neglected. The definitions of both movements as detailed above have been used to set the parameters for identifying not only the similarities, but also the differences, between the two. The thesis also offers a very brief rationale for why sixteenth-century Anabaptism did not evolve into an early Pentecostal-like movement.[306] A brief discussion on the initial reform theologies of both Luther and Zwingli and how they became the catalysts for the emergence of radical elements of both movements will begin the conclusory observations.

THE REFORMATIONS OF LUTHER AND ZWINGLI

The criticisms of Erasmus, Martin Luther, and Huldrych Zwingli of the Roman Catholic Church called for its reformation. They saw the church as spiritually impoverished based on several observations: the work of humanist scholars that had proven the Donation of Constantine to be a fraud; they believed that the Roman Catholic clergy had become corrupt and abusive; they further declared the word of God to be the last and final authority for Christians; they saw the church as having slipped into a condition of apostasy due to its redefinition of the word of God as the Bible plus the traditions of the church arbitrated solely by the pope.

---

304. Gregory, *Unintended Reformation*, 90–91.

305. Gregory, *Unintended Reformation*, 92.

306. This theory moves outside the scope of the thesis and therefore requires more research perhaps in another study.

The corruption of the clergy had to be remedied if the church was to be reformed to be compliant with Scripture. The usurpation of every Christian's prerogative to live as led by the Holy Spirit and to read and interpret Scripture was unacceptable.

Luther and Zwingli led separate reformation efforts, but both, being considered radical by Roman Catholic apologists, were very similar in their conclusions as to what it would take to reform the church. The major similarities in their respective Reformations, at least initially, were salvation through faith alone, *sola fide*, the word of God had to be the only and last arbiter of the faith, *sola scriptura*. Additionally, celibacy was seen as a great contributor to clerical moral corruption, the inefficacy of the Mass, the irrelevance of religious iconography, opposition to indulgences, the acceptance of the priesthood of the believer, and belief in the efficacy of the working of the Holy Spirit in every Christian's life.[307] A most controversial aspect of both efforts was their respective decisions to incorporate the state magistracy into the propagation of the gospel, thus coercing faith.

However, they did disagree or interpret differently some aspects of their respective efforts. When Luther saw that his initial stance on the priesthood of the believer (1 Pet 2:9) resulted in the installation of untrained and uneducated pastors when he had allowed the churches to select them from their respective congregations, he saw the various theological differences that appeared as unacceptable. He considered the word of God a higher priority than the Holy Spirit. The Spirit could not be present before the word. He also became a cessationist when he began to see the various and radical manifestations of the gifts of the Holy Spirit appear. He declared that the gifts of the Spirit listed in 1 Corinthians 12–14 were for the first church and only necessary until the development of the institutional church and a hierarchical clergy.[308] Zwingli had the same problem with congregational appointments of local pastors, but he established a Bible school to train those that were chosen to serve. Then again, he was not a cessationist, although he considered the manifestation of gifts of the Spirit a matter of studying and learning the biblical languages for the edification of the church. He was, however, very critical of the manifestation of the charismata as reported to him. He disagreed that the word was a higher priority than the Spirit, and claimed it was the Spirit

---

307. Luther, "To the Christian Nobility," 127.
308. Luther, *Commentary on the Epistle*, 238.

who led him into the truth of the word. But the greatest disagreement was over the meaning, purpose, and value of the Eucharist, the Lord's Supper. Where Luther seemed to hold closer to the Roman Catholic position of the real presence of Christ in the elements, although rejecting transubstantiation, Zwingli maintained that the communion was strictly a commemorative ceremony taken by faith alone.

Out of the German and Swiss Reformations, radical elements emerged that rejected various parts of both. Luther's radicals, the *Schwärmer*, were disaffected by the growing antinomianism that grew out of a misunderstanding of what saved by faith alone meant, understanding his position as maintaining the Catholic interpretation of the Eucharist as the real presence of Christ, as well as keeping the ritual of the Catholic Mass. Most important to this thesis is that Luther denied the efficacious currency of the charismata.

For Zwingli, it was the Anabaptists who rejected his retention of Catholic infant baptism instead of the adult baptism they believed to be more scriptural, as well as including the magistracy into the propagation of the gospel. This precluded them from taking an oath of allegiance to the city, reinforcing their concept of pacifism. Their radical literal hermeneutic can be attributed to their continued adherence to the Lutheran and Swiss Reformed initial theological positions, particularly the priesthood of the believer. It was this position of Erasmus, Luther, and Zwingli that concluded that every Christian not only should read Scripture, but interpret it as well. This led to a literal (biblicist) reading of the Bible without leaving parts out or adding things like church tradition to it.

The radical realization of both Luther and Zwingli that the Roman Catholic Church was not going to be reformed moved them to begin the establishment of a new church. For Luther it was evangelical Lutheranism, for Zwingli it was the Reformed church. The *Schwärmer*, with the exception of Schwenckfeld however, were unsuccessful in creating a new church. The Anabaptist radicals moreover, were initially able to establish numerous sectarian churches that over time coalesced into at least two separate sixteenth-century churches that have survived, the Mennonites and the Hutterites. These churches were convinced that only the restitution of the charismatic New Testament primitive church was the correct biblical answer to the perceived apostasy of the Catholic, Lutheran, and Reformed Churches. As radical elements began to read and interpret Scripture with the new hermeneutic, having already understood that the church was far from biblical compliance, they began the praxis of acting out the Scriptures in real life, particularly 1 Corinthians 12–14. This resulted in manifestations of the charismata. The Anabaptists revolted against Zwingli and became known as the Swiss Brethren.

ANABAPTIST RESTITUTION OF THE PRIMITIVE NEW TESTAMENT CHURCH

Anabaptist spirituality and theology as outlined in the dissertation, particularly that of Pilgram Marpeck, was similar to the Pentecostalism of the early twentieth century. The manifestations of the gifts of the Holy Spirit began to appear in both instances within the context of private prayer meetings in homes, small Bible studies, or in the case of the Anabaptists, conventicles.[309] In both instances they were responding to a perceived apostasy within their respective contemporary church environments. The primary gifts manifested in both movements were prophecy (Anabaptists) and speaking in tongues (Pentecostals) and for them, the absence of the manifestation of the gifts proved that there was no evidence of the indwelling of the Holy Spirit in the church. They both believed that a Christian was bound by love to share their spiritual gifts for the edification of the whole body, notwithstanding who might be the designated leader. Interpreting 1 Corinthians 14 literally, they both developed a praxis of lay participation according to Paul's instructions. Whoever had something to share could share it. The idea of a separate people and church is another shared principle. They both conceived the church as being separate from any political institution and the unsaved world in general.[310] The manifestation of the gifts of the Spirit was seen by both movements as confirmation that they were indeed facilitating the restitution of the apostolic church of the New Testament.

There is much in the way of contemporary literature that has provided a picture as to where and how these beliefs were derived, not the least of which are the early theologies abandoned by Luther and Zwingli. A few Anabaptist Reformation leaders were former priests, monks, and theologians in their own right. They had studied the church fathers, particularly Tertullian, whose doctrine concerning adult baptism was most

---

309. The conventicle was something established first by Luther and adopted by Zwingli. It was within these existing groups that Anabaptists had a ready-made forum.

310. Wacker, *Heaven Below*, 217. As described above in *The Zofingen Disputation of 1532*.

appealing. Not unlike early Pentecostalism, however, the impact of aberrant behavior, misuse, and abuse of the charismata took its toll, as the reactions of the magisterial reformers confirmed. Anabaptists themselves, as Sattler's *Schleitheim Confession* pointed out, opposed such behavior. Notwithstanding these reactions, five years after Schleitheim, Anabaptists would continue to argue that the manifestation of the gifts of the Holy Spirit defined a true Christian church at *The Zofingen Disputation of 1532*. Likewise, Pentecostals would come together in 1914 and opt for an official document outlining pertinent fundamentals of the faith, including glossolalia as the initial evidence of the baptism in the Holy Spirit. Early Pentecostalism experienced the same problem, as the misuse and abuse of the charismata instigated what William Seymour called "wild fire" and rejected the doctrine that speaking in tongues was the initial evidence of the baptism in the Holy Spirit.[311]

RESPECTIVE SPIRITUALITY AND THEOLOGY COMPARED

The comparison of early Pentecostal statements of faith and doctrines such as *The Doctrines of Discipline* written by Seymour in 1915, the early Pentecostal *Fundamentals of the Truths Approved by the [American] General Council of the Assemblies of God October 2–7 1916* on the Pentecostal side, and[312] the confessions of faith of early Anabaptists as recounted in the dissertation have been contrasted with the above statements of fundamentals. Comparison models were presented in the genres of theology and spirituality as they developed chronologically.

Those aspects of traditional Christian doctrine believed and practiced by Lutherans and Zwinglians, which in the minds of Anabaptists and Pentecostals were faithful to a biblically restored church, were acknowledged as valid. Early Anabaptism and early Pentecostalism both accepted the Protestant premise of *sola scriptura,* that the unexpurgated Bible was the inspired word of God, the revelation of God to man, the infallible rule of faith and conduct, and from that position the concept of a restored Christianity, in what the Anabaptists called *restitutio in*

---

311. Sanders, *William Seymour Papers*, 117.

312. Flower, "Statement of Fundamental Truths." The British Assemblies of God statement of faith will also be used as well as other European movements (Anderson, *Introduction to Pentecostalism*, 91–96). See also, Sanders, *William Seymour Papers*, 108.

integrum, in Pentecostal terms the *full gospel,* was embraced. Secondly, they accepted the literal interpretation of 1 Corinthians 12–14 as the natural sense and efficacy of the Holy Spirit with all that Paul described as church and life praxes. The body of Christ, the church, Paul's *eclessia,* was visible in the world, but not of the world.

The Lutheran and Reformed theology of predestination, the bondage of the will, was rejected by Anabaptists. Good works (piety) were considered evidence of the spiritual transition that had occurred in a Christian's life and not an effort to earn salvation. Evangelism based on the Great Commission of Acts 1:8 was understood literally and believed to be critical to the restitution of the primitive New Testament church. Salvation was attained by an informed conscious personal confession of an adult. Infant baptism had no biblical basis. Anabaptists believed that there were three baptisms: water, fire and blood. Water and fire were similar to Pentecostalism in that water was a sign or witness to an inner spiritual experience, while fire referred to the Holy Spirit baptism. For some Anabaptists, however, blood referred to the horrible persecutions that were being inflicted upon them. This baptism was to be expected, even anticipated, as being part of the true church in the last days, imitating the life of the "bitter Christ." For Anabaptists, evidence of the baptism in the Holy Spirit, unlike most of Pentecostalism, was thought to be the manifestation of the fruit of the Spirit as Paul described it in Galatians 5:22. They did not preclude manifestations of the charismata as important to the Christian life, but only as it edified the congregation, as Paul had indicated. Pentecostalism declared glossolalia to be the initial evidence of the baptism in the Spirit with a few exceptions. Anabaptism respected the gift of speaking in tongues, but held prophecy to be a more edifying priority. This was very similar to the early German Pentecostal position and a few others. Divine healing was another Pentecostal emphasis, and although Anabaptism again understood the value of the gift of healing, including deliverance from persecution, they simply counted it as a spiritual consequence of being a Christian.

Despite the efforts of many Anabaptist leaders to unify the movement, unification did not come to fruition in the early sixteenth century. No agreed upon systematic theology was produced. The same can be said for early Pentecostalism. Nevertheless, the characterizations as publicized by the local Los Angeles newspapers, reporting eyewitness accounts of William Seymour's Pentecostal revival on Azusa Street and other similar examples of negative publicity, were an indication of the necessity for the movement to establish more specific guidelines as to what was and was not Pentecostal.

Of all that was reported as occurring at Azusa Street, the most noted were: the interracial nature of the congregation, the kerygmatic proclamation of the gospel, loud praying, rolling in prostration, and demonstrations of "enthusiastic festive celebration, with singing, shouting, clapping, leaping, dancing, and being slain in the Spirit."[313] The manifestation of dreams, visions, and prophecies were also experienced. But the most important phenomenon reported were various participants "speaking in tongues" (glossolalia).[314] As asserted in the dissertation, with the exception of racial integration, similar phenomena were reported to have occurred during the rise of early Anabaptism. Unlike Pentecostals, Anabaptists were forced to meet in secret to avoid arrest and prosecution. This inhibited the freedom of worship, but nonetheless, reports of the same kinds of activities were reported to Catholic, Lutheran, and Reformed authorities. The Anabaptist conventicle was similar to the Pentecostal home prayer meetings of the early twentieth century. They were private affairs devoted to reading the Bible, teaching, singing, and prayer—particularly to praying in tongues in the case of the Pentecostals, and prophecy for the Anabaptists—but all within the guidelines set forth by Paul in 1 Corinthians 14:1–33. In both movements the initial inclination regarding women was to allow them to participate as any man would in speaking in tongues, prophesying, singing, exhorting, and reading the Bible. Both movements initially allowed and encouraged pastoring and evangelistic preaching by women.

It was not the intention of this dissertation to argue that early sixteenth-century Anabaptism was a Pentecostal movement. Many historians have commented on the similarities but none have provided much evidence. The purpose was to identify similar aspects of early twentieth-century Pentecostalism practiced within the early sixteenth-century Anabaptist movement, and assert that these aspects were Pentecostal in the context of 1 Corinthians 12–14. But that begs the question as to why Anabaptism didn't evolve into a Pentecostal denomination as it did in the early twentieth century? There are at least three reasons for this failure. First, the insistence that infant baptism and the Mass be discontinued by the church struck fear into the hearts of Luther and Zwingli. They

---

313. Robeck, *Azusa Street Mission and Revival*, 57.
314. Robeck, *Azusa Street Mission and Revival*, 89, 135, 73–77, 87.

along with their respective magistracies anticipated that social discord would occur and the public peace would be jeopardized. This resulted in the criminalization of the movement, which drove it into exile. Second, from its initial stages of development, the appearance of aberrant manifestations of the charismata and the misuse and abuse of them further alienated the magisterial Reformation leadership. This precipitated negative reactions condemning them, not only from the authorities, but from within the movement itself. Third, the apocalyptic Melchiorites established a legal theocracy in Münster from 1534 to 1535. This threatened a large segment of Western Europe with apocalyptic and prophetic religious chaos and brought to bear the alliance of Catholics and Lutherans that violently eliminated the threat. But the siege and destruction of Münster also threatened the extinction of Anabaptism in the broadest sense.

Anabaptism had survived murderous persecution from magisterial authorities and Catholic, Lutheran, and Zwinglian Reformed authorities for ten years. This made the Münster debacle the threshold of extinction for them in the mind of Menno Simons. When he assumed the leadership after Münster, he thought that discretion would be the better part of valor and decided to incline the movement to a more acceptable position, at least in the eyes of Protestants. He discontinued the Office of Prophet, deemphasized manifestations of the charismata, and proceeded to lead Anabaptism into being the "quiet of the land." Initially, this affected the Western European elements of Anabaptism the most. Elements of the east were less affected, including the Swiss Brethren, the Marpeckans, and the Hutterites, but it should be noted that the Mennonites were to become the major Anabaptist denomination of the twentieth century.

Early twentieth-century Pentecostalism cannot be considered heirs of early sixteenth-century Anabaptist Pentecostal-like praxes. There is no evidence that the Pentecostal movement, referred to above, had any historical knowledge of Reformation Anabaptism. There are common denominators, however, to which both movements were exposed to, and those are the initial Reformation theologies of both Martin Luther and Huldrych Zwingli. First, *sola scriptura*, the Bible is the sole and final arbiter of the Christian faith; and second, *sola fide*, the sufficiency of faith alone in the shed blood of Christ plus nothing for eternal salvation. These were the foundational elements for both Luther and Zwingli's Reformation efforts in Germany and Switzerland respectively. It was also on this foundation that the superstructure of the Radical Reformation was ultimately built.

Luther added the Petrine doctrine of the priesthood of the believer, the Holy Spirit empowerment of every Christian to read and interpret the Bible; the right of every congregation to choose their own pastor regardless of training and education; and the efficacy of Pauline pneumatology, wherein the work of the Holy Spirit was integral to a biblical church. Even though Zwingli insisted that the Swiss Reformation was entirely independent of Luther's German protest, he embraced the same theology. Within a short period of time after the inception of both Reformations, both protagonists were faced with radical adherents that acted pragmatically on the idea of the priesthood of the believer and had begun to read and act out Scripture literally. Their opposition was based on their inability to find supporting Scripture for much of the Roman Catholic liturgy, ritual, and ceremony. These radicals wanted to jettison major portions of Catholicism, including the Mass, iconography, and purgatory. The more radical these adherents became, the more obvious it became to both Luther and Zwingli that there had developed an unintended consequence to their initial theology of reform. They began to retreat from the idea of the priesthood of the believer and saw the incorporation of the local magistracies into the propagation of Protestantism as being critical to any successful reformation of the Roman Catholic Church. The further they went in this direction, the more obvious it became to the radicals that reforming Catholicism was not possible and only created a situation of compromise that imperilled any biblical restitution of the primitive New Testament church.

In the beginning, Zwingli's radical elements had convinced him of the unbiblical nature of the Mass and more importantly the lack of scriptural support for infant baptism. Their interpretation of *sola fide* meant that only adults could be baptized and that upon a personal confession of faith. These radicals became known as Anabaptists. But, when Zwingli realized that the magistracy would not agree to the elimination of the Mass or infant baptism because it would cause great social unrest among the people, he acquiesced to the magistracy. The radicals then understood that the only answer to reform was to pursue was the restitution of the New Testament primitive church as described literally in the Bible and not the reformation of the Roman Catholic Church. This description included a literal understanding of 1 Corinthians 12–14 and the manifestation of the charismata for the edification of the church. Without the charismata there was no evidence that the Holy Spirit was present, and without the Spirit there was no true church. Just as important to them was Christ's commission to evangelize the world.

Early twentieth-century Pentecostalism found itself in a similar situation. The modern major Protestant denominations had become materialistic and had developed a proclivity to a gospel that was driven more by social justice than Christian spirituality. Higher textual criticism had become the preferred methodology of biblical hermeneutics. This was perceived by many as robbing the Bible of its spiritual meaning and relying only on the empirically proven aspects of Scripture. Notwithstanding the lack of knowledge of early Anabaptism and over four centuries of lapsed time, the Pentecostals saw the answer to their dilemma the same way Anabaptists had seen it, the restitution of the primitive New Testament church. The Reformation theologies of the *sola scriptura* and *sola fide* were once again embraced as truth. This reignited the idea of the priesthood of the believer, the literal natural sense reading of Scripture by all Christians, the call to preach and pastor without theological education or training, and most importantly, the literal reading, interpretation, and practical application of 1 Corinthians 12–14, which taught the nature of the manifestation of the charismata regarding the edification of the church. Evangelization was also critically important to the movement as well. All of these similarities came from a similar literal reading and interpretation of Scripture by both movements, notwithstanding centuries of separation and lack of knowledge of each other.

Bibliography

Adogame, Afe. "Germany." In *International Dictionary of Pentecostal and Charismatic Movements*, edited by Stanley M. Burgess, 109–11. Grand Rapids: Zondervan, 2002.

Alexander, Paul. *Peace to War: Shifting Allegiances in the Assemblies of God*. C. Henry Smith Series. Edited by J. Denny Weaver. 9 vols. Telford, PA: Cascadia, 2009.

Alighieri, Dante. *Inferno*. London: J. M. Dent, 1970.

Althaus, Paul. *The Theology of Martin Luther*. Philadelphia: Fortress, 1966.

Anderson, Allan. *An Introduction to Pentecostalism*. Cambridge: Cambridge University Press, 2004.

———. *Spreading Fires: The Missionary Nature of Early Pentecostalism*. London: SCM, 2007.

———. *To the Ends of the Earth*. Oxford: Oxford University Press, 2013.

———. "Varieties, Taxonomies, and Definitions." In *Studying Global Pentecostalism*, edited by Allan Anderson, 13–29. Los Angeles: University of California Press, 2010.

Anderson, Robert Mapes. *Vision of the Disinherited: Making of American Pentecostalism*. Peabody, MA: Hendrickson, 1979.

Archer, Kenneth J. "Anabaptism-Pietism and Pentecostalism: Scandalous Partners in Protest." Scottish Journal of Theology 63.2 (2010) 185–202.

———. *A Pentecostal Hermeneutic*. Cleveland, TN: CPT, 2009.

Armour, Rollin S. *Anabaptist and Baptism*. Studies in Anabaptist and Mennonite History. Edited by John S. Oyer. 11 vols. Scottdale, PA: Herald, 1966.

Backus, Irena. "Valentine Crautwald's *Nouus Homo*." In *Colloquium on Schwenckfeld*, edited by Peter C. Erb, 327–37. Pennsburg, PA: Schwenckfelder Library, 1984.

Baille, John, ed. *Advocates of Reform*. 26 vols. Library of Christian Classics Series. Edited by John Baillie. Philadelphia: Westminster, 1953.

Bainton, Roland. "Anabaptist Contribution to History." In *Recovery of the Anabaptist Vision*, edited by Guy F. Herschberger, 317–26. Scottdale, PA: Herald, 1957.

———. *Here I Stand*. New York: Abingdon-Cokesbury, 1950.

Balserak, Jon. *John Calvin as Sixteenth-century Prophet*. Oxford: Oxford University Press, 2014.

Barge, Herman. *Andreas Bodenstein Von Karlstadt*. 1905 ed. Vol. II, Leipzig: Nieuwkoop B. De Graaf, 1968.

Barlow, William. *A Dyaloge Descrybyng the Orygyinall Ground of These Lutheran S[F] Accyons The English Experience: Its Record in Early Printed Books*. Amsterdam: Theatrum Orbis Terrarum, 1974.

Barratt, T. B. *When the Fire Fell: An Outline of My Life, 1927*. Cedar Rapids: Pentecostal Books.com, 2013.

Bartleman, Frank. *My Story: The Latter Rain*. Self-published: 2012.

Bauman, Harold E. "Charismatic Movement." http://www.gameo.org/index.php.?title=Charismatic_Movement.

Beaman, Jay. *Pentecostal Pacifism*. Hillsboro, KS: Center for Mennonite Brethren Studies, 1989.

Bell, Eudorus. N. "Is European War Justifiable?" *Christian Evangel* (December 12, 1914) 1.

Bender, Harold S. "Conrad Grebel, the Founder of Swiss Anabaptism." *Church History* 7.2 (1938) 157–78.

———. "Infant Baptism." http://www.gameo.org/index.php?title=Infant_Baptism.

———. "Ontario Mennonite Brethren in Christ." http://www.gameo.org/index.php?title=Ontario_Mennonite_Brethren_in_Christ.

Bender, Harold S., and John S. Oyer. "Historiography, Anabaptist." http://www.gameo.org/index.php?title=Historiography:_Anabaptist.

Bergsten, Torsten, and Gunnar Westin, eds. *Balthasar Hubmaier: Schriften*. Edited by Verein fur Reformationsgeschichte. Vol. xxix; Quellen zur Geschichte der Taufer, ix, Quellen Und Forschungen Zur Reformationsgeschichte. Karlsruhe, Germany: Guterslohe Verlagshaus Gerd Mohn, 1962.

Berkhof, Louis. *Principles of Biblical Interpretation: Sacred Hermeneutics*. Grand Rapids: Baker, 1950.

Blanke, Fritz. *Brothers in Christ: The History of the Oldest Anabaptist Congregation, Zollikon, Near Zurich, Switzerland*. Translated by Joseph Nordenhaug. Scottdale, PA: Herald, 1961.

Blickle, Peter. "The Popular Reformation." In *Handbook of European History: 1400–1600*, vol. 2, edited by Heiko A. Oberman, 161–92. Grand Rapids: Eerdmans, 1995.

———. "Twelve Articles." In *Oxford Encyclopedia of the Reformation*, Reformation, vol. 4, edited by Hans J. Hillerbrand, 183–84. Oxford: Oxford University Press, 1994.

Blumhofer, Edith L. *Restoring the Faith: Assemblies of God, Pentecostalism, and American Culture*. Chicago: University of Illinois Press, 1993.

Boddy, Alexander A. "Brief Items." *Confidence* 2.12 (1909) 38.

———. "Declaration of the International Pentecostal Consultative Council." *Confidence* (December 1912) 1.

———. *Laying on of Hands: 1895*. Self-published, Full Well Ventures, 2012. Kindle.

———. *Pleading the Blood: The Baptism in the Holy Ghost*. Digital 2012 ed. Amazon Kindle: Full Well Ventures, 2012.

———. *A Vicar's Testimony: "Pentecost" at Sunderland*. Digital 2012 ed.: Full Well Publishing, 2012.

———. "The War." *Confidence* 2.10 (October 1914) 191.

Booth-Clibborn. "Christian and War: Is It Too Late?" *Weekly Evangel* (April 28, 1917) 5–6.

Booze, Joyce. "Africa, North." In *International Dictionary of Pentecostal and Charismatic Movements*, edited by Stanley Burgess, 6–8. Grand Rapids: Zondervan, 2002.

Bossy, John. *Christianity in the West: 1400-1700*. Oxford: Oxford University Press, 1985.
Boyd, Stephen B. *Pilgram Marpeck: His Life and Social Theology*. Duke Monographs in Medieval and Renaissance Studies Series. Edited by Arthur B. Ferguson. Durham, NC: Duke University Press, 1992.
Brady, Thomas A. "Swabian League." In *Oxford Encyclopedia of the Reformation*, vol. 4, edited by Hans J. Hillerbrand, 124-25. Oxford: Oxford University, 1996.
Brandt, Otto S., ed. *Thomas Muntzer: Sein Leben Und Seine Scriften*, Jena, Germany: Eugen Diederichs Verlag, 1933.
Brecht, Martin. "Luther's Reformation." In *Handbook of European History*, edited by Heiko A. Oberman. Grand Rapids: Eerdmans, 1995.
———. "Martin Luther." In *Oxford Encyclopedia of the Reformation*, edited by Hans J. Hillerbrand, 460-67. Oxford: Oxford University Press, 1996.
Bromiley, Geoffrey. W. *Zwingli and Bullinger*. Vol. 24. Library of Christian Classics. Philadelphia: Westminster, 1957.
Brown, Henry B., and John M. Harlan. "Plessy V. Ferguson." In *Annals of America: 1895-1904*, edited by Mortimer J. Adler, 92-100. Chicago: William Benton, 1896.
Brumback, Carl. *Suddenly from Heaven*. Springfield, MO: Gospel, 1961.
———. *What Meaneth this?* Springfield, MO: Gospel, 1947.
Bullinger, Heinrich. *Der Widertoufferen*. Zurich: Christossel Froschower, 1561.
———. *Widertoeufferen Ursprungen/Secten* [in German]. Leipzig: Zentralantiquariat DDR, 1975.
Bundy, David. D. "Barratt, Thomas Ball." In *International Dictionary of Pentecostal and Charismatic Movements*, edited by Stanley M. Burgess, 365-66. Grand Rapids: Zondervan, 2002.
———. "Boddy, Alexander Alfred." In *International Dictionary of Pentecostal and Charismatic Movements*, edited by Stanley M. Burgess, 436-37. Grand Rapids: Zondervan, 2002.
———. "Early European Perspectives on Pentecostalism." *Bulletin of the European Pentecostal Theological Association* 5.1 (1986) 4-23.
———. "Pethrus, Petrus Lewi." In *International Dictionary of Pentecostal and Charismatic Movements*, edited by Stanley M. Burgess, 986-87. Grand Rapids: Zondervan, 2002.
Burgess, Stanley. *The Holy Spirit: Medieval Roman Catholic and Reformation Traditions*. Peabody, MA: Hendrickson, 1994.
———. *The Holy Spirit: Medieval Roman Catholic and Reformation Traditions*. Peabody, MA: Hendrickson, 1997.
———. *The Holy Spirit: Ancient Christian Traditions*. Peabody, MA: Hendrickson, 1984.
Burgess, Stanley M., and Eduard M. van der Maas. *New International Dictionary of Pentecostal and Charismatic Movements*. Grand Rapids: Zondervan, 2002.
Byrd, Charles. "Pentecostalism's Anabaptist Heritage: The Zonfingen Disputation of 1532." *Journal of the European Pentecostal Theological Association* 28.1 (2008) 49-61.
Chatfield, Adrian. "Zealous for the Lord: Enthusiasm and Dissent, Lovers and the Beloved: Brides of Christ." *Journal of Pentecostal Theology* 5 (1997) 95-109.
Clark, Matthew S. "Pentecostalism's Anabaptist Roots." In *Spirit and Spirituality*, edited by Wonsuk Ma, 194-211. London: T. & T. Clark, 2004.

Clasen, Claus-Peter. *Anabaptism: Social History, 1525–1618*. Ithaca, NY: Cornell University Press, 1972.

———. "Anabaptist Sects." *Menonnite Quarterly Review* 46 (1972) 256–79.

Conn, Charles W. *Like a Mighty Army: History of the Church of God*. Cleveland, TN: Pathway, 1996.

Corum, Fred T., ed. *Like as of Fire: Apostolic Faith Reprints*. Wilmington, MA: self-published, 1981.

Cox, Harvey. *Fire from Heaven*. New York: Addison-Wesley, 1995.

Coxe, Arthur Cleveland. "Teaching of the Twelve Apostles." In *Ante-Nicene Fathers*, edited by Alexander Roberts, 369–83. Grand Rapids: Eerdmans, 1886.

Cyril of Jerusalem. "Catechetical Lectures: 351?-358?" In *Cyril of Jerusalem and Gregory of Nazianzen*, edited by Edwin H. Gifford, 115–33. Nicene and Post-Nicene Fathers: Second Series, Vol. 7. Peabody, MA: Hendrickson, 1994.

Davies, Oliver. *God Within: Mystical Tradition of Northern Europe*. London: Darton, Longman, and Todd, 1988.

Davis, Kenneth R. *Anabaptism and Asceticism*. Eugene, OR: Wipf & Stock 1998.

———. "Anabaptism as a Charismatic Movement." *Mennonite Quarterly Review* 53.3 (1979) 219–34.

Dayton, Donald W. *Theological Roots of Pentecostalism*. Grand Rapids: Francis Asbury, 1987.

de Bakker, Willem. *Bernhard Rothmann and the Reformation in Munster, 1533–35*. Kitchener, ON: Pandora, 2009.

Depperman, Klaus. *Melchior Hoffman: Social Unrest and Apocalyptic Visions in the Age of Reformation*. Translated by Malcom Wren. Edinburgh: T. & T. Clark, 1987.

Derksen, John "Voice, Leadership, and Influence among Spiritualist and Anabaptist Women in Strasbourg, 1525–1570." *Mennonite Quarterly Review* 88.4 (2014) 423–50.

Dipple, Geoffrey. "Spiritualist Anabaptists." In *Companion to Anabaptism and Spiritualism, 1521–1700*, edited by John D. Roth, 257–98. Brill's Companions to the Christian Tradition. Leiden: Brill, 2007.

Draper, Jonathan A. "Didache." In *Writings of the Apostolic Fathers*, edited by Paul Foster, 13–41. London: T. & T. Clark, 2007.

Eder, Georg. *Evangelische Inquisition Wahrer Und Falscher Religion*. N.p.: Villingen, 1573.

Epp, Marlene. "Blumenhof Mission Hall: Manitoba Canada." http://www/gameo.org/index.php?title_blumenhof_mission_hall.

Erasmus. "Paraclesis." In *Desiderius Erasmus: Christian Humanism and the Reformation Selected Writings 1516*, edited by John C. Olin, 92–106. NY: Harper Torch, 1965.

Estep, William R. *Anabaptist Story*. 3rd ed. Cambridge: Eerdmans, 1996.

Farina, John, ed. *Johannes Tauler*. Classics of Western Spirituality. New York: Paulist, 1985.

Fee, Gordon D. *Pauline Christology*. Peabody, MA: Hendrickson, 2007.

Finger, Thomas N. *A Contemporary Anabaptist Theology*. Downers Grove, IL: InterVarsity 2004.

Fleischer, Manfred P. "Silesia." In *Oxford Encyclopedia of the Reformation*, vol.4, edited by Hans J. Hillerbrand, 59–64. Oxford: University of Oxford, 1996.

Flower, J. Roswell. "Statement of Fundamental Truths." *The Weekly Evangel* (May 9, 1914) 5–6.

———. "Statement of Fundamental Truths." *The Weekly Evangel* (December 16, 1916) 8.

———. "Statement of Fundamental Truths." *The Weekly Evangel* (December 23, 1916) 8.

———. "Statement of Fundamental Truths." *The Weekly Evangel* (January 6, 1917) 8.

Foller, O. "Martin Luther on Miracles, Healing, Prophecy, and Tongues." *Studia Historiae Ecclesiasticae* 31.2 (2005) 333–51.

Foster, Paul. "Epistles of Ignatius of Antioch." In *Writings of the Apostolic Fathers*, edited by Paul Foster, 73–87. New York: T. & T. Clark, 2007.

Franck, Sebastian. *Chronica: Zeitbuch Unnd Geschictsbibell Van Anbegyn Bisz in Diss Gegenwertig...* 2nd ed. Bavaria: Jar Verlengt, 1536.

———. "Sebastian Franck on the Anabaptists, 1536." In *Sources of South German/Austrian Anabaptism*, edited by C. Arnold Snyder, 228–52. Kitchener, ON: Pandora, 2001.

Friedmann, Robert. "Restitutionism." http://www/gameo.org/encyclopedia/contents/Restitutionism.

———. "Schiemer and Schlaffer: Two Tyrolean Anabaptist Martyr-Apostles of 1528." *Mennonite Quarterly Review* 33 (1959) 31–41.

———. *Theology of Anabaptism*. Studies in Anabaptist and Mennonite History. Edited by J. C. Wenger. 18 vols. Kitchener, ON: Herald, 1973.

Frodsham, Stanley H. "The Pentecostal Movement and the Conscription Law." *The Weekly Evangel* 201 (August 4, 1917) 6–7.

Fukuyama, Francis. *The End of History and the Last Man*. New York: The Free Press, 1992.

Fulton, Elaine. *Catholic Belief and Survival in Sixteenth-century Vienna: The Case of Georg Eder (1523–1587)*. Hampshire, UK: Ashgate, 2007.

Furcha, Edward J. *Essential Carlstadt*. Vol. 8. Classics of the Radical Reformation. Edited by H. Wayne Pipkin. Scottdale, PA: Herald, 1995.

Furcha, Edward J., ed. *Hans Denk: Selected Writings*. Pittsburgh Original Texts and Translations Series Theological Monographs. Reprint. Eugene, OR: Pickwick, 1989.

———. "Whether We Should Go Slowly and Avoid Offending the Weak." In *Essential Carlstadt*, edited by H. Wayne Pipkin, 247–68. Scottdale, PA: Herald, 1995.

Gaebler, Ulrich. *Huldrych Zwingli*. Translated by Ruth C. L. Grich. Philadelphia: Fortress, 1986.

Gamper, Rudolf. "Liebe Und Zorn: Menschliche Regungen Und Die Allmacht Gottes in Den St. Gallen Chroniken Der Reformationszeit." In *Buchwissenschaftliche Beitrage*, edited by Wolfgang Schmitz Christine Haug, und Werner Wunderlich, 41–64. Wiesbaden: Harrassowitz Verlag, 2009.

George, Timothy. *Theology of the Reformers*. Nashville: Broadman, 1988.

Gingrich, Del. "Koch, Roy Swartz." http:www.gameo.org/index.php?title=Koch,Roy Swartz1913–2010.

Goertz, Hans-Jurgen. *Anabaptists*. Translated by Trevor Johnson. London: Routledge, 1996.

———. "Scriptural Interpretation among Radical Reformers." In *Hebrew Bible/Old Testament: The History of its Interpretation: Vol. 2: Renaissance to the Enlightenment*, edited by Magne Saebo, 577–601. Gottingen: Vandenhoeck & Ruprecht, 2008.

———. *Thomas Muntzer: Apocalyptic Mystic and Revolutionary.* Edinburgh: T. & T. Clark, 1993.
Goff, J. R. "Parham, Charles Fox." In *New International Dictionary of Pentecostal and Charismatic Movements*, edited by Stanley Burgess, 955–57. Grand Rapids: Zonervan, 2002.
Goff, James R. *Fields White unto Harvest: Charles F. Parham and the Missionary Origins of Pentecostalism.* Fayetteville, AR: University of Arkansas Press, 1988.
Gohr, Glenn W. "Historical Development of the Statement of Fundamental Truths." *Assemblies of God Heritage* 32 (2012) 60–66.
Gordon, Bruce. *The Swiss Reformation.* New Frontiers in History. Edited by Mark Greengrasss Manchester, UK: Manchester University Press, 2002.
Grebel, Conrad. "Grebel Letter to Muntzer: September 5, 1524." In *Sources of Swiss Anabaptism*, edited by Leland Harder, 284–91. Classics of the Radical Reformation. Scottdale, PA: Herald, 1985.
———. "Letters to Thomas Muntzer 1524." In *Spiritual and Anabaptist Writers*, edited by George H. Williams, 71–85. Library of Christian Classics. Philadelphia: Westminster, 1957.
Green, Jonathan "Last Book of the Strasbourg Prophets." *Sixteenth-Century Journal* 46.2 (2015) 313–30.
Gregory, Brad S. *Salvation at Stake: Christian Martyrdom in Early Modern Europe.* Cambridge, MA: Harvard University Press, 1999.
———. *The Unintended Reformation.* Cambridge, MA: Belknap Press of Harvard University Press, 2012.
Greschat, Martin. "Bucer, Martin." In *Oxford Encyclopedia of the Reformation*, edited by Hans J. Hillerbrand, 221–24. Oxford: Oxford University Press, 1996.
Gritsch, Eric W. *Reformer without a Church: Life and Thought of Thomas Muntzer.* Philadelphia: Fortress, 1967.
———. *Thomas Muntzer: Tragedy of Errors.* Minneapolis: Fortress, 1989.
Hagen, Kenneth. "Omnis Homo Mendax: Luther on Psalm 116." In *Biblical Interpretation in the Era of the Reformation*, edited by Richard A. Muller, 85. Grand Rapids: Eerdmans, 1996.
Harder, Leland, ed. *Sources of Swiss Anabaptism.* Classics of the Radical Reformation. Edited by Cornelius J. Dyck. Scottdale, PA: Herald, 1985.
Harlan, Henry B., and John M Brown. "Plessy V. Ferguson." In *Annals of America: 1895–1904*, edited by Mortimer J. Adler, 92–99, Chicago: William Benton, 1896.
Hartranft, Chester D., ed. *Schwenckfeld's Juditium, 1542*, Vol. ll. Study of the Earliest Letters of Schwenckfeld. Norristown, PA: Board of Publication of the Schwenckfelder Church, 1907.
Hege, Christian. "Mandates." http://gameo.org/index.php?title=Mandates&oldid=92558.
Hillerbrand, Hans J. "Andreas Bodenstein Von Carlstadt: Prodigal Reformer." *Church History* 35.4 (1966) 379–98.
———. *A Bibliography of Anabaptism, 1520–1630.* Elkhart, IN: Institute of Mennonite Studies 1962.
———. *Reformation: Narrative History Related by Contemporary Observers.* New York: Harper and Rowe, 1964.

———. "Renato, Camillo (1500–1575)." In *Oxford Encyclopedia of the Reformation*, vol. 3, edited by Hans J. Hillerbrand, 421–22. Oxford: Oxford University Press, 1996.

Hochen, Peter. D. "Berlin Declaration." In *International Dictionary of Pentecostal and Charismatic Movements*, edited by Stanley M. Burgess, 371. Grand Rapids: Zondervan, 2002.

———. "Bjorner, Anna Larssen." In *International Dictionary of Pentecostal and Charismatic Movements*, edited by Stanley M. Burgess, 419. Grand Rapids: Zondervan, 2002.

Hollenweger, Walter J. *Pentecostalism: Origins and Developments Worldwide*. Peabody, MA: Hendrickson, 1997.

———. *The Pentecostals*. Translated by R. A. Wilson. Minneapolis: Augsburg, 1977.

Horsch, John. "An Inquiry into the Truth of Accusations of Fanaticism and Crime against the Early Swiss Brethren." *Mennonite Quarterly Review* 8.1 (1934) 26–31.

Horton, Harold. *The Gifts of the Spirit*. Springfield, MO: Radiant, 1999.

Hsia, R. Po-chia. *World of Catholic Renewal: 1540–1770*. New Approaches to European History. Cambridge: Cambridge University Press, 1998.

Hubmaier, Balthasar. "A Christian Catechism, 1526." In *Balthasar Hubmaier*, edited by H. Wayne Pipkin and John H. Yoder, 339–65. Scottdale, PA: Herald, 1989.

———. "Eighteen Theses Concerning the Whole Christian Life: 1524." In *Balthasar Hubmaier*, edited by H. Wayne Pipkin and John H. Yoder, 30–34. Scottdale, PA: Herald, 1989.

———. "Eine Christliche Lehrtafel, 1526." In *Balthasar Hubmaier: Schriften*, edited by Gunnar Westin, vol. 9, 75–84. Heidelberg: Guttersloher Verlagshaus Gerd Mohn, 1962.

———. "Letter to Oecolampadius, January 1525." In *Balthasar Hubmaier*, edited by H. Wayne Pipkin and John H. Yoder, 67–72. Scottdale, PA: Herald, 1989.

———. "Public Challenge: February 2, 1525." In *Balthasar Hubmaier*, edited by H. Wayne Pipkin and John H. Yoder, 78–80. Scottdale, PA: Herald, 1989.

Hurst, John F. *History of the Christian Church, Volume 2*. Library of Biblical and Theological Literature. 2 vols. Edited by George R. Crooks. New York: Eaton and Mains, 1897.

Hutterite Brethren. *Chronicle of the Hutterite Brethren*. Translated by the Hutterite Brethren. Rifton, NY: Plough, 1987.

Ignatius of Antioch. "Epistles." In *Ante-Nicene Fathers*, edited by A. Cleveland Coxe, 45–133. Grand Rapids: Eerdmans, 1987.

Karant-Nun, Susan. *Zwickau in Transition, 1500–1540: Reformation as an Agent of Change*. Columbus, OH: Ohio State University Press, 1987.

Karkkainen, Velli-Matti. "Missiology: Pentecostal and Charismatic." In *International Dictionary of Pentecostal and Charismatic Movements*, edited by Stanley Burgess, 877–85. Grand Rapids: Zondervan, 2002.

Kauffman, J. Howard. "Mennonite Charismatics." *Mennonite Quarterly Review* 70.4 (1996), 449–72.

Kay, William K. "Alexander Boddy and the Outpouring of the Holy Spirit in Sunderland." *European Pentecostal Theological Association Bulletin* 5.2 (1986) 44–56.

Kerry, Anthony. *Wyclif*. Oxford: Oxford University Press, 1985.

Kessler, Johann. "Sabata: 1519–1539." In *Quellen Zur Geschicte der Tauferin der Schweiz*, edited by Heinold Fast, 590–638. Zurich: Theologischer Verlag Zurich, 1911.

———. *Sabata: St. Galler Reformationgeschicte 1523–1539.* Leipzig: Verein fur, 1910.

Kirschoff, Karl-Heinz. "Munster." In *Oxford Encyclopedia of the Reformation*, vol. 3, edited by Hans J. Hillerbrand, 97–98. Oxford: Oxford University Press, 1996.

Kittelson, James M. "Strasbourg." In *Oxford Encyclopedia of the Reformation*, vol. 4, edited by Hans J. Hillerbrand, 115–18. Oxford: Oxford University Press, 1996.

Kjeldgaard-Pedersen, Steffen "Johann Agricola." In *Oxford Encyclopedia of the Reformation*, vol. 1, edited by Hans Hillerbrand, 10. Oxford: Oxford University Press, 1996.

Klaassen, Walter. *Anabaptism: Neither Catholic nor Protestant.* Waterloo, ON: Conrad, 1973.

———. *Anabaptism in Outline.* Classics of Radical Reformation. Edited by Cornelius J. Dyck Scottdale, PA: Herald, 1981.

———. *Marpeck: A Life of Dissent and Conformity.* Studies in Anabaptist and Mennonite History. Edited by Steven M. Nolt. 44 vols. Vol. 44, Scottdale, PA: Herald, 2008.

———. "Schwenckfeld and the Anabaptists." In *Schwenckfeld and Early Schwenckfeldianism*, edited by Peter C. Erb, 389–400. Pennsburg, PA: Schwenckfeld Library, 1986.

———. "Word, Spirit, and Scripture in Early Anabaptist Thought." Oxford: University of Oxford, 1960.

Klaassen, William, and Walter Klassen. *Marpeck: A Life of Dissent and Conformity.* Scottdale, PA: Herald, 2008.

———, eds. *Writings of Pilgram Marpeck.* Classics of the Radical Reformation. Edited by Cornelius J. Dyck. Waterloo, ON: Herald, 1978.

Klassen, Peter J. "Moravia." In *Oxford Encyclopedia of the Reformation*, vol. 3, edited by Hans J. Hillerbrand, 87–89. Oxford: Oxford University Press, 1996.

Klassen, William. *Covenant and Community: The Life, Writings, and Hermeneutics of Pilgram Marpeck.* Grand Rapids: Eerdmans, 1968.

Kleist, James A. "Didache." In *Ancient Christian Writers*, edited by Johannes Quasten, 22–23. Westminster, MD: Newman, 1948.

Klotzer, Ralf. "The Melchiorites and Munster." In *A Companion to Anabaptism and Spiritualism, 1521–1700*, edited by John D. Roth, 225. Leiden: Brill, 2007.

Kolb, Robert. "Augsburg Confession, 1530." In *Book of Concord: Confessions of the Evangelical Lutheran Church*, edited by Robert Kolb, 42–43. Translated by Charles Arand. Minneapolis: Fortress, 2000.

Land, Steven Jack. *Pentecostal Spirituality: A Passion for the Kingdom.* Cleveland, TN: CPT, 2010.

Lederach, Paul M. "First Mennonite Church, Norristown, PA." https://gameo.org/index.php?title=First_Mennonite_Church,_Norristown,_PA.

Lehmann, Helmut T., ed. *Luther's Works.* Philadelphia: Fortress, 1960.

Littell, Frank H. *Origins of Sectarian Protestantism.* New York: Macmillian, 1964.

Locher, Gottfried W. *Zwingli's Thought: New Perspectives.* Studies in the History of Christian Thought. Edited by Heiko A. Oberman. Leiden: E. J. Brill, 1981.

Lohse, Bernhard. *Martin Luther's Theology: Its Historical and Systematic Development.* Edinburgh: T. & T. Clark, 1999.

Lull, Timothy F. ed. *Martin Luther's Basic Theological Writings.* Minneapolis: Fortress, 2005

Lunn, John R., ed. *Bishop Barlowe's Dialogue on the Lutheran Factions:1531*. London: Ellis and Keene, 1897.

Luther, Martin. "Against the Heavenly Prophets 1525." In *Luther's Works*, vol. 39: Church and Ministry II, edited by Helmut T. Lehmann, 146. Philadelphia: Fortress, 1958.

———. "Against the Robbing and Murdering Hordes of Peasants, 1525." In *Martin Luther*, edited by E. G. Rupp, 121–26. Documents of Modern History. London: Edward Arnold, 1979.

———. "Against the Roman Papacy an Institution of the Devil: 1545." In *Luther's Works, Vol. 41: Church and Ministry III*, edited by Jaroslav Pelikan, 263, 376. Philadelphia: Fortress, 1966.

———. "The Babylonian Captivity." In *Martin Luther's Basic Theoligical Writings*, edited by William R. Russell, 210–11, 394–95. Minneapolis: Fortress, 2005.

———. "The Catholic Epistles: Lectures on the First Epistle of John." In *Luther's Works, Vol. 39: Church and Ministry I*, edited by Jaroslav Pelikan, 301–14. St. Louis: Concordia, 1967.

———. "A Christian Assembly has the Right to Choose Teachers." In *Church and Ministry 1*, edited by Erich W. Gritsch, 166. Luther's Works. Philadelphia: Fortress, 1970.

———. *Commentary on the Epistle to the Galatians 1522*. Translated by Erasmus Middleton. Edited by John P. Fallowes. 55 vols. London: Harrison Trust, 1987.

———. "Concerning the Ministry." In *Luther's Works, Vol. 40: Church and Ministry II*, edited by Conrad Bergendorf, 32–36. Philadelphia: Fortress, 1958.

———. "Confessions Concerning Christ's Supper, 1528." In *Luther's Works: Vol. 37: Word and Sacrament Lll*, edited by Helmut T. Lehmann, 216. Philadelpha: Fortress, 1961.

———. "Freedom of the Christian." In *Martin Luther's Basic Theological Writings*, edited by Timothy Lull, 394–98. Minnaeapolis: Fortress, 2005.

———. "Friendly Admonition to Peace Concerning the Twelve Articles of the Swabian Peasants, 1525." In *Protestant Reformation*, edited by Hans J. Hillerbrand, 63–66. Documentary of Western Civilization. London: Harper Torchbooks, 1968.

———. *Galatians*. Edited by Alister McGrath and J. I. Packer. Crossway Classic Commentaries. Wheaton, IL: Crossway, 1998.

———. "Letters to Almsdorf and Melanchthon." In *Luther's Works*, edited by Helmut T. Lehmann, 364–67. Philadelphia: Fortress, 1522.

———. "Letter to George Spalatin." In *Letters 1*, translated by Gottfried G. Krodel, edited by Helmut T. Lehman, 350–51. Luther's Works. Philadelphia: Fortress, 1963.

———. "Letter to the Christians at Strasbourg in Opposition to the Fanatic Spirit." In *Luther's Works, vol. 39: Church and Ministry II*, edited by Conrad Bergendorff, 63–71. Luther's Works. Philadelphia: Fortress, 1958.

———. "The Marburg Colloquy and the Marburg Articles, 1529." In *Luther's Works: Vol. 38: Word and Sacrament IV*, edited by Helmut T. Lehmann, 5–13. Philadelphia: Fortress, 1971.

———. *Schmalkald Articles, 1537*. Translated by William R. Russell. Minneapolis: Fortress, 1995.

———. "Table Talk No. 4007." In *Luther's Works, vol. 54: Table Talk*, edited by Helmut G. Tappert, 308–9. Philadelphia: Fortress, 1967.

———. "That a Christian Assembly or Congregation has the Right and Power to Judge All Teaching and to Call, Appoint, and Dismiss Teachers, Established and Proven by Scripture." In *Luther's Works: Vol. 39: Church and Ministry 1*, edited by Eric W. Gritsch, 301–14. Phildelphia: Fortress, 1970.

———. *Theologia Germanica of Martin Luther, Vol. 19*. Translated by Bengt Hoffman. Classics of Western Spirituality. 19 vols. New York: Paulist, 1980.

———. "To the Christian Nobility of the German Nation." In *Luther's Works: Vol. 44: Christian and Society I*, edited by Helmut T. Lehman, 115–219. Philadelphia: Fortress, 1970.

———. "Treatise on the New Testament, That Is, the Holy Mass 1520." In *Luther's Works: Vol. 35: Word and Sacrament I*, translated by Charles M. Jacobs, edited by E. Theodore Bachman, 86–87. Philadelphia: Fortress, 1960.

———. "Two Kinds of Righteousness." In *Martin Luther's Basic Theological Writings*, edited by William R. Russell. Minneapolis: Fortress, 2005.

Mabry, Eddie. *Balthasar Hubmaier's Doctrine of the Church*. London: University Press of America, 1994.

Macchia, Frank D. *Spirituality and Social Liberation: Message of the Blumhardts in the Light of Wuerttenberg Pietism*. Pietists and Wesleyan Studies. Edited by David Bundy. 4 vols. London: Scarecrow, 1993.

MacCulloch, Diarmaid. *Reformation: A History*. London: Penguin Group, 2004.

Marius, Richard. *Luther: Christian between God and Death*. Cambridge, MA: Harvard University Press, 1999.

Marpeck, Pilgram. "Admonition of 1542." In *Writings of Pilgram Marpeck*, translated by Walter Klaassen, edited by Walter Klaassen and William Klassen, 180. Classics of the Radical Reformation. Kitchener, ON: Pandora, 2010.

———. "A Clear Refutation." In *Writings of Pilgram Marpeck*, translated by Walter Klaassen, edited by Walter Klaassen and William Klassen, 50. Classics of the Radical Reformation. Eugene, OR: Wipf & Stock, 1999

———. "Ein Neu Gespreche/ Frag und Antwort Zwischen Ainem Predicanten und Ainem Tauffer." In Sammelband vol. A 1207/1 690–696, ed. German State Archive of Ulm, 1532.

———. "Expose of the Babylonian Whore, 1531." In *Later Writings of Pilgram Marpeck*, tranlated by Werner Packull, edited by C. Arnold Snyder, 28. Kitchner, ON: Pandora, 1999.

———. "A New Dialogue, 1532." In *Later Writings by Pilgram Marpeck and His Circle*, translated by Werner Packull, edited by Werner Packull, 50–54. Kitchener, ON: Pandora, 1999.

Matheson, Peter, ed. *The Collected Works of Thomas Müntzer*, Edinburgh: T. & T. Clark, 1988.

McConica, James. *Erasmus*. Past Masters. Edited by Keith Thomas Oxford: Oxford University Press, 1991.

McDonnell, Killian. *Christian Initiation and Baptism in the Holy Spirit*. Collegeville, MN: Liturgical, 1991.

McGee, Gary. "Initial Evidence." In *New International Dictionary of Pentecostal and Charismatic Movements*, edited by Stanley Burgess, 784–91. Grand Rapids: Zondervan, 2002.

———. "Missions Overseas (North American Pentecostal)." In *New International Dictionary of Pentecostal and Charismatic Movements*, edited by Stanley Burgess, 886–901. Grand Rapids: Zondervan, 2002.

McGinn, Bernard, ed. *Essential Writings of Christian Mysticism*. New York: Modern Library, 2006.

———. *Harvest of Mysticism in Medieval Germany, Vol. 4: Presence of God: History of Christian Mysticism*. Edited by Bernard McGinn. 6 vols. New York: Crossroad, 2005.

McGrath, Alister. *Christian Theology: An Introduction*. 3rd ed. Oxford: Blackwell, 2001.

———. *The Intellectual Origins of the European Reformation*. Oxford: Basil Blackwell, 1987.

———. *Reformation Thought*. 3rd ed. Oxford: Blackwell, 1988.

McGrath, Alister, ed. *Galatians by Martin Luther*. Wheaton, IL: Crossway, 1998.

McLaughlin, R. Emmet. *Caspar Schwenckfeld, Reluctant Radical: His Life to 1540*. London: Yale University Press, 1986.

———. "Paul in Early Anabaptism." In *Companion to Paul in the Reformation*, edited by R. Ward Holder, 217, 224, 228. Brill's Companion to the Christian Tradition, 500–1700. Leiden: Brill, 2009.

———. "Radical Reformation." In *Cambridge History of Christianity*, edited by R. Po-Chia Hsia, 42–43. Cambridge: Cambridge University Press, 2007.

———. "Reformation Spiritualism: Typology, Sources, and Significance." In *Radikaltat Und Dissent Im 16 Jahrhundert*, edited by Hans Jurgen-Goertz, 124. Berlin: Zeitschrift fur Historische Forschung, 2002.

———. "Spiritualism: Schwenckfeld." In *Anabaptism and Spiritualism*, edited by John D. Roth, 127. Leiden: Brill, 2007.

The Mennonite Church. "Holy Spirit in the Life of the Church: Mennonite Church." https://gameo.org/index.php?title=Holy_Spirit_in_the_Life_of_the_Church:_Mennonite_Church.

Menzies, William W. *Anointed to Serve*. Springfield, MO: Gospel, 1980.

———. *Bible Doctrines: A Pentecostal Perspective*. Springfield, MO: Logion, 1998.

Methuen, Charlotte. "Interpreting Nature and Scripture." In *Interpreting the Books of Nature in Medieval and Early Modern Thought*, edited by Jitse van der Meer, 159. Leiden: Brill, 2009.

———. "Interpreting the Books of Nature and Scripture in Medieval and Early Modern Thought: An Introductory Essay." In *Interpreting Nature and Scripture: History of a Dialogue in the Abrahamic Religions*, edited by Jitse van der Meer & Scott Mandelbrote, 2. Brill's Series in Church History. Leiden: Brill, 2009.

———. *Luther and Calvin: Religious Revolutionaries*. Oxford: Lion Hudson, 2011.

Miller, Gregory J. "Huldrych Zwingli (1484–1531)." In *The Reformation Theologians: An Introduction to the Early Modern Period*, edited by Carter Lindberg, 1–2. Oxford: Blackwell, 2002.

Moeller, Bernd. "Imperial Cities and the Reformation." In *Imperial Cities and the Reformation: Three Essays*, edited and translated by H. C. Erik Midelfort. Philadelphia: Fortress, 1972.

Muller, Richard. *Dictionary of Latin and Greek Theological Terms*. Grand Rapids: Baker, 2003.

Murray, Stuart. "Biblical Interpretation among the Anabaptist Reformers." In *History of Biblical Interpretation: Medieval through the Reformation Period*, edited by Alan

J. Hauser, 403. History of Biblical Interpretation Series. Grand Rapids: Eerdmans, 2009.

Musing, Hans-Werner. "Anabaptist Movement in Strasbourg, 1526–1527." *Mennonite Quarterly Review* 51.2 (1977) 91–126.

Myland, David W. *Latter Rain Covenant and Pentecostal Power*. Chicago: Evangel, 1910.

Neff, Christian. "Manuscripts." http://www.gameo.org//index.php?title=Manuscripts.

Nichol, John Thomas. *Pentecostalism*. New York: Harper & Row, 1966.

Nienkirchen, Charles W. *A. B. Simpson and the Pentecostal Movement*. Eugene, OR: Wipf & Stock, 1992.

Oberman, Heiko A. *Dawn of the Reformation*. Grand Rapids: Eerdmans, 1992.

———. *Luther: Man between God and the Devil*. New York: Doubleday, 1990.

O'Loughlin, Thomas. *Didache*. Grand Rapids: Baker Academic, 2010.

Olin, John C., ed. *Erasmus: Christian Humanism and the Reformation Selected Writings*. New York: Harper Torchbooks, 1965.

Opitz, Peter. "The Exegetical and Hermeneutical Work of Oecolampadius, Huldrych Zwingli and John Calvin." In *Hebrew Bible/Old Testament: The History of Its Interpretation*, edited by Magne Saebo, 415. Gottingen: Vandenhoeck & Ruprecht, 2008.

Ozment, Steven. *Age of Reform*. New Haven: Yale University Press, 1980.

———. *Reformation in the Cities*. London: Yale University Press, 1975.

Packull, Werner O. *Hutterite Beginnings*. Baltimore: Johns Hopkins University Press, 1995.

———. *Mysticism and the Early South German-Austrian Anabaptist Movement 1525–1531*. Reprint. Eugene, OR: Wipf & Stock, 2008.

Parham, Charles Fox. *A Voice Crying in the Wilderness*. Baxter Springs, KS: Apostolic Faith Bible College, 1910.

Pauck, Wilhelm, ed. *Luther: Lectures on Romans, Vol. 15*. Library of Christian Classics. 26 vols. Philadelphia: Westminster, 1953.

Peachy, Paul. "Answer of Some Who are Called (Ana) Baptists Why They Do Not Attend the Churches: A Swiss Brethren Tract." *Mennonite Quarterly Review* 28.1 (2008) 5–32.

Pelikan, Jaroslav, ed. *Lectures on Galatians 1535: Chapters 1–4*. Luther's Works. Vol. 26. St. Louis: Concordia, 1963.

Peters, Edward. "Introduction." In *Uldrych Zwingli*, edited by Samuel Macauley Jackson, v–xxx. Philadelphia: University of Pennsylvania Press, 1972.

Pettegree, Andrew. *Brand Luther*. New York: Penguin, 2015.

Pew Research Center: Religious and Public Life. "Global Christianity: A Report on the Size and Distribution of the World's Christian Population." http://www.pewforum.org/2011/12/19/global-christianity-exec.

Pipkin, H. Wayne, ed. *Balthasar Hubmaier: Theologian of Anabaptism, Vol. 5*. Edited by Cornelius J. Dyck. Classics of the Radical Reformation. 12 vols. Scottdale, PA: Herald, 1989.

———. *Pittsburg Theological Monographs*. 2 vols. Allison Park, PA: Pickwick, 1984.

Polman, Gerrit. R. "European War Justifiable?" In *Christian Evangel* (December 12, 1914) 1.

Potter, George. R., ed. *Huldrych Zwingli*. Documents of Modern History. London: Edward Arnold, 1978.

———. *Zwingli*. Cambridge: Cambridge University Press, 1978.

Preus, James S. "Carlstadt's *Ordinaciones* and Luther's Liberty: A Study of the Wittenberg Movement." *Harvard Theological Studies* 26.10 (1974) 315.

Radice, Betty. "Biographical Note: Erasmus." In *Praise of Folly*, translated by Betty Radice, edited by Mortimer J. Adler, ix–x. Great Books of the Western World. Chicago: Encyclopedia Britannica, 1952.

Raeder, Siegfried. "The Exegetical and Hermeneutical Work of Martin Luther." In *Hebrew Bible/Old Testament: The History of Its Interpretation: Vol. 2*, edited by Magne Saebo, 367. Renaissance to the Enlightenment. Gottingen: Vandenhoek & Ruprect, 2008.

Ratzinger, Joseph Cardinal. *Catechism of the Catholic Church*. Liguori, MO: Liguori, 1994.

Reimer, A. James. "Denominational Apologetics to Social History and Systematic Theology." *Religious Studies Review* 29.3 (July 2003) 235.

Rempel, John D., ed. *Jorg Maler's Kunstbuch: Writings of the Marpeck Circle*. Classics of the Radical Reformation. Kitchener, ON: Pandora, 2010.

Riedemann, Peter. *Peter Riedemann's Hutterite Confession of Faith, 1540*. Translated by John J. Friesen. Edited by H. Wayne Pipkin. Classics of the Radical Reformation, vol. 9. Waterloo, ON: Herald, 1999.

Rilliet, Jean. *Zwingli: Third Man of the Reformation*. London: Lutterworth, 1959.

Robeck, Cecil M. *The Azusa Street Mission and Revival: The Birth of the Global Pentecostal Movement*. Nashville: Nelson Reference and Electronic 2006.

———. "Montanism and Present Day Prophets." *Pneuma* 32.3 (2010) 418–19.

Roth, John D. "Marpeck and the Later Swiss Brethren, 1540–1700." In *A Companion to Anabaptism and Spiritualism, 1521–1700*, edited by John D. Roth and James M. Stayer, 347–88. Leiden: Brill, 2007.

———. "Recent Currents in the Historiography of the Radical Reformation." *Church History* 71.3 (September 2002) 523–35.

Roth, John D., and James Stayer, eds. *Anabaptism and Spiritualism, 1521–1700*. Brill's Companions to the Christian Tradition. Leiden: Brill, 2007.

Rothkegel, Martin. "Anabaptism in Moravia and Silesia." In *A Companion to Anabaptism and Spiritualism, 1521–1700*, edited by John D. Roth, 163–216. Brill's Companions to the Christian Tradition. Leiden: Brill, 2007.

Rowan, Steven. "Urban Communities: The Rulers and the Ruled." In *Handbook of European History: 1400–1600*, edited by Thomas A. Brady, Jr., 197–230. Grand Rapids: Eerdmans, 1994.

Rummel, Erika, ed. *The Erasmus Reader*. Toronto: University of Toronto Press, 1990.

Rupp, Gordon, and Benjamin Drewery. *Martin Luther: Documents of Modern History, Vol. 1*. 20 vols. London: Edward Arnold 1970.

Rupp, Gordon. "Andreas Karlstadt and Reformation Puritanism." *Journal of Theological Studies* 10.2 (1959) 309–26.

———. *Patterns of Reformation*. London: Epworth, 1969.

———. *Reformers in the Wings*. 2nd ed. Oxford: Oxford University Press, 2001.

Russell, William R. "Introduction: Two Kinds of Righteousness." In *Martin Luther's Basic Theological Writings*, edited by William R. Russell, 134–208. Minneapolis: Fortress, 2005.

Sanders, G. W., ed. *William Seymour Papers*. Self-published, 2006.

Sattler, Michael. "Letter to the Church at Horb." In *Martyr's Mirror*, edited by Thieleman J. van Braght, 418–20. Scottdale, PA: Herald, 1998.

Schad, Elias. "True Account of an Anabaptist Meeting at Night in a Forest." *Mennonite Quarterly Review* 58 (July 1984) 292–95.

Schaff, Philip. *History of the Christian Church: Ante-Nicene Christianity, Vol. 2*. 8 vols. Grand Rapids: Eerdmans, 1985.

Schiemer, Leonhard. "Letter to the Church of God at Rattenberg, 1527." In *Sources of South German/Austrian Anabaptism*, edited by C. Arnold Snyder, 64–80. Kitchener, ON: Pandora, 2001.

Schiess, Traugott, ed. *Kessler's Sabata: St Galler Reformationschronik 1523–1539*. Leipzig: Rudolf Haupt, 1911.

Schlaffer, Hans. "Brief Instruction for the Beginning of a Truly Christian Life, 1528." In *Sources of South German/Austrian Anabaptism*, edited by C. Arnold Snyder, 81–109. Classics of the Radical Reformation. Kitchener, ON: Pandora, 2001.

———. "Instruction on Beginning of a True Christian Life." In *Early Anabaptist Spirituality*, translated and edited by Daniel Liechty, 99–108. Classics of Western Spirituality. Mahwah, NJ: Paulist, 1994.

Schmid, Alois. "Marburg Colloquy." In *Oxford Encyclopedia of the Reformation, vol. 3*, edited by Hans J. Hillerbrand, 2–4. Oxford: Oxford University Press, 1996.

Schowalter, Paul. "Numbers of Anabaptists Martyred." http://gameo.org/index.php?title=Martyrs&oldid=92632.

Schwenckfeld, Caspar. "Ermanung Des Missbrauchs." In *Corpus Schwenckfeldianorum*, edited by Chester D. Hartranft, 62. Leipzig: Breitkopf & Haertel, 1911.

Scott, Tom. *Thomas Muntzer: Theology and Revolution in the German Reformation*. London: Macmillan, 1989.

Scribner, Robert W. "Peasants' War." In *Oxford Encyclopedia of the Reformation*, edited by Hans J. Hillerbrand, 234–37. Oxford: Oxford University Press, 1994.

Scribner, Robert W., and Ole Peter Grell, eds. *Tolerance and Intolerance in the European Reformation*. Cambridge: Cambridge University Press, 1996.

Seguenny, Andre. "Schwenckfeld." In *Reformation Theologians*, edited by Carter Lindberg, 353. Malden, MA: Blackwell, 2002.

Seymour, William. "Apostolic Faith Movement." *Apostolic Faith* 1.1 (1906) 2.

———. "Precious Atonement." *Apostolic Faith* 1.1 (1906) 2.

Shantz, Douglas H. *Crautwald and Erasmus: Study in Humanism and Radical Reform in Sixteenth Century Silesia, Vol. 4*. Bibliotheca Dissidentium. Baden-Baden: V. Koerner, 1992.

———. "Role of Valentine Crautwald in the Growth of Sixteenth Century Schwenckfeldian Reform." *Mennonite Quarterly Review* 65.3 (July 1991) 287–307.

Sider, Ronald J. *Andreas Bodenstein Von Karlstadt: Development of His Thought 1517–1525*. Studies in Medieval Thought. Vol. 11. Leiden: E. J. Brill, 1974.

Sider, Ronald J., ed. *Karlstadt's Battle with Luther: Documents in a Liberal-Radical Debate*. Philadelphia: Fortress, 1978.

Simons, Menno. *Complete Writings of Menno Simons*. Translated by Leonard Verduin. Scottdale, PA: Herald, 1984.

Simpson, Carl. "Development of the Pentecostal and Charismatic Movements in the Germanic Countries." In *European Pentecostalism*, edited by William K. Kay, 62–63. Global Pentecostal and Charismatic Studies. Leiden: Brill, 2011.

———. "Jonathan Paul and the German Pentecostal Movement." *Journal of the European Pentecostal Theological Association* 28.2 (2008) 169–82.

de Smit, Gilbert, ed. *Die Teutsch Spraach: Dictionarium Germanicolatinum Novum.* Edited by Ludwig Erich Schmitt, Documenta Linguistica: Quellen Zur Geschicte Der Deutschen Sprache Des 15. Bis 20. Jahrhunderts. Reihe 1. Worterbuch Des 15.Und 16. Jahrhunderts Hildeshiem: Georg Olms Verlag, 1971.

Snyder, C. Arnold. *Anabaptist History and Theology: An Introduction.* Kitchener, ON: Pandora, 2002.

―――. *Life and Thought of Michael Sattler.* Studies in Anabaptist and Mennonite History. 27 vols. Scottdale, PA: Herald, 1984.

―――. "Sattler, Michael." In *Oxford Encyclopedia of the Reformation*, edited by Hans J. Hillerbrand, 485–86. Oxford: Oxford University Press, 1996.

―――. "Sebastian Franck on the Anabaptists (1536)." In *Sources of South German/Austrian Anabaptism,* translated by Walter Klaassen, edited by C. Arnold Snyder, 228–52. Classics of the Radical Reformation. Kitchener, ON: Pandora, 2001.

―――. "Simple Confession: Part 2." *Mennonite Quarterly Review* 54.1 (January 2000) 87–113.

―――. *Sources of South German/Austrian Anabaptism.* Classics of the Radical Reformation.10 vols. Kitchener, ON: Pandora, 2001.

Snyder, C. Arnold, ed. *Biblical Concordance of the Swiss Brethren, 1540.* Kitchener, ON: Pandora, 2001.

―――. *Profiles of Anabaptist Women: Sixteenth Century Reforming Pioneers.* Vol. 3, Studies in Women and Religion. Waterloo, ON: Wilfrid Laurier University Press, 1996.

Spinka, Matthew, ed. *Advocates of Reform.* Library of Christian Classics. London: SCM LTD, 1954.

Stayer, James M. "Anabaptists." In *Oxford Encyclopedia of the Reformation, vol. 1,* edited by Hans J. Hillerbrand, 31–35. Oxford: Oxford University Press, 1996.

―――. *Anabaptists and the Sword.* Lawrence, KS: Coronado, 1973.

―――. *German Peasants' War and Anabaptist Community of Goods.* McGill-Queen's Studies in the History of Religion. 10 vols. Montreal: McGill-Queen's University Press, 1991.

―――. "Hubmaier, Balthasar." In *Oxford Encyclopedia of the Reformation, vol. 2,* edited by Hans J. Hillerbrand, 260–63. Oxford: Oxford University, 1996.

―――. "Monogenesis or Polygenesis." *Mennonite Quarterly Review* 49.2 (1975) 81–121.

―――. "Peasants' War 1524–1525." http://www.gameo.org/encyclopedia/contents/P44.html.

―――. "The Radical Reformation." In *Handbook of European History*, edited by Thomas A. Brady, 249–82. Grand Rapids: Eerdmans, 1996.

―――. "Swiss Anabaptism: The Beginnings." In *Companion to Anabaptism and Spiritualism, 1521–1700,* edited by John D. Roth, 45–82. Brill's Companion to the Christian Tradition. Leiden: Brill, 2007.

Steinmetz, David C. *Reformers in the Wings.* 2nd ed. Oxford: Oxford University Press, 2001.

Stephens, W. Peter. *The Theology of Huldrych Zwingli.* Oxford: Clarendon, 1986.

Stephenson, Carl, ed. *Sources of English Constitutional History.* Harper's Historical Series. London: Harper & Row, 1937.

Storms, Everek R. "Eby, Solomon, 1834–1931." http://www.gameo.org/index.php?title=Eby, Solomon. 1834–1931.

Synan, Vinson. *Century of the Holy Spirit: 100 Years of Pentecostal and Charismatic Renewal*. Nashville: Thomas Nelson, 2001.

———. *Holiness-Pentecostal Tradition*. Grand Rapids: Eerdmans, 1997.

Szczucki, Lech. "Socianism." In *Oxford Encyclopedia of the Reformation, vol. 4*, edited by Hans J. Hillerbrand, 483–87. Oxford: Oxford University, 1996.

Tabbernee, Wiliam. *Fake Prophecy and Polluted Sacraments*. Supplements to *Vigiliae Christianae*. Leiden: Brill, 2007.

Thiessen, Richard D. "Thiessen, Johann, 1869–1953." http://gameo .org/index.php?title=Theissen, Johann, 1869–1953.

Troeltsch, Ernst. *Social Teaching of the Christian Churches, Vol. 2*. Library of Theological Ethics. 2 vols. London: Westminster/John Knox, 1912.

Tucker, Albert. *A History of English Civilization*. London: Harper & Row, 1972.

van Braght, Thieleman J. *Martyr's Mirror*. Scottdale, PA: Herald, 1998.

Van Dusen, Henry P. "Third Force in Christendom." *Life Magazine* (June 9, 1958) 113–24.

Vedder, Henry C. *Balthasar Hubmaier: Leader of the Anabaptists*. New York: Putnam, 1905.

Vogler, Gunter. *Thomas Muntzer*. Berlin: Dietz Verlag, 1989.

Wacker, Grant. *Heaven Below: Early Pentecostals and American Culture*. London: Harvard University Press, 2001.

Wandel, Lee Palmer. "Zwingli." In *Oxford Encyclopedia of the Reformation, vol. 4*, edited by Hans J. Hilderbrand, 320–23. Oxford: Oxford University Press, 1996.

Ware, S. L. "Restorationism in Classical Pentecostalism." In *International Dictionary of Pentecostal and Charismatic Movements*, edited by Stanley M. Burgess, 1019–21. Grand Rapids: Zondervan, 2002.

Warrington, Keith. *Pentecostal Theology: A Theology of Encounter*. London: T. & T. Clark, 2008.

Wesley, John. *The Works of John Wesley: Letters, Vol. 12*. 13 vols. Kansas City: Beacon Hill, 1979.

———. *The Works of John Wesley: Sermons II, Vol. 6*. 3rd ed. 14 vols. Kansas City: Beacon Hill, 1979.

Williams, George H. *Radical Reformation*. Kirksville, MO: Sixteenth Century Journal, 1992.

———. *Spiritual and Anabaptist Writers*. Library of Christian Classics. Philadelphia: Westminster, 1958.

Williams, H. H. Drake, ed. *Caspar Schwenckfeld: Eight Writings*. Kitchener, ON: Pandora, 2006.

Wilson, Dwight. J. "Pacifism." In *International Dictionary of Pentecostal and Charismatic Movements*, edited by Stanley Burgess, 953–55. Grand Rapids: Zondervan, 2004.

Wondey, Wolfgang. "Pentecostalism and the Reformation: Toward a Joint Ecumenical Commemoration." *Journal of the European Pentecostal Theological Association* 37.2 (2017) 110–22.

Yoder, John Howard. *Anabaptism and Reformation in Switzerland: An Historical and Theological Analysis of the Dialogues between Anabaptists and Reformers*. Translated by David C. Stassen and C. Arnold Snyder. Kitchener, ON: Pandora, 2004.

———. "Concern 15." *Marginalia* 15 (July 1967) 77–80.

———. *Legacy of Michael Sattler*. Classics of the Radical Reformation, vol. 1. Scottdale, PA: Herald, 1973.

Yong, Amos. *Who Is the Holy Spirit: A Walk with the Apostles*. Brewster, MA: Paraclete, 2011.

Zwingli, Uldrych. *Catabaptistarum Strophas Elenchus*. Zurich: Christophori Froschouer, 1527.

———. "Clarity and Certainty of the Word of God." In *Zwingli and Bullinger*, edited by John T. McNeill and translated by Geoffrey. W. Bromiley, 49–95. Library of Christian Classics. London: SCM, 1953.

———. "Exposition and Basis of the Conclusions or Articles Published by Huldrych Zwingli, Zurich, 29 January, 1523." In *Huldrych Zwingli: Writings*, edited by E. J. Furcha, 1–373. Allison Park, PA: Pickwick, 1984.

———. "The First Zurich Disputation." In *Ulrich Zwingli: Selected Works*, edited and translated by Samuel Macauley Jackson, 40–117. Philadelphia: University of Pennsylvania Press, 1972.

———. "Of the Upbringing and Education of Youth in Good Manners and Christian Discipline: An Admonition by Ulrich Zwingli." In *Zwingli and Bullinger*, translated by G. W. Bromiley, edited by John T. McNeill et al., 96–118. Library of Christian Classics. London: SCM, 1953.

———. "On Baptism 1525." In *Zwingli and Bullinger*, edited and translated by Geoffrey. W. Bromiley, 119–75. Library of Christian Classics. Philadelphia: Westminster, 1953.

———. "The Preaching Office." In *Huldrych Zwingli: Writings*, edited and translated by E. J. Furcha, 147–86. Allison Park, PA: Pickwick, 1972.

———. "Refutation of the Tricks of the Catabaptists." In *Ulrich Zwingli, 1484–1531: Selected Works*, edited by Samuel M. Jackson, 123–258. Philadelphia: University of Pennsylvania Press, 1972.

———. *Selected Writings of Huldrych Zwingli: In Search of True Religion: Reformation, Pastoral, and Eucharistic Writings*. Translated by H. Wayne Pipkin. Pittsburgh Theological Monographs. Allison Park, PA: Pickwick, 1984.

———. "Sermon on Divine and Human Justice: June 1523." In *Sources of Swiss Anabaptism*, edited by Leland Harder, 210–20. Classics of the Radical Reformation. Scottdale, PA: Herald, 1985.

———. "Shepherd (1524)." In *Huldrych Zwingli Writings*, edited and translated by H. Wayne Pipkin, 77–126. Pittsburgh Theological Monographs. Allison Park, PA: Pickwick, 1984.

———. "Short Christian Instruction (1523)." In *Huldrych Zwingli Writings*, edited and translated by H. Wayne Pipkin, 43–76. Pittsburgh Theological Monographs. Allison Park, PA: Pickwick, 1984.

———. *Writings: Defense of the Reformed Faith, Vol. 1*. Pittsburgh Theological Monographs. 2 vols. Allison Park, PA: Pickwick, 1984.

———. *Zwingli and Bullinger*. Library of Christian Classics. Edited by G. W. Bromiley. Vol. 24. Philadelphia: Westminster, 1957.

Index

Achtzehn Slussreden (Hubmaier), 75–77
Admonition Concerning Abuse of Certain Important Articles of the Gospel (Schwenckfeld), 35
Admonition of 1542 (Marpeck), 182–83
adult baptism, 33, 63, 182
African Americans, early Pentecostals as, 110
African-American customs, Seymour's adoption of, xxvi
Agabus, 55
Against the Robbing and Murdering Hordes of Peasants (Luther), 82
Agricola, John, 160
Ain klarer/vast nützlicher unterricht (A Clear and Useful Instruction), 158
Cardinal Albrecht of Mainz, 16
alien righteousness, Luther on, 17–18
allegorical meaning, of the Old Testament for Zwingli, 51
Althaus, Paul, 17
American Constitution, first amendment, 110
American Pentecostalism. *See also* Pentecostalism
  Charles Fox Parham and, xxiv–xxv
  high priority for a Pauline pneumatology, 98
  persecution by vigilante-type groups, 111
  on speaking in tongues as a genuine foreign language, 124
  on World War I, 128
Americans, opting for conscientious objector status, 130
Anabaptism. *See also* early Anabaptism
  advent of coincided with very traumatic events, 78
  associated with the Peasants War of 1525 and the apocalyptic debacle at Münster, xxxi
  becoming legalistic and dogmatic, 182
  broke into two primary opposing groups after Münster, 198
  charismatic and Pentecostal nature of, 184
  as a charismatic movement, xvii, 201
  charismatic nature of early, 91
  church praxes, 92–94
  complicated nature of, 163
  defined using the principles of C. Arnold Snyder, xxxvii
  degenerating into a "rank spiritualism of charismatic vagaries," xvii
  difficulty of separating into distinctive categories, 141
  dilemma of pacifism faced by early, 130
  divisions within, 140, 158
  early Pentecostalism's knowledge of, 159–61
  efforts to restore the primitive church, xl–xli

Anabaptism (continued)
  emulating a Pauline ecclesiology and spirituality, xxxi
  of equal importance to the original apostolic church, xvii
  established by the initial reform theology of Zwingli and Luther, 45
  evangelization effort of, 83–84
  historiography and literature, xxxi–xxxiv
  impact of evangelism, persecution, and pacifism in, xli
  leaders including former priests, monks, and theologians, 211
  marginalization and diaspora of, 64
  as neither Protestant nor Catholic, xxix
  not evolving into a Pentecostal denomination, 214
  overcame perversions of the church of Rome, 109n18
  persecution from magisterial authorities, 215
  polygenetic origin of, 160
  in the same spiritual "family" as twentieth-century Pentecostalism, 140
  similarities with Pentecostalism, xvi, xviii, xxxix, xli, 133, 204
  solidified by rebellion, 82
  spiritualism and, 137–39
  spread of, 74, 104
  theological issues with the Roman Catholic Church and with evolving Reformation churches, xxvii
  Williams's characterization of, 143–44
"Anabaptist," meaning rebaptized or baptized again, 74n17
Anabaptist biblical literalism, 144, 158
Anabaptist conventicles. *See* conventicles
Anabaptist diaspora, 64, 87, 114
Anabaptist disputants at Zofingen, 187
Anabaptist evangelistic effort, results of, 91
Anabaptist groups, identified by Eder, 118
Anabaptist historiography, xxxvi
Anabaptist leadership of Zurich, listing of, 71
Anabaptist primary archival sources, xxxiii
Anabaptist radicalism. *See* radicalism
Anabaptist spirituality and theology, compared with Pentecostals, xv, xl, xli, 203, 206, 211, 212–17
Anabaptist tenets of faith, 75–77
Anabaptist theological positions, xxxiii
Anabaptist Vision, publication of, xxxvi
Anabaptists
  appearing more traditionally orthodox, 140, 201
  armed resistance position of Hubmaier, 87
  believed the reformed church was continuing to maintain the Catholic Church order, 197
  disobeyed mandates for continuing the Catholic forms of the Mass, veneration of images, and infant baptism, 63
  distinguishing from spirituality, 137
  disunited according to Franck, 115
  divergent views of, 89
  divided into Evangelicals, Revolutionaries, and Contemplatives by Williams, 140
  early sixteenth-century catalysts for radical reform, xxvii–xxxi
  embraced priesthood of the believer, 125
  emergence of, 60–64
  emigration to religiously tolerant regions, 119
  ensconced in Zwingli's memorial theology, 66
  evangelism of, 102, 106–7
  flocked to Münster as a holy refuge, the "New Jerusalem," 195
  forced into clandestine conventicles and constant emigration, 122

forced to meet in secret to avoid arrest and prosecution, 214
forming a new church, 67, 70
holding to the original teachings of Luther and Zwingli, 99–100, 189
incarcerated, tortured, and martyred routinely, 129
incorporated the experiential nature of the efficacy of the Holy Spirit, the manifestation of the gifts of the Spirit, and adult baptism, 89–90
insisted on the efficacy of the Spirit in the absence of the word, 102
on the manifestation of the gifts of the Holy Spirit defining a true Christian church, 212
number martyred from 1525 to 1618, 109
objecting to only allowing one person to speak in worship services, 188
pacifism of. *see* pacifism
persecution of, 108–9
position concerning Christian initiation, 63
positive characteristics of, 94
prophetic-literal hermeneutic of, 4
reasons for not attending Lutheran or Zwinglian meetings, 187
refused all participation in violence of any kind, 130
rejected the idea of a single priest, 12
rejected Zwingli's retention of Catholic infant baptism and rejected including magistracy propagation of the gospel, 210
restitution of the primitive New Testament church, 211–12
on Scripture demanding informed confession and contrition, 106
sectarianism of, 113–18
sects described by William Barlowe, 116–17
separated from the Reformations of Luther and Zwingli, 107
sorting out the various theologies, 147
speaking out against the preacher during a reformed church service, 197
taking up arms to ensure the restitution of the church in Münster, 195
testifying to physical torture, 165
testifying with their "death and blood," 108
theological propositions held by, 70
use of Paul's letters to the Romans and Galatians, 167
Zwingli's theological positions of, xviii
Anderson, Allan
defining Pentecostalism, 89
on divine healing, xxiii
on examples of Pentecostal manifestations, xxvii
"family resemblance" definition for Pentecostalism, xxxix
on opposition to charismata (Pentecostalism), xxii
on origins of Pentecostalism, xxvi
theory of the nature of Pentecostalism, xxxviii
Anderson, R. M., xxi
Anglican Pentecostals, participating in a just war, 130
anthropology, of Anabaptism, xxxvii
anti-Anabaptist historical convention, xxxi–xxxii
anti-clericalism, 1, 43, 78–79
antinomianism, xxviii, 36, 210
anti-pacifism theology, of Hubmaier, 98
anti-pedobaptism, xxxiv, 99, 100, 142
antitrinitarianism, 89, 139
apocalypse, 158, 192, 193, 200
apocalyptic Melchiorites, 215
apostasy, 208
"apostle," Zwingli's definition of, 54
apostles, appointed bishops in their time only, 171
"Apostolic," defined, xvn3
apostolic authority, 171

apostolic church, reinstitution of, 92
Apostolic Faith, 205
"Apostolic Faith" movement, xxv
The Apostolic Faith (Seymour), 131–32, 162
apostolic standards, restoration of, 205–6
apostolic succession, 14
Appolonia, prophet in Strasbourg, 192
Archer, Kenneth, 166–67, 175
Aristotelian theology, 18
armed resistance, 82, 83, 87
Arnold, Gottfried, xxxii
Artz, Wendel, 118
Ascherham, Gabriel, 143
Assemblies of God, 128, 129, 130
Augustianism, Karlstadt's conversion to, 19
Augustinian idea, of *sola scriptura* as the sole arbiter of the faith, 71–72
Augustinian theologians, on sufficiency of Scripture, 11
authority, of Scripture (*sola scriptura*), 27
Azusa Street, 213, 214
Azusa Street Pentecostal mission, xxv
Azusa Street Pentecostal revival, 130

The Babylonian Captivity of the Church (Luther), 10
Bainton, Roland, 145
Balserak, Jon, 197
ban (excommunication)
  Anabaptist misuse or abuse of, 183
  Balthasar Hubmaier on, 98
  described in the *Schleitheim Confession*, 96
  for falling into error and sin, 95
  as a form of church discipline, xxxvii
  as an instrument of punishment, 182
  letter to the Swiss Brethren on abusing, 183
  not a restorative process, 98
  not using to maintain spiritual order, 189
baptism
  first adult performed by Grebel, 63
  in the Spirit and fire described by Hubmaier, 85–86
  of water, fire and blood for Anabaptists, 213
baptism in the Holy Spirit, xxiii, xxvii, 213
Barlowe, William, 116, 117
Barmen conference of the GB, 112
Barratt, Thomas Ball, 111, 112, 130–32
Barrett, T. B., 126
Batenburg, Jan van, leader of the Batenburgers, 198
Batrtleman, Frank, 198
Beamon, Jay, 129
beliefs, of various Anabaptist groups, xxxvi
believers
  as the product of preaching, 174
  requirement for baptism, 106
believer's church, opposed to a state church, 63
Bell, E. N., 130
Bender, Harold S., xxxiii
Bender paradigm, xxxv
Bender School, xxxvi, xxxvii–xxxviii
Berlin Declaration, 112, 113
Bible. See also Scripture
  different ways of reading, 173–74
  disregarding as the final arbiter of the faith, 205
  interpreting with spiritual-prophetic literality, 133
  reading and interpreting without papal arbitration, 6
  as sole authority, xxxvii
  as spirituality irrelevant, xix
biblical commentaries, 13
biblical concordances called guides (*Zeyger*), circulation of, 175–76
biblical hermeneutics, introduced by Marin Luther and Huldrych Zwingli, xvi
biblical interpretation, not denying the efficacy of the manifestation of the gifts of the Holy Spirit, 190

INDEX

biblical languages, gifts providing the ability to understand, 55
biblical literalists, in the sense of Pauline pneumatology, 148
biblical priesthood, authority of, xx
biblical role, of the Holy Spirit, 208
biblicist interpretation of Scripture, by Simons, 200
biblicist literalism, 146
biblicists' Swiss Brethren, chose Marpeck as their new leader, 158
"bitter Christ," imitating, 213
Bjorner, Ana Larssen, 131
Blaurock, Georg, 63, 141, 154–55
Blickle, Peter, 79–80
blood, of Jesus Christ cleanseth from all sin, 87
bloody rebellion, by German commoners, 78
Blumhardt, Johann, xxiii
Blumhofer, Edith, xxii, xxxviii
Boddy, Alexander A.
   Anglican pastor at All Saints' Church, 130–31
   counseled those seeking the baptism in the Holy Spirit, 132
   first leader of British Pentecostalism, xxvii
   at the Hamburg conference in 1908, 112
   justification for England's involvement in war, 126–27
   on the near coming of Christ, 126
   providing a linkage between various groups, 132
   on reading God's holy word as a Christian duty, 173
body and blood of Christ, as physically present in the bread and wine, 66
body of Christ, 56, 213
Booth-Clibborn, Samuel H., 128
Bossy, John, 105–6, 207
Bosworth, F. F., 168, 170n151
bottom-up ecclesiastic methodology, 176
Boyd, Stephen, 153, 154, 156
Brady, Thomas, 79

Brecht, Martin, 4
Brief Apologia (Hubmaier), 86
British Assemblies of God, statement of faith, 212n312
British nonconformist Pentecostals, pacifism of, 128
Bromiley, G. W., 49, 50
Brotherly Union of a Number of Children of God Concerning Seven Articles (Sattler), 94
Brötli, Johannes, 61, 62, 84n53
Brumback, Carl, 171
Bucer, Martin, 121, 148, 193
Bullinger, Heinrich, 24, 60, 66, 118, 184
Bünderlin, Hans, 102, 157, 163
Bünderline, Johann, 144
Burgess, Stanley, 26, 135, 203
Byposten, Barratt's periodical, 132

"call" to preach, 165, 173, 174, 181
Calvin, John, 105, 139, 197
"candles, palm branches, and holy water," denying, 76
Capito, Wolfgang, 75, 121
cardinal doctrines, of Pentecostalism, 125
carnal compulsion (the call to preach), 165
carnal immorality, of priests, 76
Castelberger, Andreas, 61, 62
Castellio, Sebastian, 140
Castenbauer, Stefan (aka Boius Agricola), 152–53
Catabaptist, 113n36
Catabaptistarum Strophas Elenchus (Refutation of the Tricks of Anabaptists) (Zwingli), 63
catabaptizers, 74n17
catachresis, 51, 51n37
The Catenae (patristic interpretations), 13
Catholic cantons, proceeded to battle, 66
Catholic Church. *See* Roman Catholic Church

Catholic imagery and the Mass, Disputation of October 1523 called to debate, 62
Catholic Mass, practice of continued in Zurich, 61
Catholic theology, 15
Catholics and Lutherans, alliance of eliminated Melchiorites in Münster, 215
cause of Christ, forsaking all for, 189
"celestial flesh of Christ," 39, 150, 179, 181
celibacy, 209
ceremonies, Marpeck on, 173
cessationist, Luther as, 42, 209
charismata
  in Anabaptist conventicles in the context of evangelism, 105
  controling manifestations of reminiscent of the *Didache*, 200
  as evidence that the Holy Spirit was present, 217
  impact of aberrant behavior, misuse, and abuse of, 212
  manifestations of, xvi, xix, 4, 15, 213, 215
  Müntzer's openness to, 33
  praxis of according to Pauline pneumatology, xlii
  role in restitution, xxiii
  Zwingli critical of the manifestation of, 209
"charismatic," Williams use of the term, 141–42
charismatic biblical model, 125
charismatic Christian confession, 162
charismatic gift of prophecy. *See* gift of prophecy
charismatic gifts of the Spirit. *See* gifts of the Spirit
"charismatic" movement, early Anabaptism as, xvi
charismatic spiritual experience, of early Anabaptism, 89
Charismatics, number of in the world, xv
Emperor Charles V, 123, 152
chastity, 76

Christ. *See also* Jesus
  atoned for the sins of the whole world, 172
  being conformed to, 38
  came as a natural man, 179–80
  commanding and directing Christians to "preach, teach, and baptize," 166
  having a heavenly or celestial body, 192
  as our sole intercessor and mediator, 76
  physical humanity of critical to Marpeck, 178, 179
  salvation through the body of received by faith only, 38
Christendom, converting to primitive Christianity, 121
Christian Catechism (Hubmaier), 86, 151
Christian freedom, found in love, not law, for Zwingli, 58
Christian impiety, addressed with legal measures in Zurich, 57
Christian peace and love, tension with national patriotism, 128
Christians
  all capable of interpreting the Scripture as a priesthood of believers, 41
  bound by love to share spiritual gifts for the edification of the whole body, 203, 206, 211
  differentiated from the world, 9
  empowered by the Spirit to read and interpret Scripture, 197
  enabled to act freely by the knowledge of Christ through the Eucharist, 37
  not forbidden to have fellowship with the world for the sake of bodily nourishment, 189–90
  number of in the world, xv
  praxis of manifestation of the charismata from the first-century church, xli

INDEX 243

using neither worldly sword nor war according to Grebel and his Swiss Brethren, 83
Christology, of Marpeck, 172, 176–77
church
    as being separate from any political institution, government, and the unregenerate world, 203, 206, 211
    at the center of civic as well as religious life of a town, 119–20
    necessity of separation from the state, 67
church and state, separation of, 133–34
church cooperative, duties of the members of, 76
Church of God, resolved in 1917 "Against members going to war," 129
Clare verantwortung (A Clear Refutation), 158
Clark, Mathew, xviii
Clasen, Claus-Peter, 107, 108–9, 146
A Clear and Useful Instruction (Marpeck), 177–78, 179, 184, 185, 190
A Clear Refutation (Marpeck), 163–71, 183–84, 185, 190
clergy. *See also* priests
    Erasmus speaking out against the abuses of, 9
    no need for a hierarchical, xx
    oppressing simple peasants with superstitions, 36
coming of Christ, rejecting violent preparation for, 199
commands, of Christ according to Marpeck, 166
communal fields and arable lands, claimed by the communities, 81
communal hermeneutics, 175, 200
community, having the right to elect and dismiss clergy, 80
Comparison of Biblical Scripture (Bünderlin), 163
conduct and attitude, of Anabaptists, 92

confessions of faith
    author of the first Anabaptist, 74
    of both Hubmaier and Sattler not acceptable to all, 102
    comparisons of, 97–98
    by Sattler, 88n69
    written to unify the Anabaptist movement, 70
Confidence periodical, 132
congregational theology (*Gemeindetheologie*), 175
congregations, right to choose their own pastor, 216
Conn, Charles W., xxi, 129
conscientious objection, of British Pentecostalism, 127
conscientious objector status, 129
consecration, by a pope or bishop not making a priest, 12
Constantine
    advent of, xvn3
    conversion to Christianity, xxx
    "Donation" to Pope Sylvester, 70
    fraudulent proclamation attributed to, 68–69
Contemplatives, as an Anabaptist group, 141
continuation, of the ordinances and sacraments of the church, 185
conventicles
    Anabaptists forced into clandestine, 122
    attendees bound by love to speak out to edify the church, 187
    bottom-up ecclesiastic methodology, 176
    charismata appearing in Anabaptist, xxxviii, 105
    description of Anabaptist, 93
    established first by Luther and adopted by Zwingli, 211n309
    establishment of local radical Anabaptist, 63
    formed by Schwenckfeld, 34
    Luther's and Zwingli's idea to create local, 175
    Pentecostal-like behavior described for Anabaptist, 93

conventicles (continued)
　practices and behavior, 113
　for prayer, worship, and Bible study, and preaching for both Anabaptists and Pentecostals, 133
　similar to the Pentecostal home prayer meetings, 214
　Zwickau Prophets convening private, 31
core principles, of sixteenth-century Anabaptism, xxxvii
1 Corinthians 12–14, xlii, 134, 217
Corpus Christi (the body of Christ), 140
corpus christianum, perspective of, 140
Cox, Harvey, xxi
Coxe, Arthur Cleveland, 201
Crautwald, Valentin, 35, 37, 38–39, 65
creed, of Anabaptism, xxxvii
crimes
　enumerated in mandates, 122
　penalties for, 80
criminalization, of Anabaptists, 104, 215
Cullis, Charles, xxiii
Cusa, Nicholas, 69n2
Cyril, Archbishop of Jerusalem, 86

Dallmyer, Heinrich, 111
Darby, John N., xxvii
Davis, Kenneth R., xvii, 90
day of Pentecost, Marpeck referring to, 177
Dayton, Donald, xxii, 198
dead, raising, 108, 108n13
death, of Zwingli, 66–67
death tax, abolishing on inheritance, 81
Declaration of the International Pentecostal Consultative Council (Paul), 170–71
deifying union, as typical of medieval mysticism, 6
Denck, Hans
　appeared in Strasbourg in 1526, 150
　as a contemplative Anabaptist, 141
　as a leader of Anabaptism in 1526, 114
　perspective of Contemplative Anabaptist, 142
　proponent of Müntzer's apocalypticism, 155
　as a significant spiritualist, 102
　spent time in Strasbourg, 121
Depperman, Klaus, xxxiv, 147
detachment (*gelassenheit*), described by Karlstadt, 20
devotio moderna, 8
Dialogue or Discussion Booklet on the Infamous Abuse of the Most High Blessed Sacrament of Jesus Christ (Karlstadt and Gemser), 22
Didache, xxix, 101, 200–201
Dipple, Geoffery, 144–45
discipleship, of Anabaptism, xxxvii
disputations, of Marpeck unveiling his *via media* plan, 157–58
divine healing, xxiii, 213
"divinization," Christ lived through a gradual, 181
doctrine of God, learning direct from his own Word, 45
The Doctrines and Discipline of the Azusa Apostolic Faith Mission of 1915 (Seymour), 160, 166, 169, 173
Donation of Constantine, 69, 69n2, 208
Dowie, John A., xxiv
Drechsel, Thomas, 31
dualism, 145
Dutch Mennonites, theological concepts of, 99

early Anabaptism. See also Anabaptism
　defined, xvi
　identified by the manifestation of the charismata, 204
　on Pauline pneumatology as the foundation for restitution of the Primitive New Testament church, 136

shared a common spirituality and theology with early Pentecostalism, 137
"early church," described, xvn3
Early Modern tradition, of prophecy, 197
early Pentecostal hermeneutics, compared with early Anabaptist hermeneutics, 175
early Pentecostal statements of faith and doctrines, comparison with confessions of faith of early Anabaptists, 212
early Pentecostalism. *See also* Pentecostalism
  aberrant behavior and phenomena in, 206
  characterized by contemporary non-Pentecostal churches as heretical, 204
  defined as the initial Christian movement, xvi
  developed a similar position to that of Marpeck regarding the "call" to preach and teach the gospel by all, 173
  developed into a pneumatological movement in belief and praxis similar to early Anabaptism, 136
  embraced a similar interpretation of the gift of prophecy, 197–98
  fraught with the same issue of the multiplication of many varied renditions of the faith, 89
  knowledge of Anabaptism, 159–61
  not derivative of early Anabaptism, 136
  not following any historic Anabaptist examples, 54
  praxis of preaching "the full gospel," 53
  shared common spirituality and theology with early Anabaptism, 137
  sharing tenets with Anabaptism, 144
  similar aspects to early sixteenth-century Anabaptist movement, 214
  in a similar situation to Anabaptism, 217
An Earnest Appeal to Schaffhausen (Hubmaier), 85
ecclesia
  lost in the clerical usurpation of the priesthood of the believer, 15
  Pauline concept of the body of Christ as, 69
  as a priesthood of believers, 42
  understood in prophetic-literal Pauline terms, 5
  used throughout the book of Acts and the Pauline Epistles, 15n60
ecclesiology
  of Anabaptism, xxxvii
  of Zwingli, 56–58
Eckhart, Meister, 7
Eder, Georg, 118
eisegesis, of Scripture, rather than exegesis, 53
Eldat, 172
Enchiridion militas Christiani: Hand Book of the Christian Soldier (Erasmus), 8, 38, 59
enemies, overcome by the power of the Holy Spirit, 176–77
English Keswick movement, xxvi
Entfelder, Christian, 102, 157
Epistles of Ignatius of Antioch, xxx
Erasmian humanism, 44, 57, 75
Erasmian solution, applied by Schwenckfeld, 37–38
Erasmus, 7–10
  criticisms of the Roman Catholic Church, 208
  decried the practice of selling indulgences, 44–45
  every Christian as a theologian, 13
  influence on both Luther and Zwingli, 12, 71
  influence on Zwingli, 59
  Luther initially influenced by, 12

Erasmus (continued)
- presented theological problems regarding many accepted Catholic tenets, 72
- recognition of the disparity between the Bible and the praxes of the church, 71
- rejected Luther's confrontational style and his theology of the bondage of the will, 12, 73
- Zwingli moving away from, 83

eschatology, of Anabaptism, xxxvii
eschaton, sign of, 124
Espionage and Sedition Act, in 1917, 129
Eucharist. *See also* Lord's Supper
- controversy over, 64–66
- dispute about, 22–26
- elements of provided inward spiritual nourishment, 37
- greatest disagreement over the meaning, purpose, and value of, 210
- Schwenckfeld's spiritualistic theology of, 39

European Pentecostals, 112, 130, 132
Evangelical (Holiness) Movement (*Gemienshaftsbewegung* (GB)), 111
evangelical Anabaptist leaders, listing of, 141
Evangelical Anabaptists, connected to Müntzer, 142
evangelical order, Reformed preachers not maintaining, 189
"evangelical radical reformers," identified by Snyder, 18
evangelical radicals, uniquely of Lutheran origin, 3
Evangelical Rationalists, 89, 139
evangelical spiritualism, 143
Evangelicals, beliefs of, 140–41
Evangelische Inquisition (Eder), 118
evangelism
- of the Anabaptists, 106–7
- based on the Great Commission of Acts 1:8, 213
- as a casualty of Simons's pacifist position, 200
- contingent upon the imminent second coming of Christ, 125
- critical to the restitution of the primitive church, 71, 122, 134
- importance both Anabaptism and Pentecostalism placed on, 104
- of Pentecostals, 123–26
- unrepentant concerning the critical nature of, 107

evangelistic efforts, of Anabaptists, 74
evangelization, as critically important, 217
evidential tongues, doctrine of, xxv
executions, catalytic effect on Marpeck, 156
An Exposition of the Faith (Zwingli), 56
extra-biblical writings, implying restitution or continuance of early church charismatic praxes, xxix

faith
- Anabaptist tenets of, 75–77
- coming from what is heard, 52
- correct interpretation of the word as key to, 8–9
- evidenced by moral change demonstrated by good works, 38
- gifts of not lacking to the believers in their need, 184
- only the Holy Spirit necessary for according to radical spiritualists, 139

faith alone *sola fide*. *See sola fide*
falling in love with Jesus, Anabaptist experience of, xvii–xviii
"false brethren," 94, 95
false teachers, xxix
Fast, Heinhold, 136n2
"Father of Dutch Anabaptism," 192
female prophets, 199
Ferdinand I of Austria, 151–56
Finney, Charles, xxvi
"first born," or prophets, 192
first Christians, indwelling of the Holy Spirit, 7

INDEX

first Zurich Disputation, 61
"fish, cowl, and tonsure," denying, 76
fivefold gospel aspect, of sanctification, 162
flesh of Christ, Marpeck on, 180
foot washing, 166–67
forensic justification
   Anabaptist rejection of, 99
   of Luther, 41
   as progressive sanctification for Schwenckfeld, 36–37
   rejection of, 142
forgiveness, needing daily, 17
Foundation of Christian Doctrine, 1539–1540 (Simons), 199, 200
Fourfold Gospel, Marpeck's, 179
fourfold gospel model, for Pentecostalism, 162
fourfold sense of Scripture (the *Quadriga*), 13–14
Franck, Sebastian, 102, 114–15, 143, 155
Frankenthal Protocol of 1571, 202
Frederick the Wise, 16, 19, 20, 21
free church, 110, 133–34
Free Imperial Cities, 119
free will, 42
freedom, 38
The Freedom of a Christian (Luther), 12
The Freedom of a Christian Man (Luther), 10
Duke Friederick II of Liegnitz, 34, 35–36, 39
"fruit of the Spirit," Paul's definition of, 41
Fukuyama, Francis, 109–10
the full gospel, xxxi, 53, 213
fullness of the Spirit, xxvi
"fully God fully man" theology, 150

Gaismaier, Michael, 153
Gast, Johannes, 117–18
GB. *See* Evangelical (Holiness) Movement (*Gemienshaftsbewegung* (GB))
Gee, Donald, 127

Gelassenheit, practical and personal spiritual yieldedness to Christ, 6, 6n19
Georg Witzel, xxxi
George, Timothy, 11, 51
German Church Service Book (Müntzer), 27
German Evangelical Mass (Müntzer), 27–28
German Evangelical Pentecostalism. *See also* Pentecostalism
the *Gnadauer Verband* (GV), 111
German Pentecostal experience, 111
German Pietism, similarities with Anabaptism, xxxii, xxiin31
German rulers, objected to the Vatican taking indulgence funds, 16
Germany, court-martialed and executed pacifists in World War I, 129
Geschict-Buch, listing between 600 and 1,386 martyrdoms in the Tyrol, 109
gift of discernment, testing spirits, 165
gift of healing, 213
gift of prophecy. *See also* prophecy
   as criteria for guidance of a theocratic government, 194
   early Pentecostalism's interpretation of, 197–98
   efficacy of, 165
   as evidence for the presence of the Holy Spirit, 196
   Paul's instruction regarding, 92
   taken from 1 Corinthians 14, 54
   Zwingli rejected the manifestation of, 54–55
gift of speaking in tongues. *See* speaking in tongues (glossolalia)
gifts of the Spirit
   absence of, 211
   for the first church only, 209
   forbidding others to exercise, 188
   impact of aberrant behavior, misuse, and abuse of, 203, 206
   manifestations of, xvi, 4n12, 67, 90–92, 93, 100, 179, 199, 203, 211

gifts of the Spirit (continued)
  necessary to the restitution of a primitive New Testament church, 185
  not denied by Simons, 200
  not in cessation as the spiritualists proposed, 179
  Paul listing, 55
  for the primitive church only according to Luther, 42
  relegated to the primitive church and in cessation according to Luther, 25, 29, 46
Glossa Ordinaria, 13
glossolalia. *See* speaking in tongues (glossolalia)
God
  creative words of, 49
  everyday revelation of, 30
  making the word effective, 138
  still prophetically speaking to Christians, 29
  as truth itself, 51
"godly law," 79
God's caretaker of the saving truth, Roman Catholic Church as, 207
God's word. *See* word of God
Goertz, Hans Jurgern, 32
Goeters, J. F. G., 136n2
good works (piety), 213
Gordon, Bruce, 67
gospel, xxi, 140
Gospel of wealth, xxi
Great Commission of Christ, 104, 107, 213
Grebel, Conrad
  on baptism, 106
  corresponded with Müntzer, 33
  decided against a radical departure from the Catholic practices, 62
  described, 61
  as an evangelical Anabaptist leader, 141
  evangelizing by, 84
  exposed to Erasmian Christian humanism, 71
  letter to Thomas Müntzer to gain his support, 70
  on living in the last days, 106
  on pacifism, 83
  on the visible church as nonresistant, 97
Greek New Testament, impact of Erasmus's, 50
Gregersen, Dagmar, 111
Gregory, Brad, 83, 207–8
grievances, drafted at Memmingen meeting, 80
Gritsch, Eric, 32
GV party, refused all association with Pentecostals, 112–13

Haetzer, Louis, 141
"Hail Mary Full of Grace," brought into question by Erasmus, 9
Hamilton, Andrew, 166–67
Hätzer, Ludwig, 62, 114
Hausman, Nicholas, 31
healing. *See* divine healing
Hedio, Caspar, 117
Hege, Christian, 122
heimsuchung (divine visitation), experienced by Schwenckfeld, 34
hereditary despotism, commonplace in the sixteenth century, 110
hermeneutics
  of early Pentecostalism and early Anabaptism, xix
  of Luther and Zwingli, 13–15
  of Marpeck and Pentecostalism compared, 172–76
  of Zwingli, 45–46, 50
higher criticism, xix, 133
historical circumstances, in different locales, 144
historical records, reflected manifestations of the charismata, xxxviii
historical-literal meaning of biblical text, 4
historiographers, interpreting Anabaptism, xxxvii
historiography, of Anabaptist movement, xxxi–xxxiii
Hochen, P. D., 113
Hoffman, Bengt, 7

Hoffmann, Melchior
  apocalypticism of, 191
  on baptism, 191
  on Christ having a heavenly or celestial body, 192
  led the Melchiorites, 141, 158
  on sacramentarianism, 191–92
  as the second Elijah of the Apocalypse, 193
  in Strasbourg, 121, 193
Hofmeister, Sebastian, 77n28, 84
Holiness groups, seeking to restore experiential revivalism, xxi
Holiness Keswick convention, influenced Boddy, 130
Holiness leaders, visited the Azusa Street mission, xxvi
Holiness Movement
  advent of Pentecostalism and, xx–xxiii
  attempt to clarify difference between sanctification and the baptism in the Spirit, xxvi
  origins of early Pentecostals, 124
  as the vanguard of modern Pentecostalism, xxii
Holl, Karl, 99
Hollenweger, Walter J., xxvi
Holy Bible. *See* Scripture
Holy Spirit. *See also* Spirit
  could not come as long as Christ was here on earth, 177
  critical nature of the presence and efficacy of, 164
  critical to faith for Luther, 13
  critical to faith for Zwingli, 59
  efficacy of the work of believed in by both Anabaptists and Pentecostals, 125
  enabling every Christian to read and interpret Scripture, 12
  encouraging obedient Christlikeness, 6
  every Christian filled with, 133
  evidence of the indwelling of, 203
  experience of the working of, xvi
  experienced and defined in patristic and medieval Christianity, 143
  expounding Scripture for Luther, 137
  filling and flooding souls, 7
  as final arbiter and interpreter of the word, 53
  integral to a biblical church, 216
  parameters for the evidence of the infilling of, 168
  presence of as the mark of any true church, 188
  proclaiming God's glory, 202
  rendering physical aspects of the church no longer necessary, xxviii
  role of critical for Zwingli, 51
  salvation as an experience of the presence of, xx
  sent to lead all Christians into the truth of the word, 208
  Tauler on the infilling of, 6–7
  those within the church lacking, 164n119
  witness inward as the greatest knowledge of knowing God, 169
  work and role of in the first-century church, 135
  working in every Christian's life, 209
Holy Spirit baptism. *See* baptism in the Holy Spirit
homogeneity, of God's creation, 164
Hottinger, Margret, 91
Hubmaier, Balthasar
  in the Anabaptist movement, xli
  arrested by Ferdinand I of Austria, 151
  attempting to unify Anabaptism with *A Christian Catechism*, 151
  on the Ban, 98
  on baptism of children, 75, 75n23
  on baptism of the Holy Spirit, 86
  baptized by Wilhelm Reublin, 150
  belief in armed resistance, 82–83, 85, 87
  burned at the stake in 1528, 154
  call for a public disputation, 84
  confession of faith, 97
  fully committed to Anabaptism, 87

Hubmaier, Balthasar (continued)
    importance of the Peasants' War for, 77
    influence on Anabaptist pneumatology, 87
    initially accepted and preached Luther's reform but felt greater affinity for Zwingli, 98
    introduced Zwinglian evangelicalism by preaching open-air sermons, 75n22
    as a leader of Anabaptism, 114, 141
    managed Waldshut's defection to the Lutheran Reformation, 75
    as the most prolific writer of the developing Anabaptist theology, 74
    only admitted to expanding the articles, 81
    Pentecostal-like understanding of speaking in tongues, 85
    pneumatology of, 85–88
    sacramentarian position of, 62
    supported Zwingli, 61
    theology of Christian resistance, 82–83, 130
    trained and educated as a Catholic priest, 136
Bishop Hugo of Constance, 47
human intelligence, misunderstanding the word without the Spirit, 138
human will, Luther and Erasmus disagreed over, 10
humanist methods, 51, 71
The Humanity of Christ 1555 (Marpeck), 180
Bishop Hurst, 160–61
Hut, Hans, 102, 114, 121, 155
Hutter, Jacob, 102, 121, 141
Hutterites, 107, 121, 210

iconography, 216
images, as good for nothing, 76
imminent apocalypse, Hoffmann preached, 192
impanation, 38
Imperial mandates. *See* mandates
imperial regimes, pressure to eliminate Anabaptists, 122
Index of Prohibited Books, 9
individualism, polarized church and community, 105
indulgence controversy, 15–16
indulgences
    opposition to, 209
    popularity of, 16
    sale of, 10, 15, 44–45
infant baptism
    continued as before in Zurich, 61
    having no biblical basis, 213
    as inconceivable, 63
    Müntzer on, 30
    taught by Zwingli as a sacramental ritual, 60
infant children, congregations refused to baptize, 62
informants, hired by government officials, 122
initial evidence doctrine, xxxviii, 86
inner baptism, evidence of as the fruit of the Spirit, 178
intellectualism, xx, 148, 159
internal spirituality, 59
intimate Anabaptist love, Pentecostalism emulated, 171
invisible church, 56, 140
Invocavit Sermons (Luther), 21
Israelites, restored ancient ceremonies, 164

James, Lucy, 132
Jeffereys, George, 131
Jesus. *See also* Christ
    confronting and convincing the Samaritan woman at the well, 86–87
    gift of alien righteousness from, 17
    humanity of, 176
    "*This is my body*" establishing his real presence in the elements, 64
Jim Crow laws, 111
Joachim de Fiore, 30
Joel, making no gender exceptions, 193

Joel 2:27–32, Müntzer's acceptance of a literal Biblicist interpretation of, 26
John 13, interpreting, 167
Johnson, Andrew, 112
Joris, David, 198
Joshua, 172
Jost, Agnes, 192
Jost, Elizabeth, 192
Jost, Lienhard, 192, 193
Jost, Ursula, 192, 193
Jubilee Indulgences, 16
Jud, Leo, 60–61
Judgement and Decision (Marpeck), 183
Judicium (Schwenckfeld), 40, 182, 183
Pope Julius II, conscription of young Swiss men by, 44
justification, of inner/outer transformation, 99

Karant-Nun, Susan, 32
Karlstadt, Andreas Bodenstein von, 61
  Anabaptist correspondence with, 71
  anti-Lutheran eucharistic writings of, 149
  assumed sole leadership and responsibility for reform in Luther's absence, 20
  conducting the Christmas Mass in German, 24–25
  conforming to a more Pauline pneumatology, 21
  on the efficacy of the indwelling of the Holy Spirit, 24
  encouraged congregants to prophesy in services, 21
  first to act on Luther's theology of reform, 26
  on the indwelling of the Holy Spirit, 203
  linked the word with preaching, hearing the word, and the sacraments, 23
  not considered Anabaptist by Swiss Brethren, 147
  paraphrase of 1 Corinthians 12:29–31, 21–22
  placed greater emphasis on the inward work of the Spirit, 23–24
  on restitution of the New Testament church, 105
  reverting to the life of a lay preacher, 21
  sacramentarianism of, 191
  sided with Zwingli on the Eucharist, 22
  stressed the inwardness of the work of the Spirit, 22
  tension with Luther, 18–26
  took exception to Luther's eucharistic theology, 64
  unwilling to allow any human tradition not commanded by Scripture, 25
  warned Müntzer not to get involved in the Peasants' War, 33
  wrote pamphlets on the Lord's Supper in 1524, 22
  Zwingli's relationship with, 73–74
Keller, Ludwig, xxxii
Kessler, Johannes
  on Anabaptists in *Sabata*, 122
  described Margret Hottinger, 91, 91n82
  described the Anabaptists as being respected by non-Anabaptists, 92
  George Williams relying on for information, 90
  impression of Anabaptist evangelistic fervor, 84
  reported Pentecostal-like activities among the Anabaptists, 91
  on Spirit versus word, 102
Keswick Convention, xxvi
Kingdom of Christ, 167
Klaassen, Walter
  denied that spiritualism was the polar opposite of biblical literalism of Anabaptism, 144
  on Marpeck developing a *via media*, 202
  premature conclusion of, 50

Klaassen, Walter (continued)
  on Strauss and Castenbauer preaching together, 153
  Zwingli treating both testaments as God's whole revelation, 53
  on Zwingli's reticence to claim that preaching was the word of God, 48
Klaassen, William
  on Marpeck developing a *via media*, 202
  on the "Purification of Anabaptism," 147
  on Strauss and Castenbauer preaching together, 153
knowledge of Christ, leading to knowledge of God, 177
Korean revival, under the leadership of Methodist missionaries, xxvii
Korsets Seir (The Victory of the Cross), *Byposten* renamed to, 132, 133
Kunstbuch, or "book of understanding," found again in 1956, 136n2

laity, enabling participation in Christian worship, 24
languages of the world, power to speak all, 124
large tithe, to be administered by the community, 80
"last days," Marpeck defining, 174
Latin New Testament, of Erasmus, 9
Latin Vulgate, as the primary Bible in use, 13
"latter rain," xxiv, 180–81
lay participation, according to Paul's instructions, 211
The Laying on of Hands: A Bible Ordinance 1895 (Boddy), 173
Pope Leo, 10
Letter to the Princes of Saxony (Luther), 29
Lex Sedentium, 92–93
Liber Sententiarium, 13
library, Zwingli's still in existence, 57
life of piety, seeking evidence of, 41

life-threatening persecution, devastating to the Anabaptists, 106
literal (biblicist) reading, of the Bible, 210
literal interpretation, of 1 Corinthians 12–14, 213
literal law, demanded the physical, 22
literal meaning, of the Old Testament for Zwingli, 51
literal prophetic-spiritual sense of the word, 14
literal spiritual-prophetic style, of Zwingli, 46
literal spiritual-prophetic word, Luther relying on, 59
Littell, Franklin H., xxx, 63–64
living word, Scripture as, 27
local congregations, choosing their own pastors, 12
local pastors, chosen by their own congregations, 58–59
Locher, Gottfried, 50
Lohse, Bernard, 17
Lohse, Bernhard, 11
lords, restoring serfdom to prevent an urban migration, 79
Lord's Supper. *See also* Eucharist
  described in the *Schleitheim Confession*, 95–96
  Karlstadt's pamphlets on, 22
  partaking of unworthily, 183
  suspended by Schwenckfeld, 179
Lorenz, Gertrude, 192
Loriti, Heinrich, 71
Lost, Leinhard, 198
Lotzer, Sebastian, 80
love, 168, 170, 171
love and faithfulness, fruit of the Spirit as, 168
Luther, Martin
  attempted to achieve peace in April 1525, 82
  aware of Erasmus's position on the church, 9
  began evangelical Lutheranism, 210
  believed in a forensic justification, 41

believed in the real presence of Christ in the Eucharist, but not transubstantiation, 42, 64
biblical hermeneutics introduced by, xvi
called for reformation of the Roman Catholic Church, 208
challenged the practice of selling indulgences in 1517, 16
choice not to go against the magisterial authority of Elector Frederick, 25
classified Schwenckfeld as a Lutheran *Schwärmer*, 40
closer to the Roman Catholic position of the real presence of Christ, 210
complied with Frederick's command and restored aspects of Karlstadt's reform, 25
conclusions as to what it would take to reform the church, 209
considered gifts of the Spirit, the charismata, to be in "cessation" and unnecessary, xxii, 100–101
considered the efficacy and work of the Holy Spirit as critical to faith, 13
corresponded with Erasmus, 10
declared Karlstadt a *Schwärmer*, 25
denied Karlstadt's eucharistic theology, 149
denied the efficacious currency of the charismata, 210
diatribe against peasants encouraged them to avoid Lutheranism, 88
distancing himself from his initial acceptance of Rhenish mysticism and Pauline pneumatology, 100
emphasizing the prophetic-literal hermeneutic, 4
evolving consideration of the magistracy, 25
examination of the origins of initial theology of, xxxix–xl
excommunicated by March 1521, 19, 64
five core doctrines of the Reformation, 36, 36n160
found theological differences that appeared as unacceptable, 209
on government as necessary for the well-being of society, 57
great writings of 1520, 10–13
held onto his premise of giving word precedence, 59
hermeneutics of, 13–15
on impanation, 38
influence of the early teachings of, 154
initial encounter with the charismatic Zwickau prophets in Wittenberg, 137
initial Reformation theologies of, xviii, xl, 215
insistence on *sola scriptura* as the final arbiter of the faith, 73
insistence that infant baptism and the Mass be discontinued struck fear into his heart, 214
interests in the ideas of Rhenish mysticism, 1
on Karlstadt's decision to proceed with the Wittenberg reform in spite of Luther's absence, 24
maintained major aspects of Roman Catholicism, 5
monastic approach to Scripture as the *sacra pagina*, 14
opted to move gradually away from mystical spirituality, 73
as an orthodox Christian seeking a biblically based *ecclesia*, xxix
ostracized Karlstadt, 24
on the Petrine doctrine of the priesthood of the believer, 25, 216
preached the eight *Invocavit Sermons*, attired as an Augustinian monk, 21
as a radical protestor in the eyes of the Catholic Church, 2
reformation of the church as paramount, 41

Luther, Martin (continued)
  rejected Schwenckfeld's theology, 39
  restoring magisterial order, 105
  rumors of his kidnapping, 35
  Schwenckfeld an avid reader of the works of, 34
  searching Scripture to rectify his lack of personal peace regarding salvation, 3
  on speaking in tongues as plain reading or singing biblical texts, 101
  on the spirituality of Tauler and the *Theologia Germanica*, 31
  theology of "two kingdoms," 105
  threatened with excommunication, 19
  on the visible sending forth of the Holy Spirit, 25n107
  on who was eligible to read and interpret Scripture and who was qualified, 12
  on the word having precedence over the Spirit, 22, 46
  word inculcated Christ into the hearts of Christians, 48
Lutheran and Catholic forces, alliance of against the peasants, 107
Lutheran movement, Müntzer an asset to, 30
Lutheran radical reformers, *Schwärmer* becoming, 41
Lutheran Reformation, xxviii, 147
Lutheran Reformed city, Strasbourg made into, 148
Lutheran *Schwärmer*
  influence on the emerging Anabaptist movement, xl
  Schwenckfeld as, 40
  theological positions of, xviii
Lutheranism, emergence of radicalism within, 5

Mabry, Eddie L., 98
magisterial control, difficulty in maintaining, 101
magisterial intervention, only encouraged evangelistic efforts, 104
magisterial Lutheranism, coercing and propagating the gospel, 35
magisterial reformation
  Anabaptism rejected, xxix
  propagating the gospel by coercion, xxviii
  radicals' rejection of, 2
magisterial support, Zwingli reforming the church from a position of, 57
magisterial system of justice, Reformed using to defend themselves with the use of violence, 189
magistracy
  involving in resisting enemies of the church with violence, 97
  local, critical to any successful reformation of the Roman Catholic Church, 216
  local, pressure to eliminate Anabaptists, 122
  local and imperial continued to criminalize Anabaptism, 102
  propagating the gospel using, 57
  swearing an oath of allegiance to as tantamount to agreeing to take up the sword, 123
mandates, 63, 122, 149
manifestation, of the gifts of the Spirit, 90–92, 142, 203, 206
Mantz, Felix, 61, 62
Marburg Colloquy of 1529, 38
Margaret, prophet in Strasbourg, 192
Marian intercession, growing theology of, 58
Marius, Richard, 12–13, 16
Marpeck, Heinrich, 151–52
Marpeck, Pilgram
  Anabaptist conversion of, 154–58
  arguing against the cessation of miracles, signs, and wonders, 108
  associated himself with Reublin and the Swiss Brethren in 1528, 150

INDEX 255

attempted to develop some common ground, 135
attempting to unify Anabaptism, 121
background of, 151–52
Christology of, 176–77
conclusion against the spiritualists, 177–79
criticism of legalistic Anabaptism, 183
defining the "last days," 174
developing a *via media* between spiritualists and Anabaptists, 40, 102–3, 158
discovery of the works of, 160
emphasizing the critical importance of the external Scripture, 172
on external authority not making an apostle, 171
fled to Strasbourg, 156
future leader and theologian of the Anabaptists of Austria and Southern Germany, 34
on the gift of prophecy, 165
influence on the disputants at Zofingen, 190
interpreted Paul in a similar way to the early Pentecostals, 167
laid his foundation on 1 Corinthians, 167
life and work of, xli
on misuses of baptism, 182
one of few Anabaptists who wrote prolifically, 136
Pentecostal charismatic pneumatological perspective of, 190
on the physical humanity of Christ, 179–80
pneumatology of, 163–71
proponent of Anabaptist evangelization, 84
referring to the day of Pentecost, 177
Reformation and, 149–54
as representative of Anabaptism in general, 203–4

republishing Rothmann's *Bekentnisse van beyden Sacramenten of 1533* (Confession Concerning Both Sacraments), 202
response to Schwenckfeld's *Stillstand* and "Celestial Flesh" theology, 39–40, 182
Schwenckfeld and, 179–84
spoke out against false prophets, 202
stood behind Rothmann's work, 202n287
theology of, 159, 161–63, 206
Marpeck Circle writings, recovery of, 136n2
Marpeckan South German/Austrians, theological concepts of, 99
martyrdom, of Hubmaier by burning at the stake in 1528, 87
martyred Anabaptists, Clasen's estimated total, 109
martyrs, Anabaptist, 108
Martyr's Mirror, xxxii, 109
Mass, 47, 76, 216
material Christianity, as the default spirituality, 145
materialism, xxi, 145
Matthijs, Jan, 194, 196
McGinn, Bernard, 6
McGrath, Alister
   accusing Zwingli of indulging in eisegesis of Scripture, rather than exegesis, 53
   on the effect of Erasmus on Zwingli's hermeneutics, 51
   on Marpeck, 136
   on *schola Augustaniana moderna* emphasizing *scriptura sola*, 11
   on theologians of the Radical Reformation, 74
   on Zwingli adopting Erasmus's hermeneutic method, 46
McLaughlin, R. Emmet, 145, 167
McPherson, Aimee Semple, 205–6
Medat, 172
medieval mysticism, xl, 7, 142
Medieval tradition, on prophecy, 197
Melanchthon, Philipp, 20–21

Melchiorites
  apocalyptic and bellicose resistance theology, 191
  embraced the apocalyptic expectation but rejected self-proclaimed prophets, 199
  established a legal theocracy in Münster, 215
  gathered to Münster by van Leiden, 194
  Hoffmann responsible for the development of, 192
  interpreted the Old Testament as containing types of the restored church of the Spirit, 141
  legally gained political control of Münster, 194
  obsessed with the apocalypse, 158
Memmingen meeting, of peasant rebel fighters, 79–80
Mennonite church, xxxvi
Mennonite historians, xxxii
Mennonite scholars, xxxiii, xxxv
Mennonites, 191, 210, 215
mercenary conscription, of young Swiss men, 44
merits, of Christ, Mary, and saints under the control of the pope, 15
Methuen, Charlotte, 14, 51, 59
Meyer, Emil, 111
Miller, Gregory, 51
Miller, Kathleen, 132
miracles and signs, not the measure of truth, 164–65
missionary campaigns, initiated by Schwenckfeld, 34
Moeller, Bernd, 119–20
Monophysite Christology, of the celestial flesh of Christ, 181
Montanism, xxx, 69, 150
Moravia, 121, 149
Moravian Anabaptist confession, 157
Moravian Hutterites, theological concepts of, 99
Moriae encomium: In Praise of Folly (Erasmus), 8, 9
Moses, 172
Mukti Mission, xxvii

Müller, Hans, 81
Münster, debacle in, 194–96, 215
Müntzer, Thomas
  acting out his beliefs in rebellion, 27
  advocating Pauline pneumatology, xxviii
  attracted to Luther's Reformation theology, 30
  insights into the indwelling of the Holy Spirit, 203
  letter to, presenting Anabaptist positions, 70–71
  mind saturated in Scripture, 32
  as the most radical of Luther's *Schwamer*, 26–33
  no relationship with Zwingli, 74
  paraphrased 1 Corinthians 14:23–24 in the *Prague Manifesto*, 29
  primacy of inner baptism for, 142
  prophets known to, 20
  radical anti-Lutheranism of, 1
  replaced Luther's *sola fide* with a doctrine of the experienced cross, "the bitter Christ," 142
  took exception to Luther's eucharistic theology, 64
  on the Zwickau Prophets, 32–33
Murray, Andrew, Jr., xxvi
Murray, Stuart
  classified Anabaptists of various types, 88
  on congregational theology (*Gemeindetheologie*), 175
  identifying a more valid list of Anabaptist groups, 146
  on the transition of the charismatic (Pentecostal) phase of Anabaptism, 200
Musing, Hans-Werner, 150
Muslim nations, religions foreign to subject to civil and criminal actions, 111
Myland, David W., 162, 180–81

natural catastrophes, seen as God's punishment, 119
natural physical man, 180, 181

natural theology, 14
Nebuchadnezzar, 30
neighbor, loving, 170
neo-Pentecostals, characteristics of, xxi
A New Dialogue/Questions and Answers between a Preacher and a Baptist (Marpeck), 184, 185–86, 190, 202
"New Jerusalem," 193
New Testament, 3, 90, 176
New Testament Christianity, restitution of primitive, 2
New Testament church
  desire for restitution of, xxxviii
  literal reading of Scripture as conducive to the restitution of, 133
  restitution of the primitive, xx, 1, 69, 70
  struggle to define a restored, 88
New Testament norm, for prophecy, 198
New Testament prophets, counted by Zwingli, 55
Nichol, John T., xviii, 159
Ninety-Five Theses (Luther), 16–17
non-normative spiritualists, xxxiv
nonviolence, 130, 134
North American Pentecostal groups, appearance of diverse, 125
"Norway's Free Evangelical Mission to the Heathen," founded by Barratt, 132–33
Norwegian Pentecostal revival, influence on Boddy, 130–31

oath of allegiance, Anabaptists precluded from taking, 210
oaths, forbidden in the *Schleitheim Confession*, 96
"obedience of faith," of Anabaptists, 153
Oberman, Heiko, 16
Ochino, Bernardio, 139–40
Ockhamism, semi-Pelagian principle of medieval, 10
Oecolampadius, Johannes, 61, 75, 84

Of the Clarity and Certainty of the Word of God (Zwingli), 45, 49–50, 51–52, 138
Office of Prophet, 54, 199, 215
office of shepherd, in the church, 49
Old and New Testaments, relationship between, 53
Old Testament, 53, 141
old-time religion, of the great awakenings and spiritual revivals, xix
O'Loughlin, Thomas, 201
open participation, 92
Opitz, Peter, 50, 51, 54
The Ordinance of God, 1530 (Hoffmann), 191
ordinances. *See* sacraments
Origins of Anabaptism (Bullinger), 24
"orthodoxy," defined, 121n67
ostracism, after Anabaptism was criminalized, 113
Ozman, Agnes, xxiv

pacifism
  as accepted belief, 87, 88
  of Anabaptists, 74–77, 123
  for Anabaptists during the Peasants' War, and for Pentecostals during World War I, 134
  of British nonconformist Pentecostals, 128
  described in the *Schleitheim Confession*, 96
  as a dilemma faced by early Anabaptists, 130
  Grebel and his Swiss Brethren on, 83
  impact on Anabaptism and Pentecostalism, xli
  as a major tenet of the Mennonite faith, 123
  of Pentecostals, 126–30
  reinforcing for Anabaptists, 210
pacifist group, of Melchiorites, 199
pacifists, sought a more peaceful alternative, 198
Packull, Werner, xxxiv, 156, 185
Paracelsus, as a rational spiritualist, 143

"Paraclesis" (Erasmus), 72–73
Parham, Charles Fox
  American Pentecostalism and, xxiv–xxv
  critical of the emotional nature of the meetings at Azusa Street, xxv–xxvi
  disaffected from Methodism after experiencing healing from rheumatic fever, xxiv
  on the full Gospel, 162
  glossolalia interpreted as genuine foreign languages (xenolalia), 124
  initial evidence thesis, 170n151
  scandalized by a sexual indiscretion, xxvi
parousia
  belief in the imminence of, 33, 107
  invisible church of the Spirit awaiting, 140
  Müntzer's belief in, 26
Pastor, Adam, 141
patriotism, tension with Christian peace and love, 128
Pauck, Wilhelm, 4
Paul
  baptized the disciples of John the Baptist in the name of Jesus Christ, 85–86
  on Christians justified by faith in Christ alone, 3
  describing an early New Testament church meeting, 86
  describing the experiences and practices of the first Christian converts, 19n78
  encouraged Christians to seek after spiritual gifts, especially prophecy, 187–88
  instructions on the proper manifestation of the gifts of the Holy Spirit, 95
  spiritual truth in the writings of, 136
Paul, Jonathan, 131, 170
  advocacy of Pentecostalism, 112
  criteria for evidence of the Spirit, 168
  early western European Pentecostal model set out by, 165
  at the Hamburg conference in 1908, 112
  on the outward manifestation of the fruit of the Spirit, 169–70
  of the Pietist Holiness resurgence, 111
Pauline concept, of the body of Christ on earth, 14–15
Pauline doctrine, Müntzer agreeing with, 29
Pauline ecclesiology, Montanism and, xxx
Pauline perspective, of Erasmus, 72
Pauline pneumatology, 31, 121, 216
Paulinism, 2n3, 72
Peacock, Reginald, 69n2
peasants
  drafted the "Twelve Articles," 80–81
  failure to consolidate battle victories, 82
  grappling with an emerging urban middle class, 78
  more attracted to urban life, 79
Peasants' War
  began as an act of civil disobedience, 81–82
  disaffected veterans looking to Anabaptism to continue to seek redress, 88
  ended in ignominious defeat for the peasants in 1526, 87
  focused on regions where the Roman Catholic Church was a significant land holder, 79
  intersection of Anabaptism and, 74
  as a military reality for Hubmaier, 77
  Müntzer as a leader of, 27
  occurred in the midst of a turbulent social, economic, and cultural conditions, 78
  pointed to the reality of the genuine parousia for Müntzer, 33

INDEX

pedobaptism (the baptism of infants)
  Karlstadt criticizing Luther regarding the continued practice of, 24
  maintained by both Luther and Zwingli, 68
  precluded an information response, 42
  rendered evangelism moot within the Western European Catholic Church, 106
  Zwingli's willingness to accept causing a major radical schism, 58
penance, 9, 15
Pentecostal and charismatic phenomena, not accepted by Luther or Zwingli, 101
Pentecostal Anglican Church of England brethren, on World War I as justified, 128
Pentecostal aspects, defined early or classical Pentecostalism, xvi
Pentecostal cardinal doctrines, 125
Pentecostal Consultative Council 1912, 169–70
Pentecostal Greetings (Pfingstgrüsse), 112
Pentecostal historiography, current, xxxviii–xxxix
Pentecostal Missionary Union, 132
Pentecostal Sunderland Convention, 131
Pentecostal terms, as being beyond liminal Anabaptism, xxxv
Pentecostalism. *See also* American Pentecostalism; early Pentecostalism; German Evangelical Pentecostalism
  apostasy of the early twentieth-century church perceived by, 15
  as a close parallel to Anabaptism, xvii
  declared glossolalia to be initial evidence of the baptism in the Spirit, 213
  defining, 89
  devoted to the restitution of the primitive church, xxxi
  early adopted missionary evangelism as a spiritual calling, 123–26
  early dilemma juxtaposing biblical tenets of peace against war, 75n20
  early issues similar to the early Reformation, 4
  early twentieth-century defined by using the term "classic," 4n12
  as an empowering religious response to contemporary sociological conditions, xxxviii
  "family resemblance" theory of, xxxvi
  had no historical knowledge of Reformation Anabaptism, 215
  historical development of early similar to that of early sixteenth-century Anabaptism, 135
  historical roots in sixteenth century Anabaptism, xviii
  Holiness Movement and, xx–xxiii
  impact of evangelism, persecution, and pacifism in, xli
  initially produced several variations, 124
  primary gifts manifested in were speaking in tongues and prophecy, 203
  similarities with early Anabaptism, 133
  struggle with pacifism, 126
Pentecostal-like aspects, of early Anabaptism, 98
Pentecostal-like behavior, described for Anabaptist conventicles, 93
Pentecostal-like missiology, of Anabaptism, 69
Pentecostal-like perspective, of Schlaffer's statements from prison, 156
Pentecostal-like practices, of Karlstadt, 21, 24
Pentecostals
  connection between evangelism and the second coming, 125
  embraced priesthood of the believer, 125

Pentecostals (continued)
  evangelistic and missionary zeal of the early, 125
  incarcerated under military conscription laws, 129
  most sided with Christian pacifists, 129
  number of in the world, xv
  opting for an official document outlining pertinent fundamentals, 212
  persecution of American and European, 109–13
  rarely martyred, 129
  responding to a perceived apostasy, 211
  saw the answer the same way Anabaptists had seen it, 217
  sola scriptura opening doors to, 15
perfectionism, 143
persecution
  of American and European Pentecostals, 109–13
  of Anabaptists, 106, 108–9, 213
  from other Christian denominations, 110
  suffered by early Pentecostals, 133
Peter, quoting Joel making no gender exceptions, 193
Pethrus, Petrus Lewi, 131
Petrine doctrine, of the Priesthood of the Believer, xviii–xix, xx, 4, 58, 208, 216
Philips, Dirk, 141, 199
Philips, Obbe, 199
Phillip of Hesse, 65, 194
Philosophi Christi, of Erasmus, 13
physical things, as perceptible, 65
"physic-realist" sense, of deification, 143
piety
  Anabaptists' theology of, 162, 213
  contradictions of witnessed by Seymour, 168
  evidence of a life of, 41
Piper, William H., 170n151
plague, at the end of the fourteenth century, 78

pneuma, 5
pneumatic gifts of the Spirit, 95, 98
pneumatology
  of Anabaptism, xvii, xxxvii
  of Anabaptist core theology and ecclesiology, 99
  of Hubmaier, 85–88
  increased emphasis by Anabaptists on, xxxvii
  of Marpeck, 163–71
  similarities between Marpeck's and early Pentecostal theology and praxis, 184–85
  of Zwingli, 50–56
Polhill, Cecil, 112, 132
political reality, Zwingli's confrontation with, 66
Polman, Gerrit R., 112, 127
polygamous theocracy, of the New Jerusalem, 141
polygamy, 196, 199
polygenesis of Anabaptism, support for, xxxvi
polygenetic origins, difficulty in defining movements of, xxxviii
popes
  creating positions such as prince-bishops, 119
  as formidable even to royalty, 10
  Luther challenged the authority of, 16
  merits under the control of, 15
practical or present meaning, of the Old Testament for Zwingli, 51
Prague Manifesto of 1521 (Müntzer), 27, 28, 29
preachers, according to Zwingli, 54
preaching, 23, 133, 165
"The Preaching Office" (Zwingli), 55
The Precious Atonement (Seymour), 124
predestination, 99, 213
premillennialism, xxiv
priesthood of the believer
  acceptance and belief in the doctrine of, 207, 209
  acting on the doctrine of, 197
  Anabaptists' adoption of, 105, 133

INDEX 261

Anabaptists continued adherence to, 210
common denominator of, 125
confirmation of the concept of, 52
described, 6
embraced thoroughly, 99
enabling Luther's initial concepts of, 36
encouraged many radical Christians, 175
in Hubmaier's tenets of faith, 76
idea of, 217
Karlstadt on, 21, 24
magisterial Reformation's initial concept of, 136
Petrine doctrine of, xviii–xix, xx, 4, 58, 208, 216
radical adherents acted pragmatically on, 216
resulted in the installation of untrained and uneducated pastors, 209
scriptural concept of, 12
theological concept of, 83
priests. *See also* clergy
all who are baptized consecrated as, 12
distributing only the letter of the word according to Müntzer, 28
external, audible word of not the word of God but their own, 32
forbidding marriage to, 76
talked as if God had become silent according to Müntzer, 29
Zwingli articles on, 47
primary source material, xix, xxxiii, xixn17
primitive New Testament Christianity, restitution of, xxix, 41, 205
primitive New Testament church
Anabaptist restitution of, 211–12
charismatic in nature and needed *restitutio in integrum*, 190
described, xvn3
desire to restore critical to early Pentecostalism, 162
Karlstadt's insistence on the restitution of, 25

middle round to the restitution of, 135
opting for the restitution of, 69
restitution of, xix, 18, 217
restitutional position regarding, 25
printing, as a great catalyst, 105
progressive sanctification, 17, 99
pro-laity radicalism, 146
proper righteousness, Luther on, 18
prophecy. *See also* gift of prophecy
evolved into a more supernatural ecstatic experience, 198
as instruments of the revelation of the divine will, 30
meaning to interpret, 55–56
medieval and early modern, 196–201
more edifying for Anabaptists, 213
as most effective for evangelization and edification of, 196
as the primary gift for the Anabaptists, 203
prophet(s)
evidence required to recognize, 165
as an interpreter of Scripture, 197
known and active in Strasbourg, 192
managing the ministries of itinerant charismatic, 201
preaching special spiritual insights in Wittenberg, 20
role of for Zwingli, 54
at the time of the apostles, 55
prophetic word, 53, 56
prophetic-literal ecclesiology and pneumatology, developed by Luther, 5
prophetic-literal meaning of biblical text, 4
Prophezei school, of Zwingli, 54
Protestant denominations, xix, xxi, 217
Protestant Reformation, 64, 152
Protestantism, xx
Protestation or Proposition (Müntzer), on faith, 28
psalms, translation of, 27–28, 76
psychical (soul), 181

psychopannychism (soul sleep), 89
public preaching, 133
punishments, in mandates, 122
Purgatory
    not existing, 76
    purification occurring in, 15
    radicals wanted to jettison, 216
    true Holy Scriptures knowing nothing of according to Zwingli, 47
"Purification of Anabaptism," 147

"Quiet of the Land," Anabaptists becoming, 200, 215

racial discrimination, against early Pentecostals, 110
racial integration, Seymour's encouragement of, xxvi
racism, caused by divisive white men, 168–69
"radical," defined, 2
radical adherents, of Luther following his mystical inclinations, 1
radical Anabaptism, many renditions of, 102
radical Anabaptist conventicles, establishment of, 63
radical Christians, felt empowered by the Holy Spirit to read and interpret Scripture, 146
radical congregations, emerging as free believers' churches in a primitive New Testament sense, 100
radical detractors, of Zwingli, 58
radical hermeneutics, evolution of, 175
Radical Reformation
    described, 139
    equality of women participating in, 192–93
    historians coining the phrase, xxxiv
    leaders including former priests, monks, and theologians, 203
The Radical Reformation (Williams), 139
radical reformers
    active in Strasbourg, 120, 148

    categorizing, 139–46
    differentiating from each other, 3
    dismissed the idea of reforming Roman Catholicism, 69
    rejected the idea of a single priest, 12
radical religious landscape, 146
radical sacramentarians, became Melchiorite Anabaptists, 194
radical sectarianism, principal groups of, 139
radical sects, appearance of consequent to the persecution and diaspora of Anabaptism, 114
radicalism
    attributed to exposure to Erasmian humanism and Lutheranism, 67
    categorizing, 144
    definition of, 2n3
    emergence within Lutheranism, 5
    Marpeck's acceptance of, 154–58
    pro-laity, 146
    on reading and interpreting Scripture without clerical authority, 4
    rejected the idea of a professional clergy, 205
    Schwenckfeld's influence on, 34
    Swiss, 43–44
radicals
    emerging to challenge Zwingli, 61
    establishing numerous sectarian churches, 210
    Luther and Zwingli opening the door to, 2
    pursued the restitution of the New Testament primitive church and not the reformation of the Roman Catholic Church, 216
    questioning the efficacy of a reformation of Catholicism, 41
raising the dead, Anabaptist position comparable to that of early Pentecostalism, 108n13
Ramabai, Pandita, xxvii, 132
rational evangelical spiritualist, Ziegler as, 150
rational spiritualists, 143

INDEX

real living word of God, winning over the unbeliever, 29
Reasons Why Carlstadt Remained Silent (Karlstadt), 23
Rebstock, Barbara, 192, 193
reform (*reformatio*), sought by Luther, 5
reform effort, core of Luther's, 6
reform theology, Luther's turn away from his initial, 18
Reformation. *See also specific Reformations*
    goals of Schwenckfeld's, 36
    of Luther and Zwingli, 208–11
    Marpeck and, 149–54
    more than fifty of free cities officially recognized, 119
    principles of, 16
    social issues reflected the religious concerns of, 78
Reformation Anabaptism. *See* Anabaptism
The Reformation and the Old Reformationists (Keller), xxxii
Reformation era, 7, 29–30
Reformation historians, heretical label assigned to Anabaptists, xxxii
Reformation theological principles, first application to a sociopolitical issue, 80
Reformed churches, reasons for not attending, 185
regeneration, for Schwenckfeld, 37
regular priest, ordained for the work of pastoring, 44n2
Reid, William, 129
Reimer, A. James, xxxvi
religious externalities, Karlstadt's devaluation of, 19
religious iconography, irrelevance of, 209
religious objector status, provision for in the U. S., 129
Rempel, John R., xxxiin61
resistance, Hubmaier's theology of, 74–77
restitutio in integrum, 5, 5n14, 213

restitution (*restitutio*)
    of the New Testament's description of the first-century Christian movement, xvn3
    Pentecostal concept of, 205
    of the primitive New Testament church, xv, xxxi, 5, 24, 42, 68
restitutionism, many examples of, xxix
restorationists, xxii
Reublin, Wilhelm
    assumed the leadership of the Swiss Brethren in Strasbourg, 150
    conducting a larger baptism with Hubmaier, 84–85
    described, 61
    Marpeck's alignment with, 157
    ostracized from Zurich, 62
revelation, preacher needing, 29
revenge, as no longer permitted, or even necessary, 176
revival movements, with Pentecostal manifestations, xxvii
revolutionary, or charismatic, spiritualists, experienced the Spirit as a driving power, 141–43
revolutionary Anabaptists, beliefs of, 141
Rhegius, Urbanus, 75
Rhenish mysticism, 5, 6, 7, 46, 73
Riedemann, Peter, 105
right living, from charity infused in the hearts, 19
righteous, having nothing to do with evil matters, 163
righteousness, 3, 17–18
Rinck, Melchior, 114
Robeck, Cecil, xxx, 114n39
Roberts, Evan, xxvii
Roman Catholic Church
    advocacy of extreme changes in, 2
    as the antichrist, 163
    clergy as corrupt and abusive, 57, 208, 209
    insisting on a two-source definition of the word, 14
    no supporting Scripture for much of the ritual and ceremony, 216

Roman Catholic Church (continued)
  as not the visible church on earth according to Zwingli, 56
  political power and ecclesiastical ascendency from of a fraudulent proclamation, 68–69
  reformation of out of the question, xix
  spiritualists' rejection of the rituals of, 167
  willingness to go to war to protect, 66
Romans, Luther's lectures on, 3
Roth, John
  on congregational theology (*Gemeindetheologie*), 175
  on "normative" and "evangelical" Anabaptists, xxxiii
  on Pilgram Marpeck, 203–4
  on the polygenesis theory, xxxv
Rothkegel, Martin, 203–4
Rothmann, Bernhard, 194, 195, 202
royalty, selling royal offices, 119
"Rule of Life," based on Scripture sans commentary, 175
Rupp, Gordon
  on Karlstadt's and Luther's concepts of faith, 23
  on Karlstadt's commentary on Augustine's *Spirit and Letter*, 22
  on Karlstadt's future mystical spirituality, 19
  on Karlstadt's mysticism, 21
  on Storchian influence on Müntzer, 32
Russell, William, on kinds of righteousness, 17

Sabata (Kessler), 90–91, 102, 122
sacra pagina, 14
sacraments, 178, 182
salvation, xxxvii, 170, 213
Samaritan woman, at the well, 86–87
sanctification
  achieving, 37
  doctrine of, xxii–xxiii
  fivefold gospel aspect of, 162
  as the goal and achievement of Christian life, 143
  made possible by the work of the Holy Spirit, 42
  separated from the baptism in the Holy Spirit, xxiii
Sanford, Frank, xxiv
"*sapientia experimentalis*," 7
Sattler, Michael
  on aberrant behavior, 201
  Anabaptist confession of faith of, 87–88, 94
  arrested with Grebel and other Anabaptist leaders in Zurich, 151
  arrived in Strasbourg, 150–51
  convicted of being an Anabaptist, 94
  as an evangelical Anabaptist leader, 141
  exhorting his brethren not to forget to assemble, 95
  pleaded with Bucer and Capito for the release of Anabaptist prisoners in Strasbourg, 151
  position on the sword and oath adopted by the Swiss Anabaptists, 123
  spiritual selfishness of, 206
  stayed in Strasbourg, 120–21
  uncompromising position on the separation of church and state, 151
Schad, Elias, 93
Schappeler, Christoph, 80
Scharnschlager, Leupold, 156, 158
Schiemer, Leonhard, 151, 155
Schlaffer, Hans, 64, 151, 155–56
Schleitheim Articles (Sattler), 201
Schleitheim Confession (Sattler), 94–97, 151, 212
scholasticism, enhanced by the advent of printing, 14
Schowalter, Paul, 108, 109
Schuggers, Thomas, 117
Schwärmer
  acted out their differences, 42
  beliefs of, 99
  believed in acts of piety, 41

detrimental to Luther's original reform intent, 2
disaffected by the growing antinomianism, 210
on the efficacy of the elements of the Eucharist, 42
experience of the Spirit, 141
identifying those who embraced the manifestation of the gifts of the Holy Spirit, 2n2
initially in agreement with Luther's five tenets of reform, 41
Luther's, xviii, xl, 18, 40
rejected Luther's protest, 11
theological positions of, xviii
took issue with Luther, 73
uniquely of Lutheran origin, 3
unsuccessful in creating a new church, 210
Schwenckfeld, Caspar
adopted Crautwald's theology of the "*Nouus homo*," 37
advocating aspects of Pauline pneumatology, xxviii
beliefs of, 36
critical of the Anabaptists' tendency toward accepting self-proclaimed saints and prophets, 181
on the Eucharist, 38–39, 65
as an Evangelical spiritualist, 142, 143
influence of, 34, 155
initially attracted to the Anabaptists, 181
Marpeck and, 40, 179–84
opposed to Anabaptists' baptismal theology, 39, 102
radical anti-Lutheranism of, 1
seeking a theology with a more pious outcome, 40
spent time in Strasbourg, 121
tracts written by, 35
Schwenckfeldianism, Friedrich suppressed, 39
Scott, Thomas, 32
scriptural language, difference between translating and interpreting, 56

scriptural principles, in everyday life in peasant thinking, 88
Scripture. *See also* Bible
acting out in real life resulting in manifestations of the charismata, 211
biblicist approach to, 67
critical nature of, 173
critical to faith for Müntzer, 28
every Christian's responsibility to read in their respective vernaculars, 59
as the final arbiter of the faith by the Holiness Movement, xx
general acceptance of the literality or natural sense of, 207
Hoffmann having the prophetic gift for interpreting, 193
interpreted Scripture for Luther, 137
interpreted Scripture with only the aid of the Holy Spirit, 148
as a key to restitution of the primitive church for Schwenckfeld, 36
messengers and teachers having witness of, 173
Müntzer's personal core belief regarding, 27
Müntzer's proclivity to rely on, 32
opening the door to the Christian laity to read and interpret, 5
priesthood of, 72
ranking higher than the church for Luther, 11
value of searching, 174
as a witness to the word, 19
as the word of God for Müntzer, 27
Zwingli accepting as the judge, 48
"second blessing," Wesley's doctrine of, xxii
second coming of Christ, belief in the imminence of, 133
"secret rapture," of the church as believable, xxvii
sectarianism, of Anabaptists, 113–18
secular authorities, protecting true believers with the sword according to Hoffmann, 192

secular priest, ordained for the monastic life, 44n2
secularism, replacing personal piety and public ministry, xxi
secularization, of many former ecclesiastic responsibilities during the Reformation, 105
Seebass, Gottfried, 81
Séguenny, on Schwenckfeld, 37
Seid, Katherine, prophet in Strasbourg, 192
self-indulgence, of "false brethren," 94
separation, from evil and wickedness of the world, 96
separatist nonresistant stance, of Sattler's *Schleitheim Confession*, 123
serfdom, 78, 80
Sermon to the Princes (Müntzer), 29–30
sermons of Tauler, classified by the church as mystical, 7
Servetus, Michael, 139
Seymour, William Joseph, xxv–xxvi
  Apostolic Address of 1915, 115
  article entitled *The Precious Atonement*, 124
  criteria for evidence of the Spirit, 168
  described the early Pentecostal movement, 98
  early example of the Pentecostal concept of restitution, 205
  experience of being baptized in the Spirit and speaking in tongues, 114n39
  on going by signs and voices, 206
  on the illumination one receives when baptized with the Holy Spirit, 86–87
  paraphrasing church history on the gift of tongues, 160
  on racism caused by divisive white men, 168–69
  on Sacraments, 166
  on the second coming, 125–26
  on seeking to displace dead forms and creeds, 170
  on speaking in tongues, 212
  on spiritual qualifications of those who were called to preach, 173
  on standing for the restoration of the faith once delivered unto the saints, 162
  witnessed many contradictions of piety, 168
shepherd of the church, duties described in the *Schleitheim Confession*, 96
"The Shepherd" sermon (Zwingli), 49
Sider, Ronald, 22, 23
Silesian Reformation, 34–36
Simons, Menno
  in the Anabaptist movement, xli, 215
  as an evangelical Anabaptist leader, 141
  marginalization of the role of women, 200
  rejected the Münster experience, 199
  rescued Anabaptism from extinction, 136–37, 191
  scriptural guidance for not swearing an oath, 123
  trained and educated as a Catholic priest, 136
  wrote against the "Blasphemy of Jan van Leyden" and the many mistakes in Münster, 199
"simple congregants," 192
Simpson, A. B., xxiii, 162
Simpson, Carl, 169
simul peccaor et iustus, simultaneously righteous and sinful, 17
singing, of the word, 28
sinner, compared to a sick man, 17
Sitzerrecht (lex sedentium), 92–93, 95
sixteenth-century church, as something other than that depicted in Scripture, 69–70
sixteenth-century primary sources, availability of, xix
Sixty-Seven Articles (Zwingli), 46, 77
slain in the Spirit, in early Pentecostalism, 114
small tithe, abolishment of, 80

Snyder, C. Arnold
   on Anabaptist pneumatology, 99
   analysis of the *Frankenthal Protocol of 1571*, 202
   common core of systematic theological and doctrinal categories for examining Anabaptism, xxxvii
   on the definition of Anabaptism, 89
   on early Anabaptism, xvi, 167–68
   on Karlstadt, Müntzer, and Schwenckfeld as "evangelical" radical reformers, 3
   on the "learned" or scholastic theology of the church, 161
   on the Melchiorite "pacifist" wing, 199
   on not all Anabaptists seeing church and the world from an apocalyptic worldview, 202
   on similarities between the Anabaptists and the Lutheran radical archetypes, 99
   on Williams's methodology in categorizing radicalism, 144
Social Darwinism, xxi
social relationships, women redefining, 193
Socianism, 139
sola fide
   Christians saved by, 73
   complying with, xxviii
   described, 1
   doctrine forced radical recognition of the lack of personal piety and antinomianism among the reformed, 41
   due to the Bible alone, *sola scriptura*, 11
   embraced as truth, 217
   preventing from evolving into antinomianism, 35
   salvation through faith alone, 209
   sufficiency of faith alone in the shed blood of Christ, 215
   as the work of the Spirit first, 41
sola fide and *sola scriptura*, acceptance by Luther and Zwingli, xxxix

sola scriptura
   adopted by both Luther and Zingli, 13
   application of by Luther and Zwingli, 15
   the Bible as the sole arbiter of the faith, 207, 215
   City Council convinced by Zwingli of the validity of, 48
   complying with, xxviii
   declaration of, 5
   described, 1, 6
   embraced as truth, 217
   insufficiency of as a spiritual catalyst, 23
   Karlstadt reiterating the authority of, 23
   as key to true Christian faith for Zwingli, 44
   Luther's doctrine of, xx
   obviating the necessity of a trained and educated clergy, 207
   as open to all Christians for interpretation, 175
   opening the door to a New Testament spirituality, 2–3
   Protestant premise of, accepted by early Anabaptism and early Pentecostalism, 212
   shared commitment to, entailed a hermeneutical heterogeneity, 208
   some spiritualists adhered to, xxxiv
   thoroughly embraced, 99
   word of God as the only and last arbiter of the faith, 209
soteriology, of Zwingli, 59
Sozzini, Fausto, 139
Spalatin, Georg, 20
speaking in tongues (glossolalia)
   Anabaptism respected, 213
   considered heresy or demon possession, xxii
   as evidence of the empowerment of the Holy Spirit, 125
   German phrase for, xxxv

speaking in tongues (continued)
  incidents described by Zwingli, 113–14
  as initial evidence of the infilling of the Holy Spirit, 204
  as initial evidence of the Spirit baptism, xxiv, xxv, 212
  known to Anabaptists, 203
  manifestations of between 1525 and 1526, 90
  as the most important phenomenon reported, 214
  reported at Azusa Street proving one was "filled with the Holy Spirit," 204
  speaking known but unlearned languages (xenolalia), xxiv, 101n112
  spoken by Paul, 86
  sporadically experienced during the Welsh revival, xxvii
  by two or three at most with one interpreter, 55
  Zwingli interpreted as biblical languages, 85, 101
Spirit. *See also* Holy Spirit
  brought faith and understanding to the word for Müntzer, 28
  consulting the mind of, 138–39
  defined the word, 142
  enabled all Christians as believer priests, 148–49
  first in priority relative to Scripture for Zwingli, 52
  having precedence over word, 19
  led into the truth of the word for Zwingli, 210
  poured forth over all the present and future world until the last judgment, 174
  revealing the truth of the secrets of the law, 23
  speaking to man for Müntzer, 142
  Zwingli led by, 138
Spirit and Letter (Augustine), 22
Spirit and word, as inclusive, 52, 138
spirit of the law, 22–23
Spirit possession, 140, 141
Spirit-empowered laity, xxviii
spiritual and theological praxes, in common between early sixteenth-century Anabaptism and early twentieth-century Pentecostalism, 149
spiritual behavior, of racist white men, 169
spiritual meaning, 9, 46
spiritual praxes, with Pentecostal-like aspects, xvi
spiritual realm, depending upon the inner power which Christ alone gives, 171
spiritualism
  Anabaptism and, 137–39
  defining, 137, 145
  divisions within, 140
  Seymour on winding up in, 169
  as variegated and complex, 146
spiritualist Anabaptists (biblicists, or biblical literalists), 97, 144, 148
"Spiritualistic," defined, 21n88
spiritualists
  chose to reject Catholicism, Protestantism, and rapidly growing Anabaptism, 137
  complaints about the *Schleitheim Confession*, 97
  contention that there was no apostolic authority to create an apostolic succession, 171
  could not state who commissioned them to teach, write, travel, and use Scripture, 167
  declared the miracles of the New Testament to be in cessation, 164
  denying externalities, 166
  desired to stop up the well of the Spirit, 172
  divisions of, 141
  on the fall of the New Testament church was precipitated with the advent of Constantine, 205
  focused on the future of the church, 140

held to the condemnation of the material rites and ceremonies of the church, 158
individualistic nature of, 170
lacking the true knowledge of Christ, 166
Marpeck's conclusion against, 163, 177–79
preaching their respective gospels, 102
pushed the limits of traditional Christian orthodoxy, 88–89
rejected the idea of a single priest, 12
sought to abolish too much of the external, 172
spirituality, Karlstadt's as mystical, 19
spirituality and theology, of Pentecostals and Anabaptists compared, 212–17
spiritual-prophetic hermeneutic, of Luther, 16, 207
spiritual-prophetic literalism, Anabaptist approbation of, 190
spoken word, existed prior to the recorded word, 49
spoken word of God, directly related to Scripture for Müntzer, 27
Stadler, Ulrich, 141
state magistracy, incorporating into the propagation of the gospel, 209
Statement of Faith and Belief (Seymour), 170
Staupitz, Johannes, 19
Stayer, James
  on Anabaptist beliefs, 99
  on evidence that Hubmaier was not the sole author of the "Twelve Articles," 81
  on the Peasants' War, 81–82
  published "From Monogenesis to Polygenesis" challenging Bender's Anabaptist paradigm, xxxiv
  on Williams use of "the left wing of the Reformation," 145
Stephens, W. P., 50, 53

Stillstand (suspension)
  discontinued church practices for spiritualists, 205
  of the Eucharist (and eventually baptism) declared by Schwenckfeld and other Silesian reformers, 39
  extended by Schwenckfeld to include baptism, 181–82
  Marpeck attacked Schwenckfeld's, 179
Stone's Folly Bible school, xxiv
Storch, Nicolaus, 31–33
Storchians. *See* Zwickau Prophets
Strasbourg
  1525–1545, 147–49
  Anabaptist experience in, 198
  attracted and tolerated the residence of many Anabaptists, spiritualists, and other types of religious radicals, 120
  city council sought Hoffmann's arrest, 193
  Melchiorites led by Leinhard Jost, 198
  prophet(s), 192–93
Strauss, Jacob, 153
Stübner, Marcus, 31, 33
study groups (conventicles), formed by Schwenckfeld, 34
Stumpf, Simon, 63
Summa Theologica (Thomas Aquinas), 14
Swabian League, 79, 82
The Swearing of Oaths (Simons), 123
Swiss Anabaptism, Conrad Grebel as founder of, 33
Swiss Brethren
  Anabaptists became known as, 211
  attempts to contact Luther's *Schwärmer*, 71
  becoming legalistic and dogmatic, 182
  first early Anabaptist adherents, 63
  as the initial Anabaptists, *der Wiedertaufer*, 74, 74n17
  Müntzer attracted the attention of, 30

Swiss Brethren (continued)
  ostracism from Zurich in 1525, 104
  in Strasbourg, 147
  theological concepts of, 99
Swiss Brethren Anabaptist confession, Moravian confession in opposition to, 157
Swiss Brethren (Anabaptists) church, 63
Swiss Brethren Zwinglians, 69
Swiss mercenaries, deserted the Swabian League, 79
Swiss radicalism and the resultant Anabaptist movement, predicated upon Zwingli's initial reform theology, 43–44
Swiss Reformation
  distancing from Luther, 57
  initiation of, 43
  men of significance supporting Zwingli's, 61
  rejected infant baptism and embraced adult rebaptism, xvi, 67
Swiss Reformed Protestant economic blockade, 66
sword of the Spirit, Reformed not having, 189
Pope Sylvester I, 69n2, 70
synecdoche, 51, 51n37
systematic theology, 161, 213

Tabbernee, William, xxx
Tauler, Johannes, 2, 6, 9
Taulerian doctrine of reception of the Holy Spirit, 31
Teaching of the Twelve Apostles, xxix
teachings, non-scriptural as invalid, 76
tenets of faith, Anabaptist, 75–77
tension, between the word and the Spirit for Müntzer, 33
Tertullian, xxx, 90, 203, 211–12
Tetzel, Johann, selling indulgences, 16
textual criticism, 217
Thelle, Agnes, 111
theocentrists, 89

theocratic government, with charismatic gift of prophecy as main criteria for guidance, 194
Theologia Germanica, 6, 7, 31
theological aspects, of Pentecostalism, xvi
theology, of Zwingli, 51, 58–60
"third blessing"
  beyond "entire sanctification," xxiv
  combined the second blessing of sanctification and the baptism with fire, xxvi–xxvii
Thomas Aquinas, 14
"Throng of apostolic messengers," unable to sin, 192
tithes, 61, 78, 80
To the Christian Nobility of the German Nation (Luther), 10
Toleration Act of 1689, by the English Parliament, 111
Tract on the Supreme Virtue of Gelassenheit (Karlstadt), 20
transubstantiation, 42, 210
Troeltsch, Ernst, xxxii–xxxiii
tropes, misuses of distinguished by Zwingli, 51
True and False Religion (Zwingli), 65
true apostolic church, going back to, xxxi
The True Christian Faith, 1541 (Simons), 199–200
"Twelve Articles," 80–81, 88, 97
"Two Kinds of Righteous," sermon of Luther, 17–18
typological approach, of Williams, 144

Unitarianism, originators of, 139
United Nations, 110
"unmerited grace and pure Scripture," combined by Luther, 16
Unpartisan History of Church and Heresy (Arnold), xxxii

Vadian, 49, 61, 75
Valla, Lorenzo, 69n2
Van Dusen, xvii
van Leiden, Jan, 194, 195, 196, 199

INDEX

Verantwortung (Response) (Marpeck), 39–40
Verein für Reformationgeschicte, xxxiii
Vermanung (Admonition), by Marpeck, 40
via media, of Marpeck, 35, 40, 102–3, 157–58, 159, 202
Vindication and Refutation (Müntzer), 29
Virgin Mary, as gracious (*gratiosa*) and not full of grace (*gratia plena*), 9
visible church, 56–57
Voget, C. O., 127
von Karlstadt, Andreas Bodenstein, xxviii, 1
von Watt, Joachim, 49, 61, 117

Wacker, Grant, xxi, xxii, 53, 161
Bishop Waldeck, 194, 195
Waldron, Clarence, 129
Warrington, Keith, 198
water baptism, 105, 179, 181
Weigel, Valentine, 143
Welsh revivals, xxvii, 130
Weniger, Martin, 190
Wesley, John, xxii
Wesleyan Pentecostals, 124
Wesleyan position, on the second blessing, xxvi
Western European Pentecostals, priority for a Pauline pneumatology, 98
what is heard, coming by the preaching of Christ, 52
Whitsuntide Conventions in Sunderland, 132
"Whole troop of pastors," 192
Williams, George H.
  beliefs categorized as universal, 145
  coined the term "Radical Reformation," 139
  on concerns of Schwenckfeld, 36
  describing Anabaptism, xvii, 90
  on Müntzer's *Sermon to the Princes*, 29
  on the Radical Reformation, 2, 145
  on radical reformers finding a place for the ministry of prophets, 121
  on the reputation of Strasbourg for penal moderation, 120
  on the Schappeler/Lotzer theory, 80
  on Schwenckfeld's alteration of Luther's doctrine of justification by faith alone, 37
  set the term Radical over against a Magisterial Reformation, 145
"witnesses," absence of the two as prophesied in the Bible, 196
Wölff, Hans, 147, 150
women, participating in the Radical Reformation, 192–93, 199–200, 214
word
  capable of creating and supporting faith, 64
  critical to any manifestation of the gifts in terms of confirmation, 102
  different ways of reading, 173–74
  reading and singing of paramount for Müntzer, 28
  understood by the Spirit for Schwenckfeld, 40
  as what is heard that comes by the preaching of Christ, 138
word and Spirit, held in simultaneous tension, 199
word of God
  Catholicism's two-source concept of, 5
  defined as Scripture plus tradition as arbitrated by the pope, 207
  denying or silencing for temporal gain, 77
  established among most Protestants as *sola scriptura*, 207
  as a higher priority than the Holy Spirit for Luther, 209
  as the last and final authority for Christians, 208
  and sacraments as inseparable, 64
  as sure and strong for Zwingli, 49
  understood without any human direction, 52

word-over-Spirit position, of Luther, 25
"working of the Holy Spirit," xxxix
works, as evidence of faith, 38
World War I, the Great War, caused consternation among Pentecostals, 126
worldwide revival, referred to as the "latter rain," xxiv
written word, as a "hearable" sign, 105
Wycliffe, John, on Constantine, 69n2
Wyttenbach, Thomas, 44–45

xenolalia, xxiv–xxv, 124

Yoder, John Howard, xxxvi, 147

Zell, Matthew, 150
Ziegler, Clement, 147, 149–50
Zofingen Disputation of 1532 (Marpeck), 166, 184, 190, 202, 212
Zungen Reden, translated as unintelligible speech or language, xxxv
Zurich City Council
  allowing images to remain and the Mass to proceed, 62
  declaring the Ave Maria to be nonbinding, 57
  enacted the death penalty against any adult who had been re-baptized upon a confession of their new faith, 122
  mandated the baptism of all infants within eight days as a civic duty, 62
  ordering the radical Anabaptists to cease and desist from teaching, 71
  ruling that Ulrich Zwingli continue to proclaim the holy Gospel and the correct divine Scriptures, 48
  Zwingli's political power and control over, 58
Zwickau Prophets, 31, 141
Zwingli, Huldrych
  appointed preacher under the direct control of the Zurich city council, 61
  articles presented at the first Zurich Disputation, 47–48
  on aspects of applying the process of interpreting the word, 138–39
  began the Reformed church, 210
  biblical hermeneutics introduced by, xvi
  called for reformation of the Roman Catholic Church, 208
  careful but insistent opposition to the Catholic Church, 45
  challenged by radical reformers from among his own followers, 73
  challenging church's teachings, 57–58
  as chaplain to the Swiss mercenaries from Glarus, 44
  conclusions on what it would take to reform the church, 209
  considered the manifestation of gifts of the Spirit a matter of studying and learning the biblical languages, 209
  considering preaching to be the word of God, 50
  on corruption of the Catholic church, 57
  on the current manifestation of gifts by every Christian, 101
  death of, 66–67
  declared the Spirit to be first in priority relative to Scripture, 138
  difficulty restoring magisterial order, 105
  distanced himself from anti-pedobaptism, 60
  distancing himself from Luther, 57
  ecclesiology of, 56–58
  on the enabling role of the Holy Spirit, 50
  established a Bible school to train local pastors, 209
  on the Eucharist (communion), 65, 210
  eventually eschewed humanism for a more spiritual hermeneutic, 50
  examination of the origins of initial theology of, xxxix–xl
  excommunicated under the Edict of Worms by 1528, 64

founded a theological college and began teaching both testaments in the humanistic style, 54
gave Karlstadt a more positive hearing, 149
on government as necessary for the well-being of society, 57
hermeneutics of, 13–15, 45–46
incorporated aspects of both medieval and humanistic methodologies, 51
on infant baptism, 60
influence of the early teachings of, 154
influenced by Erasmian humanism, 13
initial Reformation theologies of, xviii, 215
initial theology, xl, 67
insistence that infant baptism and the Mass be discontinued struck fear into his heart, 214
insisting on the precedence of the Spirit, 59
list of biblical illustrations of instances where the word of God was spoken, 49
on methodology of applying the process of interpreting the word, 52–53
moving away from his relationship with Erasmus, 83
on only one person speaks to the edification of the church, 55
as an orthodox Christian seeking a biblically based *ecclesia*, xxix
petitioning for grievances regarding the abuses and non-biblical practices of the pope and the church's hierarchical priesthood, 43
on preaching as the word of God, 48–49
on the prophet's role, 55
published a refutation of Anabaptist (*Catabaptists*) beliefs and practice in 1527, 113–14
as a radical, 2, 46
realized that the magistracy would not agree to the elimination of the Mass or infant baptism, 216
refused to be labeled a Lutheran, 46
retreated from the idea of the priesthood of the believer, 216
role of the Spirit in the hermeneutics of, 138
on the selling of indulgences, 45
on *sola scriptura* as interpreted by the Holy Spirit, 73
soliciting the authority of various canton magistracies to coerce compliance and acceptance of his reforms, 66
theology of, 58–60
understanding of being able to speak in other tongues, interpretation, or prophecy, 114
used the Latin word *ecstasia* in his Catabaptist pamphlet which is also translated "trance," 114n39
utilized the magistracy in reforming and protecting the church, 48, 61, 67
Zwinglian Reformation, xxviii
Zwinglian Reformed churches, radicals disruptive in, 62
Zwinglian theologians, summoned Anabaptist preachers to a disputation, 184
Zwinglianism, Hubmaier's affinity for, 75

www.ingramcontent.com/pod-product-compliance
Lightning Source LLC
Chambersburg PA
CBHW061429300426
44114CB00014B/1608